Guided Comprehension
in the
Primary
Grades

Maureen McLaughlin

INTERNATIONAL READING ASSOCIATION

800 BARKSDALE ROAD, PO BOX 8139
NEWARK, DE 19714-8139, USA
www.reading.org

The International Reading Association attempts, through its publications, to provide a forum for a wide spectrum of opinions on reading. This policy permits divergent viewpoints without implying the endorsement of the Association.

Executive Editor, Books   Corinne M. Mooney
Developmental Editor   Charlene M. Nichols
Developmental Editor   Tori Mello Bachman
Developmental Editor   Stacey L. Reid
Editorial Production Manager   Shannon T. Fortner
Design and Composition Manager   Anette Schuetz

Project Editor   Matthew W. Baker

Art   Cover Design: Linda Steere; Cover Photography (clockwise from left): Maureen McLaughlin, Maureen McLaughlin, Jamie Fialcowitz; Interior Photography (pages 1, 77, 189): Maureen McLaughlin

Copyright 2010 by the International Reading Association, Inc.

All rights reserved. No part of this publication may be reproduced or transmitted in any form or by any means, electronic or mechanical, including photocopy, or any information storage and retrieval system, without permission from the publisher.

The publisher would appreciate notification where errors occur so that they may be corrected in subsequent printings and/or editions.

Library of Congress Cataloging-in-Publication Data

McLaughlin, Maureen.
  Guided comprehension in the primary grades / Maureen McLaughlin. -- 2nd ed.
        p. cm.
  Includes bibliographical references and index.
  ISBN 978-0-87207-715-7
  1. Reading comprehension--Study and teaching (Primary)--United States--Handbooks, manuals, etc. I. Title.
  LB1525.7.M35 2010
  372.47--dc22
                              2010016999

Suggested APA Reference
McLaughlin, M. (2010). *Guided Comprehension in the primary grades* (2nd ed.). Newark, DE: International Reading Association.

For Ann Burke and Thomas J. McLaughlin

CONTENTS

APPENDIXES   189
Guided Comprehension Resources

ABOUT THE AUTHOR

 **Maureen McLaughlin** is a professor of reading education at East Stroudsburg University of Pennsylvania in East Stroudsburg, Pennsylvania, USA. She earned her doctorate at Boston University in reading and language development. Prior to her tenure at East Stroudsburg University, Maureen spent 15 years as a classroom teacher, reading specialist, and department chair in a public school system.

A member of the Board of Directors of the International Reading Association from 2005–2008 and recipient of IRA's 2010 Jerry Johns Outstanding Teacher Educator in Reading Award, Maureen is the author of numerous publications about the teaching of reading, reading comprehension, and content area literacies. Another of her recent books is *Content Area Reading: Teaching and Learning in an Age of Multiple Literacies* (Allyn & Bacon, 2010). A frequent speaker at international, national, and state conferences, Maureen is a consultant to schools and universities throughout the world.

PREFACE

Thank you for joining me in welcoming the second edition of *Guided Comprehension in the Primary Grades*. Guided Comprehension is based on the idea that reading is a social constructivist process. Underpinned by current research and beliefs about best practice, the Model provides a detailed, research-based, classroom-tested process for teaching reading in the primary grades from a comprehension-based perspective. When we use the Model, we teach students to become active, strategic readers by providing explicit strategy instruction, numerous opportunities for engagement, and a variety of texts and instructional settings.

Writing this edition has provided me with opportunities to update the research base, integrate 16 new Guided Comprehension lessons, share ideas for differentiating instruction, present all new theme resources, and include new examples of student work. It also has afforded me an opportunity to revise the appendixes. Evidence of this can be found in the updated information concerning the five building blocks of literacy (Appendix B), the all new teaching examples in Appendix C, the revised forms for organizing and managing centers and routines (Appendix D), and the updated sources of leveled texts (Appendix F).

Although this book is filled with innovations, I have, simultaneously, continued to focus on our ultimate goal: helping primary students to become good readers—readers who actively engage with text and naturally use a variety of skills and a repertoire of strategies to facilitate the construction of meaning.

We know from a variety of research studies that comprehension strategies and the skills that support them can be taught. We also know that Guided Comprehension, a context in which students learn comprehension skills and strategies in a variety of settings, has emerged as a highly successful teaching framework. The Model fosters students' transactions with text by integrating explicit and guided instruction of comprehension strategies, multiple levels and types of text, and varied opportunities for strategy application.

This new edition is divided into two parts. Part One features a detailed description of the Guided Comprehension Model for the primary grades, including its research base, multiple stages, assessment connections, and use of leveled texts. Sixteen theme-based Guided Comprehension lessons are presented in Part Two. The lessons, which focus on four themes, also include student examples, assessment possibilities, and ideas for differentiating instruction. Resources that support the Guided Comprehension Model and facilitate its use in the primary grades are featured in the appendixes.

The six chapters in Part One focus on the Guided Comprehension Model and the research that supports it.

- Chapter 1 introduces Guided Comprehension, a context in which students and teachers engage in reading as a strategy-based thinking process. The chapter also explains the Guided Comprehension Model and the research-based tenets that underpin it.

- Chapter 2 delineates the three stages of the Model. This discussion includes the presentation of the comprehension strategies and related teaching ideas.

- Chapter 3 focuses on comprehension centers. A wide variety of ideas for creating centers and related activities are described, and student writing samples are featured.
- Chapter 4 explains comprehension routines, including Literature Circles, Reciprocal Teaching, and Cross-Age Reading Experiences. The components of each routine are detailed and ideas for classroom implementation are presented.
- Chapter 5 discusses the multiple roles of assessment in Guided Comprehension, makes connections to state assessments, and describes a variety of practical measures.
- Chapter 6 discusses the various roles of leveled text in Guided Comprehension. Factors that influence student accessibility and text type and structure are presented.

Chapters 1–6 are also linked to practical, reproducible resources in the appendixes.

In Part Two, which includes Chapters 7–10, sixteen lessons focused on four new Guided Comprehension themes are introduced:

1. Click, Clack, WOW! The Stories of Doreen Cronin
2. Animals Aplenty: The Informational Text of Seymour Simon
3. Giggles Galore: The Humor of Dav Pilkey
4. Oceans Alive: Sea Creatures, Coral Reefs, Ecology, and More!

Each theme includes the following elements:

- Theme description
- Theme-based plan for Guided Comprehension
- Four new Guided Comprehension lessons
- Planning forms
- Teacher commentaries and think-alouds
- Samples of student work
- Ideas for differentiating instruction
- Theme-based resources including related texts, websites, performance extensions across the curriculum, and culminating activities.

The appendixes are filled with resources for teaching reading in the primary grades. Appendix A contains the Primary-Level Developmental Continuum for Reading and Writing that was developed by the International Reading Association and the National Association for the Education of Young Children. Appendix B focuses on the research bases and practical teaching ideas related to the five building blocks of literacy: phonemic awareness, phonics, fluency, vocabulary, and comprehension. New samples of student work are featured in Appendix C, which provides strategy descriptions, graphic organizers, and reproducible blacklines. Resources for organizing and managing comprehension centers and routines are presented in Appendix D. Assessment materials and leveled text resources are the focus of Appendixes E and F. Home–school connections are featured in Appendix G, and Guided Comprehension planning and scheduling forms are presented in Appendix H.

This edition of *Guided Comprehension in the Primary Grades* is designed to be a teacher-friendly comprehensive resource. Whether you are a classroom teacher, staff developer, reading specialist, literacy coach, or teacher educator, this is a book that will remain on your desk and emerge dog-eared and well used over the years. It contains everything you need to teach Guided Comprehension in the primary grades.

Acknowledgments

As always, there are many people to thank for making this book possible. I express my appreciation to them now for their insight, their understanding, and their support.

I am particularly grateful to the following people:

- Suzy Park
- Christine Godiska
- Susan Brink
- Jackie Ackerman
- Katie Lime
- Nancy Sun
- Dayle Henry
- Casey Paone
- Rebecca Norman
- Megan Walp
- Kasey Pohl
- Barbara Snyder
- Stroudsburg School District, Stroudsburg, Pennsylvania
- Stephanie Lukan
- Dina Evans
- Michele Kirias
- Rebecca Flores
- Michael Neu
- Sue Mirrione
- Lisa Jaferis
- Beth Gress Watkins
- My family, colleagues, and friends
- Shannon Fortner, IRA Editorial Production Manager, for her extraordinary knowledge of the publication process
- Matt Baker, Project Manager, for his insight, patience, and unparalleled editorial expertise

Finally, I thank you for joining me as we continue our search for greater understanding of reading comprehension. I hope you find this second edition to be a valuable teaching resource, one that you and your colleagues will use to further our common goal of helping primary-grade students understand what they read.

—*MM*

Guided Comprehension: A Teaching Model for the Primary Grades

Part One provides a detailed description of the Guided Comprehension Model for Grades K–3, including its research base, multiple stages, assessment connections, and use of leveled text.

Theoretical Underpinnings: In Chapter 1, the 10 research-based tenets that support the Guided Comprehension Model's emergence from research and current beliefs about best practice in the primary grades are presented. Guided Comprehension connections are made to each tenet.

The Guided Comprehension Model for Grades K–3: In Chapter 2, the three stages of the Model are explained. This discussion includes the presentation of the comprehension strategies and related teaching ideas.

Comprehension Centers: Comprehension centers are the focus of Chapter 3. A wide variety of ideas for creating centers and related activities are described, and student writing samples are featured. How to organize and manage comprehension centers is a special emphasis of this chapter.

Comprehension Routines: Literature Circles, Reciprocal Teaching, and Cross-Age Reading Experiences are explained in Chapter 4. The components of each routine are detailed and ideas for classroom implementation are presented. Grade-level examples are also shared.

Assessments: In Chapter 5, the multiple roles of assessment in Guided Comprehension are discussed, connections are made to state assessments, and a variety of practical measures are described. Guided Comprehension connections are provided for each assessment. Then the Guided Comprehension Profile, an organizational framework for documenting student progress, is introduced.

Leveled Texts: The various roles of leveled text in Guided Comprehension are presented in Chapter 6. Factors that influence student accessibility and text type and structure are discussed. This is followed by descriptions of elements essential for choosing books for student success. Finally, methods of leveling and organizing classroom texts are delineated.

CHAPTER 1

Reading Comprehension in the Primary Grades

As grade K–3 teachers, our primary responsibility is to teach our students to become active, engaged readers. We want them to enjoy being read to and reading on their own. We want them to be motivated to listen to and read a variety of texts and use a repertoire of strategies to construct meaning. We want to hear them giggle when they read Shel Silverstein's "Sarah Cynthia Sylvia Stout" from *Where the Sidewalk Ends*, David Wiesner's *The Three Pigs*, and Jon Scieszka and Lane Smith's *The Stinky Cheese Man and Other Fairly Stupid Tales*. We want to hear our students express their emotions when they read *The Lemonade Club* by Patricia Polacco and *The Wall* by Eve Bunting. We want to see their looks of amazement as they read Seymour Simon's *Wolves* or Gail Gibbons's *Tornadoes!* We want to see their faces bursting with pride as they read sentences and stories they have written or share their ideas in discussion. Helping students to become active, strategic readers is a challenging process, but to be successful, one aspect is clear: We need to teach comprehension skills and strategies right from the start. The Guided Comprehension Model for the Primary Grades, a teaching framework in which students learn comprehension skills and strategies in a variety of settings using multiple levels and types of text, provides a viable format for such instruction.

Reading comprehension researchers including Duke and Pearson (2002), Hilden and Pressley (2002), and Pressley (2001) note that reading comprehension strategies can be taught in the primary grades. Pressley (2001) suggests that students begin learning comprehension skills and a few strategies as early as kindergarten. Pearson (2001b) reports that the three most important things we have learned about comprehension in the past 30 years are that (1) students benefit from using comprehension strategies and routines; (2) having opportunities to read, write, and talk matters; and (3) knowledge helps comprehension by providing a starting point—where readers are and what they know.

A variety of other sources support the need to teach comprehension strategies in the primary grades. The Continuum of Children's Development in Early Reading and Writing in *Learning to Read and Write: Developmentally Appropriate Practices for Young Children* (International Reading Association [IRA] & National Association for the Education of Young Children [NAEYC], 1998) suggests that students use reading skills and strategies as early as kindergarten (see Appendix A). Continuums that delineate students' achievement of state standards have been authored by a variety of educational teams. Examples of these include the following:

- The Pennsylvania Department of Education and Pennsylvania Association of Intermediate Units' *Early Childhood Learning Continuum Indicators* (Partnership for Educational Excellence

Network, 2001; see www.wpsd.k12.pa.us/parents/newseventslib/EarlyChildhood Continuum.pdf)

- School districts such as Washington's Mercer Island School District's Grade Level Curriculum, Reading Targets Grades K–5 (see www.misd.k12.wa.us/curriculum/gradelevel/ targets/readingtargetsk_5.html)
- Canadian provincial groups, such as Manitoba Education, Citizenship and Youth (see www .edu.gov.mb.ca/k12/cur/ela/drc/drc_poster3.pdf)

Further, the National Reading Panel (National Institute of Child Health and Human Development [NICHD], 2000) suggests that we focus our teaching on five areas: phonemic awareness, phonics, fluency, vocabulary, and comprehension. Students' understanding of the first four areas contributes to comprehension, so it is only logical to include such aspects of literacy when discussing reading comprehension in the primary grades. The National Reading Panel emphases permeate the Guided Comprehension themed lessons. A variety of resources for phonemic awareness, phonics, fluency, and vocabulary—including definitions, practical teaching ideas, and related resources—are included in Appendix B.

In this chapter, Guided Comprehension's natural emergence from current research is delineated. To illustrate this relationship, 10 research-based comprehension tenets are presented. Each is followed by a brief discussion of its relationship to the Guided Comprehension Model for the Primary Grades.

Tenets of Reading Comprehension

Studies have shown that multiple factors affect successful reading comprehension. The following research-based tenets describe the current most influential elements (McLaughlin & Allen, 2009):

- Comprehension is a social constructivist process.
- Comprehension strategies and skills can be taught.
- Differentiated reading instruction accommodates students' needs, including those of English learners and struggling readers.
- Excellent reading teachers influence students' learning.
- Good readers are strategic and take active roles in the reading process.
- Reading should occur in meaningful contexts.
- Students benefit from transacting daily with a variety of texts at multiple levels.
- Vocabulary development and instruction affect reading comprehension.
- Engagement is a key factor in the comprehension process.
- Dynamic assessment informs comprehension instruction.

Although the tenets have strong research underpinnings, they are also designed to inform instruction. In the sections that follow, each tenet is discussed and connections are made between theory and practice.

Comprehension Is a Social Constructivist Process

From a constructivist perspective, learning is understood as "a self-regulated process of resolving inner cognitive conflicts that often become apparent through concrete experience, collaborative discourse, and reflection" (Brooks & Brooks, 1993, p. vii). Constructivists believe that learners make sense of their world by connecting what they know and have experienced with what they are learning. They construct meaning through these connections when educators pose relevant problems, structure learning around primary concepts, seek and value students' ideas, and assess students' learning in context (Brooks & Brooks, 1993).

According to Short and Burke (1996), constructivism frees students of fact-driven curricula and encourages them to focus on larger ideas, allows students to reach unique conclusions and reformulate ideas, encourages students to see the world as a complex place with multiple perspectives, and emphasizes that students are responsible for their own learning and should attempt to connect the information they learn to the world around them through inquiry.

Cambourne (2002, p. 26) notes that constructivism has three core theoretical assumptions:

1. What is learned cannot be separated from the context in which it is learned.
2. The purposes or goals that the learner brings to the learning situation are central to what is learned.
3. Knowledge and meaning are socially constructed through the processes of negotiation, evaluation, and transformation.

Constructivists believe that students construct knowledge by linking what is new to what is already known. In reading, this concept is reflected in schema-based learning development, which purports that learning takes place when new information is integrated with what is already known. The more experience learners have with a particular topic, the easier it is for them to make connections between what they know and what they are learning (Anderson, 1994; Anderson & Pearson, 1984). From a constructivist perspective, comprehension is viewed as

> the construction of meaning of a written or spoken communication through a reciprocal, holistic interchange of ideas between the interpreter and the message in a particular communicative context. Note: The presumption here is that meaning resides in the intentional problem-solving, thinking processes of the interpreter during such an interchange, that the content of meaning is influenced by that person's prior knowledge and experience, and that the message so constructed by the receiver may or may not be congruent with the message sent. (Harris & Hodges, 1995, p. 39)

Vygotsky's principles enhance the constructivist perspective by addressing the social context of learning (Dixon-Krauss, 1996). According to Vygotsky, students should be taught within their zones of proximal development (Forman & Cazden, 1994; Vygotsky, 1978). Instruction within the zone should incorporate both scaffolding and social mediation. As Dixon-Krauss (1996) notes when explaining this Vygotskian principle, "It is through social dialogue with adults and/or more capable peers that language concepts are learned" (p. 155). Such social interaction encourages students to think and share their ideas.

Constructivism is manifested in classrooms that are characterized by student-generated ideas, self-selection, creativity, interaction, critical thinking, and personal construction of meaning

(McLaughlin & Allen, 2002b). In such contexts, authentic literacy tasks assimilate real-world experiences, provide a purpose for learning, and encourage students to take ownership of learning (Hiebert, 1994; Newmann & Wehlage, 1993).

Cambourne (2002) suggests that instructional principles emerge from constructivist theory. These principles include the following:

- Creating a classroom culture that encourages deep engagement with effective reading
- Using strategies that are a blend of explicitness, systematicity, mindfulness, and contextualization
- Creating continuous opportunities to develop intellectual unrest
- Encouraging students to develop their conscious awareness of how text functions and how we create meaning
- Designing and using tasks that will support the authentic use of the processes and understandings implicit in reading behavior

Guided Comprehension Connection The Guided Comprehension Model is based on the view of comprehension as a social constructivist process. This is demonstrated in the Model in numerous ways, including the ultimate goal of students' transaction with text and the value placed on learning in a variety of social settings.

Comprehension Strategies and Skills Can Be Taught

Durkin's research in the late 1970s reported that little if any comprehension instruction occurred in classrooms (Durkin, 1978). Instead, comprehension questions, often at the literal level, were assigned and then corrected; comprehension was assessed but not taught. Studies have demonstrated that explicit instruction of comprehension strategies improves students' comprehension of new texts and topics (Hiebert, Pearson, Taylor, Richardson, & Paris, 1998).

We know that research supports the teaching of reading comprehension strategies in the primary grades (Duffy, 2001; Duke & Pearson, 2002; Hilden & Pressley, 2002; McLaughlin, 2003). In fact, Duke and Pearson (2002) suggest incorporating "both explicit instruction in specific comprehension strategies and a great deal of time and opportunity for actual reading, writing, and discussion of text" (p. 206). Guided Comprehension strategies include the following:

- *Previewing*: Activating background knowledge, predicting, and setting a purpose
- *Self-questioning*: Generating questions to guide reading
- *Making connections*: Relating reading to self, text, and others
- *Visualizing*: Creating mental images while reading
- *Knowing how words work*: Understanding words through strategic vocabulary development, including the use of the graphophonic, syntactic, and semantic cue systems to figure out unknown words
- *Monitoring*: Asking "Does this make sense?" and clarifying by adapting strategic processes to accommodate the response
- *Summarizing*: Synthesizing important ideas
- *Evaluating*: Making judgments about the text

Pressley (2001) states that comprehension instruction should begin in the early grades with the teaching of comprehension skills, such as sequencing and questioning, and that instruction in a few strategies, such as predicting and summarizing, should occur as early as kindergarten. Linking skills and strategies can facilitate comprehension. Comprehension strategies are generally more complex than skills and often require the orchestration of several skills. Effective instruction links comprehension skills to strategies to promote strategic reading. For example, the comprehension skills of sequencing, making judgments, noting details, making generalizations, and using text structure can be linked to summarizing, which is a comprehension strategy (Lipson, 2001). These and other skills including generating questions, making inferences, distinguishing between important and less important ideas, and drawing conclusions facilitate students' use of one or more comprehension strategies. For example, students' ability to generate questions permeates all the Guided Comprehension strategies. (See Chapter 2, particularly Figure 2 on page 22, for more detailed information about questioning.)

Fielding and Pearson (1994) recommend a framework for comprehension instruction that encourages the gradual release of responsibility from teacher to student. This four-step approach includes teacher modeling, guided practice, independent practice, and application of the strategies in authentic reading situations. This framework is supported by Vygotsky's (1978) work on instruction within the zone of proximal development and by scaffolding, the gradual relinquishing of support as the students become more competent in using the strategies.

After explaining and modeling strategies, teachers scaffold instruction to provide the support necessary as students attempt new tasks. During this process teachers gradually release responsibility for learning to the students, who, after practicing the strategies in a variety of settings, apply them independently.

Guided Comprehension Connection This tenet is a core underpinning of Guided Comprehension because the Model is designed to promote comprehension as a strategy-based thinking process. It incorporates the explicit teaching of comprehension strategies and the skills that enable their use. The Model also provides multiple opportunities for practice and transfer of learning.

Differentiated Reading Instruction Accommodates Students' Needs, Including Those of English Learners and Struggling Readers

Duke and Pearson's (2002) work reminds us that learners need different kinds and amounts of reading comprehension instruction. As teachers, we understand this. We know that we have students of differing capabilities in our classes and we strive to help them to comprehend to the best of their abilities.

Differentiated instruction enables us to accommodate the diversity of students' needs (Gibson & Hasbrouck, 2008; Tyner & Green, 2005). To develop environments that promote differentiated instruction, Gibson and Hasbrouck (2008) suggest that we do the following:

- Embrace collaborative teaching and learning
- Use whole-class and small-group explicit strategy instruction
- Establish consistent routines and procedures
- Scaffold student learning

- Increase student engagement
- Teach students how to learn, as well as what to learn
- Change the way teaching occurs

We can differentiate a number of instructional components to support students as they gain competence and confidence in learning. These include *content*—the information being taught, *process*—the way in which the information is taught, and *product*—how the students demonstrate their learning (Tomlinson, 1999).

When we differentiate instruction we create multiple pathways to learning. This supports our goal of helping students to perform to their maximum potentials.

Guided Comprehension Connection Differentiated instruction is embedded in the Guided Comprehension Model. Flexible small-group instruction, multiple levels of text, and differentiated tasks are three examples of how we can accommodate individual students' needs when teaching Guided Comprehension. Examples of ideas for differentiating instruction are presented at the start of each theme in Chapters 7–10.

Excellent Reading Teachers Influence Students' Learning

Excellent reading teachers are valued participants in the learning process. As the National Commission on Teaching and America's Future (1997) has reported, the single most important strategy for achieving U.S. education goals is to recruit, prepare, and support excellent teachers for every school.

The teacher's knowledge makes a difference in student success (IRA, 1999). A knowledgeable teacher is aware of what is working well and what each student needs to be successful, and he or she knows the importance of every student having successful literacy experiences.

The teacher's role in the reading process is to create experiences and environments that introduce, nurture, or extend students' literacy abilities to engage with text. This requires that teachers engage in explicit instruction, modeling, scaffolding, facilitating, and participating (Au & Raphael, 1998).

Both reading researchers and professional organizations have delineated the characteristics of excellent reading teachers (Fountas & Pinnell, 1996; IRA, 2000; Ruddell, 1995). The following characterization of such reading teachers integrates these ideas.

Excellent reading teachers believe that all children can learn. They base their teaching on the needs of the individual learner. They know that motivation and multiple kinds of text are essential elements of teaching and learning. They understand that reading is a social constructivist process that functions best in authentic situations. They teach in print-rich, concept-rich environments.

Such teachers have in-depth knowledge of various aspects of literacy, including reading, writing, and discussion. They teach for a variety of purposes, using diverse methods, materials, and grouping patterns to focus on individual needs, interests, and learning styles. They also know the strategies good readers use, and they can teach students how to use them.

Excellent reading teachers view their teaching as multifaceted and they view themselves as participants in the learning process. They integrate their knowledge of the learning cycle, learning styles, and multiple intelligences into their teaching.

These teachers understand the natural relation between assessment and instruction, and they assess in multiple ways for a variety of purposes. They use instructional strategies that provide formative feedback to monitor the effectiveness of teaching and student performance. They know that assessment informs both teaching and learning.

Guided Comprehension Connection Teachers who engage in Guided Comprehension are knowledgeable not only about the concept but also about their students. They know that students read at different levels, and they know how to use the Guided Comprehension Model to accommodate each reader's needs. These educators are participants in the reading process. They know how to use a variety of materials in a variety of ways, within a variety of settings. Guided Comprehension provides a context for such teaching.

Good Readers Are Strategic and Take Active Roles in the Reading Process

Numerous reading researchers have reported that much of what we know about comprehension is based on studies of good readers (Askew & Fountas, 1998; Duke & Pearson, 2002; Pearson, 2001a; Pressley, 2000). They describe good readers as active participants in the reading process who have clear goals and constantly monitor the relation between the goals they have set and the text they are reading. Good readers use comprehension strategies to facilitate the construction of meaning. In Guided Comprehension, these strategies include previewing, self-questioning, making connections, visualizing, knowing how words work, monitoring, summarizing, and evaluating. Researchers believe that using a repertoire of such strategies helps students become metacognitive readers (Duke & Pearson, 2002; Palincsar & Brown, 1984; Roehler & Duffy, 1984).

Good readers read from aesthetic or efferent stances and have an awareness of the author's style and purpose (Rosenblatt, 1978, 2002). They read both narrative and expository texts and have ideas about how to figure out unfamiliar words. They use their knowledge of text structure to efficiently and strategically process text. This knowledge develops from experiences with different genres and is correlated with age or time in school (Goldman & Rakestraw, 2000).

These readers spontaneously generate questions at different points in the reading process for a variety of reasons. They know that they use questioning in their everyday lives and that it increases their comprehension. Good readers are problem solvers who have the ability to discover new information for themselves.

Good readers read widely. This provides exposure to various genres and text formats, affords opportunities for strategy use, increases understanding of how words work, provides bases for discussion and meaning negotiation, and accommodates students' interests.

Good readers construct and revise meaning as they read. They monitor their comprehension and know when they are constructing meaning and when they are not. When comprehension breaks down because of lack of background information, difficulty of words, or unfamiliar text structure, good readers know a variety of fix-up strategies to use. These strategies include rereading, changing the pace of reading, using context clues, cross-checking cueing systems, and asking for help. Most important, good readers are able to select the appropriate strategies and to consistently focus on making sense of text and gaining new understandings.

Helping students to become active, strategic readers is the ultimate goal of Guided Comprehension, and students fully participate in the process. Students' roles are extensive and include engaging in comprehension as a thinking process and transacting with various levels of text in multiple settings. Students then incorporate the strategies they learn into their existing repertoire and use them as needed.

Reading Should Occur in Meaningful Contexts

Duke (2001) has delineated an expanded understanding of context for present-day learners. She suggests that context should be viewed as curriculum, activity, classroom environment, teachers and teaching, text, and society. One of the interesting aspects of this expanded notion of context is the number of influences that impact student learning. As Cambourne (2002) reminds us, "what is learned cannot be separated from the context in which it is learned" (p. 26).

Lipson and Wixson (2009) suggest that the instructional context encompasses settings, practices, and resources. The instructional settings include teacher beliefs and literate environment, classroom interaction, classroom organization, and grouping. Instructional goals, methods, activities, and assessment practices are part of instructional practice. Commercial programs, trade materials, and technology are viewed as instructional resources.

More specific, literacy-based descriptions of context include ideas offered by Gambrell (1996), Hiebert (1994), and Pearson (2001a). They suggest that the classroom context is characterized by multiple factors including classroom organization and authentic opportunities to read, write, and discuss. They further note that the instruction of skills and strategies, integration of concept-driven vocabulary, use of multiple genres, and knowledge of various text structures are other contextual components.

Guided Comprehension is a context for teaching and learning comprehension strategies. It incorporates a variety of settings, practices, and resources. Students have numerous opportunities to read, write, and discuss using multiple genres and levels of text.

Students Benefit From Transacting Daily With a Variety of Texts at Multiple Levels

Students need to engage daily with multiple levels of texts. When such levels of text are being used, teachers scaffold learning experiences and students receive varying levels of support, depending on the purpose and context of the reading. When text is challenging, students have full teacher support. For example, teachers can share the text through read-aloud. When the text is just right for instruction, students have support as needed, with the teacher prompting or responding as necessary. Finally, when the text is just right for independent reading, little or no support is needed. (For a more detailed discussion of leveled text, see Chapter 6.)

Transacting with a wide variety of genres enhances students' understanding. Experience reading multiple genres provides students with knowledge of numerous text structures and improves their text-driven processing (Goldman & Rakestraw, 2000). Gambrell (2001) notes that transacting with a wide variety of genres—including biography, historical fiction, legends, poetry, and brochures—increases students' reading performance.

 In Guided Comprehension, students have opportunities to engage with a variety of texts at independent, instructional, and challenging levels on a daily basis.

Vocabulary Development and Instruction Affect Reading Comprehension

Vocabulary development and instruction have strong ties to reading comprehension. As the National Reading Panel (NICHD, 2000) notes, "Reading comprehension is a complex, cognitive process that cannot be understood without a clear description of the role that vocabulary development and vocabulary instruction play in the understanding of what has been read" (p. 13). Snow, Burns, and Griffin (1998) support this view, observing, "Learning new concepts and words that encode them is essential to comprehension development" (p. 217).

Harris and Hodges (1995) describe students' ever-growing knowledge of words and their meanings as *vocabulary development*. They note that vocabulary development also refers to the teaching–learning processes that lead to such growth. Vocabulary development is also influenced by the amount and variety of text students read (Baumann & Kame'enui, 1991; Beck & McKeown, 1991; Snow et al., 1998). Teacher read-alouds, which offer students access to a variety of levels of text, contribute to this process (Hiebert et al., 1998).

Blachowicz, Fisher, Ogle, and Watts-Taffe (2006) suggest that effective vocabulary instruction is characterized by the following:

- An environment that fosters word consciousness—"the awareness of and interest in learning and using new words and becoming more skillful and precise in word usage" (Graves & Watts-Taffe, 2002, p. 144)
- Students who actively participate in the process
- Instruction that integrates vocabulary with the curriculum and word learning throughout the day and across subject areas
- Instruction that provides both definitional and contextual information
- Teachers who provide multiple exposures to words
- Teachers who provide numerous, ongoing opportunities to use the words

Baumann and Kame'enui (1991) suggest that explicit instruction of vocabulary and learning from context should be balanced. The instruction should be meaningful to students, include words from students' reading, and focus on a variety of strategies for determining the meanings of unfamiliar words (Blachowicz & Lee, 1991). Another important aspect of such teaching is making connections between the vocabulary and students' background knowledge.

In Guided Comprehension, students are immersed in words. They engage daily with texts at multiple levels in a variety of settings, and they learn words through both explicit instruction and use of context. They also learn vocabulary strategies in scaffolded settings that provide numerous opportunities for practice and application, paired and group reading, and teacher read-alouds.

Engagement Is a Key Factor in the Comprehension Process

The engagement perspective integrates cognitive, motivational, and social aspects of reading (Baker, Afflerbach, & Reinking, 1996; Baker & Wigfield, 1999; Guthrie & Alvermann, 1999). Engaged learners achieve because they want to understand, they possess intrinsic motivations for interacting with text, they use cognitive skills to understand, and they share knowledge by talking with teachers and peers (Guthrie & Wigfield, 1997). Engaged readers are motivated by the material offered, use many strategies to comprehend the text they are reading, and are able to construct new knowledge after making connections with the text (Casey, 2008).

Engaged readers transact with print and construct understandings based on connections between prior knowledge and new information. Tierney (1990) describes the process of the mind's eye and suggests readers become part of the story within their minds. Teachers can nurture and extend this by encouraging students to read for authentic purposes and respond in meaningful ways, always focusing on comprehension, personal connections, and reader response. Baker and Wigfield (1999) note that "engaged readers are motivated to read for different purposes, utilize knowledge gained from previous experience to generate new understandings, and participate in meaningful social interactions around reading" (p. 453).

Pitcher and Fang (2007) suggest, "Motivation to read is a complex construct that influences readers' choices of reading material, their willingness to engage in reading, and thus their ultimate competence in reading, especially related to academic reading tasks" (p. 379). There are seven instructional practices that increase student motivation in reading and reading comprehension: Setting content goals, allowing students to choose what they read, picking a topic of interest, allowing social interactions, caring about what students do, using some extrinsic rewards, and reading for mastery goals (Guthrie et al., 2006). Edmunds and Bauserman (2006) recommend that teachers can increase their students' motivation to read by allowing students to select their own books, by paying attention to the characteristics of the books offered, by acknowledging students' personal interests and their access to the books, and by allowing active involvement of others during the reading process.

Motivation is described in terms of competence and efficacy beliefs, goals for reading, and social purposes of reading (Baker & Wigfield, 1999). Motivated readers believe they can be successful and are willing to take on the challenge of difficult reading material. They also exhibit intrinsic reasons for reading, such as gaining new knowledge about a topic or enjoying the reading experience. Motivated readers enjoy the social aspects of sharing with others new meanings gained from their reading.

Gambrell (1996) suggests that "classroom cultures that foster reading motivation are characterized by a teacher who is a reading model, a book-rich classroom environment, opportunities for choice, familiarity with books, and literacy-related incentives that reflect the value of reading" (p. 20). Gambrell, Palmer, Codling, and Mazzoni (1996) note that highly motivated readers read for a wide variety of reasons including curiosity, involvement, social interchange, and emotional satisfaction.

Guided Comprehension Connection The Guided Comprehension Model is based on students' active engagement. It integrates the cognitive, motivational, and social aspects of reading. Students use strategies to think through text. Students are motivated, because their interests and opportunities for success are embedded in the Model. Guided Comprehension is social because students negotiate meaning and interact with teachers and peers on a daily basis.

Dynamic Assessment Informs Comprehension Instruction

Dynamic assessment captures students' performance as they engage in the process of learning. It is continuous, provides an ongoing record of student growth, and has the ability to afford insights into students' understandings at any given point in the learning experience. Dynamic assessment reflects constructivist theory and is viewed not as an add-on but rather as a natural component of teaching and learning (Brooks & Brooks, 1993).

Dynamic assessments, which are usually informal in nature, can be used in a variety of instructional settings. These include scaffolded learning experiences in which students have varying degrees of teacher support. Assessing in this context captures the students' emerging abilities and provides insights that may not be gleaned from independent settings (Minick, 1987).

Guided Comprehension Connection Assessment permeates the Guided Comprehension Model, occurring for multiple purposes in a variety of settings. Dynamic assessment provides insights into students' thinking as they engage in all stages of the Model. This, in turn, informs future teaching and learning.

As delineated in this chapter, the Guided Comprehension Model for the Primary Grades has a sound theoretical framework. It is dynamic in nature, accommodates students' individual needs, employs a variety of texts and settings, and uses active, ongoing assessment. Chapter 2 details the Model by describing its three stages: teacher-directed whole-group instruction, teacher-guided small-group instruction and student-facilitated independent practice, and teacher-facilitated whole-group reflection and goal setting.

CHAPTER 2

The Guided Comprehension Model for the Primary Grades

Guided Comprehension is a context in which students learn comprehension skills and strategies in a variety of settings using multiple levels and types of text. It is a three-stage process focused on explicit instruction, application, and reflection. In Stage One, teachers use a five-step explicit instruction process: explain, demonstrate, guide, practice, and reflect. In Stage Two, students apply the strategies in three settings: teacher-guided small groups, student-facilitated comprehension centers, and student-facilitated comprehension routines. In Stage Three, teachers and students engage in reflection and goal setting. Student engagement with leveled text and placement in small groups are dynamic and evolve as students' reading abilities increase.

The Guided Comprehension Model for the Primary Grades is a framework designed to help teachers and students think about reading as a strategy-based process. The Model is based on existing research, knowledge of best practice, and personal experience. It integrates the following:

- Explicit instruction of comprehension strategies
- Leveled independent, instructional, and challenging texts
- Dynamic assessment
- Scaffolded instruction (varying levels of teacher support, with gradual release of control to students)
- Various genres and text types
- Reading, writing, and discussion
- Strategy instruction and application in a variety of settings
- Independent practice and transfer of learning in multiple settings
- Reflection and goal setting

Structurally, the Model has three stages that progress in the following sequence:

Stage One: Teacher-directed whole-group instruction

Stage Two: Teacher-guided small-group instruction and student-facilitated comprehension centers and comprehension routines (independent practice)

Stage Three: Teacher-facilitated whole-group reflection and goal setting

The Guided Comprehension Model is active for both teachers and students. For example, teachers engage in explicit instruction and select texts and strategies based on student needs, which

The Guided Comprehension Model

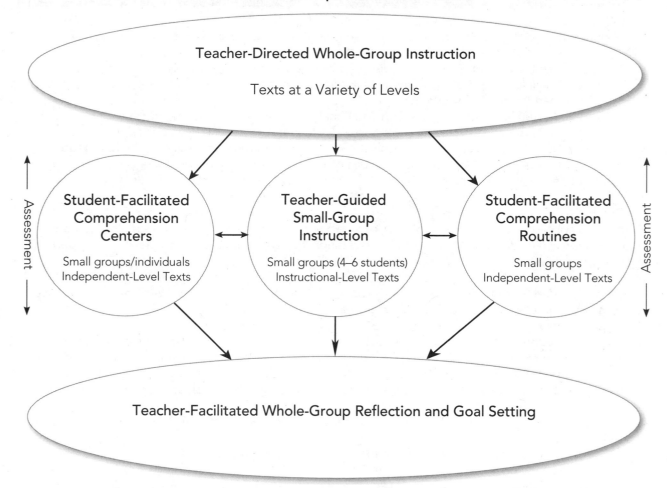

Teacher-Directed Whole-Group Instruction

Texts at a Variety of Levels

Assessment

Student-Facilitated Comprehension Centers

Small groups/individuals
Independent-Level Texts

Teacher-Guided Small-Group Instruction

Small groups (4–6 students)
Instructional-Level Texts

Student-Facilitated Comprehension Routines

Small groups
Independent-Level Texts

Assessment

Teacher-Facilitated Whole-Group Reflection and Goal Setting

are assessed continually. Teachers also participate by facilitating students' engagement in reading, writing, and discussion. Students' active roles in Guided Comprehension include thinking through the reading process, using strategies, transacting with text in multiple settings, and responding in a variety of ways.

The Guided Comprehension Model includes opportunities for whole-group, small-group, paired, and individual literacy experiences. Students transact daily with texts at a variety of levels. Teachers direct whole-group instruction, explicitly teach comprehension skills and strategies, and work daily with Guided Comprehension small groups. Teachers also observe and assess students as they engage in their independent comprehension activities.

The Model progresses from explicit teaching to independent application and transfer (see Figure 1). All stages of the Model are necessary to ensure that students can independently apply comprehension strategies in multiple settings. Assessment permeates every aspect of the Model, facilitating the gathering of information about student progress, which continually informs teaching and learning.

The Guided Comprehension Model for the Primary Grades is adapted from the original Guided Comprehension Model, which was developed for grades 3–8 (McLaughlin & Allen, 2002a). The primary-grade Model differs from the original Model in a number of ways. First, shared reading

Figure 1. Overview of Guided Comprehension Instruction in the Primary Grades

STAGE ONE

Teacher-Directed Whole-Group Instruction—Teaching a comprehension strategy using independent, instructional, or challenging text.

> **Explain** the current strategy and discuss how it relates to the class goal.
>
> **Demonstrate** the strategy using a Think-Aloud, a read-aloud, and a visual—chalkboard, chart, overhead slide, or PowerPoint.
>
> **Guide** student practice by reading additional sections of text aloud and encouraging pairs of students to apply the strategy with support. Monitor students' applications.
>
> **Practice** by asking students to apply the strategy to another section of text you have read, providing minimal support. Applications can occur in pairs or individually.
>
> **Reflect** by inviting students to think about how they can use this strategy on their own.

STAGE TWO

Students apply the comprehension strategies in teacher-guided small groups and student-facilitated comprehension centers and routines. In these settings, students work with varying levels of support and use appropriate instructional- and independent-level texts.

Teacher-Guided Small-Group Instruction—Applying comprehension strategies with teacher guidance using instructional-level texts and dynamic grouping (four or five students).

> **Review** previously taught strategies and focus on current strategy.
>
> **Guide** the students to apply the current strategy as well as previously taught strategies as they read sections of the instructional-level (just right) text or the text in its entirety. Prompt the students to construct and share personal meanings. Scaffold as necessary, gradually releasing support as students become more proficient. Encourage discussion and repeat this process with other sections of text.
>
> **Practice** by inviting students to work in pairs or individually to apply the strategy. Encourage discussion.
>
> **Reread, Retell, and Reflect** by inviting students to engage in a second reading of the text, retell what they read, and share ways in which the current strategy and the other strategies they know helped them to understand the text. Talk about ways in which students can apply the current strategy in comprehension centers and routines.

Student-Facilitated Comprehension Centers and Routines—Applying comprehension strategies individually, in pairs, or in small groups using independent-level (easy) texts.

> **Comprehension Centers** are independent activities that provide opportunities to practice strategy application and extend understandings.
>
> **Comprehension Routines** are procedures that foster habits of thinking and promote the comprehension of text.

STAGE THREE

Teacher-Facilitated Whole-Group Reflection and Goal Setting—Reflecting on performance, sharing experiences, and setting new goals.

> **Share** performances from Stage Two.
>
> **Reflect** on students' ability to use the strategy.
>
> **Set new goals** or extend existing ones.

ASSESSMENT OPTIONS

Use authentic measures in all stages.

Note. Adapted for the primary grades from McLaughlin & Allen, 2002a.

and interactive read-alouds are often integrated into explicit instruction in this Model. Second, teacher-guided small-group instruction has been expanded to include rereading and retelling. The comprehension centers include a variety of language-based activities. The comprehension routines have also been adapted; they now include Literature Circles, Reciprocal Teaching, and Cross-Age Reading Experiences.

Stage One: Teacher-Directed Whole-Group Instruction

In Stage One of Guided Comprehension, the teacher engages in explicit instruction by using a five-step process: explain, demonstrate, guide, practice, and reflect. The class is organized as a whole group during the first two steps, but flexible grouping occurs in the guide and practice steps. Stage One concludes with whole-class reflection. During this stage, the level of text may be easy, just right, or challenging because the teacher is reading aloud.

Organizing for Stage One

In Stage One of the Model, whole-group instruction provides students with a positive sense of belonging to a community of learners. The sense of community is fostered by student–teacher and student–peer interactions, print-rich environments, opportunities to engage with authentic texts from a variety of genres, students who are active learners, and teachers who are knowledgeable about their students and current best practice.

Because the instruction in Stage One of Guided Comprehension is teacher directed and allows us to fully support student learning, we can choose to teach from texts that range in level from easy to challenging. For example, if we choose a text that is interesting to the students and works well when teaching a particular strategy but is challenging in nature, we can share it with students through a read-aloud.

Engaging in Explicit Instruction

In working with a wide variety of literacy professionals, I have heard many say that reading educators often describe teaching comprehension strategies as "going over" the strategies with students, "telling" the students about the strategies, or just sharing blacklines. Effectively teaching comprehension strategies requires more than "going over" these ideas; it requires explicit instruction—explaining, demonstrating, guiding, practicing, and reflecting.

When engaging in explicit instruction, we use authentic text, and assessment is a natural part of the process. As previously noted, there are a variety of comprehension strategies incorporated into the Model. They include previewing (activating prior knowledge, setting a purpose for reading, and predicting), self-questioning, making connections, visualizing, knowing how words work, monitoring, summarizing, and evaluating. Which strategies are taught will depend on the students' stage of literacy development and their abilities. For example, the focus in kindergarten is often on teaching comprehension skills and just a few strategies—usually previewing and summarizing. To facilitate teaching comprehension strategies at your students' levels, consider active, strategic readers in the intermediate grades, take a step back, and contemplate what you can teach your students to help them become such readers.

Steps in Explicit Instruction

Regardless of the skill or strategy being taught, the explicit instruction process remains the same. It includes the following steps:

1. *Explain the skill or strategy*: Describe how the skill or strategy works and how it contributes to text comprehension. Describe a related teaching idea (see Appendix C) and explain how it works.

2. *Demonstrate the skill or strategy*: When introducing a skill or strategy at the primary level, use a read-aloud, a Think-Aloud, and an overhead projector, chalkboard, whiteboard, or poster paper. Using a Think-Aloud allows us to share our reasoning process with our students and to provide a model for students to think through their strategy use. As we think aloud, we orally explain precisely what is triggering our thoughts and how it is affecting our understanding. (For a detailed description of Think-Alouds, see Appendix C, pages 241–242.) This can lead to the development of personal connections, questions for clarification, and refined predictions. Duffy (2001) notes the importance of wording the Think-Aloud. For example, he suggests using the following format when modeling predicting:

   > Let me show you how I would make a prediction about this book. When I read the title, *The Very Hungry Caterpillar*, I know from having seen a caterpillar that it is a small insect. I also know that caterpillars turn into butterflies. The secret of making predictions is to think about what you already know from your own experience with caterpillars and butterflies. (n.p.)

   When using the Think-Aloud to demonstrate strategies, we need to explain our thinking so students have a clear idea of the cognitively active process readers experience as they transact with text.

3. *Guide the students to apply the strategy*: Read aloud the next section of the text and guide the students to apply the strategy just taught, prompting and offering assistance as necessary. When the students are comfortable with the strategy, continue scaffolding instruction by having the students work in pairs or small groups.

4. *Practice the skill or strategy*: Students begin to practice the skill or strategy independently in small groups, as we gradually relinquish control of the process.

5. *Reflect on strategy use*: Invite the students to reflect on how using the strategy helped them to understand the text. Discuss the ideas shared.

When engaging in explicit instruction, always focus on the following:

- Explaining the skill or strategy and how it works
- Demonstrating using a Think-Aloud
- Guiding students to practice, prompting and offering assistance as necessary
- Providing settings for group, paired, and independent practice
- Affording opportunities to reflect on strategy use

This stage also provides multiple opportunities for authentic assessment. These often include observation, discussion, informal writing, and sketching.

Throughout this framework, students' learning is scaffolded—responsibility is gradually released to the students. When students learn how the strategy works, they have our total support. When they engage in guided practice, they have our support as necessary. When they apply the strategy independently, our support is diminished and the students are in control.

Comprehension Strategies: Focus on Teaching

During Stage One of the Model, a number of teaching ideas can be used to clarify and reinforce students' understanding and application of the comprehension skills and strategies. Although these ideas are used as frameworks for teaching individual strategies, our goal is for students to eventually develop a repertoire of strategies they can use independently. This section provides a definition of each comprehension strategy and a list of related teaching ideas. These lists are not exhaustive, but they do include those that are used most frequently at the primary level. Appendix C contains a step-by-step process for explicit instruction of each teaching idea, as well as the idea's links to comprehension strategies, types of text, and reading stages.

Previewing is a way of introducing the text. It includes activating background knowledge, setting a purpose for reading, and predicting. The following teaching ideas support this strategy:

- Anticipation/Reaction Guide
- Predict-o-Gram
- Probable Passages
- Semantic Map
- Semantic Question Map
- Story Impressions
- Storybook Introductions

Self-questioning involves generating questions to guide thinking while reading. Teaching ideas that support this strategy include the following:

- "I Wonder" Statements
- K–W–L and K–W–L–S
- Paired Questioning
- Question–Answer Relationships (QAR)
- Thick and Thin Questions

Making connections occurs when students think about the text in relation to connections they can make to self, to texts, and to others. Teaching ideas that support this strategy include the following:

- Coding the Text
- Connection Stems
- Double-Entry Journal
- Draw and Write Connections

Visualizing is creating mental images while reading. Teaching ideas that support this strategy include the following:

- Draw and Write Visualizations
- Graphic Organizers/Visual Organizers
- Guided Imagery
- Open-Mind Portrait
- Sketch to Stretch

Knowing how words work is understanding words through strategic vocabulary development, including the use of the graphophonic, syntactic, and semantic cueing systems to figure out unknown words. The graphophonic cueing system involves creating grapheme (written letter)–phoneme (sound) matches. The syntactic cueing system deals with the structure of the language. The semantic cueing system focuses on meaning. Readers use all three cueing systems, along with other knowledge of words, to effectively engage with text. Ideas that support this comprehension strategy include the following:

- Concept of Definition Map
- Context Clues
- List–Group–Label
- RIVET
- Semantic Feature Analysis
- Text Transformations
- Vocabulary Bookmark

Monitoring involves asking, "Does this make sense?" and clarifying by adapting strategic processes to accommodate the response. Monitoring is knowing if meaning is being constructed and what to do if it is not. The following teaching ideas support this strategy:

- Bookmark Technique
- Cueing Systems Check
- Patterned Partner Reading
- Say Something
- Think-Alouds

Summarizing involves extracting essential information, including the main idea and supporting details, from text. Teaching ideas that support this strategy include the following:

- Bio-Pyramid
- Lyric Retelling and Lyric Summary
- Paired Summarizing
- QuIP (Questions Into Paragraphs)
- Retelling

- Story Map
- Story Pyramid
- Summary Cube

Evaluating means making judgments about text. The following teaching ideas support this strategy:

- Evaluative Questioning
- Journal Responses
- Mind and Alternative Mind Portraits
- Persuasive Writing
- Venn Diagram

Skills That Underpin the Comprehension Strategies

As noted earlier, comprehension strategies are more complex than skills and may require the orchestration of several comprehension skills. In the primary grades, students often begin by learning comprehension skills and then progress to learning strategies. The following list of skills is not exhaustive, but it offers a good sampling of the kinds of skills that underpin comprehension strategies:

- Decoding
- Generating Questions
- Recognizing Text Structures
- Sequencing
- Distinguishing Important From Less Important Ideas

These skills are essential components of the reading process, and they need to be taught. For example, the ability to generate questions is a skill that underpins every comprehension strategy (see Figure 2). For this reason, we should ensure that the students understand how to create questions by engaging in explicit instruction.

When teaching students about questioning, we can explain what questions are, discuss their purposes, and delineate their multiple levels. We can explain that there are many reasons for generating questions, including information seeking, connected understanding, historical speculation, imagination, and research. Busching and Slesinger (1995) note that the best way to help students develop meaningful questions is to encourage them to engage extensively in reading, writing, speaking, listening, and viewing.

Ciardiello (1998; 2007) suggests that students generate questions at four levels: memory, convergent thinking, divergent thinking, and evaluative thinking. He also provides the following signal words and cognitive operations for each category:

Memory Questions

Signal words: *who, what, where, when?*

Cognitive operations: naming, defining, identifying, designating

Figure 2. Generating Questions: A Skill That Supports Comprehension Strategies

Comprehension Strategy	Narrative Text (*The Fourth Little Pig* by Teresa Celsi)	Informational Text (*Wolves* by Seymour Simon)
Previewing	What is the story about? What might happen in this story?	What do I already know about wolves?
Self-Questioning	There are usually three little pigs. Who is the fourth little pig? Why is she wearing a cowgirl hat?	How are wolf packs like families?
Making Connections	What connections can I make between this story and the original little pigs story?	What connections can I make between the text description of wolves and the text illustrations and the video we saw about wolves? To the article we read in *National Geographic World*?
Visualizing	Is my mental picture of the fourth little pig still good? Why should I change it?	What do arctic wolves look like? How do they compare/contrast with _____ wolves?
Knowing How Words Work	Does the word *budge* make sense in the sentence?	What clues in the text can I use to figure out the word _____?
Monitoring	Does what I'm reading make sense? If not, what can I do to clarify?	Does what I'm reading make sense? If not, what can I do to clarify?
Summarizing	What has happened so far?	What is the most important information in the book?
Evaluating	Thinking about all the little pigs stories that I know, how would I rank the fourth little pig's story? Justify your response.	Do you think wolves will become extinct? Justify your response.

Note. Adapted for the primary grades from McLaughlin & Allen, 2009.

Convergent Thinking Questions

Signal words: *why, how, in what ways?*

Cognitive operations: explaining, stating relationships, comparing and contrasting

Divergent Thinking Questions

Signal words: *imagine, suppose, predict, if/then*

Cognitive operations: predicting, hypothesizing, inferring, reconstructing

Evaluative Thinking Questions

Signal words: *defend, judge, justify/what do you think?*

Cognitive operations: valuing, judging, defending, justifying

The teacher explains each question type and then models, first with life experiences and then with authentic text. Students engage in guided practice in a variety of settings and finally engage in independent application and transfer.

Stage Two: Teacher-Guided Small-Group Instruction and Student-Facilitated Comprehension Centers and Routines

Stage Two of the Guided Comprehension Model focuses on three instructional settings: teacher-guided small groups, student-facilitated comprehension centers, and student-facilitated comprehension routines.

Organizing for Stage Two

In Stage Two of Guided Comprehension, students have opportunities to apply the comprehension skills and strategies in a variety of settings with varying levels of support. Texts in this stage vary from the instructional level texts used in the teacher-guided small groups to the independent level texts used when students work independently in comprehension centers and routines.

Because students can work in three different settings in this stage, having an organizational plan is essential. One way to manage this time is to use a chart that illustrates the settings in which students should be at given times (see Figure 3). (Other organizational plans can be found in Appendix D.)

Teacher-Guided Small-Group Instruction

Although Stage Two is characterized by three different instructional settings, only one is teacher-guided. In this small-group setting, students of similar abilities apply their knowledge of strategies to leveled texts to become active, engaged readers. Students are dynamically grouped and progress at individual rates, changing groups as they become prepared to transact with increasingly challenging levels of text.

When organizing for teacher-guided small-group instruction, we need to consider the following factors:

- All students in the group need to have similar instructional levels; this means that all the students in this Guided Comprehension setting should be able to read the same texts with some teacher support.
- What we are teaching is determined by students' needs and use of skills and strategies while constructing meaning.
- While teaching in this setting, we also need to monitor students who are working independently in the comprehension centers and routines.

Figure 3. Organizing for Stage Two

Centers	Session 1	Session 2
ABC	☐ ☐ ☐ ☐	☐ ☐ ☐ ☐
Drama	☐ ☐ ☐	☐ ☐ ☐
Making Words	☐ ☐ ☐	☐ ☐ ☐
Theme	☐ ☐	☐ ☐
Writing	☐ ☐ ☐	☐ ☐ ☐

Routines	Session 1	Session 2
Literature Circles	☐ ☐ ☐ ☐	☐ ☐ ☐ ☐
Reciprocal Teaching	☐ ☐ ☐ ☐	☐ ☐ ☐ ☐
Cross-Age Reading Experiences	☐ ☐ ☐	☐ ☐ ☐

Teacher-Guided Small Groups	Session 1	Session 2
	☐ ☐ ☐ ☐ ☐ ☐	☐ ☐ ☐ ☐ ☐ ☐

Once the small groups are formed and the appropriate text is matched to students' abilities, the teacher meets with one or more guided small groups every day. During this time with the students we should use the following Guided Comprehension small-group lesson format:

- *Review* previously taught strategies and focus on the strategy of the day.
- *Guide* the students to apply the strategy being taught, as well as previously taught strategies, as they read a section of the instructional level text or the text in its entirety. Prompt the students to construct personal meanings. Incorporate word study as needed. (See Appendix B and selected centers in Chapter 3 for examples of teaching ideas to use for word study.) Scaffold as necessary, gradually releasing support as students become more proficient. Encourage discussion and repeat this process with other sections of text.
- *Practice* by having the students work in pairs or individually to apply the skills and strategies as they read the text (silently or in whisper tones).
- *Reread, retell, and reflect* by inviting students to do a second reading of the text, retell it, and share ways in which the skill or strategy helped them to understand the text. Extend learning by incorporating word study (see Appendix B), discussion, and related activities (see Appendix D). Discuss the text and ways in which the students can apply the skill or strategy in the comprehension centers and routines. The second reading of the text offers an opportunity to complete a running record with a student. (See Chapter 5 for information on running records.)

Review the strategies. Begin each guided group by reminding students about skills and strategies that have been taught previously. It is helpful to have these posted on a chart in the classroom or listed on a bookmark or other quick reference for the students. Keene and Zimmermann (1997) suggest creating "Thinking Records" using the following steps:

- Use chart paper to create a separate record for each strategy.
- Record strategy definitions.
- Include examples generated by children.
- Add questions and insights about the use of the strategy.
- Display the Thinking Records in the classroom.
- Add information about the strategies as they are learned and used.

This review is designed to remind students that even though they need to learn each strategy, the ultimate goal is to use them in concert—developing a repertoire of strategies to use as needed to construct personal meaning. After this quick review, the focus shifts to revisiting the strategy and related teaching idea featured in that day's whole-group setting.

Guide students. Begin by introducing the text and helping students preview. When the students will be reading narrative text, Marie Clay's Storybook Introduction (1991; see Appendix C, pages 218–220) can be used to introduce the text. Then ask each student to read silently or in whisper tones a designated portion of the text. Encouraging the students to read in whisper tones allows you to check on fluency and observe strategy use. After reading, integrate word study as needed and guide students to discuss understandings. To facilitate this, you may revisit predictions, verbalize connections, or share visualizations. You may ask, "What does this remind you of?" "Have you ever had an experience like this?" "How is this character like...?" You can also revisit students' original predictions and have students determine why their thinking has changed or remained the same. After this, the students read another predetermined section of the text and stop for more guided discussion.

Practice. When students are actively engaging with the text and constructing meaning, they practice reading and using the focus strategy. For example, they may make connections as they finish reading the text independently and then discuss it with the members of the small group. If the text appears challenging for the students, you may choose to continue guiding their comprehension until they are more successful.

Reread, retell, and reflect. The final component of teacher-guided small-group instruction includes rereading the text, retelling it, and reflecting on the text and strategy through discussion. Students may make personal responses and share new information or insights at this point. You may choose to incorporate word study and guide students to make broader connections to other texts and extend their understandings. These may be documented through writing, drawing, dramatization, or oral response. Students reread the text to enhance understanding and practice fluency. The rereading also provides an opportunity to do a running record with one of the students. This is also a good time to observe student responses and connections; this information will inform dynamic grouping, future student–text matches, and instructional planning. During discussion, it is important to ask students to reflect on their reading and to review the strategies they used to make sense of the text. This will remind students to transfer what they have learned in whole-class instruction and in their Guided Comprehension small groups to their reading of other texts. The Guided Comprehension Model provides students with two settings for such independent practice: comprehension centers and comprehension routines.

Student-Facilitated Comprehension Centers and Routines

Comprehension centers provide purposeful, authentic settings for students to integrate and apply their comprehension strategies. Students may work in small groups, with partners, or on their own when they are engaged in the centers. Theme-based center activities promote the integration of reading, writing, and discussion. Ideas for organizing and managing centers as well as descriptions of a variety of centers are presented in Chapter 3.

Students also practice and transfer what they have learned in comprehension routines. Comprehension routines are those habits of thinking and organizing that facilitate reading and response in authentic contexts. These are independent settings: This implies that students are knowledgeable about the strategies and routines, that they are provided with texts at their independent levels, and that they have ample time for practicing and transferring these processes. Routines used in Guided Comprehension at the primary level are described in detail in Chapter 4.

Stage Three: Teacher-Facilitated Whole-Group Reflection and Goal Setting

In this stage of the Model, the students and teacher gather to reflect on what they have learned. This stage follows a three-step process: share, reflect, and set new goals.

Organizing for Stage Three

In this setting we encourage students to think about what they have accomplished in the first and second stages of the Model. We want them to actualize their learning and be accountable for it. Bringing the class together also provides opportunities for closure and celebration of new knowledge.

The cyclical process of setting goals, engaging in learning experiences, reflecting on performance, and setting new goals helps students to perceive themselves as empowered, successful learners. It encourages students to think critically, observe progress, and take ownership of their learning.

It is these active roles that students are taking, not reflection itself, that is new to the educational process. In 1933, Dewey suggested that teachers become reflective practitioners to gain better understandings of teaching and learning. In 1987, Schön noted that reflection offers teachers insights into various dimensions of teaching and learning that can lead to better understanding. In the 1990s, when reflection became a valued component of evolving assessment practices, students were encouraged to engage actively in the process (Darling-Hammond, Ancess, & Falk, 1995; Hoyt & Ames, 1997; McLaughlin, 1995).

Self-reflection focuses on what students have learned and how they feel about their learning (Cooper & Kiger, 2001). It includes both self-assessment, which addresses process and product, and self-evaluation, which makes judgments about performance. Questions raised for self-assessment purposes include "What is confusing me?" and "How did I contribute to the discussion?" Questions that foster self-evaluation include "What did I do well?" and "Did I achieve my goal?"

Self-reflection offers insights into students' thinking. It not only illustrates that they are thinking but also details *how* they are thinking. According to Hoyt and Ames (1997), "Self-reflection offers students an opportunity to be actively involved in internal conversations while offering teachers an insider's view of the learning and the student's perception of self as learner" (p. 19). This focus on internal conversations parallels Tierney and Pearson's (1994) idea that "literacy learning is an ongoing conversation with oneself.... If we view learning as dynamic in character, as that evolving dialogue with oneself, then even major shifts become little more than the natural, almost inevitable, consequence of human reflection" (p. 514).

Reflection and Goal Setting in Guided Comprehension

Goal setting is a natural outgrowth of reflection. As Hansen (1998) notes, "Learning proceeds from the known to the new" (p. 45). What students have learned to a given point influences what they learn next; this is the foundation of goal setting. Students reflect on what they have learned and set future personal goals for continuous improvement. When students actively engage in creating both personal and class goals, they appear to be more motivated and take more responsibility for their learning (Clemmons, Laase, Cooper, Areglado, & Dill, 1993; Hill & Ruptic, 1994).

Because explicit instruction of reflection and goal setting is necessary, we apply the steps shared in Stage Two to this process. This is especially important in the primary grades, because students may not have strong background experiences in reflection; in fact, many may not even be familiar with the concept.

- *Explain* what reflection is and how it works.
- *Demonstrate* how to reflect.
- *Guide* students to apply reflection to something they have learned. Reflection forms can be used to facilitate this process (see Appendix E).
- *Practice* by providing students with multiple opportunities for application.

After engaging in reflection, students create new personal goals. The following are examples of new goals that were shared in student–teacher conferences in various grade levels:

- My goal is to read a book with my friend. (kindergarten)
- My new goal is to write a trifold story. (grade 1)
- My new goal is to ask better questions. (grade 2)
- My new goal is to share more in Literature Circle. Ask bigger questions, ones that have bigger answers. (grade 3)

When students become comfortable with reflection and goal setting, they engage in transfer of their learning. In Guided Comprehension, students have opportunities to reflect on their performance as members of a whole group, small group, or pair, as well as individually. (See Appendix E for reproducible blacklines for Reflection and Goal Setting, page 353, and Student Self-Reflection and Goal Setting in Guided Comprehension, page 352.)

Because reflection and goal setting are essential components of Guided Comprehension, it is important to maintain student interest in them. The following are additional teaching ideas to foster students' engagement in these processes.

Vary the components. When planning reflection and goal setting, we make selections from the following four categories:

1. *Type of goal*: individual or whole group, short term or long term
2. *Reflection setting*: whole group, small group, paired, or individual
3. *Reflection mode*: speaking, writing, illustrating, or dramatizing
4. *Sharing setting*: whole group, small group, paired, or individual

Choices can vary according to lesson content, student learning styles, or student interest. For example, students can create new personal goals by working in pairs to reflect on their learning, create sketches to illustrate their thinking, and then share them with a small group.

There are several formats for engaging students in written reflection, two of which are Guided Comprehension Journals and Tickets Out.

Guided Comprehension Journals: Students can use Guided Comprehension Journals during all stages of the Model. For example, they can use the journals to record notes for Literature Circles, jot down questions that arise during the stages of Guided Comprehension, and engage in reflection. In Stage Three, students can use the journals to record their reflections and set new goals.

Tickets Out: This is a favorite teaching idea because it fosters reflection, helps monitor students' learning, and takes very little time. It is called Tickets Out because students hand their tickets to the teacher as they exit the classroom at the end of the period or the end of the day. To participate in this activity, students use a half sheet of paper. On the first side, they write the most important thing they learned that day. On the other side, they write one question they have about something they learned that day. Whether students put their names on their tickets is the teacher's choice.

To complete this activity, students need only about five minutes. As the students leave the room, collect the tickets with side one facing up. After students have left the room, read side one of their tickets first. This is the side on which they record the most important thing they learned that day. During this part of Tickets Out, put aside any tickets that need clarification. Remember to discuss them at the start of the next day's class.

Next, turn over the entire pile of tickets and read the questions students have about their learning. Some days, more than one student will raise the same question, and other days, not every student will have a question. During this part of Tickets Out, put aside questions that you deem valuable. Respond to these questions, which usually number between four and six, at the start of the next day's class. This helps students understand that we value their thinking and also enhances the continuity from class to class.

Tickets Out is not a time-consuming process, but it does provide valuable information. For example, it offers insight into what students value about their learning and also gives us an opportunity to monitor and clarify any misconceptions they may have. (A reproducible graphic organizer for Tickets Out can be found in Appendix E, page 354.)

Provide prompts. Providing prompts can assist students when reflecting and creating new goals in a variety of settings. Prompts help to focus students' thinking on various dimensions of learning.

Questions to Guide Reflection
- What was your goal today? Did you reach it?
- What did you learn today?
- What did you do today that you have never done before?
- What strategies did you find most helpful?
- What confused you today? How did you figure it out?
- How did your group do? What contributions did you make to your group? What contributions did others make?
- What questions do you have about what you learned today?
- How do you think you will use what you learned today?

Reflection Stems

- I was really good at…
- The best thing I learned today was…
- I found out that…
- I contributed…to our literature discussion.
- I read…and found out that…
- When I was confused today, I…

Questions to Guide Goal Setting

- What do you need to work on?
- Where will you start next time?
- What do you hope to accomplish?
- What is your new goal?

Goal-Setting Stems

- I need more work on…
- Tomorrow, I hope to…
- My goal for tomorrow is to…

Students can think about one or more of these prompts and then share their responses. Sharing can take place with a partner, a small group, or the whole class. I often use Think–Pair–Share (McTighe & Lyman, 1988) as a framework for this. Students *think* about their learning, *pair* with a partner to discuss ideas, and then *share* their thoughts with the class. Students also can write their reflections in their Guided Comprehension Journals and then use Think–Pair–Share. This technique can be adapted for goal setting. First, students *think* about their performance and new goal(s), then they write it. Next, they *pair* with a partner to discuss their new goal(s). Finally, they *share* their goal(s) with the whole class. Sharing with the whole class is beneficial because it shows that everyone values reflection and goal setting and provides good models for the other students.

The Guided Comprehension Model for the Primary Grades provides a variety of settings for student learning. These include student-facilitated comprehension centers and routines, settings in which the students engage in independent practice. These components of Stage Two are examined in detail in Chapters 3 and 4.

CHAPTER 3

Creating, Organizing, and Managing Comprehension Centers

Comprehension centers provide purposeful, authentic settings for students to independently apply their comprehension strategies. Students may work in small groups, with partners, or on their own in this setting. Comprehension centers promote the integration of reading, writing, and discussion and provide a variety of ways for students to integrate and practice their comprehension strategies.

Student-facilitated comprehension centers are described in detail in this chapter. It begins by explaining the nature of the primary-level centers and delineating their purposes. Next, issues related to organization and management, including scheduling and student accountability, are explored. Finally, descriptions of a variety of comprehension-based centers and sample activities are presented.

Creating Guided Comprehension Centers

The time students spend in comprehension centers should be meaningful. This means that we need to be aware of students' abilities to work independently, create engaging activities, and provide accessible text. It is important to take time to teach students about the purpose of each center and how it functions. The five steps of explicit instruction—explain, demonstrate, guide, practice, and reflect—facilitate this process.

Center activities should accommodate a variety of learning levels, be open-ended, and be able to be completed independently—in small groups, in pairs, or individually. The activities should be purposeful, address a variety of interests and intelligences, and help students to think critically and creatively. The activities also should be engaging, foster discussion, extend learning, and promote decision making and student ownership of learning.

The centers are usually located around the perimeter of the classroom and away from the area used for teacher-guided small-group instruction (Guided Reading). The centers vary in appearance from tabletop tri-fold displays to file folders, pizza boxes, and gift bags. It is important to remember that the content of the center is more important than its physical appearance.

A variety of centers can be used when implementing the Guided Comprehension Model. Some centers may be specific to reading skills such as the ABC center; others, such as the mystery center, represent a theme-related genre; still others, such as the listening center and the writing center, are process based. Centers may be permanent throughout the year, but the topics addressed may change with themes. For example, in the poetry center, the resources could change from poems about families to poems about seasons, depending on the current theme.

During center time, students can work independently or in small groups to make words, apply strategies while reading theme-related texts, write stories or poems, complete projects, or engage in other theme-related activities. The teacher should provide a structure for these projects but make sure that the activity is open-ended to allow for students to apply thinking and personal interpretations.

Although there are many activities that can be completed in literacy centers, in Guided Comprehension, center activities are designed to promote students' development and application of comprehension skills and strategies. (A graphic organizer to facilitate planning literacy centers can be found in Appendix D, page 300. Suggested centers, accompanying open-ended projects, and other extensions for learning are described in this chapter; additional center activities are embedded in the theme lessons in Part Two.)

ABC Center

Students participate in a wide variety of language activities ranging from word sorts to creating alphabet books of varying levels of complexity.

A-B-C Watch Me Read! (Page, 2001): Students fold a piece of paper into eight sections. At the top of each section, they write one of their favorite lowercase letters. Next, they look around the room and in familiar literature to find words they can read that begin with each of the chosen letters. Then they copy the words onto their charts.

Alphabet Books—Individual: When students know 10 letters, they begin making their own alphabet books. They continue adding to the books as they learn the remaining letters.

Students continue making alphabet books through the elementary grades. These books are often theme based. Titles of student books might include *My Favorite Author Alphabet Book*, *My ABC Book of Friends*, or *My Community Alphabet Book*. (See Appendix D, page 297, for a list of published alphabet books that serve as great models for this activity.)

Class Alphabet Book: Students can create individual pages to contribute to a class alphabet book. The class alphabet books might be based on a theme, favorite author, or favorite genre.

Sentence Strips: Sentence strips from a variety of stories are kept at this center. Students can use these for numerous activities including practicing sequencing; reviewing the beginning, middle, and end structure of stories; and reading and retelling the story.

Sorts: A variety of sorts can be kept at this center. Students may use these cards or manipulatives to create sound, word, or concept sorts. (For more information about sorts, see Appendix B.)

Art Center

Students use materials at the art center to visually represent their understandings of texts or to create illustrations for the texts they are writing. A variety of materials and examples of specific art techniques should be available at the center. The following materials are suggested:

- All kinds of paper—colored, lined, construction, large, textured, adhesive notes
- All kinds of writing and illustrating utensils—markers, crayons, paints, colored pencils, pencils, water colors, texture paints
- Scraps of fabric, scraps of wallpaper, contact paper, cotton balls, and macaroni (and other items to provide texture for illustrations)
- Glue sticks, white glue, tape
- Scissors—straight and patterned—and hole punchers
- Stamps—alphabet, textures, symbols, designs
- Printmaking supplies
- Wire, yarn, sticks with rounded edges, ribbon, rubber bands
- Magazines, catalogs

The center should include samples and directions for a variety of art techniques, such as drawing, collage, painting, printmaking, and puppetry.

Drama Center

In this center, students use acting to demonstrate their understandings. They can plan and rehearse their acting performances. The following are some ideas for implementing drama in the classroom.

Puppet Theater: Students use puppets provided at this center to engage in storytelling and retelling. Puppets may be created from paper bags, wooden spoons, or other materials.

Readers Theatre: Students use minimal theatre to dramatize stories. They first transcribe a story or other text into a play format, and then they rehearse the dramatization using voice, facial expressions, and movement to portray characterizations. They use scripts during the performance.

Genre Center

The focus of the genre center changes as the year progresses. Possible topics include biography, traditional and transformational fairy tales, fantasy, folk tales, mystery, and poetry. (For examples of genre centers, see the descriptions of mystery center and poetry center in this section.)

Making Words Center

Students use a variety of activities to construct words. (For related blackline masters, see Appendix D, pages 316–317.)

Making Words (Cunningham, 2008): Students manipulate the letters of a mystery word to create other words. They begin with short words and progress to longer ones. They may create the words based on clues or just list as many words as possible. Then they guess the mystery word. When creating the words, students may manipulate plastic letters, arrange magnetic letters on a cookie sheet, or use letter tiles.

Making and Writing Words (Rasinski, 1999a): In this adaptation of Making Words, students write the words they create from the letters in a mystery word. Making and Writing Words provides students with opportunities to practice their handwriting and spelling.

Making and Writing Words Using Letter Patterns (Rasinski, 1999b): In this adaptation of Making and Writing Words, students use rimes (word families) and other patterns as well as individual letters to create words. Then students transfer their knowledge to create new words. Finally, they cut up the organizer to create word cards, which they use to practice the words in games and sorts.

For example, in a unit on mysteries, students might read *Cam Jansen and the Mystery Writer Mystery* (Adler, 2007), and *theater* (p. 52) might be the mystery word. The letters in the word would be shared in random order. Then the students would be asked to make and write as many words as they can using the letters in that word (only once unless a letter was repeated in the mystery word). Following are some of the words they might create.

- Two-letter words: *at, he*
- Three-letter words: *tea, tee, tar, eat, ate, art, rat*
- Four-letter words: *rate, heat, tear, hare*
- Five-letter words: *threat*
- Six-letter words: *heater*
- Mystery word: *theater*

Mystery Center

Students read mysteries and use the elements of the genre to create mysteries in a variety of formats. Mysteries students write can be placed in the classroom library or students can share them with the class in Author's Chair.

Create-a-Mystery: Label bags or boxes with the major components of a mystery (such as suspects, clues, victims, detectives, criminals, motives, crimes, and crime scenes). Teachers record on index cards examples of each from mysteries they have read, and then they place the index cards in the appropriate bag or box. Students select one index card from each box and use that information to create a mystery. After writing the mystery, students can illustrate it and share it with the class. The students can then extend this activity by participating in a Mystery Theater.

Suspicious Suspects: The students organize their thoughts about the suspects in a mystery by completing the Mystery Suspect Organizer (see Appendix D, page 320). Based on the clues, the students can easily come to a conclusion about who committed the crime. The organizer also can be completed as a planner for writing a mystery.

Write Your Own Mystery: The students will use the Write Your Own Mystery graphic organizer to record information to help them plan mysteries they will write (see Appendix D, page 336). The organizer also can be used to help students summarize a mystery they are reading. On the organizer they draw, describe, or explain the crime scene. They write two clues and describe a main character, and they also write a brief description of how the mystery is solved. As an alternative writing activity, students can create mysteries based on photos or story starters placed at the center. Following is a mystery written by a second-grade student:

The Case of the Missing Grapes
by Cody Baker

Red grapes are my favorit. They were in the fruit bowl when my family went to a fotball game. It was a great game. We had lots of fun and our team won. After the game, we went back to my house and my mom said that my brother and I could have some fruit before dinner. I ran to the fruit bowl to get my grapes, but when I got there, the grapes were missing. I asked my brother if he had taken them, but he's my yunger brother and he hadn't even reached the fruit bowl yet. Then I asked my dad if he ate them and he said he saw them on top of the fruit bowl when we left, but he didn't eat them. Next, I asked my mom and she said they had to be in the bowl, because that is where she put them. So, she checked the bowl, and they really were gone. My mom said this is quite a mystery.

I wondered what happened to the grapes. I looked in the refrdgerator and in the cupburds, but I couldn't find them anywhere. Then I went to my room to play with my Wi and the mystery was solved! I started seeing grapes on the floor one by one and when I went in my room, our cat was sitting in the middle of the floor eating the grapes. I told my family and we all laughed.

Mystery Poetry: Students write poems about various aspects of mysteries using formats such as acrostics, cinquains, definition poems, or diamantes (see Appendix D, pages 323–327, for poetry forms). For example, students may write an acrostic about one of the suspects in a mystery by writing the name and using the letters in the suspect's name as starters for the clues related to this suspect. Students can contribute their poems to a class book of mystery poems or use their poems for a Poetry Theater presentation.

Mystery Pyramid: Students can manipulate language by trying to fit all the elements of a mystery into a Mystery Pyramid (see Appendix D, page 319). Students enjoy completing this activity with a partner or in trios.

Mystery Theater: The students practice a scene from a mystery they have read, and then perform it for the class. The audience tries to guess which mystery the scene is from and the characters involved.

Word Detective: Using the Word Detective Sequential Roundtable Organizer, the students can create a master list or word wall of mystery words from mysteries read (see Appendix D, page 335). The completed list can then be used to support students' writing or mystery theme word sorts.

Listening Center

Students can independently apply their comprehension strategies as they listen to a variety of theme-related audio books at this center.

Making Books Center

Students can retell key events from stories, gather data and create reports on content area topics, or write creative pieces that can be published. These may be self-created or follow a familiar structure, such as alphabet books. The following is a list of book types and suggestions for using them:

- *Accordion*: retelling, content area facts, creative stories with illustrations
- *Origami*: word books, retelling, facts, short stories, story elements

- *Flip/flap*: word work (parts of speech, antonyms, synonyms, rhymes, prefixes/suffixes, story elements, riddles)
- *Slotted*: journals, reading response, word books, alphabet books
- *Dos à dos*: dialogue or buddy journal, research and report, compare/contrast
- *Stair-step*: riddle books, sequence story events, time lines

(See Appendix D, pages 307–309, for directions for making books.)

Pattern Book Center

Students use a pattern from a familiar book and retell the story or share information using the pattern. Some effective patterns are those used in *Fortunately* by Remy Charlip (1993) and *The Important Book* by Margaret Wise Brown (1990). Providing specific organizers for pattern books helps students plan these books (see Appendix D, pages 321–322).

Poetry Center

Keep a large supply of poetry books and poetry cards at this center. Provide lots of copies of poems that students can read, act out, or illustrate. The following are activities students will enjoy completing at the Poetry Center.

Poetry Forms: Students create their own poems using structured formats such as bio-poems, cinquains, and diamantes. Blacklines of poem formats (see Appendix D, pages 323–327) for students to use and examples of completed poems are available at this center.

Poetry Frames: Students create their own versions of published poems. The teacher can create frames in which students can write their own words, keeping the structure but changing the content of the original poem. (See Appendix D, page 312, for a poetry frame for "If I Were in Charge of the World.")

Poem Impressions: Students write poems based on a series of clues provided from an existing story poem, and then they share their poems. Finally, the original poem is read and discussion focuses on comparing and contrasting the impressions with the original poem.

Poetry Theater: In small groups, students plan and practice acting out a poem. These dramatizations include minimal theatrics and props and maximum expression through voice and actions.

Poetry Turnabouts: Students can work with partners to change a story poem into a written story or picture book. For example, students might read "Sick," a story poem by Shel Silverstein in which little Peggy Ann McKay pretends to be sick so she can stay home from school. Then at the end of the poem, she learns that it is Saturday and she suddenly is feeling just fine and is going out to play. The following is a student example of a Poetry Turnabout for "Sick":

> Little Peggy Ann McKay thought she could stay home from school if she pretended to be sick. So she said she had a long list of reasons to be sick like measles, mumps, and purple bumps. Then someone said it was Saturday and she knew there was no school, so she stopped pretending to be sick and went out to play.

Project Center

Students work on specific extensions or projects related to the theme or current events. These may include multiple modes of response such as reading, writing, illustrating, and dramatizing. Various reference materials, from encyclopedias to books to the Internet, should be readily available.

Book Cubes: Students use the Summary Cube (see Appendix C, pages 249–250 and 291) to present essential information about a book. For example, students can record the title, author, main character(s), setting, summary statement, and illustration.

Bookmarks: Students create bookmarks about the book they read. They may choose what to include on the bookmark or the teacher can provide guidelines. For example, information for narrative texts may include title, author, main character(s), the student's thoughts about the book, and illustrations of characters or events. For informational texts, students can include the title, author, key ideas learned, their reactions, and illustrations.

Book Mobile: Students create mobiles about books they have read. Students may create the mobile on their own or use the Book Mobile Organizer (see Appendix D, page 298) to format the information. Information may include the title, author, setting, characters, problem, resolution, and illustration. Students may also use the mobile format to share information about the author, focus on a single narrative element (e.g., character mobiles), or review a book. Because the mobiles will be suspended from the ceiling, students can record information on both sides of the paper.

Newspaper/Newsletter: Students write newspaper articles related to a topic of study and publish them in a newspaper format. Examples include articles about pollution during an oceans theme, reviews of a new book or book-based movie such as *Cloudy With a Chance of Meatballs*, and collections of comic strip summaries presented as the comics section of the newspaper.

Press Conference (McLaughlin, 2010): This inquiry-based activity promotes oral communication. Students choose a topic to investigate. Then they peruse newspapers, magazines, or the Internet to find at least two sources of information about the topic. After reading the articles, focusing on essential points, raising questions, and reflecting on personal insights, the student presents an informal summary of his or her research to a group of classmates or the entire class. Members of the audience then raise questions that can lead to "I Wonder" Statements that students can record in their investigative journals (see the Press Conference Summary blackline in Appendix D, page 328). Students can use Questions Into Paragraphs (QuIP) to organize the information for their Press Conference (see Appendix C, pages 245–246).

Open-Mind Portraits (Tompkins, 2006): Students draw two or more portraits of one of the characters in a story. One drawing is a regular face of the character; the other drawings include one or more representations of the mind of the character at important points in the story. The mind pages include words and drawings representing the character's thoughts and feelings.

Questions Into Paragraphs (QuIP) (E.M. McLaughlin, 1987): Students ask questions related to the topic and use two or more sources to find answers to each question. The information is recorded on a QuIP Research Grid (see Appendix C, pages 245–246 and 284) and then used to write a summary paragraph or to organize research for a Press Conference.

ReWrite (Bean, 2000): In this activity, students write songs before and after content area study. For example, students write a song based on what they think they know about bats. Then they read to learn about bats and rewrite their lyrics based on the new information. The rewrite represents how students' knowledge, perceptions, and feelings have changed after studying the topic. Tunes may include familiar songs or instrumental tapes.

Choose Your Own Project: Students make selections from a list of ideas to extend their thinking about what they have read (see Appendix D, page 304).

Storytelling Center

Students can engage in storytelling, in which they focus on the narrative elements (characters, setting, problem, attempts to resolve the problem, and resolution) with a partner or small group. It is a good idea to provide a tape recorder at this center, so students can listen to themselves tell stories.

Wordless Picture Books: Students tell the story of wordless picture books, such as Alexandra Day's *Carl Goes to Daycare* (1995) and *Carl's Masquerade* (1992), or David Wiesner's *Tuesday* (1991), *Sector 7* (1999), *The Three Pigs* (2001), and *Flotsam* (2006). Students may work in pairs or tape record their storytelling.

Storytelling Gloves: Students use Storytelling Gloves with Velcro-backed characters and other representations of the narrative elements to sing familiar songs and share rhymes and tales. Commercially available Storytelling Gloves include "Old MacDonald Had a Farm," "The Three Little Pigs," "Five Green and Speckled Frogs," "Five Little Ducks," "The Three Bears," "The Itsy Bitsy Spider," "Baa Baa Black Sheep," and "The Gingerbread Man." (Storytelling Gloves and Lapboards are available from Lakeshore at www.lakeshorelearning.com.)

Teaching Center

In this center, students work with partners and take turns being the teacher. A variety of activities can be used in this center.

Transparency Talk (Page, 2001): In this center, a student assumes the role of the teacher. He or she places transparencies containing onsets and rimes, sentences, messages, or stories the classroom teacher has prepared on the overhead projector. The "teacher" then uses these for a variety of activities including finding and lifting words he or she can read, finding all the words that begin or end with a particular sound or pattern, or reading along with a partner. (Place the projector on the floor and use a white piece of paper for a screen.)

Read the Room: The "teacher" uses a pointer and the "student" and "teacher" take turns reading room labels, the word wall, bulletin board, or morning message as the "teacher" points to it. Then the partners switch roles.

Shared Reading: The "teacher" uses a pointer as he or she and the "student" read a Big Book together.

Theme Center

Books at a variety of levels related to the theme of study are housed in this center. Students may self-select a book to read and use it to practice and transfer comprehension strategies. Students may also select the mode of reading they will use. This often includes using the following patterns from Patterned Partner Reading:

- *Predict–Read–Discuss*: Partners make predictions about material, read to confirm or disconfirm their predictions, discuss the outcome, and then renew the cycle.

- *Read–Pause–Make a Connection*: Partners take turns making connections to the text they are reading.

- *Read–Pause–Retell*: Partners read, stop to think, and retell what they have read to that point.

- *You Choose*: Partners select which mode to use.

(To learn more about Patterned Partner Reading, see Appendix C, pages 239–240.)

Vocabulary Center

This center may have a word wall or other display of words that can be the focus of study. These words may be structurally similar (rhymes, prefix, suffix, roots) or may be theme-related. Sentences also may be displayed, so students can use context clues to "Guess the Covered Word" (Cunningham, 2008).

This center also may include interesting word books (such as *The Weighty Word Book* by Paul Levitt [1990], *Animalia* by Graeme Base [1996], or books by Fred Gwynne, Ruth Heller, or Marvin Terban) that can provide the impetus for word study. Students work on learning, using, and making connections to these new vocabulary words. The following are activities students can complete at the vocabulary center.

Acrostics: Students write the name of a topic or character vertically, and then write words or phrases to describe the topic, each description starting with one of the letters in the name. The focus can include characters, places, people, or any other topic related to areas of study. Students can also use the acrostic form to retell key events of a story in sequential order.

Invent a Word: Students use their knowledge of prefixes, suffixes, and roots to create new words and their meanings. Then students illustrate the new word's meaning.

Word Bingo: Students put 16 vocabulary words on a Bingo sheet. Clues such as definitions, synonyms, antonyms, or rhymes are listed on cards and placed in a bag or box. One at a time, a student pulls out a card and reads the clue, and students cover the word with a marker. The first student to get four in a row wins.

Word Sorts: Students sort vocabulary words into categories provided by the teacher (closed sort) or by self-selected categories (open sort). These might include rhyming words, parts of speech, vowel sound, syllables, and specific theme subtopics. This may be completed in a hands-on fashion, using word cards; then students can record their ideas on a word-sort sheet. This activity also may be completed in writing on a web or other organized structure.

Word Storm: A visual display—such as a picture from a book, a piece of art, or a poster—provides the impetus for word brainstorming. Students look at the visual and brainstorm and record words that come to mind. Then they use some or all of the words to create a detailed sentence or paragraph about the visual.

Writing Center

This center is a place for free and structured writing. Students may write informally or use the writing process. You may also structure the writing using one or more of the following ideas.

Informational Writing: Students write restaurant menus and checks; create brochures about theme-related topics; write newspaper articles; write letters; and develop book, movie, and music reviews.

Journals: Students write about self-selected topics or respond to teacher-provided prompts.

Patterned Writing: Students use patterned books, poetry forms, fractured fairy tales, and nursery rhymes as formats for writing.

Sticker or Stamp Stories: Students use stickers or stamps to create an illustration with action and then write a story to accompany the picture.

Story Bag: Students pull out one item at a time from a bag of story-related props the teacher has prepared. They create a story based on the props as they remove them from the bag.

Story Collages: Instead of writing a story and then illustrating it, students create textured illustrations first and then develop stories based on them. Because the illustrations are textured (pine cones, aluminum foil, felt, sand), students can use their tactile modalities (Brown, 1993).

Story Impressions: Students write a story based on approximately 10 clues from a story. Each clue is from three to five words, and the clues are placed sequentially and connected with downward arrows. The title of the original story may or may not be shared. When the story is completed and the students read it, the original author's story is read for comparison and contrast (see Appendix C, pages 217–218).

Story Trifold: Students write a story using a graphic that folds into three labeled parts: beginning, middle, and end (see Appendix D, page 334).

Organizing and Managing Comprehension Centers

Students can move from center to center in a variety of ways, depending on the structure of the literacy schedule and the students' level of independence. The following methods are used frequently.

Menu Board: One way to organize center time is to use a menu board that provides a visual organizational overview of Stage Two (see Figure 3 on page 24). The students who will meet for teacher-guided small-group instruction are listed on the menu board. Center choices are also provided and students put their names under the center name where they will work. The number of students who may work at a given center or at a given activity within a center is designated at that center and on the menu board. For example, three is the designated number of students for the making words center as posted at the activity site and on the menu board. Students continue working at their assigned center until they complete the work they have scheduled for that day. For example, students may choose to work on word study at the ABC center or use a partner-reading pattern to read a book at the theme center. This assures that choice is being accommodated on multiple levels: Students can choose what goals they are trying to achieve that day, which centers to visit, how long to stay, and how to manage their time.

Required and Optional Centers: We can also provide students with a framework for required and optional centers (see Appendix D, page 333). Sometimes we may choose to assign students to the centers where they will begin, but they may choose to move later, as openings at other centers occur.

Rotating Schedule: Some teachers prefer to move the students using a rotating schedule. With this setup, students move among three or four activities, changing every 15 to 20 minutes. This rotational format provides maximum control by the teacher, but limits students' opportunities for choice and for learning to manage their own time.

Student Accountability

Students need to be accountable for the time they spend at the centers. Using a record-keeping system helps to keep track of which centers each student visits during the week. We can use a whole-group chart to monitor who visits which centers each week, or we can place charts at individual centers for students to record their visits. Students may also keep track of their work in their Guided Comprehension Journals (see cover sheet in Appendix D, page 311).

Student self-assessment can also contribute to our understanding of how students used their center time. Providing self-assessment forms that indicate which centers students visited, what they did, and how they think they progressed toward their goal on a particular day facilitates this process (see Appendix D, page 303).

Students can keep their center work and reflections in a two-pocket folder, where the teacher can review them weekly or biweekly. Students also can share their work with the teacher in individual conferences. Including a checklist, rubric, or other evaluative tool at each center facilitates this process (see Appendix D). At the end of Stage Three, selected works will be transferred to the students' Guided Comprehension Profiles.

Regardless of what the comprehension centers include or how they are managed, they are places for independent exploration by students. The centers should accommodate a variety of abilities, be open-ended, have clear directions, be motivational, and provide activities that are familiar to students so they can use them independently.

Ford and Opitz (2002) suggest the following guidelines for using centers to facilitate this process:

- Operate with minimal transition time and management concerns.
- Encourage equitable use of centers and activities among learners.
- Include a simple built-in accountability system.
- Allow for efficient use of teacher preparation time.
- Build the centers around classroom routines.

In the next chapter, another setting in which students independently apply reading skills and strategies, student-facilitated comprehension routines, is described in detail. The comprehension routines discussed include adapted versions of Literature Circles, Reciprocal Teaching, and Cross-Age Reading Experiences.

CHAPTER 4

Organizing and Managing Comprehension Routines

Comprehension routines are habits of thinking and organizing that facilitate reading and response in authentic contexts. These routines provide another context in which students can practice their reading comprehension strategies independently. Their purpose is to help students gain a deeper understanding of the text and to equip students with a set of strategies they can use with other texts on their own. These are independent settings, which implies that students are able to work on their own, are knowledgeable about comprehension skills and strategies, know how to use the routines, have access to texts at their independent levels, and have ample time for practicing and transferring these processes.

Over time, routines become courses of action that are so ingrained that they can be used successfully on a regular basis. Routines that are most effective for promoting comprehension in both whole-group and small-group settings at the primary level are Literature Circles, Reciprocal Teaching, and Cross-Age Reading Experiences.

Before students can use these comprehension routines independently, they need to understand the purpose of the routines, why they are engaging with them, and how the routines function. These needs can be accommodated by using the five-step explicit instruction process— explain, demonstrate, guide, practice, and reflect—to teach the routines. This process of gradual release ensures that students' learning is scaffolded. The teacher can begin by offering total support, and, as learning progresses, he or she gradually releases control of the routines to the students.

It is important to note that students engage in the various routines as appropriate for their developmental stage. For example, students can begin engaging in Cross-Age Reading Experiences in kindergarten, but they may only begin to learn some skills associated with the other routines at that level. For this reason, teaching models for Literature Circles and Reciprocal Teaching for each grade level are included.

Literature Circles, Reciprocal Teaching, and Cross-Age Reading Experiences are described in this chapter. These routines, along with Directed Reading–Thinking Activity and Directed Listening– Thinking Activity, are presented in a step-by-step teaching process in Appendix C.

Literature Circles: What We Know

Literature Circles enable students to use discussion and interaction to better comprehend what they are reading. Meeting independently in small groups provides opportunities for students to become more engaged in conversation and make connections to their own experiences (Brabham

& Villaume, 2000; Ketch, 2005). In Literature Circles, groups of students share their insights, questions, and interpretations of the same or theme-related texts. The goal of Literature Circles is to provide students with a setting in which to converse about texts in meaningful, personal, and thoughtful ways (Brabham & Villaume, 2000). In Guided Comprehension, this means that students are integrating their comprehension skills and strategies as they construct personal meaning.

Implementing Literature Circles

To facilitate students' use of Literature Circles, we need to explicitly teach the concept and actively demonstrate how to engage with text (Stien & Beed, 2004). Brabham and Villaume (2000) caution against a cookie-cutter version of how to implement Literature Circles and instead recommend designing and using them in ways that emerge from our students' needs and challenges. These circles may not all have the same format, but they all encourage the implementation of grand conversations about texts (Peterson & Eeds, 1990). It is particularly important to remember this when using Literature Circles in the primary grades. Although the procedural decisions about the implementation of Literature Circles need to emerge from specific classrooms, there are some structures that do facilitate their use. (Literature Circle models designed by primary-grade teachers are presented later in this chapter.)

Literature Circles are a time of exploration and construction of personal meaning for the students. This routine is not a list of literal questions to be answered after reading. Students' personal interpretations drive the discussion. The focus is on students' inquiries, connections, and interpretations. During explicit instruction, we should make a point of modeling how to converse in critical ways during the demonstration step. Using Think-Alouds facilitates this process.

Daniels (2002) and Tompkins (2006) suggest guiding principles for using Literature Circles:

- Students self-select the books they will read.

- Temporary groups are formed based on book choice.

- Each group reads something different.

- Groups meet on a regular basis, according to predetermined schedules.

- Students use drawings or writings to guide their conversations.

- Students determine the topics for discussions and lead the conversations.

- The teacher acts as a facilitator, not an instructor or leader.

- Assessment can be completed through teacher observation or student self-reflection.

- Students are actively involved in reading and discussing books.

- After reading the books, the students share their ideas with their classmates, choose new books to read, and begin the cycle anew.

When implementing Literature Circles, it is also important that students engage in an activity in which they can get to know each other before meeting to discuss the book. This encourages students to build positive relationships with group members (Clarke & Holwadel, 2007; Daniels & Steineke, 2004).

Choice, literature, and response are Tompkins's (2001) suggestions for the key features of Literature Circles. Each of these is detailed in the following sections.

Choice. Clarke and Holwadel (2007) note the importance of having students choose the texts they will read, but students also make other choices in Literature Circles. They select the group they will join, the schedule they will follow, and the direction of the conversation. We can set the parameters for students to make these choices by providing a variety of texts at multiple levels for student selection, setting minimum daily or weekly reading requirements, and prompting ideas for conversations. However, the ultimate responsibility for each group rests with the students.

Literature. The books from which the students choose should be high-quality authentic literature or informational text that relates to their experiences. The literature should also help students make personal connections and prompt critical reflection (Brabham & Villaume, 2000). The books should include interesting stories with well-developed characters, rich language, and relevant themes that are engaging and meaningful and that generate interest from students (Noe & Johnson, 1999; Samway & Wang, 1996).

While reading, students can jot ideas in their Guided Comprehension Journals to share during discussion. Providing prompts to help students focus their thoughts is beneficial. Examples of prompts include the following:

- I wonder...
- I want to ask my group about...
- I think it is funny (sad, surprising, scary) that...
- I think it is interesting that...
- I think it is confusing that...
- The illustrations in this text...
- A vocabulary word I think our group should talk about is...
- This book reminds me of...

Using the Bookmark Technique (McLaughlin & Allen, 2002a) is a viable alternative for documenting students' ideas (see Appendix C, page 238). In this activity, students record their thoughts on four different bookmarks. The first contains their ideas about what they found most interesting; the second features a vocabulary word they think the group needs to discuss; the third provides information about something that was confusing; and the fourth contains ideas about illustrations, maps, or other graphics featured in the text (see Appendix C, pages 259–260, for Bookmark blacklines). The students record the page number and their thoughts on the bookmarks and place them at appropriate points in the text. Then the students use the completed bookmarks to support their contributions to the discussion.

Response. After reading, students gather in their small group to share understandings from the text and make personal connections. This public sharing, in the form of a conversation, helps the students to broaden their interpretations and gain new perspectives from the other members of the group.

Noe and Johnson (1999) suggest that after Literature Circle discussions have concluded, we should expand students' opportunities to respond to text by encouraging them to participate in extension activities. These activities provide students with another mode for exploring meaning, expressing their ideas about the text, making connections, and using a variety of response formats. Examples of extension projects adapted for use at the primary level include the following.

Book Poster: Students create an illustrated poster about the book. They include the title and author, draw or collage ideas, and include comments about what they thought of the book.

Quilt Square: Students design a quilt square to represent the book and add it to the class book quilt. They include the book's title and author and create an illustration to represent the book. They use the yarn provided to connect their square to the existing quilt. Competed class book quilts may feature theme-related texts, be genre-specific (such as favorite poetry books, biographies, or mysteries), or focus on the work of a favorite author.

What We Thought of Our Book: Students orally present information about their book. They use drawings, make connections, and retell the story or summarize the information they read. They conclude by explaining why they would or would not suggest that other students read the book.

(For more ideas about extending students' thinking after reading, see Appendix D and the Theme Resources sections of Chapters 7–10.)

Organizing and Managing Literature Circles

There are several ways to structure and manage Literature Circles. There is no right way, but rather choices must be made to accommodate the needs and challenges of not only each grade level but also of each student in the class. Any of the existing plans for Literature Circles may be used to create successful formats. Specific models for using Literature Circles in the primary grades appear in the next section. Once a meaningful plan has been selected, we make decisions about text choice, forming groups, and structuring the conversations.

Text selection. Texts for Literature Circles can be picture books, chapter books, and poetry books, but students may also read high-quality informational text (McLaughlin, 2010; Stien & Beed, 2004). Text choices should relate to students' experiences, help them make personal connections, contain relevant themes and rich language, and prompt critical reflection (Brabham & Villaume, 2000; Noe & Johnson, 1999; Samway & Wang, 1996). These books should also be engaging, meaningful, interesting, and accessible for students. Including theme-based leveled texts ensures that students will be able to engage in the circles independently—without teacher assistance. Although students in Literature Circles usually read the same text, they can also read similar texts about the same theme or a variety of theme-related genres on multiple levels. The texts that are selected will need to accommodate a wide range of student interests and abilities.

There are multiple options for selecting texts for Literature Circles. One way is to choose books that relate to a theme, topic, genre, or author. When using this method, the teacher should choose several texts on varying levels, and the students should make reading choices based on interest and ability. Another way to select text is to create collections of text sets related to a theme or topic. Texts within each set are related but can vary in level of difficulty. Students select the theme or topic and then choose the reading material from within that set. A third way to choose reading material is to allow students to self-select and then form groups based on text similarities.

Introducing text. After selecting the texts to be used in Literature Circles, we match the books with readers. Although there are various methods for doing this, book passes and book talks are especially effective.

Book passes: Several books are passed among students. Each student peruses a book for a few minutes, noting the title, reading the book cover, and leafing through it. If the students find a book appealing, they jot the title in their Guided Comprehension Journal and pass the book to the next person. After previewing several titles, students make choices. Groups are then formed on the basis of the book selections.

Book talks: This is a short oral overview of the book, focusing on the genre, the main characters, and the plot. After the book talks, students make choices and groups are formed.

We may need to guide some students in making appropriate text choices. If text sets are used, we can introduce the theme of the set and the kinds of texts that are in it. If selections are used from an anthology, we can introduce them through book talks.

Grand conversations: Schedules, talk, and roles. Once the Literature Circles are formed, students meet and develop a schedule to determine how much they will read and to create meeting deadlines. At first, the teacher can provide the schedule as a way to model how to set these goals. Once reading goals are set, students read the text on their own or with a partner. At the designated group meeting time, the students gather to discuss the texts. Notes or sketches from their reading that have been recorded in their Guided Comprehension Journals or their Literature Circle Bookmarks inform this discussion. Prior to this point, we model how to respond to text and how to use these responses to get the group conversations started.

The time spent in Literature Circles varies by length of text, but usually 10 to 20 minutes is sufficient. We can use a minilesson to demonstrate a particular literary element—such as plot, theme, or characterization—on which the students may focus their discussion. It is important, though, that we allow each group's conversation to evolve on its own.

Gilles (1998) has identified four types of talk that often occur during Literature Circles: talk about the book, talk about the reading process, talk about connections, and talk about group process and social issues. Teachers can encourage all types of talk with demonstrations and gentle prompts during the Literature Circle conversations.

Some teachers prefer to use assigned roles and responsibilities as a way to guide the conversations. Daniels (2002) has found that the following roles, which students rotate, provide a wide level of conversation within the Literature Circle:

- The *discussion director* takes on the leadership of the group and guides the discussion. Responsibilities include choosing topics for discussion, generating questions, convening the meeting, and facilitating contributions from all members.

- The *literary luminary/passage master* helps students revisit the text. Responsibilities include selecting memorable or important sections of the text and reading them aloud expressively.

- The *connector* guides the students to make connections with the text. Responsibilities include sharing text–self, text–text, and text–world connections and encouraging others to do the same.
- The *illustrator/artful artist* creates a drawing or other symbolic response to text. Responsibilities include making the visual response and using it to encourage others to contribute to the conversation.

The advantage of using these roles is that they represent response in a variety of learning modes, including linguistic, dramatic, and visual. The disadvantage is that this structure may stifle responses. I have found that starting with clearly defined roles and then relaxing or relinquishing them as the students gain competence in Literature Circles is effective. Daniels (2002) concurs, noting that role-free discussions are the ultimate goal.

Assessment in Literature Circles

There are several ways to assess students' comprehension, contributions, and cooperation within Literature Circles. Options include self-reflection, observation, discussion, and response sheets or journal entries.

- Students may self-reflect on their contributions to the circle and the group's ability to function. Providing forms for students to record their self-reflections facilitates this process (see Appendix D, pages 314–315).
- Although the students meet independently, we can observe their conversations and make anecdotal notes or keep a checklist of the content and depth of discussions (see Appendix E, page 349). We can note who is contributing to the discussion and if full participation is lacking. We can use this data to teach the students additional ways to include all group members. We also can observe the scope of the discussion. If the students are focused on basic recall of story events, we can choose to do a minilesson on making meaningful connections with texts.
- Students' response sheets, Guided Comprehension Journals, or Literature Circle Bookmarks (see Appendix D, page 313) provide another opportunity for assessment. In this format, students take notes about the text, document understandings, and make personal connections to bring to the discussion. These written or drawn artifacts provide a window into the students' thinking about the text.

The most important thing to remember about assessment in Literature Circles is to use the assessment results. These should contribute to decisions about future instruction.

Using Literature Circles in the Primary Grades

When working with primary-grade students, adaptations can be made to Literature Circles. I always suggest observing intermediate-grade Literature Circles, taking a step back, and contemplating what we could teach in third grade, second grade, first grade, and kindergarten to help students function successfully in those settings.

For example, in kindergarten, the focus may be teaching students the importance of personal response when discussing read-alouds. Teachers may even choose to have students arrange their chairs in a circle and describe such discussion times as Literature Circles. In first grade, teachers may build on what students learned in kindergarten by having the whole class meet in small groups to discuss texts read aloud by the teacher, texts read in teacher-guided small groups, or texts from shared reading. During this process, teachers may monitor the groups' discussions, prompting as necessary. As time progresses, students may discuss texts they have read independently. Second-grade teachers may choose to build on and refine this process. Third-grade teachers may then find themselves working with students who are very familiar with the Literature Circle process. Self-assessment can also be integrated in first grade and become more refined and detailed as the students' progress through the grades. (Forms to facilitate student self-assessment can be found in Appendix D.)

This section features teacher-designed models for using Literature Circles in the primary grades. These models are working successfully in the grades designated, but it is important to note that your students' needs and abilities will inform your decision to use one of these models or adapt one or more of them for use in your classroom. For an additional resource for using Literature Circles at the primary level, see the lesson plan "Literature Circles With Primary Students Using Self-Selected Reading" at www.readwritethink.org, a website maintained by IRA and the National Council of Teachers of English.

Model One: Angela Brake's Kindergarten Class

Format for discussion: I began engaging my students in Literature Circles by asking them to sit in one large circle while I read aloud. Then we all contributed to the discussion, often building on one another's ideas. The students liked our Literature Circles and always seemed eager to participate.

Preparation: When I planned for our Literature Circles, I began by choosing a motivational text. I often chose a humorous or theme-related Big Book. I have read both narrative and informational texts and my students seem to enjoy them equally. I began by introducing the book. Then we engaged in discussion as I read aloud the text in segments. We all made predictions, made connections, and contributed ideas to the retelling of the story. We also often responded to the reading by drawing our connections or visualizations.

We also predicted and confirmed, used picture clues to develop meaning, and drew pictures to help express our ideas. We talked about words that were new or about which students had questions, and we did word searches with the Big Books, often placing Wikki Stix (yarn coated with wax) around the words.

Text: We read narrative and informational text. The students seemed equally interested in both.

Comments: We recently read *Pigs*, an informational text by Gail Gibbons (2000), during our Literature Circle, and the discussion was amazing. The day before, a truck filled with pigs had overturned on a regional highway and all the television channels showed the state troopers creating a makeshift pen and gathering the pigs. It was the perfect time to be reading and learning about pigs. We learned a lot of facts about them, made connections to them, drew them, and discussed them. I think my students will always use discussion to learn.

Model Two: Leslie Fisher's First-Grade Class

Format for discussion: I began teaching Literature Circles as a whole-class activity, and then, when I felt the students were confident in the process, I organized the students into groups of four or five for Literature Circles. Students took turns being the discussion director, word finder, connector, illustrator, and summarizer. The discussion director developed his own questions, although I did teach students how to develop effective questions before we began using Literature Circles. The word finder located and discussed tricky words. The connector found the part of the text to which she could make a connection, shared it with the group, explained what her connection was, and why she selected it. The group then used it as a point of discussion. The illustrator created a drawing in response to the text and encouraged the group to discuss it. The summarizer shared the most important ideas from the text and the discussion. Students often wrote or sketched in their Guided Comprehension Journals while reading. They used this information to support their contributions to the discussion. I use explicit instruction to teach students about Literature Circles.

Each group had a Literature Circle folder that contained the group's schedule, role rotation, student work, and group assessments. I reviewed this at the end of each day that we did Literature Circles. If the group accomplished all of its tasks and worked well together, I placed a sticker in the folder.

Students chose each time whether they would read the text chorally, individually, or with a buddy. When they finished reading, each student assumed one of the roles.

When the discussions were complete, students engaged in an extending activity. They chose a way to share what they read with the class. They have shared poster-size story maps, alternative endings, murals, lyric summaries, and talk-show segments about texts they have read.

Preparation: I find that my first-grade students are accustomed to talking about what they read, but I did spend time reviewing or teaching skills they needed to effectively participate in Literature Circles. For example, we practiced guidelines for cooperative learning, including speaking one at a time, respecting everyone's ideas, and ensuring that everyone has opportunities to contribute to the discussion. We also discussed each group member's responsibility to the group as a whole and practiced using group reflections for assessment purposes.

Text: Students read and discussed theme-based trade books and a variety of leveled texts. We began by reading narrative text, but as the students became more comfortable, we also read informational text.

Comments: My first graders were very enthusiastic about Literature Circles. They enjoyed reading and sharing their ideas. I used explicit instruction to teach the students about Literature Circles, and I continued to scaffold their learning by providing support as needed when they were in their groups. I should note that once students became totally comfortable with this routine, they seemed to take pride in helping their circle be successful, and they enjoyed working independently.

One of the most interesting things I have observed is students negotiating meaning through discussion. This has also been evident when they have worked on their extension activities. For example, when one group completed a poster-size Draw and Label Retelling to share a reading with the class, group members discussed the characters, setting, problem, and solution in great depth, ensuring that all the important details were present in the sketches and sentences.

Model Three: Victoria Principe's Second-Grade Class

Format for discussion: Students worked independently in groups of four. No roles other than book club leader were used. The leaders opened the conversations with a question or statement either by using a prompt card or creating one of their own. This role was explained and modeled for students prior to their engaging in Literature Circles independently.

Preparation: Students need to know how to have a conversation, choose texts, and work cooperatively in order to have successful experiences in Literature Circles. I explicitly taught these processes prior to beginning Literature Circles.

Text: We had a book club board in our classroom. The students signed up in the morning for the text set of their choice. The text sets may be collections of books written by the same author, different versions of the same story, or books about a particular genre, theme, or concept. For example, we had poetry books, Jan Brett books, books about the ocean, and books about the moon. Six text sets are being used at one time, and the sets are rotated until the children have had a chance to read at least one book from each set. The children understand that if they are not able to use a particular text set on a certain day, they will have an opportunity to use it soon.

Comments: I engaged in explicit instruction of Literature Circles to scaffold students' learning and ensure that students understand the process. I also made some modifications and adaptations to accommodate my students. These include the following:

- Audio books for nonreaders are provided for students who have difficulty reading so they may be included in the discussions.

- Partners for reading, including peers, upper-grade students, parent helpers, and tutors, are available if needed.

- General prompts to promote discussion are provided for each group. Questions include "How are the characters the same?" "How are they different?" "How were the stories alike and different?" "If you were in the story, which character would you want to be? Explain your choice." The question prompts help the students stay on task and promote discussions, while leaving it open-ended at the same time.

Model Four: Joseph Walsh's Third-Grade Class

Format for discussion: Students worked independently in small groups of four. They took turns assuming the roles of discussion director, word finder, connector, and illustrator.

Preparation: Even though my students used Literature Circles in second grade, I engaged in a very detailed review of the skills, strategies, and processes necessary for Literature Circles to function successfully. This helped the students to reconnect with the process and refine their understanding before they engaged in Literature Circles independently. I also introduced the text sets and reminded students that writing ideas and drawing sketches in their Guided Comprehension Journals while reading will help them to engage in more meaningful discussions.

I found that it was beneficial to review self-assessment techniques before students engaged in Literature Circles independently. I explained and modeled how to use a self-reflection form to record ideas about personal and group performance (see Appendix D, pages 314–315). After discussing this process, I guided students through their initial use of the form and focused on how to use their reflections to set new goals. I found that self-assessment helped students to understand that they were accountable for the time they spend in Literature Circles.

Text: My students used text sets as the basis of their Literature Circles. The sets were theme-based and supported whatever theme we were studying.

Comments: When I first started using Literature Circles, I was truly surprised by the depth and quality of student discussion in this independent setting. They assume their roles, contribute meaningful ideas to discussion, and engage in negotiation of meaning.

I did provide adaptations to accommodate students' needs. These included the following:

- I recorded many of the books in the text sets on CD as a resource for English learners, struggling readers, and special needs students. I am grateful to parent volunteers and upper-grade students for their help in facilitating this.

- Students chose which text set they wanted to read after we engaged in book passes. I made certain that every text set contained titles that accommodated students' reading levels.

Regardless of whether you use one of the models presented here or create your own adaptation, it is important to remember that we share common goals when using Literature Circles. We are promoting student exploration, fostering reader response, and encouraging students to be independent thinkers.

Reciprocal Teaching: What We Know

Reciprocal Teaching involves scaffolded instruction and discussion of text based on four comprehension strategies: predicting, questioning, clarifying, and summarizing. The students as well as the teacher take on the role of "teacher" in leading the discussion about the text (Palincsar & Brown, 1984).

Reciprocal Teaching has three purposes:

1. To help students participate in a group effort to bring meaning to a text

2. To teach students that the reading process requires continual use of the four strategies (predicting, questioning, clarifying, summarizing) for effective comprehension

3. To provide students with the opportunity to monitor their own learning and thinking

Duke and Pearson (2002) describe a Reciprocal Teaching session in the following way:

> A typical Reciprocal Teaching session begins with a review of the main points from the previous session's reading, or if the reading is new, predictions about the text based on the title and perhaps other information. Following this, all students read the first paragraph of the text silently. A student assigned to act as teacher then (a) asks a question about the paragraph, (b) summarizes the paragraph, (c) asks for clarification if needed, and (d) predicts what might be in the next paragraph. During the process, the teacher prompts the student/teacher as needed, and at the end provides feedback about the student/teacher's work. (p. 225)

Implementing Reciprocal Teaching

In Guided Comprehension, students learn Reciprocal Teaching through explicit instruction before using it as an independent comprehension routine. The following steps will facilitate this process:

- Explain the procedure and the four strategies, noting their definitions, why they are important, and how they help us comprehend.
- Model thinking related to use of the four strategies by using an authentic text and Think-Alouds.
- Guide the students, in a whole-class setting, to think about their reading by providing responses for each of the strategies using verbal prompts, such as those suggested by Mowery (1995):

  ### Predicting
  I think...
  I bet...
  I wonder...
  I imagine...
  I suppose...

  ### Questioning
  Who? Where? When? What? How? Why?

  ### Clarifying
  I did not understand the part where...
  I need to know more about...
  This changes what I thought about...

  ### Summarizing
  This paragraph is about...
  The important ideas in what I read are...

- Practice by organizing the students in groups of four, and provide each group with a text to read and use as the basis of their Reciprocal Teaching.
- Assign one of the four strategies and suggested prompts to each group member.
- Have students engage in Reciprocal Teaching using the process modeled.
- Reflect by providing time for discussion and self-assessment forms (see Appendix D) to facilitate students' thinking about how strategy use affected their comprehension and what their future goals will be.

This process provides students with opportunities to share their thinking in a reciprocal fashion. While students are participating in their groups, we can monitor their activity and scaffold the dialogue when appropriate. Once the students are skilled at using Reciprocal Teaching, they can use it as an independent comprehension routine.

Studies by Palincsar and Brown (1984) demonstrate that students with a wide variety of abilities can use Reciprocal Teaching successfully. Although originally designed to help students who could decode well but had weak comprehension skills, all students benefit from this type of instruction because it allows them to read and understand more challenging texts (Palincsar & Brown, 1984).

Text Selection

In Reciprocal Teaching, the level of text is determined by students' abilities and the instructional setting in which this routine is being used. For example, when students have learned how to use Reciprocal Teaching and teacher support is available, narrative texts should have complex story lines and require critical thinking. Expository texts should have complex organizations and enough information for students to distinguish essential from nonessential information. When students are learning how to use Reciprocal Teaching in a whole-class setting or if students are using Reciprocal Teaching independently to practice using multiple comprehension strategies, texts should be at students' easy or independent reading levels.

Assessing Reciprocal Teaching

Teachers can assess students in Reciprocal Teaching groups by observing their ability to successfully use the strategies (see Appendix E, page 350). Students may self-reflect on contributions (see Appendix D, page 332) or may keep notes of the ideas they contributed. These data will help teachers create whole-class or small-group minilessons on using the strategies.

Using Reciprocal Teaching in the Primary Grades

Although Reciprocal Teaching is used more often in the intermediate and middle grades, it also can be used successfully in the primary grades (Palincsar & Brown, 1986). Observing an intermediate class successfully using Reciprocal Teaching as an independent routine may inform how you will use Reciprocal Teaching in your primary classroom. While observing, consider your students' needs and abilities and what you can do to help prepare them for using Reciprocal Teaching.

For example, kindergarten teachers may support the process by teaching related comprehension skills—such as generating questions and sequencing—as well as how to predict and retell. Students may also practice assuming the role of the teacher in center activities such as Transparency Talk and A-B-C Watch Me Read! In first grade, students may learn additional skills and strategies and use the Reciprocal Teaching process as a heavily scaffolded whole-group activity. Second graders may begin using Reciprocal Teaching as an independent routine, a process that may be refined and extended in third grade. Teachers at all levels may wish to create Thinking Records (Keene & Zimmermann, 1997) for each strategy. This involves defining the strategy on a long piece of paper that is attached to the wall. Students complete the Thinking Records by providing examples of how they used the strategies while reading. When engaging in Reciprocal Teaching, students may also benefit from using Reciprocal Teaching Bookmarks (Allen, 2002; see Appendix D, pages 330–331), which contain the four strategies and prompts that facilitate their use.

Examples of teachers' ideas for using Reciprocal Teaching in the primary grades follow. Each teacher provides some information about the class he or she taught and what was done to promote students' engagement in Reciprocal Teaching.

Model One: Nancy Sun's Kindergarten Class

In kindergarten, we are busy laying the foundation for Reciprocal Teaching. Before I began teaching some of the fundamentals with my students, I observed two third-grade classes that were using Reciprocal Teaching. I knew what this comprehension routine was, but I wanted to learn about how it looked and what it sounded like. After that, I visited second- and first-grade classes. After talking with the teachers of those classes, I discussed Reciprocal Teaching with our other kindergarten teachers. Then I thought about my students' needs and abilities. I realized that I should begin by revisiting two of the strategies my students already knew how to use.

I began by using a whole-class setting to review predicting and summarizing, the two strategies with which my students already had a lot of practice. When I explained the role of the teacher, the students seemed to enjoy the possibility of one day having that role. Then we used "I Wonder" Statements to form our predictions. The students always enjoy "wondering." As I read aloud, I modeled questioning and clarifying. I prompted the students to engage in the remaining strategies and offered my full support. The students delighted in taking turns being the teacher when we predicted and summarized.

Model Two: Adriah Lynch's First-Grade Class

When I was preparing to introduce Reciprocal Teaching to my students, I already knew that the kindergarten teacher focused on providing a foundation of strategies, such as previewing and summarizing. So, I decided to observe Reciprocal Teaching in action in second and third grade. When I finished my observations, I decided to build on what my students knew and to use highly motivational text to capture their interest.

I was using the Guided Comprehension Model to teach my students, so, as they progressed in understanding and using the strategies, I began teaching Reciprocal Teaching in a whole-class setting. I provided copies of an easy text for the students in the class as well as the members of my demonstration group. The demonstration group consisted of students I had invited to learn about Reciprocal Teaching earlier in the week and with whom I had practiced the routine on multiple occasions. The students in the demonstration group represented a variety of reading levels. I began by reviewing the comprehension strategies involved in the process and reminded the students about the variety of ways we had learned to apply the strategies. I used Think-Alouds as I modeled the "teacher" role in Reciprocal Teaching—first in a demonstration group and then with the whole class. I repeated similar demonstrations several times so every student in the class would be a member of the demonstration group. I also varied the type of text I used in each session.

The demonstration lessons seemed to help the students understand Reciprocal Teaching. It also helped me to observe that the students understood the routine well enough to successfully participate. Then I guided students to assume the role of the teacher in similar demonstration sessions. In the spring, I began organizing Reciprocal Teaching groups of four students within the whole-class setting. We used a read-think-write pattern throughout the process. We would read a paragraph, pause to think and write an idea in our Guided Comprehension Journals, and then engage in the four-step strategy process. We ended our sessions with whole-class sharing and reflection.

Model Three: Stephanie Dunbar's Second-Grade Class

One of the great things about teaching Reciprocal Teaching in second grade is that I was able to continue to build on what my students had learned in kindergarten and first grade. I began by reviewing the comprehension strategies and focusing on how we would be using four strategies in Reciprocal Teaching. I explained that we would begin by organizing Reciprocal Teaching groups in a whole-class setting and then, when we were all comfortable participating in it, we would add Reciprocal Teaching to the Literature Circles and Cross-Age Reading Experiences we used as independent small-group routines in Stage Two of Guided Comprehension. I observed that the students were able to use the strategies and that they thoroughly enjoyed the role of the teacher. I think that building on what they already knew and modeling Reciprocal Teaching numerous times helped the students to be successful.

Once the students were comfortable with Reciprocal Teaching as a routine, they began using the self-assessment of individual performance (see Appendix D, page 332). They shared the highlights of their Reciprocal Teaching experiences, as well as their other routines and comprehension centers, in Stage Three of Guided Comprehension.

Model Four: Connor Watkins's Third-Grade Class

When I began talking with my students about Reciprocal Teaching, I knew that most of them had learned about it in previous grades. So, my goals included reviewing the routine and the strategies it involved, organizing and managing the routine, and teaching the students how to be accountable when participating in Reciprocal Teaching. I was also careful to ensure that I took additional time to teach Reciprocal Teaching to the few students who were not familiar with it. When working with the whole class, I began by describing the multiple-strategy nature of Reciprocal Teaching, reviewing the strategies, and demonstrating the process. After I explained and demonstrated, we practiced by engaging in Reciprocal Teaching in groups of four within a whole-class setting. Students used Reciprocal Teaching Bookmarks (Allen, 2002; see Appendix D, pages 330–331), which featured strategy prompts during this process. We did this on several occasions before integrating Reciprocal Teaching into our comprehension routines. During this process, students also practiced reflecting on individual and group performances during Reciprocal Teaching. Once we began using Reciprocal Teaching as one of our routines, it became a natural part of our Guided Comprehension lessons.

How you support students' use of Reciprocal Teaching will depend on their needs and abilities. To decide what you will do to contribute to students' understanding and use of this routine, you may wish to meet with your fellow primary-grade teachers. This will provide an opportunity to develop a general plan for integrating Reciprocal Teaching across the primary grades. The plan may be revised during the year, as students have opportunities to demonstrate their abilities.

Cross-Age Reading Experiences: What We Know

Cross-Age Reading Experiences generally involve a novice working on a specific task with a more knowledgeable person for a particular period of time. This type of learning is especially applicable in education, in which practitioners frequently model and scaffold learning for less-experienced learners. Forman and Cazden (1994) note that such educational practices reflect Vygotsky's thinking about adult–child relationships and offer an alternative to traditional adult–child interactions. In educational contexts, there are a variety of people who may play the role of the more knowledgeable other in cross-age relationships with our students. These people include community volunteers, upper-grade students, and classroom aides.

In Guided Comprehension, Cross-Age Reading Experiences are routines that involve exploration, strategy application, and the construction of personal meaning. The resulting learning experiences are meaningful and memorable for all involved.

Implementing Cross-Age Reading Experiences

When planning Cross-Age Reading Experiences, there are options to consider. To begin, the cross-age partners must be identified. Students from upper grades, community volunteers, and classroom aides are among those who may volunteer for this position. Once the partners are selected, a few informal training sessions should be held. These meetings may focus on modeling read-alouds, reviewing comprehension strategies, demonstrating upcoming teaching ideas, and discussing the role of the partner in the cross-age experience. It is important that the partners understand that this routine is part of the Guided Comprehension Model and that it is a time for students to practice and transfer comprehension strategies. It is also helpful to introduce a range of texts to the partners.

Scheduling is another important consideration. The partners will need to be available during the reading/language arts block. Community volunteers and classroom aides should be able to work with students on a consistent basis. Upper-grade students may be available only once a week for a limited amount of time, but they still provide important models for students. Examples of Cross-Age Reading Experiences situated within theme-based Guided Comprehension lessons can be found in Chapters 7–10.

Text Selection

The texts used in Cross-Age Reading Experiences will vary by type and genre according to the theme of study. However, they should be easy-level texts so the students can use them without teacher assistance.

Assessment in Cross-Age Reading Experiences

Self-assessments similar to those that emerge from Literature Circles and Reciprocal Teaching also can be used for Cross-Age Reading Experiences (see Appendix D, page 306, and Appendix E, page 348).

Using Cross-Age Reading Experiences in the Primary Grades

Cross-Age Reading Experiences are easily situated in the primary grades. They provide a setting for a wide variety of meaningful comprehension-related activities, including student read-alouds and skill and strategy applications, including multiple modes of response. When first beginning Cross-Age Reading Experiences, primary teachers often organize them as a whole-class activity.

Model: Mary Ellen Cadden's First- and Fifth-Grade Reading Buddies

Twice a month my first-grade students have Cross-Age Reading Experiences with fifth-grade students. We meet in an open area in the elementary school. The fifth-grade students walk to our school to meet with us. Before our program begins, I go to the fifth-grade class for a period, while the fifth-grade teacher meets with my class. I talk to the fifth graders about when they learned how to read and what they remember. We talk about the different strategies they use when they read and I teach them the strategies I want them to use when helping my first graders with their reading. I give them each a strategy bookmark with pictures that will help guide their first-grade readers when they get stuck on a word. I also talk to them about helping to motivate their readers by using positive talk and by making the reading experience fun for them. We talk about questioning and ways to get the first graders thinking about the story. I usually meet with the fifth graders two or three times before they begin working with their first-grade buddies.

When the buddies meet, my students bring two books on their independent level to read *to* their buddies and two books at their instructional level to read *with* their buddies. The fifth graders also bring a book that they think their buddy would enjoy. They often check out books from the school library or borrow books from our classroom. The buddies read to each other and read together. Discussion and strategy use permeate the readings. The students use strategies such as previewing, making connections, visualizing, and summarizing. A few days before the students meet, the teacher gives the fifth-grade students time to select a book, practice reading it, and think about related questions and strategies.

Our Cross-Age Reading Experience ends with a celebration. The students have lunch together and then share their favorite books with other buddies. The fifth-grade teacher and I give the students photo albums and certificates celebrating their Cross-Age Reading Experiences, and our parent organization gives books to all the participants. The students share their thoughts about the program, and the building principal commends all who were involved.

Everyone involved in this program truly values it. The first graders are in awe of the fifth graders and hang on their every word. The fifth graders feel great about helping the first graders, and all the students enjoy the reading. The school administrators are extremely helpful, and the parents are very pleased with the success of the program. As teachers, the benefits of Cross-Age Reading Experiences become clear to us every time we see the students reading, smiling, giggling, and eagerly anticipating the next book they will read.

Stage Two of Guided Comprehension provides students with a variety of meaningful settings in which to practice comprehension skills and strategies. In teacher-guided small-group instruction, students' reading has teacher support as needed. In student-facilitated comprehension centers and routines, students engage in independent applications. Student assessment and leveled texts are integral components of all three of these settings.

In the next chapter, the roles of assessment in Guided Comprehension are discussed. Connections to state standards and a variety of practical assessment measures are also presented.

CHAPTER 5

Assessment in Guided Comprehension

ssessment is a natural component of teaching and learning. It helps us gain insights into students' abilities, needs, experiences, and interests. We use assessment results to inform our teaching and help students to achieve their maximum potentials.

When we are teaching, we use assessments for a variety of purposes. For example, before teaching we use diagnostic assessments to determine what students know, to learn about their interests, and to identify approximate reading levels. While we are teaching we use formative assessments to document student progress and check for understanding. After we have taught, we use summative assessments to determine what students have learned, to gain insights into how successful our teaching has been, and to make decisions about what to teach next.

In this chapter, the focus is on a practical approach to student assessment. To begin, the dynamic nature of assessment and its multiple roles in Guided Comprehension are discussed. Next, how the Guided Comprehension Model supports student performance on state assessments is presented. Then a number of practical, informative assessments and their connections to Guided Comprehension are discussed. Finally, Guided Comprehension Profiles—tools to organize and manage student progress—are explained. Throughout the chapter, connections to Appendix E, which contains a variety of reproducible assessments and assessment forms, are made.

The Multiple Roles of Assessment in Guided Comprehension

Assessment in Guided Comprehension is dynamic in nature. It occurs in an ongoing manner, offers insights into students' thinking, chronicles student development, and is a natural component of teaching and learning (McLaughlin, 2002). This aligns with constructivist thinking about purposeful assessments (Brooks & Brooks, 1993; Tierney, 1998) and supports Vygotsky's belief that assessment should extend to scaffolded experiences to capture students' emerging abilities (Minick, 1987).

Assessment in Guided Comprehension has several purposes, including the following:

- To provide an approximate range of reading levels for students
- To offer insights into student attitudes and interests
- To facilitate student–text matches
- To inform grouping for teacher-guided instruction

- To check for student understanding
- To provide insights into students' thinking
- To document students' performance
- To provide information for evaluative purposes

Assessment permeates every stage of the Guided Comprehension Model and occurs in a variety of forms and settings. For example, we use diagnostic assessments to determine approximate student reading levels and analyze students' use of skills and strategies to decode and comprehend. These assessments provide valuable information for grouping students for small-group instruction in Stage Two and for guiding our decisions about which texts to use and which strategies to teach. We employ formative measures to monitor student learning as we are teaching and guiding. These assessments allow us to check for student understanding in a continuous, ongoing manner, and to adjust our teaching to better meet the needs of our students. We use summative assessments to examine what students have learned over time and to help us make instructional decisions for future lessons.

Connections to State Assessments

Since 2000, U.S. students in grades 3 and up have been required to show adequate yearly progress (AYP) on standardized measures as part of the No Child Left Behind Act. This high-stakes testing environment has put pressure on students to do well and on teachers to ensure that students demonstrate proficiency. Although the pressure is great, we should resist the temptation to teach to the test and instead focus on providing excellent reading instruction. This, coupled with the knowledge that the single most important influence in student learning is the teacher (Gambrell, Malloy, & Mazzoni, 2007), will produce the desired results. Guided Comprehension supports student performance on these measures by focusing on student understanding, explicit strategy instruction, and multiple types and levels of text. It also emphasizes knowledge of text structure and encourages question generation at multiple levels. In addition, Guided Comprehension promotes student writing. When we view reading and writing as inextricable processes, students become more aware of how they think and more adept at sharing their thoughts.

In the next section, descriptions of the assessments most frequently used in Guided Comprehension are discussed.

Practical Assessment Measures

When preparing to teach Guided Comprehension, we assess for a variety of purposes. We gather information to learn about students' reading backgrounds and interests, to determine approximate range of reading levels, and to gain insights into students' knowledge of strategies and their ability to apply them. Results of these assessments inform several aspects of our planning, including lesson content, student–text matches, and grouping students for guided instructional settings.

A number of practical, effective assessments are presented in this section. A description of each measure, an explanation of its functions, and details of its connection to Guided Comprehension are featured.

Assessments to Learn About Students' Backgrounds and Interests

Some assessments provide insights into students' pasts that enable us to better understand their present attitudes toward and performance in reading. Examples of these measures include attitude surveys, interest inventories, literacy histories, and motivation profiles. (Reproducible copies of these measures are included in Appendix E.)

Attitude surveys. Attitude surveys are designed to illuminate students' feelings about reading and writing and the resulting impact on motivation and effort. The most common formats are question and response, sentence completion, and selected response. Information we can obtain from attitude surveys includes how students feel about various aspects of reading and writing, how they would define reading and writing, and how they would describe successful readers and writers. Information gleaned from these surveys also provides insights into factors that may have contributed to students' current attitudes toward literacy. (Reproducible reading and writing attitude surveys can be found in Appendix E, pages 338 and 339.)

Guided Comprehension Connection The completed attitude surveys provide information about students' perceptions of literacy processes. They also offer information about students' reading preferences that we can use when making student–text matches and selecting texts for Stages One and Two.

Interest inventories. Interest inventories are informal surveys designed to provide information about students' personal interests. They usually include topics such as students' reading preferences, hobbies, and special interests. The most common formats for interest inventories are question and response or incomplete sentences. These surveys are relatively easy to complete, and they provide information about numerous topics including the following: genre and author preferences, what students are currently reading, and whether students choose to read beyond required assignments. (Examples of interest inventories appropriate for grades K–3 can be found in Appendix E, pages 342 and 343.)

Guided Comprehension Connection Completed interest inventories provide information about students' backgrounds. We can use that knowledge to make decisions related to motivating students and making student–text matches.

Literacy histories. Literacy histories chronicle students' literacy development from earliest memory to present day (McLaughlin & Vogt, 1996). They facilitate students' ability to make connections between their past literacy experiences and their current beliefs.

To create their personal literacy histories, students engage in questioning and reflection. Sources they use to construct their histories range from family memories to early-grade writing samples to copies of favorite books. Students can choose the mode of presentation; they have submitted everything from time lines to scrapbooks filled with family photos. To model this assessment, we, as teachers, share our own literacy histories and provide students with prompts to guide the process. (Reproducible copies of the literacy history prompts are included in Appendix E, page 344.)

Guided Comprehension Connection Literacy histories help us learn about the present by examining the past. They provide students' personal insights into their literacy development and contribute to our understanding of students' current attitudes toward literacy.

Motivation to Read Profile.

The Motivation to Read Profile (Gambrell et al., 1996) consists of two instruments: the Reading Survey and the Conversational Interview. The cued response survey, which requires 15 to 20 minutes for group administration, assesses the self-concept of a reader and value of reading. The interview, which features open-ended free response questions and requires 15 to 20 minutes for individual administration, assesses the nature of motivation, such as favorite authors and interesting books. The Conversational Interview (included in Appendix E, pages 345–347) has three emphases: narrative text, informational text, and general reading.

Guided Comprehension Connection Knowledge of what motivates students to read both narrative and informational text enhances our understanding of our students and informs meaningful text selection.

Attitude surveys, interest inventories, literacy histories, and motivation profiles provide background information that informs our understanding of individual students and their literacy needs. These measures contribute vital information as we seek to provide optimum literacy experiences for our students. These assessments are easy to administer, require little time, and provide insights that may not be discerned from other literacy assessments.

Assessments to Learn About Students' Reading Levels and Strategy Use

Some measures provide information about how students use cueing systems, and others pair miscue analysis with comprehension assessments. Examples of these measures include oral reading assessment with miscue analysis, running records, and published leveled passages kits such as the Qualitative Reading Inventory–5, Developmental Reading Assessment 2: Grades K–3, and Fountas and Pinnell Benchmark Assessment System: Grades K–2 and 3–8.

Miscue analysis.

Miscue analysis (Goodman, 1997) helps us to assess students' use of the graphophonic, syntactic, and semantic cueing systems. Miscues indicate how a student's oral reading varies from the written text. In miscue analysis, students read aloud, and we record their attempts, self-corrections, and miscues. Recording the students' attempts and analyzing the miscues provides us with valuable information for our teaching.

To analyze miscues, Goodman, Watson, and Burke (1987) suggest we use the following four questions:

1. Does the miscue change the meaning?
2. Does the miscue sound like language?
3. Do the miscue and the text word look and sound alike?
4. Was an attempt made to self-correct the miscue?

To facilitate the use of the miscue analysis, we select some "anchor books"—both fiction and nonfiction at varying levels—and invite students to do an informal oral reading, which we tape record. At this point we code and analyze all their attempts, self-corrections, and miscues. We also ask the students to do a brief retelling of this text. These two pieces of information provide approximate student reading levels and insights into their strategy use and comprehension. There are some defined accuracy percentages that may influence the determination of a reader's range of levels: below 90%, frustration; 90–95%, instructional; 96–100%, independent. When assessing students' levels, we also need to consider factors such as background knowledge about the content, interest in the text, and supports within the text.

 Miscue analysis provides approximate reading levels, helps us to make matches between readers and texts, and informs instruction.

Running records.

Running records were developed by Marie Clay (1993a) as a way to observe, record, and analyze what a child does in the process of reading. The teacher assumes the role of a neutral observer for the purpose of taking a record of the child's independent reading behavior. Running records provide qualitative and quantitative information about what a reader knows and what needs to be learned next. In addition, running records help the teacher to make informed decisions concerning instructional needs, approximate reading levels, grouping for guided reading, and making student–text matches. (To learn how to use running records, see *Running Records: A Self-Tutoring Guide* [2000] by Johnston and *Assessment and Instruction of Reading and Writing Difficulties: An Interactive Approach* [2009] by Lipson and Wixson.)

 Running records are used to assess students for placement and advancement purposes in teacher-guided small groups and to inform the teacher's understanding of students' reading.

Qualitative Reading Inventory–5.

The Qualitative Reading Inventory–5 (Leslie & Caldwell, 2010) is a comprehensive assessment that ranges from preprimer to high school. It includes both narrative and informational leveled passages, questions to assess prior knowledge, and word lists. To assess comprehension, students can retell passages or respond to implicit and explicit questions. The leveled passages and word lists enable the teacher to estimate students' reading levels, match students with appropriate texts, and verify suspected reading difficulties. Because there are so many components to this measure, we need to make choices when using it. For example, we may choose to do the miscue analysis and then use either the retelling checklist or the comprehension questions that accompany each leveled passage to determine students' instructional levels. The leveled passages also can be used to assess silent reading comprehension.

 This assessment provides information necessary to place students in teacher-guided small groups and to create student–text matches.

Developmental Reading Assessment 2: Grades K–3.

The Developmental Reading Assessment 2: Grades K–3 assessment kit (Beaver & Carter, 2009) includes a variety of fiction and nonfiction texts at primary grade levels. Detailed record-keeping forms help the teacher document student levels, reading behaviors, and comprehension over time.

 This assessment provides information necessary to determine student placement in teacher-guided small groups and to create student–text matches.

Fountas and Pinnell Benchmark Assessment System: Grades K–2 and 3–8. The
Fountas and Pinnell Benchmark Assessment System: Grades K–2 and 3–8 assessment kits (Fountas & Pinnell, 2008) provide graded word lists, fiction and nonfiction leveled readers, and detailed forms for analyzing and recording students' comprehension, writing, and fluency over time.

 This assessment helps us to determine approximate reading levels for students in teacher-guided small groups. This, in turn, helps us to make student–text matches and plan appropriate instruction.

Assessments to Learn About Students' Everyday Progress

Other assessments are more informal. These measures can be used every day to provide insights into students' progress. Examples of these measures include student writing and teacher observation.

Student writing. Student writing is a flexible assessment. It can be used for numerous purposes including creating a writing–comprehension match, applying strategies, summarizing and synthesizing information, documenting student thinking, recording personal responses, and as a mode of reflection and goal setting. We observe and analyze student writing for multiple purposes including content, focus, organization, language structure, use of vocabulary, and knowledge of sight words and spelling patterns.

 Writing is a mode of expression that informs all stages of the Guided Comprehension Model. It documents students' thinking and provides evidence of learning.

Observation. Observation is one of the most flexible assessments because it can offer information about virtually any aspect of literacy in which students engage. For example, we can observe students as they read, write, and discuss. We can also monitor their ability to stay on task when working independently, and use observation to assess their fluency, record ideas about their engagement, or comment on their roles during cooperative learning activities.

Before we begin observing, we need to establish a purpose and determine how we will record the information gleaned from this measure. For example, if we are observing a student who is doing an oral retelling, we can use a checklist that includes information such as the characters, setting, problem, attempts to resolve the problem, resolution, and a section for us to record additional comments. In contrast, if we are observing a student's contribution to a cooperative activity, our checklist might include items such as the student's preparation for the group's work, engagement with peers, and contributions to the group. (Reproducible observation guides for comprehension routines can be found in Appendix E, pages 348–350.)

Guided Comprehension Connection Observation is an informal technique that can be used in all stages of the Model to gain insights into students' performance and inform our planning of future learning experiences.

What we want to know about our students determines which assessments we use. Therefore, our goal is not to use all these measures to assess each reader, but rather to make choices and use the measures that provide the information we need.

The assessments described in this section are practical, can be used for multiple purposes, and offer valuable insights into students' backgrounds and abilities. In addition to these measures, informal assessment opportunities, including strategy applications, are embedded in all stages of the Guided Comprehension Model. These formative measures are situated in a variety of instructional settings and provide occasions for students to demonstrate what they know through multiple modes of response including reading, writing, discussion, sketching, drama, and singing.

Guided Comprehension Profiles

We use Guided Comprehension Profiles to organize and manage student assessments. These profiles are strategy-based collections of assessments and indicators of student progress. Maintaining the profiles is an active process for both the students and teacher. As our students transact with texts and people in multiple settings in a variety of modes, we collect information to document their progress. Although Guided Comprehension offers numerous opportunities for assessment, there are some measures such as student writing, oral reading fluency, and comprehension that we systematically include. We use the results of these assessments to document student progress, refine guided instruction groups, and inform future instruction.

We store the students' assessments and work samples in pocket folders and we use a Profile Summary Sheet to organize assessment information. This offers an at-a-glance overview of student progress and facilitates reporting student progress. (A reproducible copy of this organizer is included in Appendix E, page 341.)

In Guided Comprehension, assessment is viewed as a natural part of instruction, a dynamic process in which both students and teacher actively participate. In the next chapter, using assessments to create student–text matches is discussed. Reader and text factors that influence our selection of leveled texts are also explained.

CHAPTER 6

Leveled Text: An Essential Resource for Reading Comprehension

I f we want our primary students to achieve at their maximum potentials, we need to use leveled, accessible, engaging text. Providing students with text they *can* read and *want* to read promotes achievement. This implies that students should have access to a rich and varied collection of leveled texts in addition to core programs and classroom libraries.

Leveled texts lead to successful reading, and to students who are motivated to read. This type of text is a critical component of reading comprehension instruction. If the text is accessible, students can read it. If the text is leveled, students can read it at their instructional level during teacher-guided small groups or at their independent level when they engage in independent practice. For example, when students are participating in Guided Reading, they can read instructional-level texts with some assistance from the teacher. When students are engaged in independent practice, such as centers or routines, they can read independent-level texts with no assistance from the teacher. If the text is of interest, students will choose to read it.

The focus of this chapter is the role of text selection in reading comprehension instruction. Student reading levels, student interests, and text selection are the first considerations discussed. Next, the reader and text factors that influence accessibility are shared. Then the rationale for using leveled texts, suggestions for making decisions about the ease or difficulty of text, and ideas for organizing texts are presented.

Student Reading Levels, Student Interests, and Text Selection

When considering which texts to use during Guided Comprehension, it is important to begin by determining the reading levels and interests of our students. There are a number of informal reading assessments that we can use to help determine students' approximate reading abilities. We also use informal measures to learn about students' interests. Details about these assessments and measures can be found in Chapter 5.

Student Reading Levels

There are general guidelines for determining students' reading levels related to word accuracy, comprehension, and fluency. For *word accuracy*, the text is considered easy if students can read it with 95%–100% accuracy, provided the fluency and comprehension are appropriate. The instructional level is reached when students can read most of the text, but there are some challenges with words or content. This is usually between 90% and 94% accuracy. Students who read a text below 90% accuracy often struggle with fluency and comprehension because they must use so much of their cognitive focus to figure out unknown words. This is considered a frustration level. At this level, key words are often misunderstood and comprehension is compromised.

In addition to word accuracy, *comprehension* must also be assessed. This often involves determining students' background knowledge as well as their ability to retell or summarize what was read, effectively discuss the text, or predict what will happen next. If a student is unable to successfully complete such tasks, the text may be too difficult.

Fluency, the third factor, is directly related to comprehension. In fact, Rasinski (2010) notes that fluency is the ability to read accurately and expressively at a natural rate with good phrasing and good comprehension. Fluency checks, which can easily be completed during Guided Reading, contribute to our understanding when creating appropriate student–text matches. We can complete fluency checks by asking individual students to whisper read during teacher-guided small groups.

When we assess students' word accuracy, comprehension, and fluency, we gain insights into their reading abilities. Although the results of these informal measures are approximations, they do provide a starting point for making appropriate student–text matches for guided and independent practice.

Student Interests

Student interests are essential considerations when making student–text matches. We can easily learn about students' interests by engaging our students in informal conversations or inviting them to complete interest inventories (see Chapter 5 and Appendix E, pages 342 and 343, for examples). When students are reading texts that interest them, they are more motivated to read and generally have more background knowledge about the topic of the text. This makes reading the text easier and more enjoyable for students.

Text Selection

Once we have determined students' reading levels and interests, we can begin considering texts that will contribute to students' reading success. A common way to do this is to use leveled texts, reading materials that begin at a certain level and become progressively difficult (Brabham & Villaume, 2002). The criteria for leveling text may be standards set by well-respected literacy professionals such as Marie Clay or Irene Fountas and Gay Su Pinnell, or they may involve the use of readability formulas, such as the Fry Readability Graph (1977), which consider length of text, length of sentences, and complexity of vocabulary. Another approach is to level text by considering a variety of text or reader factors. Whichever method is used, leveled text is an essential resource when we create student–text matches.

Students can usually engage with multiple levels of text depending on the setting in which they are reading. For example, when students read on their own, they can read independent-level or "easy" text. At this level, students have familiarity with the genre and content, can read all or most of the words, and can comprehend with no help. When students are reading with the support of a teacher, they can read instructional-level or "just right" text. At this level, students have some familiarity with the content and genre, know most of the words, and can comprehend with some teacher support. Students can also experience independent, instructional, and challenging texts when the teacher reads to them in teacher-directed whole-group instruction or during daily read-alouds. This means that even though students should not read challenging or frustration-level texts on their own, they can experience such texts when we share them through read-alouds or books on CD. Figure 4 illustrates how leveled texts are generally situated in the Guided Comprehension Model. It is important to remember that these text levels are approximations, and that factors beyond the text influence student accessibility.

Factors That Influence Accessibility

There are several factors that influence the accessibility of a text; some reside in the reader, others are determined by the text. Reader factors include interest and motivation, background knowledge, and sociocultural identities (Dzaldov & Peterson, 2005; Pitcher & Fang, 2007). Text factors include text type and structure, text length, content, vocabulary, language, and literary features (Brabham & Villaume, 2002; Dzaldov & Peterson, 2005; Rog & Burton, 2001; Tompkins, 2006). Considering these factors helps us to make good text selections for reading instruction as well as independent practice.

Figure 4. Text Levels and the Guided Comprehension Model

Text Level	Teacher Support	Guided Comprehension
Independent	No teacher support needed. (Just right when students are reading on their own and practicing strategy application.)	Stage Two: Independent Centers and Routines
Instructional	Some teacher support needed. (Just right when guiding small groups.)	Stage Two: Teacher-Guided Small Groups
Challenging	Full teacher support needed. (Just right when doing teacher read-alouds in whole group.)	Stage One: Teacher-Directed Whole Groups

Reader Factors

Reader factors such as interest and motivation, background knowledge, and sociocultural identities influence text selection. Dzaldov and Peterson (2005) suggest that these factors are as important as text features when making text choices for students. Similarly, Pitcher and Fang (2007) report that knowing students' interests, instructional backgrounds, experiential backgrounds, and sociocultural identities is as important or more important than text features and levels when making good matches between readers and texts.

Interest and motivation. Students who read materials on topics of interest tend to read more, can read more difficult materials, and are more motivated to read (Wigfield & Guthrie, 1997). Reading motivation is influenced by several factors, including content goals, student book choice, social structures for learning, teacher involvement, and rewards (Guthrie et al., 2006). When students are interested, they will work harder at constructing meaning. In addition, student self-efficacy, a student's belief about his or her ability to be successful, is a crucial factor in reading motivation that is connected to interest in reading and amount of time spent reading (Bogner, Raphael, & Pressley, 2002). Student motivation is influenced by students' previous experience with texts. Students who have spent years reading textbook chapters and answering the questions at the end can have negative feelings when asked to read for information. This is also true for students who have had stories so segmented for vocabulary study or detail recall that the major themes and meaning have been lost. Students who have had positive, successful experiences with texts have greater motivation to read, and therefore tend to read more, often trying longer or more challenging texts.

Background knowledge. Readers' background knowledge of text content, language, and text type influences accessibility. When students have a great deal of experience with a specific topic or type of text, they have a network of ideas in their minds that allows them to make connections with the new information. This often helps them to make predictions and inferences while reading. They also have knowledge of specific vocabulary and language patterns that helps them to read with meaning at a good pace. This is true for both narrative and informational texts and is influenced by the amount of time spent reading each type.

Sociocultural identities. Social and cultural identities influence students' interests as well as their ability to read and understand texts. When characters and contexts are familiar, students can make connections to the content or story line, and that makes the text easier to read. Dzaldov and Peterson (2005) report that students who are not familiar with certain versions of fairy tales struggle to read and understand these texts, even if texts were at a lower level than versions more familiar to the students.

Alvermann, Phelps, and Ridgeway (2007) suggest that teachers who consider students' social and cultural backgrounds when planning instruction create learning environments in which students feel engaged and successful. Holmes, Powell, Holmes, and Witt (2007) recommend having classroom libraries that represent a variety of races and people, which will help students build awareness of and greater sensitivity toward one another.

Text Factors

When considering students' abilities and interests, it is important to match those with the supports and challenges present in the text. Text features to consider when deciding on appropriateness of a book for a particular student include text type and structure, text length, language and literary features, complexity of the content, and uniqueness of the vocabulary (Brabham & Villaume, 2002; Dzaldov & Peterson, 2005; Rog & Burton, 2001; Tompkins, 2006).

Text type and structure. Texts are organized in different ways depending on their purpose. Narrative text tells a story and usually includes the basic story elements: characters, setting, problem, attempts to resolve the problem, and resolution. This format is very familiar to students because they have heard and read many stories. This knowledge of the text structure helps students anticipate what might happen next in the story and, consequently, the story is often easier for students to read. On the other hand, informational texts provide facts about a topic. There are five main informational text structures: description, sequence, cause and effect, compare and contrast, and problem and solution (Vacca & Vacca, 2008). These are often less familiar to students and, consequently, may be more challenging to read. Additionally, the syntax and vocabulary in these texts may be more difficult for students.

Goldman and Rakestraw (2000, p. 321) have drawn the following three conclusions from existing research on students' knowledge of text structure:

1. Readers use their knowledge of structure in processing text.
2. Knowledge of structural forms of text develops with experience with different genres, and is correlated with age/time in school.
3. Making readers more aware of genre and text structure improves learning.

Text length. As students become more competent readers, they are able to read longer texts. These stories are more complex and may have many characters and multiple story lines. Longer informational texts often include several subtopics and many more facts. Although a long text is not always a more difficult text, length is one factor to consider when thinking about the appropriateness of text for a particular reader. We also need to consider the setting in which the student will be reading. For example, in Guided Reading, which usually lasts only 20 minutes, shorter texts usually work better.

Text content. Text content is a critical factor in text selection because readers must be able to make connections between what they know and what they are reading. This requires that students either have background knowledge about the topic or gain some knowledge about it before they begin reading. For stories, this may include knowledge of how narrative texts work, such as character and plot development, or conflict and resolution. Additionally, much of the story may be told with dialogue between and among characters, making inferential thinking important to understand the plot. In informational texts, content includes the topic and how it is presented. As such texts get more challenging, the information is presented in more detail, with many more complex and abstract concepts. Also, the number of content-specific words generally increases. We must consider the content and how it is presented in the text when trying to determine text level and student accessibility. The size of print, the number or availability of pictures or other visual cues, the range of punctuation, the layout and organization of print, and the number of words per page are also influential factors in this category.

Vocabulary, language structure, and literary features. To understand and make meaning from a text, students need to be able to understand most of the words they read. If they come to a word they do not know, they need to be reading with enough understanding to infer the meaning of the unknown word. When there are too many unknown words, students lose the meaning of the text and focus more of their working memory on decoding. As texts become more challenging, the vocabulary usually becomes more complex. For example, there are differences in the types of words students encounter in narrative and informational text. In a narrative text, there may be several difficult words, but they often represent other concepts that the students already understand (Hiebert, 2006). That is not usually true with informational text. Many of the difficult words in informational texts are content-specific words that are critical to understanding.

We should also think about the complexity of the language structure when creating student–text matches. Compound and complex sentences may be more challenging for students when reading about particular topics. Other factors we should think about when deciding if a more challenging text is a good match for a student include literary features, such as figurative language, plot twists, and dialogue (Dzaldov & Peterson, 2005; Rog & Burton, 2001).

Considering all these text features is essential when we choose texts and create student–text matches. Figure 5 features a list of the text features and prompts we can use to determine the appropriateness of text when making these matches.

Choosing Texts to Promote Student Success

Before making student–text matches, we need to assess our students, be aware of their interests, and ensure that we have a wide range of engaging texts at a variety of levels available for student use. We also need to consider how to organize the texts so students can easily access books at the appropriate levels.

Student Information

Before planning meaningful Guided Comprehension instruction, we need to determine each student's independent and instructional level and gather information about his or her interests and background. We use this information for three purposes: to form teacher-guided small groups, to provide appropriate text for students to read when working in the comprehension-based centers and routines, and to inform text selection for teacher-directed whole-group instruction. Miscue analysis (Goodman, 1997), which we can use to assess students' oral reading and comprehension, is a viable source of this information. There are also several commercially prepared assessment tools that allow teachers to assess students' reading levels, fluency, and comprehension. (For further discussion of a variety of these assessments, see Chapter 5.)

Figure 5. Factors to Consider When Matching Students and Text

Reader Factors	Questions to Consider
Interest and Motivation	• Is the topic of interest to students? • Will students find the text engaging?
Background Knowledge	• Is the story or topic familiar? • What previous experiences with reading and reading instruction have students had? • How much experience have students had with this genre or type of text? • Do students know the vocabulary necessary to construct meaning from this text?
Sociocultural Identities	• Is the text culturally connected to students? • Is the language simple and direct? • Is the vocabulary familiar to students? • Are there illustrations to help students understand the text?

Text Factors	Questions to Consider
Length of Text	• Do students have the stamina to read this text? • Will students be able to maintain interest in this text?
Text Type and Structure	• Are students familiar with this type of text? • How much experience have students had reading this type of text? • Do students understand the structure of this text? Can they use the structure to help set a purpose or understand what they read?
Page Layout	• Do students know how to use picture and other visual cues to help them read and understand? • Is the text considerate toward the students? Is it appropriate for their developmental and achievement levels?
Text Content	• How much background knowledge do students have about this topic? • How much experience do they have with this content? • How familiar are the students with the language patterns and vocabulary used in this text? • Are students familiar with the format in which the content is presented?
Vocabulary and Literary Features	• Are there many difficult words in this text? • Do students have the background knowledge to infer the meanings of many of the words? • Do students have enough knowledge of language to make inferences and understand the subtle messages in the text? • Do students understand the use of literary devices and how authors use them to tell the story?

Hunt (1996) suggests that students also contribute to determining text accessibility. He recommends that students engage in self-evaluation during independent reading by responding to questions such as the following:

- Did you have a good reading period today?
- Were you able to concentrate as you read independently?
- Did the ideas in the book hold your attention?
- Were you bothered by others or outside noises?
- Could you keep the ideas in the book straight in your mind?
- Did you get mixed up in any place? Were you able to fix it?
- Were there words you did not know? How did you figure them out?
- Were you hoping the book would end, or were you hoping it would go on and on?

Although these questions require only yes or no responses, they do provide insights into students' perceptions of their performance. Other ways to gather similar information include holding individual student–teacher conferences and using informal measures such as quick writes and Tickets Out (see Appendix E, page 354).

We also need to gather data about student experiences and interests. As noted earlier, this can be accomplished through interviews, observations, or interest inventories. (See Chapter 5 for a more complete discussion of diagnostic measures.)

Text Information

Once we have the appropriate information about our students, we need to consider what texts we will use. We use the following steps to facilitate this process:

1. *Identify the texts available in the classroom*: These may include but not be limited to core programs, anthologies, trade books, textbooks, magazines, newspapers, online text, poetry books, and picture books.

2. *Organize the texts to facilitate Guided Comprehension*: We use the following questions to accomplish this:

   - Does this text add to existing content area study or knowledge?
   - Can this text be used in a genre study?
   - Does this text exemplify a particular style, structure, language pattern, or literary device?
   - Can this text be used to teach a comprehension strategy?
   - Are there multiple copies of the text available?
   - Does this text match a particular student's interests?
   - Is this a good example of a text structure?
   - Is this text part of a series?
   - Is it written by a favorite author?

These questions can be used with both narrative and informational texts. This includes individual stories in literature anthologies, as well as individual articles within magazines.

3. *Acquire additional materials to ensure ample accessible texts for all readers*: It is important to have some sets of books to use during teacher-guided comprehension small groups, but it is also necessary to have a wide array of texts, varying in type, genre, length, content, and level. All students should have a multitude of accessible books within the classroom, including picture books, informational texts, poetry books, and magazines. We keep in mind the following ideas when adding to classroom collections:

- Content areas—informational and narrative text to supplement studies in math, science, and social studies
- Student interests—a variety of texts (narrative, informational, poetry) about diverse topics to match students' interests
- Read-aloud—texts that offer examples of a variety of text structures and engaging story lines to be used to demonstrate comprehension processes and fluency
- Anchor books—texts used in whole-group and small-group instruction to demonstrate a specific strategy or routine
- Sets of books—four to six copies of the same title to be used in Guided Comprehension teacher-guided small groups; these should be based on students' levels and interests, as well as the strategies that can be taught using them
- Text sets—series books, favorite author, genre, topic; several books that have a common characteristic

Once we have accumulated the texts, we need to organize them to accommodate all stages of the Guided Comprehension Model.

Methods for Leveling Texts

All text levels are approximations, and there is no specific rule for determining them. Text ease or difficulty is determined by both text and reader factors. Each text will need to be evaluated with specific readers in mind. Leveling systems, teacher judgment, paralleling books, and using leveled lists developed by others facilitate this process.

Leveling Systems

Several systems exist that will help determine the approximate level of a text. These take into consideration factors such as format, language structure, and content (Weaver, 2000). The following are examples of these formulas: the Fry Readability Index (Fry, 1977), Lexile Framework for Reading Book Database (www.lexile.com), and Scholastic's Teacher Book Wizard (bookwizard.scholastic.com/tbw/homePage.do). The Fry Readability Index takes into consideration sentence length and number of syllables for three random 100-word selections within a text. These two numbers are plotted on a graph and an approximate reading level is provided for each selection. The Lexile Framework for Reading Book Database has thousands of books leveled using the Lexile leveling system. This system takes into consideration word frequency and sentence length. The higher the Lexile score, the more difficult the text is related to those two features. Scholastic's Teacher Book Wizard allows teachers to enter a book title and find an approximate level based on their leveling system. In addition, you can enter a book title and find other books that have similar levels. Leveling systems provide helpful information about the ease or difficulty of a text, and also help to find books that may be similar in levels. For examples of books from these websites and other website resources for leveled texts, see Appendix F.

Teacher Judgment

Although these leveling systems provide a starting point, teacher judgment may be the method used most frequently in leveling texts for the primary grades. When we engage in leveling, it is important to identify reader factors, such as familiarity with content or genre, as well as motivation to read, when trying to match a text with a reader.

We often use the following processes for leveling texts:

- Separate books into narrative, informational, and poetry.
- For each type of book, divide the books into harder and easier.
- Take each pile of books and sort by hardest to easiest (repeat this process as necessary).
- Label or color-code levels for student access.

Although these methods do not provide exact text levels, they do allow us to organize our books by type and by degree of difficulty. This information is very helpful when teaching students to select texts, or for us to guide students in that selection process.

Paralleling Books

Another way to level texts is to match classroom books with published leveled texts that have similar text features, such as length, font size, number of illustrations, and genre. This process, called paralleling books, provides a format for informally identifying approximate levels of existing classroom materials. In Appendix F, we provide lists of model books that represent approximate levels.

Published Lists and Websites for Leveled Books

Many publishers provide lists of leveled titles that we can use in creating student–text matches and in all stages of Guided Comprehension. We can use these lists as resources for identifying anchor books as well as for assessment purposes. Many of these sets of leveled books, which include narrative and informational texts, are available for purchase. (Information about these sources is provided in Appendix F.)

Classroom Text Organization

Once we have leveled our classroom collections, our goal is to organize the texts efficiently to promote their optimum use. This includes texts for use in whole-group and small-group teaching, as well as texts for students to use during comprehension centers and routines. To facilitate accessing text for our teaching, Harvey and Goudvis (2000) suggest accumulating a master list of titles and organizing them according to what they have to offer as teaching models. Approaches to such organization include listing books by strategy to be modeled, by book title, by genre and level, and by topic and level.

To provide accessible texts for student-facilitated comprehension centers and routines, we use the following methods of organization:

- *Class book baskets*: Creating book baskets by author, series, content, or approximate reading level is one method. With our help, students can then make selections from a whole collection of books in the basket.

- *Individual book baskets*: We can also help students to create individual book baskets in which they keep an ongoing collection of books they want to read. This eliminates any "down time" when students need to select text for independent reading.

- *Individual student booklists*: Students keep these lists in the back of their Guided Comprehension Journals. Titles can be added to the list in an ongoing manner to accommodate student progress. This often happens when students share ideas from their reading in Stage Three of the Guided Comprehension Model or when we share book talks of new and favorite books.

To further facilitate text organization, Szymusiak and Sibberson (2001) recommend that books in classroom collections be placed face out so that readers can easily see the covers and preview the texts and that sections for fiction, nonfiction, and poetry be marked clearly.

The two most important factors in matching students with appropriate texts are students' reading levels and interests. We can determine students' range of approximate reading levels by using informal assessments. Additionally, we can learn much about students' interests through simple inventories. This information helps us to create meaningful matches between students and texts.

PART TWO

Theme-Based Guided Comprehension Lessons

Focus: Situating Guided Comprehension in a variety of themes.

Theme Overviews: The planning graphic that appears at the start of each theme is based on Wiggins and McTighe's (2008) belief that we should begin the planning process by identifying the desired results. In this case, the desired results are expressed as the theme's goals and resulting connections to state standards. The next step is determining acceptable evidences; these are listed as assessments on the graphic.

The final step is planning learning experiences and instruction. These are represented by the texts, comprehension strategies, teaching ideas, and instructional settings such as comprehension centers and routines. Technology resources complete the plan.

Themes: Four Guided Comprehension lessons are provided for each theme. The lessons were written and taught by teachers in grades K–3. You will notice a change in voice as each teacher speaks about his or her classroom teaching experience. The Guided Comprehension Lesson Overviews are plans these teachers wrote for their lessons. The lessons focus on a variety of comprehension skills and strategies and multiple types and levels of theme-related texts. The lessons also include multiple modes of representation and critical and creative thinking. Theme-based resources including related texts and websites, suggestions for performance extensions across the curriculum, and a culminating activity follow each set of lessons. The chart at right presents an overview of the themes, including the comprehension strategies and teaching ideas that are embedded in each lesson.

Theme Topics, Strategies, and Teaching Ideas

Chapter 7: Click, Clack, WOW! The Stories of Doreen Cronin
Self-Questioning: "I Wonder" Statements
Making Connections: Connection Stems
Monitoring: Patterned Partner Reading
Summarizing: Draw and Write Retelling

Chapter 8: Animals Aplenty: The Informational Text of Seymour Simon
Previewing: Semantic Question Map
Self-Questioning: Draw and Write Wonders
Monitoring: Say Something
Summarizing: Questions Into Paragraphs (QuIP)

Chapter 9: Giggles Galore: The Humor of Dav Pilkey
Previewing: Story Impressions
Knowing How Words Work: Vocabulary Bookmark
Making Connections: Draw and Write Connections
Summarizing: Lyric Retelling

Chapter 10: Oceans Alive: Sea Creatures, Coral Reefs, Ecology, and More!
Previewing: Anticipation/Reaction Guide
Knowing How Words Work: Concept of Definition Map
Self-Questioning: Paired Questioning
Visualizing: Draw and Write Visualizations

CHAPTER 7

Click, Clack, WOW! The Stories of Doreen Cronin

From the moment we read *Click, Clack, Moo* and learned that cows could type, we and our students have been fans of Doreen Cronin's stories. They are engaging, funny tales that often focus on somewhat different views of life on a farm. Needless to say, in that setting the animals always seem to outsmart Farmer Brown. Betsy Lewin's illustrations not only bring the farm to life, but also show that Duck's talents extend beyond the farmyard when he wins a talent contest and is elected president of the United States. Beyond her cow and duck titles, Doreen Cronin has provided us with humorous insights into the personal thoughts of the main characters in *Diary of a Worm*, *Diary of a Spider*, and *Diary of a Fly*. These books, which are illustrated by Harry Bliss, make it easy for us and our students to make connections to the characters' families, friends, school lives. The unique photo album excerpts featured inside the front and back covers serve as Connection Stems, and our students can relate to all of them.

The sample Theme-Based Plan for Guided Comprehension: Click, Clack, WOW! The Stories of Doreen Cronin (see Figure 6) offers an overview of the lessons and resources that support this theme. The plan begins by listing theme goals and making connections to state standards. The student goals for this theme include the following:

- Use appropriate comprehension skills and strategies
- Interpret and respond to text
- Communicate effectively

These goals support the following state standards:

- Learning to read independently
- Reading, analyzing, and interpreting text
- Types and quality of writing
- Speaking and listening

Sample assessments in this theme include observation, running records, student writing, skill and strategy applications, and student self-assessments. The Guided Comprehension lessons are based on the following strategies and corresponding teaching ideas:

- Self-Questioning: "I Wonder" Statements
- Making Connections: Connection Stems

Figure 6. Theme-Based Plan for Guided Comprehension: Click, Clack, WOW! The Stories of Doreen Cronin

Goals and Related State Standards

Students will

- Use appropriate comprehension skills and strategies. Standard: learning to read independently
- Interpret and respond to text. Standard: reading, analyzing, and interpreting text
- Communicate effectively. Standards: types and quality of writing; speaking and listening

Assessment

The following measures can be used for a variety of purposes, including diagnostic, formative, and summative assessment:

Connection Stems
Draw and Write Retelling
"I Wonder" Statements
Observation

Patterned Partner Reading
Running Records
Student Self-Assessments
Student Writing

Text

Text	Title	Level
1.	Click, Clack, Moo	PreK–3
2.	Diary of a Worm	PreK–3
3.	Thump, Quack, Moo: A Whacky Adventure	PreK–3
4.	Giggle, Giggle, Quack	PreK–3

Technology Resources

Author Study
www.emints.org/ethemes/resources/S00002140.shtml
Doreen Cronin Biography
childrens-books.lovetoknow.com/Doreen_Cronin_Bio
Doreen Cronin Biography
www2.scholastic.com/browse/contributor.jsp?id=2887

Comprehension Strategies

1. Self-Questioning
2. Making Connections
3. Monitoring
4. Summarizing

Teaching Ideas

1. "I Wonder" Statements
2. Connection Stems
3. Patterned Partner Reading
4. Draw and Write Retelling

Comprehension Centers

Students will apply the comprehension strategies and related teaching ideas in the following comprehension centers:

ABC Center
Listening Center
Making and Writing Words Center
Making Books Center
Poetry Center

Storytelling Center
Teacher Center
Theme Center
Writing Center

Comprehension Routines

Students will apply the comprehension strategies and related teaching ideas in the following comprehension routines:

Literature Circles
Reciprocal Teaching
Cross-Age Reading Experiences

- Monitoring: Patterned Partner Reading
- Summarizing: Draw and Write Retelling

Click, Clack, Moo: Cows That Type (2000), *Diary of a Worm* (2003), *Thump, Quack, Moo: A Whacky Adventure* (2008), and *Giggle, Giggle, Quack* (2002) are the texts used in Stage One for teacher-directed whole-group instruction. Numerous additional theme-related resources, including texts, websites, performances across the curriculum, and a culminating activity, are presented in the Theme Resources at the end of the chapter.

Examples of comprehension centers students use during Stage Two of Guided Comprehension include ABC, listening, making and writing words, making books, poetry, storytelling, teacher, theme, and writing. Students also engage in strategy application in comprehension routines such as Literature Circles, Reciprocal Teaching, and Cross-Age Reading Experiences. Website resources complete the overview.

In this chapter, all the lessons focus on books authored by Doreen Cronin. The lessons are appropriate for all learners, including English learners, struggling readers, and students with special needs. To accommodate these learners, the lessons include multiple modes of response (such as singing, sketching, and dramatizing), working with partners, books on CD, cross-age experiences, and extra guided instruction. Ideas used to differentiate instruction in these lessons include the following:

- Content—the information being taught

  - Using leveled text to accommodate students' abilities in teacher-guided small groups, centers, and routines

  - Providing leveled texts that accommodate student interest and help motivate students to read

- Process—the way in which the information is taught

  - Activating prior knowledge and/or providing background information

  - Scaffolding student learning by using the Guided Comprehension Model

  - Reading the text aloud during Stage One to make it accessible to all students

  - Using visuals to support students' construction of meaning

  - Adapting graphic organizers; providing paragraph frames

  - Encouraging students to work with peers in pairs and small groups to provide additional support

  - Preteaching students who may need additional support to use the strategies and skills—such as sequencing and generating questions—at multiple levels

- Product—how the students demonstrate their learning

  - Integrating alternative modes of representation, such as art, drama, poetry, or music

  - Providing opportunities for students to use computers when creating projects

Guided Comprehension Lessons

Click, Clack, WOW! The Stories of Doreen Cronin
Guided Comprehension Strategy: Self-Questioning
Teaching Idea: "I Wonder" Statements

STAGE ONE: Teacher-Directed Whole-Group Instruction

Text: *Click, Clack, Moo: Cows That Type* (2000)

Explain: I began by explaining self-questioning and how "I Wonder" Statements (see Appendix C, page 220) can help us self-question as we read. I explained that we can express our wonders in several ways, and that today we would be saying them.

Demonstrate: I demonstrated "I Wonder" Statements by using a read-aloud, a Think-Aloud, and an overhead projector. I shared the cover and title of *Click, Clack, Moo: Cows That Type.* Then I invited students to make connections. Many students related to the animals, but they also wondered what the machine was that the animals seemed to be using like a computer. I took a few minutes to explain that before we had computers to input information, we used typewriters. Then I pointed out that it was a typewriter that the animals were using. Michael said, "That makes sense. It would be too expensive for the animals to have a computer." Then the students noticed the paper in the typewriter and decided that it looked as if the animals were typing a letter. That was when I began demonstrating "I Wonder" Statements. I said, "I wonder who the animals will send their letter to. Let's read to find out." Then I began reading aloud, stopping periodically to verify wonders and create new ones. For example, I read aloud to page six. Then I stopped and said,

> I have an answer for my "I Wonder" Statement. I wondered who the animals were writing to. Now I know they were writing to Farmer Brown. In their letter they said that they would like some electric blankets because the barn is so cold. I wonder if Farmer Brown is going to give the blankets to the animals.

Then I read the next page aloud and discovered that Farmer Brown would not give the blankets to the animals. The cows said they were going on strike and they would not give Farmer Brown any milk. As I continued to read aloud, an illustration showed the cows typing again. So, I said, "I wonder what the cows are typing now." Then I read on to verify or find an answer to my wonder. It turned out they were writing another note to Farmer Brown. This time the cows said the hens were cold and they wanted electric blankets. When the farmer didn't respond, the hens went on strike, too.

Guide: As I continued to read aloud, we learned that Farmer Brown was angry, so he typed his own note. I guided the students to work with partners to create "I Wonder" Statements. Rachel and Connor said, "We wonder what the Farmer's note said." Others had similar ideas, so I read on and we learned that Farmer Brown wrote that he would not give the animals the blankets and that he expected them to give him milk and eggs. By this point, we were all wondering if the animals would ever get the blankets and if Farmer Brown would get the eggs and milk.

Practice: I continued to read aloud and the students continued to wonder with their partners. For example, they wondered how Farmer Brown would get his message delivered to the animals. Then they wondered what response the animals would send. We learned that Duck delivered the

Guided Comprehension: Click, Clack, WOW! The Stories of Doreen Cronin
Self-Questioning: "I Wonder" Statements

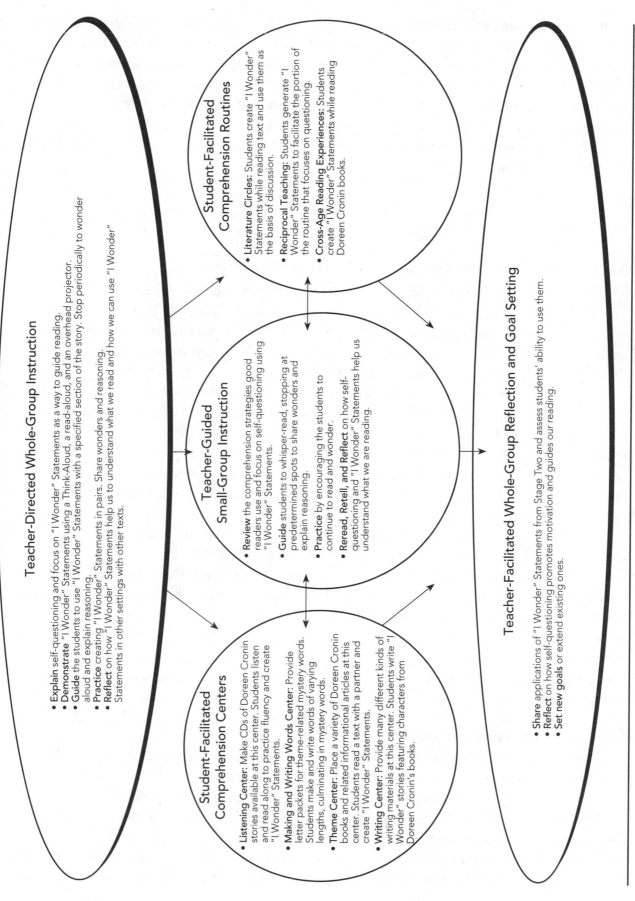

Teacher-Directed Whole-Group Instruction

- **Explain** self-questioning and focus on "I Wonder" Statements as a way to guide reading.
- **Demonstrate** "I Wonder" Statements using a Think-Aloud, a read-aloud, and an overhead projector.
- **Guide** the students to use "I Wonder" Statements with a specified section of the story. Stop periodically to wonder aloud and explain reasoning.
- **Practice** creating "I Wonder" Statements in pairs. Share wonders and reasoning.
- **Reflect** on how "I Wonder" Statements help us to understand what we read and how we can use "I Wonder" Statements in other settings with other texts.

Student-Facilitated Comprehension Routines

- **Literature Circles:** Students create "I Wonder" Statements while reading text and use them as the basis of discussion.
- **Reciprocal Teaching:** Students generate "I Wonder" Statements to facilitate the portion of the routine that focuses on questioning.
- **Cross-Age Reading Experiences:** Students create "I Wonder" Statements while reading Doreen Cronin books.

Teacher-Guided Small-Group Instruction

- **Review** the comprehension strategies good readers use and focus on self-questioning using "I Wonder" Statements.
- **Guide** students to whisper-read, stopping at predetermined spots to share wonders and explain reasoning.
- **Practice** by encouraging the students to continue to read and wonder.
- **Reread, Retell, and Reflect** on how self-questioning and "I Wonder" Statements help us understand what we are reading.

Student-Facilitated Comprehension Centers

- **Listening Center:** Make CDs of Doreen Cronin stories available at this center. Students listen and read along to practice fluency and create "I Wonder" Statements.
- **Making and Writing Words Center:** Provide letter packets for theme-related mystery words. Students make and write words of varying lengths, culminating in mystery words.
- **Theme Center:** Place a variety of Doreen Cronin books and related informational articles at this center. Students read a text with a partner and create "I Wonder" Statements.
- **Writing Center:** Provide many different kinds of writing materials at this center. Students write "I Wonder" stories featuring characters from Doreen Cronin's books.

Teacher-Facilitated Whole-Group Reflection and Goal Setting

- **Share** applications of "I Wonder" Statements from Stage Two and assess students' ability to use them.
- **Reflect** on how self-questioning promotes motivation and guides our reading.
- **Set new goals** or extend existing ones.

farmer's message and that the animals didn't reply until the next morning. They said they would return the typewriter to Farmer Brown if he would give them the electric blankets. Then the students wondered what the farmer would do. As I continued to read aloud, we learned that the farmer gave the animals the blankets, but the animals did not return the typewriter. Instead they wrote another note asking for a diving board, which, according to the last illustration, the farmer also supplied.

Reflect: We discussed the story and how "I Wonder" Statements help us to understand what we read. Phillippe said,

> If you're wondering, you can't stop reading until you find out what happens to the very last wonder. Even after you finish reading, you can still wonder about the story. Like now. The story is over, but I am still wondering what the animals will ask for next.

STAGE TWO: Teacher-Guided Small-Group Instruction

Text: *Duck for President* (2008) (Texts varied according to students' abilities.)

Review: I reminded the students about the comprehension strategies that good readers use and focused on self-questioning using "I Wonder" Statements. I reminded the students that we would be saying our wonders and when they came to a little stop sign sticker in their books, they should stop and wonder with other group members.

Guide: I introduced the text and invited the students to wonder about the title and book cover. They wondered if Duck was running for president of the United States and if he would win. I said that we should read to see if our wonders are verified. I guided the students to silently read *Duck for President*. Then students read the first few sections of text, as I monitored and provided help when requested. We stopped after each section to discuss the students' wonderings and reasoning. For example, they wondered when Duck became governor, if he would stay with that job, because the book title was *Duck for President*.

Practice: Students continued to read the rest of the story, stopping at designated points to create "I Wonder" Statements and explain their reasoning. After a brief discussion of their ideas, they continued reading, wondering, and discussing until they finished reading the story.

Reread, Retell, and Reflect: We engaged in a whisper reread of the story and engaged in an oral retelling. I used that time as an opportunity to do a running record with one of the students. Next, we reflected on how creating "I Wonder" Statements helped guide our reading and kept us engaged with the text. We thought about how to use "I Wonder" Statements with other types of text. Then Alicia said, "When we wonder we have to keep reading. We always want to know if the author has an answer for our wonder in the story."

Student-Facilitated Comprehension Centers

Listening Center: The students chose partners and listened to various Doreen Cronin stories on CD. While reading along with the story, the partners stopped at designated points to share "I Wonder" Statements. Then they completed the Center Reflections (see Appendix D, page 301).

Making and Writing Words Center: Students engaged in Making and Writing Words by manipulating letters to create words of increasing length and then writing them on the Making and Writing Words Response sheets (see Appendix D, pages 316 and 317). Some students engaged in Making Words and manipulated three-dimensional magnetic letters to form two-, three-, four-, and five-letter words until they reached the mystery word. Both activities concluded with students guessing a theme-related mystery word.

Theme Center: Students used Patterned Partner Reading to read Doreen Cronin books or related informational texts. They used the Read-Pause-Wonder pattern, stopping at designated points to share their wonderings and reasoning.

Writing Center: Students worked either with a partner or individually to write and illustrate "I Wonder" stories related to Doreen Cronin books they had read. Students had the option of using story starters such as "I wonder what the cows are typing now..." and "I wonder what Duck is doing now...."

Student-Facilitated Comprehension Routines

Literature Circles: The students created "I Wonder" Statements as they read their Literature Circle books and used them to prompt their discussion. After reading the book, the students created advertisements for it as an extension activity and shared them with the class.

Reciprocal Teaching: Students generated "I Wonder" Statements to facilitate the portion of the routine that focuses on questioning. They also predicted, clarified, and summarized.

Cross-Age Reading Experiences: Students practiced using "I Wonder" Statements with their cross-age partners as they read theme-related texts. Some partners used "I Wonder" Bookmarks (see Appendix C, page 274).

STAGE THREE: Teacher-Facilitated Whole-Group Reflection and Goal Setting

Share: We shared students' applications of "I Wonder" Statements from Stage Two in small groups. Then we shared selected examples with the whole class.

Reflect: We reflected on how self-questioning and "I Wonder" Statements helped guide our reading and helped us understand what we read. We also discussed how "I Wonder" Statements motivated us to keep reading to verify our wonders and create more.

Set New Goals: The students felt confident in their ability to use "I Wonder" Statements to engage in self-questioning when reading stories, so we decided to extend our understanding of "I Wonder" Statements by using them with informational text.

Assessment Options

I listened carefully to students' wonderings and reasoning. I observed students throughout the lesson in whole-group, small-group, and paired settings. I read and commented on their projects. I reviewed and commented on their self-assessments, which were very helpful in understanding students' abilities to self-question. I also completed fluency checks and running records with selected students.

Click, Clack, WOW! The Stories of Doreen Cronin
Guided Comprehension Strategy: Making Connections
Teaching Idea: Connection Stems

STAGE ONE: Teacher-Directed Whole-Group Instruction

Text: *Diary of a Worm* (2003)

Explain: I began by engaging in direct explanation of making connections. I explained that the connections we make are usually text–self, text–text, and text–world, and that today we would be focusing on text–self connections and text–text connections. I explained that a Connection Stem (see Appendix C, pages 225–226) is part of a sentence that connects something that happened in the story with an experience we might have had. It could also be an experience someone else might have had, or it might remind us of something that happened in another book. Then I introduced the Connection Stems and read each one aloud:

- That reminds me of...
- I remember when...
- I have a connection to...
- An experience I have had like that is...
- That character reminds me of...

Demonstrate: I introduced *Diary of a Worm* by sharing the cover and reading the title. We talked about worms and diaries. Then I asked pairs of students what they thought the story would be about. Julianna and Olivia said that they thought it would be about a worm that writes in a diary like we write in our journals. Ryan and Michael said they thought it would be about a worm that lives underground and keeps a diary. Next, I used a Think-Aloud, a read-aloud, and a chalkboard to share my connections to *Diary of a Worm*. I began by thinking aloud about the cover, the title, and the first few pages of the story. As I spoke, I noted that on the book cover the worm is sitting at a table or desk. So I said, "Seeing the worm sitting at the table or desk and writing reminds me of when we sit at our desks and write." Then I noticed that the worm is sitting on a bottle cap. I said, "Seeing the worm sitting on a bottle cap reminds me of how small worms are." Finally, after reading the first two pages aloud, I said, "An experience I have had like Worm's mother giving him advice is when my mother gives me advice." Then I asked the students if their moms, dads, other family members gave them advice. Many of the students replied that they did. Jordyn said, "My mom is always telling me to be careful crossing the street." Xavier said, "My dad is always telling me to take care of Earth by recycling."

Guide: I guided the students to work with a partner to think of a connection they could make to the section I was about to read aloud. I encouraged the students to use the stem "We have a connection to..." when sharing their connections. Then I read aloud. Here are some examples of the students' connections:

> Sasha and Angie: "We have a connection to...the girls the worm scared in the park. We would run away if we saw a worm where we were playing, too."

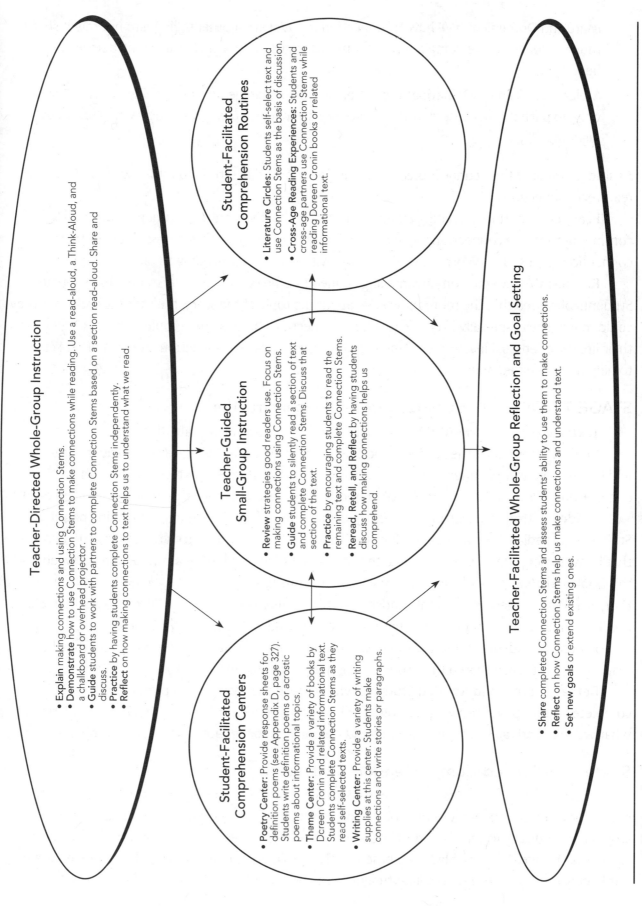

Teacher-Directed Whole-Group Instruction

- **Explain** making connections and using Connection Stems.
- **Demonstrate** how to use Connection Stems to make connections while reading. Use a read-aloud, a Think-Aloud, and a chalkboard or overhead projector.
- **Guide** students to work with partners to complete Connection Stems based on a section read-aloud. Share and discuss.
- **Practice** by having students complete Connection Stems independently.
- **Reflect** on how making connections to text helps us to understand what we read.

Student-Facilitated Comprehension Routines

- **Literature Circles:** Students self-select text and use Connection Stems as the basis of discussion.
- **Cross-Age Reading Experiences:** Students and cross-age partners use Connection Stems while reading Doreen Cronin books or related informational text.

Teacher-Guided Small-Group Instruction

- **Review** strategies good readers use. Focus on making connections using Connection Stems.
- **Guide** students to silently read a section of text and complete Connection Stems. Discuss that section of the text.
- **Practice** by encouraging students to read the remaining text and complete Connection Stems.
- **Reread, Retell, and Reflect** by having students discuss how making connections helps us comprehend.

Student-Facilitated Comprehension Centers

- **Poetry Center:** Provide response sheets for definition poems (see Appendix D, page 327). Students write definition poems or acrostic poems about informational topics.
- **Theme Center:** Provide a variety of books by Dcreen Cronin and related informational text. Students complete Connection Stems as they read self-selected texts.
- **Writing Center:** Provide a variety of writing supplies at this center. Students make connections and write stories or paragraphs.

Teacher-Facilitated Whole-Group Reflection and Goal Setting

- **Share** completed Connection Stems and assess students' ability to use them to make connections.
- **Reflect** on how Connection Stems help us make connections and understand text.
- **Set** new goals or extend existing ones.

Guided Comprehension in the Primary Grades (Second Edition) by Maureen McLaughlin. © 2010 by the International Reading Association. May be copied for classroom use.

Marc and Domenico: "We have a connection to...Worm's mother telling him not to eat so much garbage before going to bed. Our moms tell us not to eat so much junk before going to bed."

Melanie and Gina: "We have a connection...to the dance the worms were doing. They could only do part of it because they don't have arms and legs, but we do all of it when we go to weddings."

As students shared their connections, we discussed them and determined if they were text–self or text–text connections.

Practice: I continued reading aloud to the end of the book, and the students practiced by continuing to create connections with a partner and share them with the class. Most of their connections focused on Worm's never getting cavities and never needing to take a bath.

Reflect: We reflected on how making connections helped us to understand what we read. Students observed that the more they knew about the topic of the story, the more connections they could make. They especially liked the text–self connections because they could make connections to their life experiences. Finally, we reflected on how we could use Connection Stems in other settings to help us understand what we read.

STAGE TWO: Teacher-Guided Small-Group Instruction

Text: *Diary of a Spider* (2005) (Texts varied according to students' abilities.)

Review: I reminded the students about the comprehension strategies good readers use and focused on using Connection Stems. We reviewed how to make text–self and text–text connections. We noted the examples of Connection Stems from Stage One that were still on display.

Guide: I introduced *Diary of a Spider* by sharing the cover and reading the opening pages. Students immediately noted connections to the pencil the spider used to write in his diary and that he was using a leaf as a sail. I asked the students if they could make a connection between this book and another book, and they made connections to Eric Carle's *The Very Busy Spider* and *Diary of a Worm*. Then I guided the students as they silently read *Diary of a Spider*. They stopped at predetermined points to make and share connections, and we discussed their ideas.

Practice: Students continued to use Connection Stems to make connections until they finished reading the text. They shared their connections and we discussed the story.

Reread, Retell, and Reflect: Students whisper read the story with a partner and we completed a group oral retelling. We reflected on how Connection Stems helped us to understand what we read and talked about how we could use making connections with informational texts.

Student-Facilitated Comprehension Centers

Poetry Center: Students worked in pairs to read short informational texts about topics such as cows, ducks, hens, farmers, worms, spiders, or flies that relate to Doreen Cronin's books. Students stopped periodically to make connections as they read. Then they wrote definition poems (see Appendix D, page 327, for a blackline) based on the informational text they read, and posted them in our Poetry Corner, where we display student-authored poems.

Theme Center: Students chose from a variety of Doreen Cronin books or related informational texts and completed Connection Stems as they read. They recorded their connections on a response sheet I provided.

Writing Center: Students worked either on their own or with a partner to make connections to one of Doreen Cronin's farm and diary books or related informational texts. Then they wrote a story or an informational paragraph. Story titles included *Diary of a Dog, Duck for Principal*, and *Click, Clack, Ta-da: Kids That Type!* When they finished writing, students completed Center Student Self-Evaluations (see Appendix D, page 303).

Student-Facilitated Comprehension Routines

Literature Circles: Students selected theme-related books and read them in Literature Circles. As they read, the students completed at least three Connection Stems. They also completed the Literature Circle Bookmarks (see Appendix D, page 313). When they finished reading their books, students engaged in extension projects, such as creating an acrostic retelling of the story that they illustrated, an illustrated book review in which they presented their thoughts about the book, and a Lyric Retelling. The students presented their completed projects to the class in Stage Three. Students also completed Literature Circle Group Evaluations (see Appendix D, page 314).

Cross-Age Reading Experiences: Students worked with cross-age partners to read Doreen Cronin books or related informational texts. As they read, students completed Connection Stems. After reading, they completed Cross-Age Reading Experience Self-Evaluations (see Appendix D, page 306).

STAGE THREE: Teacher-Facilitated Whole-Group Reflection and Goal Setting

Share: We began by sharing Connection Stems and projects from Stage Two. The students enjoyed sharing the connections they had made. All the students seemed confident in their abilities, and their applications from Stage Two supported their thinking.

Reflect: We reflected on how Connection Stems helped us to understand what we read. Students also talked about how we can use Connection Stems with many different kinds of text including poetry, song lyrics, newspaper articles, and what we read on the Internet.

Set New Goals: We decided to extend our goal about making connections to learning how to use Draw and Write Connections.

Assessment Options

I observed students in all settings during Guided Comprehension, focusing on topics such as student responses, student–text matches, fluency, and ability to work with others. I reviewed and commented on students' written connections and projects. During teacher-guided small groups, I did occasional fluency checks and running records. I used the assessment results to inform future teaching.

Click, Clack, WOW! The Stories of Doreen Cronin
Guided Comprehension Strategy: Monitoring
Teaching Idea: Patterned Partner Reading

STAGE ONE: Teacher-Directed Whole-Group Instruction

Text: *Thump, Quack, Moo: A Whacky Adventure* (2008) (Texts varied according to students' abilities.)

Explain: I began by explaining that monitoring is a reading comprehension strategy that involves asking, "Does this make sense?" Next, I explained that Patterned Partner Reading (see Appendix C, pages 239–240) helps us monitor our reading. Then I said, "When we use Patterned Partner Reading, we take turns reading with our partner and, when we finish reading our sections, we use patterns, such as Read–Pause–Retell, Read–Pause–Make a Connection, and Read–Pause–Say Something. I reminded students that we had already learned how to retell, make connections, and say something.

Demonstrate: I demonstrated by using a Think-Aloud and a read-aloud of *Thump, Quack, Moo: A Whacky Adventure.* I demonstrated with Maddy, a student from the class with whom I had met the previous day. I had taught her how to engage in Patterned Partner Reading and explained that we would be focusing on just three patterns during our demonstration. I introduced the book and encouraged the students to look at the cover and read the title. Then I invited students to make predictions about the book. They concluded that the book would be another adventure in which Duck outsmarts Farmer Brown. I suggested that Maddy and I read aloud so we could find out if the students' predictions could be verified. I explained that when we read, we would be engaging in Patterned Partner Reading, using the Read–Pause–Make a Connection pattern. I began reading aloud. After reading a few pages, I paused. Then I said, "I can make a connection to the cows helping Farmer Brown paint the barn, because when we needed to paint our house, our friends and family came to help." Then Maddy said, "I can make a connection to Farmer Brown wanting his maze to be perfect, because my father takes care of our lawn and bushes and he works hard to make sure they are perfect." We discussed our connections with the class and Maddy read the next section. When she paused, she said, "I can make a connection to Farmer Brown and Duck measuring carefully before they cut, because our art teacher always tells us that when we are doing projects." Then I said, "I can make a connection to the mice following the weather report, because the maze is in the cornfield and bad weather could be a problem." We discussed our connections with the class.

Guide: I read another few pages aloud and guided the students to join Maddy and me in making connections when we paused. The students made very good connections. Then I invited pairs of students to engage in Patterned Partner Reading using the Read–Pause–Make a Connection pattern. They read two sections and each partner made connections. We discussed their responses.

Practice: I encouraged the students to practice Patterned Partner Reading until they read to the end of the book. Then we discussed how we would use other patterns, such as Read–Pause– Retell and Read–Pause–Say Something when engaging in Patterned Partner Reading. They used the patterns successfully and seemed to enjoy monitoring their understanding in this way.

Reflect: We reflected on what we knew about monitoring and how using Patterned Partner Reading helped us to monitor our reading and focus our understanding. Joseph said, "This is a lot

Guided Comprehension: Click, Clack, WOW! The Stories of Doreen Cronin
Monitoring: Patterned Partner Reading

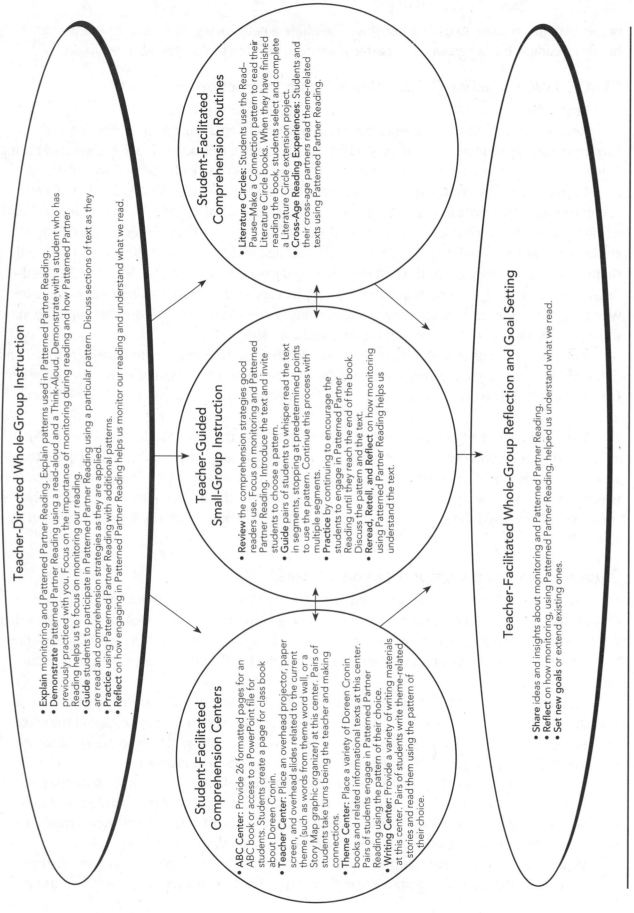

Teacher-Directed Whole-Group Instruction

- **Explain** monitoring and Patterned Partner Reading. Explain patterns used in Patterned Partner Reading.
- **Demonstrate** Patterned Partner Reading using a read-aloud and a Think-Aloud. Demonstrate with a student who has previously practiced with you. Focus on the importance of monitoring during reading and how Patterned Partner Reading helps us to focus on monitoring our reading.
- **Guide** students to participate in Patterned Partner Reading using a particular pattern. Discuss sections of text as they are read and comprehension strategies as they are applied.
- **Practice** using Patterned Partner Reading with additional patterns.
- **Reflect** on how engaging in Patterned Partner Reading helps us monitor our reading and understand what we read.

Student-Facilitated Comprehension Routines

- **Literature Circles:** Students use the Read–Pause–Make a Connection pattern to read their Literature Circle books. When they have finished reading the book, students select and complete a Literature Circle extension project.
- **Cross-Age Reading Experiences:** Students and their cross-age partners read theme-related texts using Patterned Partner Reading.

Teacher-Guided Small-Group Instruction

- **Review** the comprehension strategies good readers use. Focus on monitoring and Patterned Partner Reading. Introduce the text and invite students to choose a pattern.
- **Guide** pairs of students to whisper read the text in segments, stopping at predetermined points to use the pattern. Continue this process with multiple segments.
- **Practice** by continuing to encourage the students to engage in Patterned Partner Reading until they reach the end of the book. Discuss the pattern and the text.
- **Reread, Retell, and Reflect** on how monitoring using Patterned Partner Reading helps us understand the text.

Student-Facilitated Comprehension Centers

- **ABC Center:** Provide 26 formatted pages for an ABC book or access to a PowerPoint file for students. Students create a page for class book about Doreen Cronin.
- **Teacher Center:** Place an overhead projector, paper screen, and overhead slides related to the current theme (such as words from theme word wall, or a Story Map graphic organizer) at this center. Pairs of students take turns being the teacher and making connections.
- **Theme Center:** Place a variety of Doreen Cronin books and related informational texts at this center. Pairs of students engage in Patterned Partner Reading using the pattern of their choice.
- **Writing Center:** Provide a variety of writing materials at this center. Pairs of students write theme-related stories and read them using the pattern of their choice.

Teacher-Facilitated Whole-Group Reflection and Goal Setting

- **Share** ideas and insights about monitoring and Patterned Partner Reading.
- **Reflect** on how monitoring, using Patterned Partner Reading, helped us understand what we read.
- **Set new goals** or extend existing ones.

better than just reading to each other. If we don't have a pattern, we don't need to listen when our buddy is reading, but when we have patterns we need to listen to do what we need to do."

STAGE TWO: Teacher-Guided Small-Group Instruction

Text: *Diary of a Fly* (2007) (Texts varied according to students' abilities.)

Review: I reviewed the strategies good reader use and then focused on monitoring and Patterned Partner Reading. I reminded students about some of the examples we had created during Stage One, and explained that the pattern we would use would be Read–Pause–Say Something.

Guide: I began by doing a quick picture walk through the opening sections of *Diary of a Fly*, and encouraging students to make connections. We had already read *Diary of a Worm* and *Diary of a Spider*, so they readily made connections to the cover and opening pages. Then I guided pairs of students to use Patterned Partner Reading while reading the first section of the book. I reminded them to stop when they got to the first stop sign I had placed in their books and to use the Read–Pause–Say Something pattern. Students were very focused as they read, and were very attentive when their partners read. When they said something, they focused on Fly's concerns about opening day of school and having hundreds of brothers and sisters.

Practice: Students read the subsequent sections and used the pattern until they got to the end of the book. Their "Say Somethings" included Fly wanting to be a superhero and the support of her friends, Worm and Spider; a number of facts about flies; and Fly's relationship with her brothers and sisters.

Reread, Retell, and Reflect: We began by reflecting on the story. Students enjoyed *Diary of a Fly* and thought it was every bit as good as *Diary of a Worm* and *Diary of a Spider*. They liked that it was Fly's friends who supported her in her quest to become a superhero. They also appreciated the way that Doreen Cronin made it seem as if Fly, Worm, and Spider have many of the same problems they do. Students used the pattern well and were eager to try other patterns in the centers and routines.

Student-Facilitated Comprehension Centers

ABC Center: Pairs of students created pages for our class ABC book about author Doreen Cronin and illustrators Betsy Lewin and Harry Bliss. I bookmarked selected websites. I also provided the students with access to a PowerPoint slide show in which I had already included 27 slides—one for each letter of the alphabet and a cover slide. When the book was completed, we put it in our classroom library.

Teacher Center: Pairs of students took turns being the teacher at the center. The first "student" read the theme-related word wall list that I had placed on overhead transparencies, and the second "student" completed a Story Map based on a Doreen Cronin book that I had also prepared for the overhead projector. The "teacher" supported the "student" in these endeavors.

Theme Center: Pairs of students read Doreen Cronin books and related informational texts using Patterned Partner Reading at this center. They selected one of three patterns to use: Read–Pause–Make a Connection, Read–Pause–Say Something, or Read–Pause–Retell. When they finished reading, they completed Center Reflections (see Appendix D, page 301).

Writing Center: Students worked either on their own or in pairs to self-select theme-related topics and write stories at this center. When they completed their stories, they read them using

Patterned Partner Reading. The students chose the pattern they wanted to use. The completed stories were shared with the class and hung in our gallery, where students could read them.

Student-Facilitated Comprehension Routines

Literature Circles: The students used Patterned Partner Reading using the Read–Pause–Make a Connection pattern when reading to prepare for Literature Circles. When they finished reading their book, the students engaged in extension activities such as creating puppets out of paper bags to retell the story for the class.

Cross-Age Reading Experiences: Students and their cross-age partners used Patterned Partner Reading when reading theme-related stories and informational text. The partners chose the pattern they wanted to use.

STAGE THREE: Teacher-Facilitated Whole-Group Reflection and Goal Setting

Share: Students discussed their applications and shared their projects from Stage Two with the class. Then we viewed and discussed our student-authored electronic ABC book. We applauded after each author explained his or her page. We were all very proud of our book.

Reflect: We discussed how monitoring helps us to understand what we read. Several students noted that Patterned Partner Reading helped them to think about what they were reading while they were reading.

Set New Goals: Students felt confident with their ability to use Patterned Partner Reading to monitor their understanding. So we decided to extend our understanding of monitoring by learning how to use Double-Entry Journals.

Assessment Options

I used observation throughout this lesson and listened carefully to students as they engaged in Patterned Partner Reading. I also reviewed and commented on students' work from Stage Two, which included the pages they had created for our class ABC book, their Literature Circle extensions, and their self-assessments.

Click, Clack, WOW! The Stories of Doreen Cronin
Guided Comprehension Strategy: Summarizing
Teaching Idea: Draw and Write Retelling

STAGE ONE: Teacher-Directed Whole-Group Instruction

Text: *Giggle, Giggle, Quack* (2002)

Explain: I explained summarizing to the students and focused on retelling (see Appendix C, pages 246–247). I offered several examples from our lives when we might retell something, including if a friend missed a day at school, a sport practice, or an episode of a favorite television show, and we later shared what had happened from beginning to end. I pointed out that whenever we engage in retelling, it is important to remember to tell what happened in the same order or sequence in which it occurred. Then I demonstrated how we use retellings in our everyday lives by retelling what happened in school yesterday for a student who had been absent. Next, I explained that when we retell stories, we need to make sure that we include who was in the story, where it took place, what happened, and how it ended.

Demonstrate: I demonstrated by using a Think-Aloud, a read-aloud, and a poster-size sticky note that I had pressed to the chalkboard. I had previously sketched the Draw and Write Retelling on the large note, and began by introducing the organizer and its components: who was in the story, where it took place, what happened, and how it ended. Next, I introduced *Giggle, Giggle, Quack* by sharing the book cover and reading the first three pages. The students predicted that because Farmer Brown's brother, Bob, was in charge while the farmer was on vacation, that this time instead of outsmarting Farmer Brown, Duck would outsmart his brother. I reminded students that as I was reading we should be thinking about what information from the story we would need to include in our retellings. I again referred them to the Draw and Write Retelling I had created on the poster attached to the chalkboard. I also shared the Draw and Write Retelling blackline (see Appendix C, page 270) with the students. Then I continued reading the book aloud.

When I had finished reading the book aloud, I used the Draw and Write Retelling format I had created on the poster to review all the elements we would need to include. Then I started to sketch the characters in the first frame of the Draw and Write Retelling organizer. I drew pictures of Farmer Brown, Bob, Duck, cows, chickens, and pigs. When I finished, I wrote, "*Duck, Bob, Farmer Brown, cows, chickens, pigs.*" In the frame marked "Where?" I drew a picture of the farm and wrote "*farm.*"

Guide: I guided the students to work with a partner to complete the third frame—What happened?—on the blacklines I had provided. They sketched and wrote a variety of ideas, but most agreed that Duck had tricked Bob, so I sketched a picture of Duck writing a note and I wrote, "*Duck tricked Bob by writing notes.*"

Practice: The students worked with their partners to complete the fourth frame—How did it end? Their drawings showed Farmer Brown rushing home from vacation in cars, on trains, and on planes. So I sketched Farmer Brown looking angry because he knew what Duck had done. Then I wrote, "*Farmer Brown found out and came home.*" I reviewed my completed Draw and Write Retelling for the class and we orally summarized the story. Following this, the students reviewed the frames they had completed for their retellings with another set of partners. Figure 7 contains our completed Draw and Write Retelling for Stage One.

Guided Comprehension: Click, Clack, WOW! The Stories of Doreen Cronin
Summarizing: Draw and Write Retelling

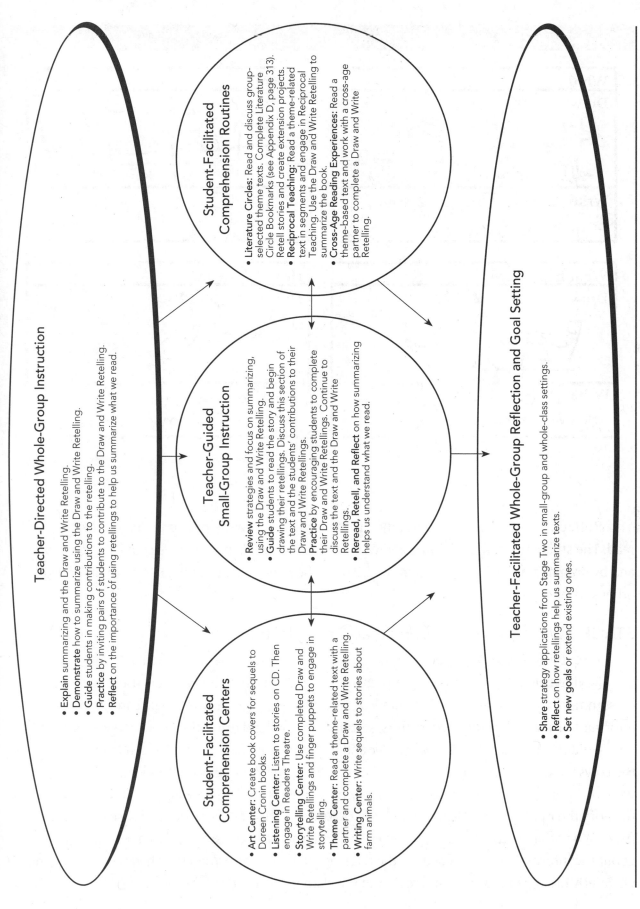

Teacher-Directed Whole-Group Instruction

- **Explain** summarizing and the Draw and Write Retelling.
- **Demonstrate** how to summarize using the Draw and Write Retelling.
- **Guide** students in making contributions to the retelling.
- **Practice** by inviting pairs of students to contribute to the Draw and Write Retelling.
- **Reflect** on the importance of using retellings to help us summarize what we read.

Student-Facilitated Comprehension Routines

- **Literature Circles:** Read and discuss group-selected theme texts. Complete Literature Circle Bookmarks (see Appendix D, page 313). Retell stories and create extension projects.
- **Reciprocal Teaching:** Read a theme-related text in segments and engage in Reciprocal Teaching. Use the Draw and Write Retelling to summarize the book.
- **Cross-Age Reading Experiences:** Read a theme-based text and work with a cross-age partner to complete a Draw and Write Retelling.

Teacher-Guided Small-Group Instruction

- **Review** strategies and focus on summarizing, using the Draw and Write Retelling.
- **Guide** students to read the story and begin drawing their retellings. Discuss this section of the text and the students' contributions to their Draw and Write Retellings.
- **Practice** by encouraging students to complete their Draw and Write Retellings. Continue to discuss the text and the Draw and Write Retellings.
- **Reread, Retell, and Reflect** on how summarizing helps us understand what we read.

Student-Facilitated Comprehension Centers

- **Art Center:** Create book covers for sequels to Doreen Cronin books.
- **Listening Center:** Listen to stories on CD. Then engage in Readers Theatre.
- **Storytelling Center:** Use completed Draw and Write Retellings and finger puppets to engage in storytelling.
- **Theme Center:** Read a theme-related text with a partner and complete a Draw and Write Retelling.
- **Writing Center:** Write sequels to stories about farm animals.

Teacher-Facilitated Whole-Group Reflection and Goal Setting

- **Share** strategy applications from Stage Two in small-group and whole-class settings.
- **Reflect** on how retellings help us summarize texts.
- **Set** new goals or extend existing ones.

Guided Comprehension in the Primary Grades (Second Edition) by Maureen McLaughlin. © 2010 by the International Reading Association. May be copied for classroom use.

Figure 7. Teacher Draw and Write Retelling

Who?	Where?
Draw:	Draw:
Write: Duck, Bob, Farmer Brown, Cow, chicken, pig	Write: Farm

What happened?	How did it end?
Draw:	Draw:
Write: Duck tricked Bob by writing notes.	Write: Farmer Brown found out and came home.

Reflect: We reflected on how summarizing using retellings helped us understand what we read. The students enjoyed drawing and writing to retell. I explained that we could also retell orally and by dramatizing and singing. Then we discussed how we could use retellings with other texts in other settings.

STAGE TWO: Teacher-Guided Small-Group Instruction

Text: *Dooby Dooby Moo* (2009) (Texts varied according to students' abilities.)

Review: First, I reviewed the comprehension strategies that good readers use, and focused on summarizing using retellings. I reminded the students that we needed to be careful to include information about the story's characters, setting, problem, and resolution when we were retelling.

Guide: I introduced *Dooby Dooby Moo* and had a brief discussion with the students about why the cows were on stage singing in front of microphone on the book cover. Students predicted they were recording a song, singing karaoke, or trying out for *American Idol*. I suggested we read the book to verify their predictions. Next, I shared the Draw and Write Retelling blacklines (see Appendix C, page 270) with the students and guided them to whisper read the story. I reminded them to think about the information we needed for the retelling while reading. When they had finished reading, we briefly discussed the story and reviewed the elements needed for the Draw and Write Retelling.

Practice: The students practiced by completing their Draw and Write Retellings and sharing them with the group. Then we created a group oral summary based on the retellings they completed. Dayle's Draw and Write Retelling is featured in Figure 8.

Reread, Retell, and Reflect: Students used Patterned Partner Reading to reread the story, and we used our Draw and Write Retellings to do a group oral retelling. During our remaining time, we reflected on how we can use retellings to help us understand what we read.

Student-Facilitated Comprehension Centers

Art Center: At this center, students created covers for the sequels they wrote in the Writing Center. They used a variety of watercolors to simulate Betsy Lewin's artistic style. When the covers dried, we attached them to the stories and displayed them in our classroom library.

Listening Center: Students listened to Doreen Cronin stories on tape or CD and read along to practice fluency. After that, if time permitted, they worked with three other students to record a Readers Theatre version of a story.

Storytelling Center: Students worked with partners and used Draw and Write Retellings they had already completed to tell a Doreen Cronin story. They used finger puppets they had previously made in art class during the retelling.

Figure 8. Student Draw and Write Retelling

Who? Draw: Write: Farmer Brown, Duck.

Where? Draw: Write: They went to the fair.

What happened? Draw: cow Pig Write: They all Singed and dance.

How did it end? Draw: Write: They Played with a trampoline!

Theme Center: Students worked in pairs to read a theme-related text and complete a Draw and Write Retelling. Then they shared and discussed their retelling with another pair.

Writing Center: Students wrote sequels to stories about farm animals and shared them with another student author. Students also completed Center Reflections (see Appendix D, page 301).

Student-Facilitated Comprehension Routines

Literature Circles: The students selected a theme-related text and read it in preparation for Literature Circles. They discussed the book in their circles and each group created a Draw and Write Retelling after reading. Then each group created an extension project. For example, some groups chose to do transmediations and changed the picture books they had read into acrostic poems or murals.

Reciprocal Teaching: Students engaged in reciprocal teaching—predicting, clarifying, questioning, and summarizing. Then they completed a group Draw and Write Retelling to summarize the book.

Cross-Age Reading Experiences: Pairs of students worked with cross-age partners to read a theme-related text. As they read, they paused at predetermined spots to make connections. After reading, they completed Draw and Write Retellings and used them to orally summarize the story.

STAGE THREE: Teacher-Facilitated Whole-Group Reflection and Goal Setting

Share: Students shared their Draw and Write Retellings and projects from Stage Two in small groups. Then each group shared selected applications with the whole class.

Reflect: We reflected on how Draw and Write Retellings help us understand what we read. Carl said, "Doing the four drawings is a good idea, because that makes us think about those parts of the story. Then we write about them. It all helps to make the story easier to remember."

Set New Goals: The students decided they were comfortable using the Draw and Write Retellings. Their work throughout the lesson supported this, so we decided to expand our understanding of summarizing by learning how to use Story Pyramids (see Appendix C, pages 248–249 and 290).

Assessment Options

I observed students retelling and summarizing during all stages of Guided Comprehension. I reviewed and commented on students' applications from Stage Two and was especially careful to provide positive feedback for student writing. I also engaged selected students in running records when they appeared ready to move to another level in teacher-guided small groups. I did fluency checks with several students and paid particular attention to student–text matches.

Final Thoughts About the Doreen Cronin Theme

Observing the lessons in the Doreen Cronin theme being taught by a number of primary-grade teachers was an extraordinary experience. During the lessons, it was abundantly apparent that the students, the teachers, and I were thoroughly engaged in Cronin's writing. During this theme, the classrooms were giggle-filled and the students were highly motivated.

As noted earlier in this book, a number of skills underpin the comprehension strategies that serve as the focus of this theme. Although space constraints prohibited sharing lessons at the skill level, it is important to note that lessons on a variety of aspects of language development and skills such as sequencing, generating questions, and distinguishing important from less important ideas were embedded in the theme. For example, Cronin's *Click, Clack, Quackity-Quack* was used in kindergarten lessons to promote phonemic awareness. (For ideas about using literature to teach phonemic awareness, phonics, and fluency, see Appendix B.) Titles such as *Dooby Dooby Moo* and *Thump, Quack, Moo* served as the basis of lessons about sequencing, and students engaged in repeated readings of many of Cronin's books to practice fluency. Other Cronin titles such as *Diary of a Worm* and *Diary of a Spider* piqued students' interest in writing in diary format. Betsy Lewin's and Harry Bliss's illustrations in Cronin's books also sparked students' interest and creativity. In addition, teachers adapted lessons for prereaders and prewriters by engaging in read-alouds and encouraging response through a variety of modes including discussion, drawing, painting, singing, dancing, and dramatizing.

Theme Resources

Books

Cronin, D. (2000). *Click, clack, moo: Cows that type*. New York: Simon & Schuster.

Cronin, D. (2002). *Giggle, giggle, quack*. New York: Atheneum.

Cronin, D. (2003). *Diary of a worm*. New York: HarperCollins.

Cronin, D. (2005). *Diary of a spider*. New York: HarperCollins.

Cronin, D. (2005). *Wiggle*. New York: Atheneum.

Cronin, D. (2006). *Click, clack, splish, splash*. New York: Simon & Schuster.

Cronin, D. (2007). *Bounce*. New York: Atheneum.

Cronin, D. (2007). *Diary of a fly*. New York: HarperCollins.

Cronin, D. (2008). *Click, clack, quackity-quack: A typing adventure*. New York: Little Simon.

Cronin, D. (2008). *Duck for president*. New York: Atheneum.

Cronin, D. (2008). *Farmer Brown's barnyard: A bestselling board book gift set*. New York: Little Simon.

Cronin, D. (2008). *Thump, quack, moo: A whacky adventure*. New York: Atheneum.

Cronin, D. (2009). *A busy day at the farm*. New York: Little Simon.

Cronin, D. (2009). *Dooby dooby moo*. New York: Atheneum.

Cronin, D. (2009). *Stretch*. New York: Atheneum.

Websites About Doreen Cronin

Author Study

www.emints.org/ethemes/resources/S00002140.shtml

Doreen Cronin Personal Website

    www.doreencronin.com/doreen.html

HarperCollins Children's: Authors & Illustrators

    www.harpercollinschildrens.com/Kids/AuthorsAndIllustrators/ContributorDetail
    .aspx?CId=21225

Love to Know: Children's Books

    childrens-books.lovetoknow.com/Doreen_Cronin_Bio

Pippin Properties: Authors/Illustrators

    www.pippinproperties.com/authill/cronin/

Scholastic Biography

    www2.scholastic.com/browse/contributor.jsp?id=2887

Web English Teacher

    www.webenglishteacher.com/cronin.html#

Performance Extensions Across the Curriculum

Art

- Students will draw their favorite farm animal on a square piece of fabric or construction paper. Each piece will be woven together to create a classroom farm animal quilt.

- Create a farm wall mural. Invite students to add paintings of a barn, ducks, cows, hens, horses, pigs, a farmer, and other things you would find on a farm.

Math

- Pairs of students will create and solve math problems based on Doreen Cronin's books. For example, students might create problems similar to this:

    If there is one duck, six cows, and two hens on a farm, how many animals are there? (Answer: 9)

- Write clues of different types about farm and zoo animals on index cards (e.g., I like to play in the mud and have a curly tail. What animal am I?). Students can take turns solving each clue and categorizing each animal by farm animal or zoo animal. When all the animals have been guessed, students count how many animals were in each category and create a graph contrasting the amounts.

Music

- Read a book about farm animals as a class. Students (or you) can generate a list of important ideas from the information learned. This can be completed as a whole-class activity or students can work in small groups. Students select a simple, popular song the class or their small-group members all know, and then write a Lyric Summary (see Appendix C, pages 243–244 and 278).

- Students work with partners or in small groups to present a musical talent show based on Doreen Cronin's *Dooby Dooby Moo*. They can sing songs, write their own songs, play instruments, create their own instruments, and choose to be in other creative acts during the show.

Science

- Students will work in a small group to engage in The Rest of the Story. Each group will choose one type of farm animal and gather information about it. Students will explore topics such as eating habits, living conditions, care, parts of the body, and interesting facts. Bookmark websites such as All About Farm Animals on Kiddyhouse.com (www.kiddyhouse.com/Farm), so students can easily access them. Small groups will present information to the class through a creative format of their choice.

- Students will use the Internet to research worms, spiders, and flies. Then they will compile what they have earned in a class book that will be kept in the class library.

Social Studies

- Students will complete the first two columns in a K–W–L–S (What I Know–What I Want to Know–What I Learned–What I Still Want to Know) chart about farm life before reading. They can do this as a class, in small groups, or with partners. After reading a text about farm life, students will use the information students have learned to complete the final two columns of the chart. Discuss the K–W–L–S with students when it is in progress and when it is completed. Bookmark websites and encourage students to use them to find responses to "what they still want to know."

- Invite a farmer to be a guest speaker in your classroom. Work with students to develop a list of questions they will ask the farmer after his presentation. After the interview, invite students to record what they have learned in a creative presentation such as a collage about farms.

Culminating Activity

Click, Clack, WOW! Reading Fun for All! Students will design, create, and deliver invitations for their families to attend this celebration. Students' projects will be presented at different stations throughout the classroom, and a Doreen Cronin mural will be hanging in the hallway to welcome guests. Students will share with their families selected projects, including poems they have written and books the class has created. Refreshments will be served and the entire event will take only one hour. Photos of students reading, writing, dramatizing, and working with their cross-age partners will be featured. The classroom computers will be open, so parents, siblings, and friends can provide feedback on the celebration. The students will give one of the class books to their families as a gift.

CHAPTER 8

Animals Aplenty: The Informational Text of Seymour Simon

Seymour Simon has been providing us with wonderfully engaging informational text for decades. If we are interested in learning intriguing facts about animals, outer space, land formations, severe weather, human organs, and myriad other topics, Seymour Simon is our author of choice. Breathtaking photographs and amazing illustrations complement his words and bring his texts to life. As we strive to balance narrative and informational text in our teaching, the work of Seymour Simon is an invaluable resource.

The sample Theme-Based Plan for Guided Comprehension: Animals Aplenty: The Informational Text of Seymour Simon (see Figure 9) offers an overview of the lessons and resources that support this theme. The plan begins by listing theme goals and making connections to state standards. The student goals for this theme include the following:

- Use appropriate comprehension skills and strategies
- Interpret and respond to text
- Communicate effectively

These goals support the following state standards:

- Learning to read independently
- Reading, analyzing, and interpreting text
- Types and quality of writing
- Speaking and listening

Sample assessments in this theme include observation, running records, student writing, skill and strategy applications, and student self-assessments. The Guided Comprehension lessons are based on the following strategies and corresponding teaching ideas:

- Previewing: Semantic Question Map
- Self-Questioning: Draw and Write Wonders
- Monitoring: Say Something
- Summarizing: Questions Into Paragraphs (QuIP)

Figure 9. Theme-Based Plan for Guided Comprehension: Animals Aplenty: The Informational Text of Seymour Simon

Goals and Related State Standards | Students will

- Use appropriate comprehension skills and strategies. Standard: learning to read independently
- Interpret and respond to text. Standard: reading, analyzing, and interpreting text
- Communicate effectively. Standards: types of writing; quality of writing; speaking and listening

Assessment

The following measures can be used for a variety of purposes, including diagnostic, formative, and summative assessment:

Draw and Write Wonders   Say Something
Observation   Semantic Question Maps
Questions Into   Student Self-Assessments
  Paragraphs (QuIP)   Student Writing
Running Records

Text	Title	Level
1. Baby Animals		PreK–3
2. Whales		PreK–3
3. Dogs		PreK–3
4. Wolves		PreK–3

Technology Resources

Seymour Simon
  www.seymoursimon.com
Seymour Simon Biography
  www2.scholastic.com/browse/contributor.jsp?id=2232
A Video Interview With Seymour Simon
  www.readingrockets.org/books/interviews/simon

Comprehension Strategies | Teaching Ideas

1. Previewing
2. Self-Questioning
3. Monitoring
4. Summarizing

1. Semantic Question Map
2. Draw and Write Wonders
3. Say Something
4. Questions Into Paragraphs (QuIP)

Comprehension Centers

Students will apply the comprehension strategies and related teaching ideas in the following comprehension centers:

ABC Center   Poetry Center
Art Center   Theme Center
Listening Center   Transmediation Center
Making and Writing Words Center   Writing Center
Making Books Center

Comprehension Routines

Students will apply the comprehension strategies and related teaching ideas in the following comprehension routines:

Literature Circles
Reciprocal Teaching
Cross-Age Reading Experiences

Baby Animals (2002), *Whales* (2006), *Dogs* (2009), and *Wolves* (2009) are the texts used in Stage One for teacher-directed whole-group instruction. Numerous additional theme-related resources, including texts, websites, performances across the curriculum, and a culminating activity, are presented in the Theme Resources at the end of the chapter.

Examples of comprehension centers students use during Stage Two of Guided Comprehension include ABC, art, listening, making and writing words, making books, poetry, theme, transmediation, and writing. Students also engage in strategy application in comprehension routines such as Literature Circles, Reciprocal Teaching, and Cross-Age Reading Experiences. Sample websites complete the overview.

In this chapter, all the lessons focus on books authored by Seymour Simon. The lessons are appropriate for all learners, including English learners, struggling readers, and students with special needs. To accommodate these learners, the lessons include multiple modes of response (such as singing, sketching, and dramatizing), working with partners, books on CD, cross-age experiences, and extra guided instruction. Ideas used to differentiate instruction in these lessons include the following:

- Content—the information being taught

  - Using leveled text to accommodate students' abilities in teacher-guided small groups, centers, and routines

  - Providing leveled texts that accommodate student interest and help motivate them to read

- Process—the way in which the information is taught

  - Activating prior knowledge and/or providing background information

  - Scaffolding student learning by using the Guided Comprehension Model

  - Reading the text aloud during Stage One to make it accessible to all students

  - Using visuals to support students' construction of meaning

  - Adapting graphic organizers; providing paragraph frames

  - Encouraging students to work with peers in pairs and small groups to provide additional support

  - Preteaching students who may need additional support to use the strategies and skills—such as sequencing and generating questions—at multiple levels

- Product—how the students demonstrate their learning

  - Integrating alternative modes of representation, such as art, drama, poetry, or music

  - Providing opportunities for students to use computers when creating projects

Guided Comprehension Lessons

Animals Aplenty: The Informational Text of Seymour Simon
Guided Comprehension Strategy: Previewing
Teaching Idea: Semantic Question Map

STAGE ONE: Teacher-Directed Whole-Group Instruction

Text: *Baby Animals* (2002)

Explain: I began by explaining previewing, and how we use it to predict and set purposes for reading a text. Then I focused on Semantic Question Maps (see Appendix C, page 217) and how they can help us learn and organize information.

Demonstrate: I demonstrated by using a read-aloud, a Think-Aloud, and a large poster board. I introduced the text by sharing the cover illustration and reading the title. Then I invited the students to make connections. The students and I discussed different types of baby animals they knew of. Next, I referred students to a Semantic Question Map graphic organizer that I had drawn on the poster board before class. There was a centered oval for the focus word and webbed question categories including *What are baby animals called? How many are born at a time? At what age do they walk?* and *What are some special facts about baby animals?* I said, "I will write *baby animals* inside the oval because that is the focus of our Semantic Question Map." Then I said, "Now I need to think about what I already know about baby animals." I read the first question, "*What are baby animals called?*" and I said, "I know that different baby animals have different names. For example, baby dogs are called puppies. I know I cannot write every baby animal name, so I will write what we call baby animals born to dogs, cats, pigs, and horses." Then I thought aloud about what I knew about each of the remaining categories and wrote the following underneath each one in clockwise order: "*multiple babies*," "*from hours to weeks*," and "*Kittens and puppies are born blind and deaf.*" I explained to the students that I would read aloud information about baby animals and revisit the Semantic Question Map to revise the ideas I had written on it, if necessary, and to include additional information we might learn from reading the text. Then I read aloud a section of text. When I finished, I returned to the Semantic Question Map and noted that the information I had included on the map so far was correct. Then I reviewed each category to see if I had new information to add. The students also contributed suggestions based on the reading. For example, we added, "*A puppy's sense of smell is more than 100 times better than a person's*" beneath the fourth question, *What are some special facts about baby animals?*

Guide: I guided pairs of students to think about information to add to each category of our Semantic Question Map as they listened to me read aloud another section. Then we discussed that section of text and I asked the students what they would like to add to our Semantic Question Map. Their suggestions included that pigs roll in the mud to keep cool and foals are fully grown at 3 to 4 years old. I wrote our responses on the map.

Practice: Students practiced by listening and thinking about more information to add to our Semantic Question Map, as I continued reading sections of text. When I finished, we added more information to our map. Students also reported that some of the information that we had written

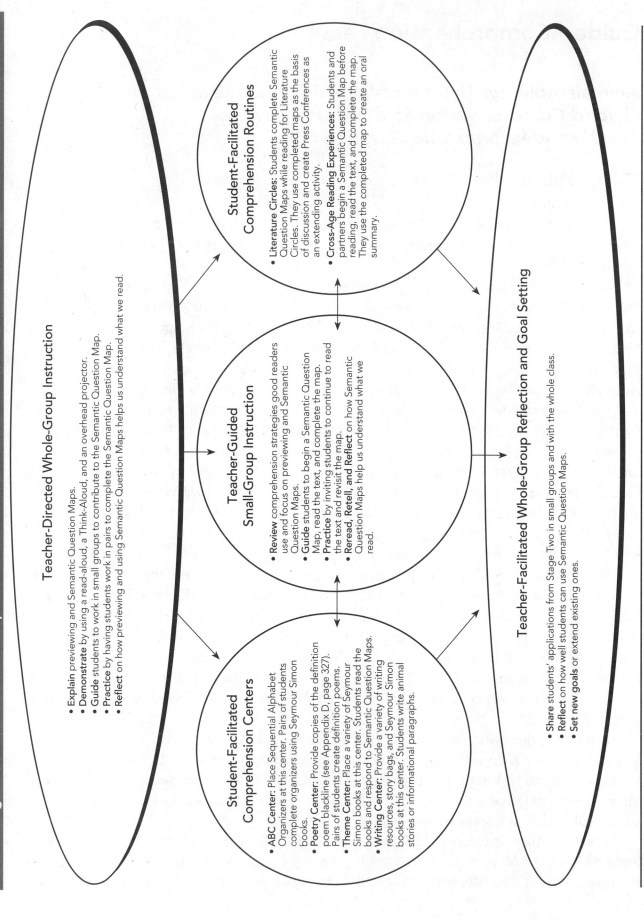

Guided Comprehension: Animals Aplenty: The Informational Text of Seymour Simon Previewing: Semantic Question Map

Teacher-Directed Whole-Group Instruction

- **Explain** previewing and Semantic Question Maps.
- **Demonstrate** by using a read-aloud, a Think-Aloud, and an overhead projector.
- **Guide** students to work in small groups to contribute to the Semantic Question Map.
- **Practice** by having students work in pairs to complete the Semantic Question Map.
- **Reflect** on how previewing and using Semantic Question Maps helps us understand what we read.

Student-Facilitated Comprehension Centers

- **ABC Center:** Place Sequential Alphabet Organizers at this center. Pairs of students complete organizers using Seymour Simon books.
- **Poetry Center:** Provide copies of the definition poem blackline (see Appendix D, page 327). Pairs of students create definition poems.
- **Theme Center:** Place a variety of Seymour Simon books at this center. Students read the books and respond to Semantic Question Maps.
- **Writing Center:** Provide a variety of writing resources, story bags, and Seymour Simon books at this center. Students write animal stories or informational paragraphs.

Teacher-Guided Small-Group Instruction

- **Review** comprehension strategies good readers use and focus on previewing and Semantic Question Maps.
- **Guide** students to begin a Semantic Question Map, read the text, and complete the map.
- **Practice** by inviting students to continue to read the text and revisit the map.
- **Reread, Retell, and Reflect** on how Semantic Question Maps help us understand what we read.

Student-Facilitated Comprehension Routines

- **Literature Circles:** Students complete Semantic Question Maps while reading for Literature Circles. They use completed maps as the basis of discussion and create Press Conferences as an extending activity.
- **Cross-Age Reading Experiences:** Students and partners begin a Semantic Question Map before reading, read the text, and complete the map. They use the completed map to create an oral summary.

Teacher-Facilitated Whole-Group Reflection and Goal Setting

- Share students' applications from Stage Two in small groups and with the whole class.
- Reflect on how well students can use Semantic Question Maps.
- Set new goals or extend existing ones.

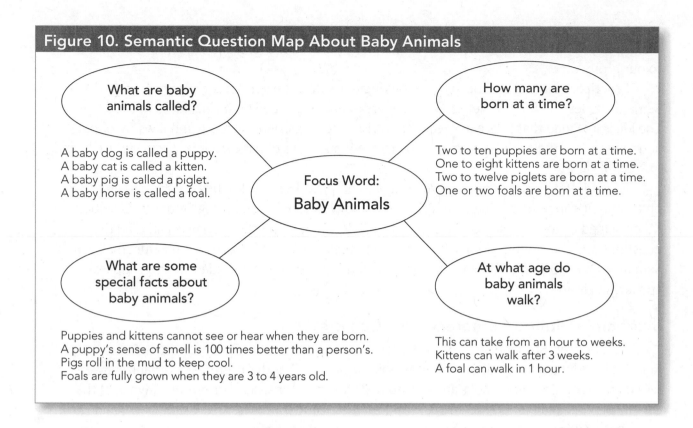

Figure 10. Semantic Question Map About Baby Animals

What are baby animals called?

A baby dog is called a puppy.
A baby cat is called a kitten.
A baby pig is called a piglet.
A baby horse is called a foal.

Focus Word: Baby Animals

How many are born at a time?

Two to ten puppies are born at a time.
One to eight kittens are born at a time.
Two to twelve piglets are born at a time.
One or two foals are born at a time.

What are some special facts about baby animals?

Puppies and kittens cannot see or hear when they are born.
A puppy's sense of smell is 100 times better than a person's.
Pigs roll in the mud to keep cool.
Foals are fully grown when they are 3 to 4 years old.

At what age do baby animals walk?

This can take from an hour to weeks.
Kittens can walk after 3 weeks.
A foal can walk in 1 hour.

on our map was verified by ideas in this text. Then we used our completed map to create an oral summary. A completed Semantic Question Map about baby animals, which Nancy and Rachel completed, appears in Figure 10.

Reflect: We reflected on what we had learned about baby animals and how the Semantic Question Map helped us to organize our thinking. We decided that we would leave our Semantic Question Map on display and add new information to the categories as we learned more about baby animals. We also talked about how the organization of the map helped us to remember the information. Finally, we discussed how we would use Semantic Question Maps in other settings.

STAGE TWO: Teacher-Guided Small-Group Instruction

Text: *Amazing Bats* (2005) (Texts varied according to students' abilities.)

Review: I began by reviewing the comprehension strategies good readers use and focused on previewing using Semantic Question Maps. Then I introduced *Amazing Bats*. I shared the cover and title, showed the pages of the book through a picture walk, and engaged the students in making connections. Then I briefly discussed the book with the students. We decided we should use bats as the focus of our Semantic Question Map. I wrote the word *bats* in the center oval of the poster-board Semantic Question Map I had prepared before our lesson. I also added four questions based on what we would read: *How do we describe bats? What do bats eat? How do bats get their food? What are some kinds of bats?* Finally, I explained to students that we would be completing a group Semantic Question Map to which we would all contribute.

Guide: We briefly discussed what we already knew about bats. Students' responses generally focused on bats flying at night and hanging upside down. We wrote those descriptors on our map and decided to read silently to find out more detailed information about bats. Students read silently and I offered support as needed. Then we discussed the text, and students added ideas to our group map.

Practice: Students practiced by continuing to read the text and record their ideas on the Semantic Question Map. When they finished reading, they added their final ideas to the map. The ideas included that bats eat insects, fruit, fish, and frogs, and use teeth and jaws, swooping, and fangs to get their food. The map also included four types of bats: *fruit, vampire, pipistrelle,* and *Australian ghost.*

Reread, Retell, and Reflect: We used our completed Semantic Question Map to create an oral summary about bats. Then we reflected on how previewing and using Semantic Question Maps helped us to understand what we read. Alberto said, "I like this map. We can read the questions and think about them as we read. That makes it easier for us to learn." Our small group's Semantic Question Map about bats, as it appeared at the end of our guided small-group lesson, appears in Figure 11.

Student-Facilitated Comprehension Centers

ABC Center: Students worked with partners to contribute to ABC Center Sequential Roundtable Alphabet organizers (see Appendix D, page 296) at this center. The organizers were based on Seymour Simon books and related texts about outer space. For example, while at the center, Daphne and Pietro read and contributed these terms: *asteroids, black hole, comet,* and *Earth.*

Poetry Center: Students worked with partners to write definition poems based on Seymour Simon books and related texts. They recorded their poems on copies of the definition poem

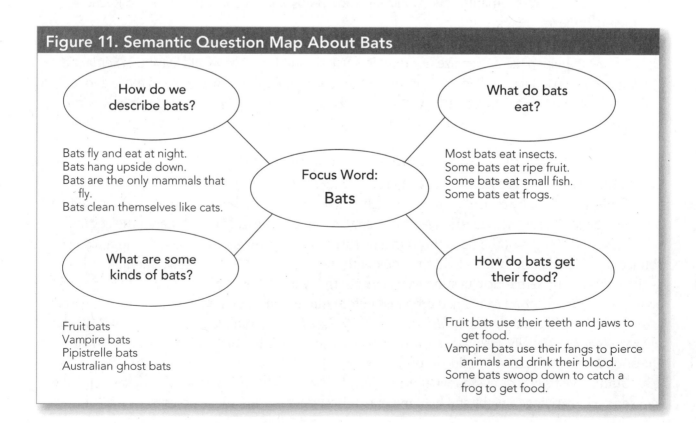

Figure 11. Semantic Question Map About Bats

How do we describe bats?

Bats fly and eat at night.
Bats hang upside down.
Bats are the only mammals that fly.
Bats clean themselves like cats.

What do bats eat?

Most bats eat insects.
Some bats eat ripe fruit.
Some bats eat small fish.
Some bats eat frogs.

Focus Word: Bats

What are some kinds of bats?

Fruit bats
Vampire bats
Pipistrelle bats
Australian ghost bats

How do bats get their food?

Fruit bats use their teeth and jaws to get food.
Vampire bats use their fangs to pierce animals and drink their blood.
Some bats swoop down to catch a frog to get food.

Figure 12. Definition Poem About Wolves

What is a wolf?

Furry
Fast
Loyal
Howling
Lives in a pack
Is part of the dog family
Cares for young pups

That is a wolf!
---

blackline (see Appendix D, page 327). Maureen and Tom's definition poem about wolves appears in Figure 12.

Theme Center: Students read Seymour Simon books and related informational text. When they selected the book they would read, Semantic Question Maps were tucked inside the cover. The maps contained focus words and questions I had developed for the students. Students at this center also completed Center Reflections (see Appendix D, page 301).

Writing Center: Students engaged in one of two activities. They either used Story Bags about animals as resources when writing and illustrating animal stories, or they used Seymour Simon books as resources and wrote informational paragraphs based on the book they chose.

Student-Facilitated Comprehension Routines

Literature Circles: Students used the Semantic Question Map to take notes as they read the text the group had selected. After reading the text and completing the maps, students used the questions and their responses to facilitate discussion. They used websites I had bookmarked to further investigate the topic of the book they read. Then they presented Press Conferences (McLaughlin, 2010), which are oral presentations, to the class (see Appendix D, page 328, for a Press Conference Summary blackline).

Cross-Age Reading Experiences: Students read Seymour Simon books or related texts with cross-age partners. I provided focus words and questions for the Semantic Question Maps. Students and their partners began completing the map prior to reading and added information as needed during and after reading. Then they used the completed map to create an oral summary.

STAGE THREE: Teacher-Facilitated Whole-Group Reflection and Goal Setting

Share: Students shared their completed Semantic Question Maps from Stage Two in small groups, and then shared selected maps, poems, paragraphs, and stories with the whole group.

Reflect: We reflected on how completing Semantic Question Maps helped to guide our reading and how well we could use them. The students seemed to like the large Semantic Question Maps I had created on poster board.

Set New Goals: Students felt confident using the Semantic Question Map. They appreciated the way the questions helped to set purposes for their reading. We decided to extend our goal of learning how to preview and self-question by learning how to use "I Wonder" Statements.

Assessment Options

I used a variety of assessments, including observation, running records, students' strategy applications, and student self-assessments, during this lesson. I observed students in multiple instructional setting and conducted fluency checks with individual students during teacher-guided small groups.

Animals Aplenty: The Informational Text of Seymour Simon
Guided Comprehension Strategy: Self-Questioning
Teaching Idea: Draw and Write Wonders

STAGE ONE: Teacher-Directed Whole-Group Instruction

Text: *Whales* (2006)

Explain: I began by explaining self-questioning and Draw and Write Wonders to my students. I made connections between "I Wonder" Statements (see Appendix C, page 220), which we had previously learned, and Draw and Write Wonders. I explained that this time we would be drawing or sketching our wonders and then writing about them underneath our drawings. Next, I focused on how such wonders could help us understand what we are reading.

Demonstrate: I demonstrated Draw and Write Wonders by reading aloud the title and showing the students the cover of the book. I said, "The title and illustration remind me of whales I have seen on television and in other books." Then I asked the students if they would work with partners to share their connections. Students offered a number of ideas, including that several of them had family members that had seen whales during whale-watching excursions or they had seen friends' or relatives' videos of such events. Then I looked at the book cover again and asked the students to share with partners what they thought the whale was doing. Everyone agreed the whale was jumping out of the water. I explained that there was a special word we use to describe when whales jump almost all of the way out of the ocean and then splash down in a huge spray of foam. I said, "The special word we use to describe that is *breaching*." Maria said, "*Breaching* sounds like *reaching*, and that's how I'll remember it because when the whale jumps it looks as if he is reaching for the sky." After a bit more discussion, I began reading the book aloud, pausing occasionally to Draw and Write Wonders. For example, after I read the first few pages, I paused to draw a whale breaching and write my wonder about it. While I was sketching the whale, I reminded students that when we sketch in our Draw and Write Wonders, our goal is to use simple lines and shapes to convey our ideas. I explained that we don't need to be accomplished artists to do that. Then I wrote, "*I wonder how many different types of whales there are.*" Figure 13 features my first Draw and Write Wonder.

I discussed what I drew and wrote with the students and then I read another segment aloud and completed a second Draw and Write Wonder.

Guide: I guided students to work with a partner to complete Draw and Write Wonders after I read the next segment. I provided the Draw and Write Wonders blackline (see Appendix C, page 272). The wonders students wrote included "*I wonder...if there are different kinds of whales*" and "*I wonder...if whales are still hunted and if they could disappear if they are hunted.*" Their writings supported their drawings. As students shared, we discussed their wonders.

Practice: I continued to read the book aloud while students practiced creating Draw and Write Wonders. As I finished reading each segment, we discussed their sketches and wonders and whether our previous wonders had been verified in the segment I had just read. We continued this practice until we reached the end of the book. Examples of students' wonders included the following:

Guided Comprehension: Animals Aplenty: The Informational Text of Seymour Simon
Self-Questioning: Draw and Write Wonders

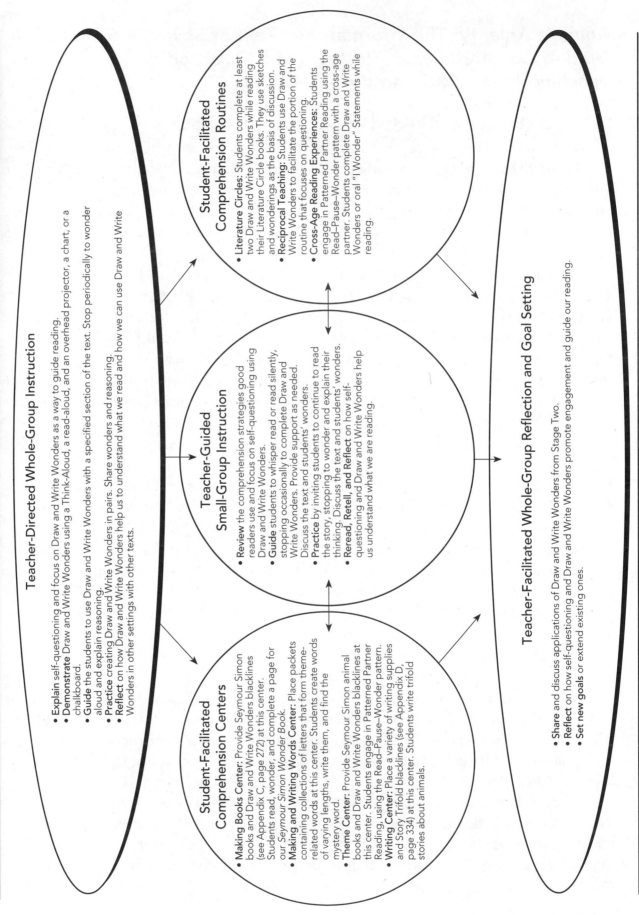

Teacher-Directed Whole-Group Instruction

- **Explain** self-questioning and focus on Draw and Write Wonders as a way to guide reading.
- **Demonstrate** Draw and Write Wonders using a Think-Aloud, a read-aloud, and an overhead projector, a chart, or a chalkboard.
- **Guide** the students to use Draw and Write Wonders with a specified section of the text. Stop periodically to wonder aloud and explain reasoning.
- **Practice** creating Draw and Write Wonders in pairs. Share wonders and reasoning.
- **Reflect** on how Draw and Write Wonders help us to understand what we read and how we can use Draw and Write Wonders in other settings with other texts.

Student-Facilitated Comprehension Centers

- **Making Books Center:** Provide Seymour Simon books and Draw and Write Wonders blacklines (see Appendix C, page 272) at this center. Students read, wonder, and complete a page for our *Seymour Simon Wonder Book.*
- **Making and Writing Words Center:** Place packets containing collections of letters that form theme-related words at this center. Students create words of varying lengths, write them, and find the mystery word.
- **Theme Center:** Provide Seymour Simon animal books and Draw and Write Wonders blacklines at this center. Students engage in Patterned Partner Reading, using the Read–Pause–Wonder pattern.
- **Writing Center:** Place a variety of writing supplies and Story Trifold blacklines (see Appendix D, page 334) at this center. Students write trifold stories about animals.

Teacher-Guided Small-Group Instruction

- **Review** the comprehension strategies good readers use and focus on self-questioning using Draw and Write Wonders.
- **Guide** students to whisper read or read silently, stopping occasionally to complete Draw and Write Wonders. Provide support as needed. Discuss the text and students' wonders.
- **Practice** by inviting students to continue to read the story, stopping to wonder and explain their thinking. Discuss the text and students' wonders.
- **Reread, Retell, and Reflect** on how self-questioning and Draw and Write Wonders help us understand what we are reading.

Student-Facilitated Comprehension Routines

- **Literature Circles:** Students complete at least two Draw and Write Wonders while reading their Literature Circle books. They use sketches and wonderings as the basis of discussion.
- **Reciprocal Teaching:** Students use Draw and Write Wonders to facilitate the portion of the routine that focuses on questioning.
- **Cross-Age Reading Experiences:** Students engage in Patterned Partner Reading using the Read–Pause–Wonder pattern with a cross-age partner. Students complete Draw and Write Wonders or oral "I Wonder" Statements while reading.

Teacher-Facilitated Whole-Group Reflection and Goal Setting

- **Share** and discuss applications of Draw and Write Wonders from Stage Two.
- **Reflect** on how self-questioning and Draw and Write Wonders promote engagement and guide our reading.
- **Set** new goals or extend existing ones.

Figure 13. Teacher's Draw and Write Wonder

Drawing:

I wonder...

how many different types of whales there are.

- "I wonder how baleen whales, the biggest ones, survive on such small food."
- "I wonder if any other whales or dolphins eat through grubbing like the gray whale does."
- "I wonder if the countries that still allow whales to be hunted will cause the whales to disappear."

Reflect: We reflected on what we had learned from Seymour Simon's books and our wonders. The students "wondered" if we could use Draw and Write Wonders in other subjects, as we did with "I Wonder" Statements. They were happy to learn that we could. Then we reflected on how Draw and Write Wonders helped us understand what we read.

STAGE TWO: Teacher-Guided Small-Group Instruction

Text: *Gorillas* (2009) (Texts varied according to students' abilities.)

Review: I reminded students that we would be focusing on self-questioning and briefly recalled a few examples of our Draw and Write Wonders from Stage One.

Guide: I introduced *Gorillas* by showing the cover and title of the book and asking the students what they might predict. They focused on the illustration and noted that the photograph appeared to include a mother gorilla and a baby gorilla. Then, because the title was *Gorillas*, they predicted the text would be about gorilla families and their lives. I guided students to whisper read a segment of the text. I reminded them to stop when they saw the stop sign I had placed in the text to create Draw and Write Wonders. When students shared their drawings and wonders, we discussed them. Their responses included the following:

- "I wonder...how much gorillas weigh."
- "I wonder...how gorillas get bananas from trees."
- "I wonder... if gorillas run from danger and how fast they can run."

Then we repeated the process.

Practice: Students practiced by continuing to whisper read and create Draw and Write Wonders. An example of a student's Draw and Write Wonder about *Gorillas* is featured in Figure 14.

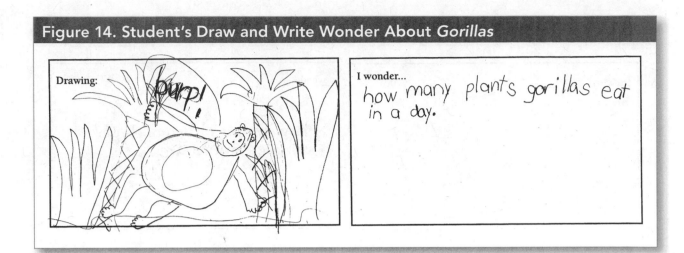

Figure 14. Student's Draw and Write Wonder About *Gorillas*

Drawing: purpl

I wonder... how many plants gorillas eat in a day.

Reread, Retell, and Reflect: We reread selected segments of the text together and then engaged in an oral group retelling. We discussed the text and how the photographs supported our understanding. Then we discussed how self-questioning and Draw and Write Wonders helped us understand what we read.

Student-Facilitated Comprehension Centers

Making Books Center: Students selected a Seymour Simon book, read the cover, and completed a Draw and Write Wonder. Then they added it as a page in our *Seymour Simon Wonder Book*. Students continued reading and wondering about the book they selected in the theme center.

Making and Writing Words Center: Students worked with partners to manipulate packets of three-dimensional letters to spell words of varying lengths. Then they used the Making and Writing Words response sheet (see Appendix D, page 316) to record two-, three-, and four-letter words until they used all the letters provided to guess the mystery word.

Theme Center: Students engaged in Patterned Partner Reading, using the Read–Pause–Wonder pattern. They read Seymour Simon books or related informational text. When they paused, they completed, shared, and discussed their Draw and Write Wonders.

Writing Center: Students worked with partners to write stories using Story Trifolds. This organizer focuses on three sections of a story (beginning, middle, end; see Appendix D, page 334).

Student-Facilitated Comprehension Routines

Literature Circles: Students completed at least two Draw and Write Wonders while reading their Literature Circle books. They used their drawings and wonders as the basis of discussion. As an extension activity, some groups created murals that summarized the book they read in pictures and words.

Reciprocal Teaching: Students used "I Wonder" Statements while engaging in Reciprocal Teaching. They used it in the portion of the routine that focuses on questioning.

Cross-Age Reading Experiences: Students read with their cross-age partners using Patterned Partner Reading. The pattern they used was Read–Pause–Wonder. As they read, they completed

Draw and Write Wonders or created oral "I Wonder" Statements. Students also completed Center Reflections (see Appendix D, page 301).

STAGE THREE: Teacher-Facilitated Whole-Group Reflection and Goal Setting

Share: Students shared their Draw and Write Wonders from Stage Two in small groups. Then we discussed their wonder-related projects as a whole class.

Reflect: We reflected on how self-questioning and using Draw and Write Wonders can motivate us and guide our reading. We discussed how Draw and Write Wonders can help us understand what we read. Bernie said, "Draw and Write Wonders are like 'I Wonder' Statements with sketches. Doing the sketches first helps me share my idea through my drawing. Then I write about it."

Set New Goals: The students appeared confident in their use of this teaching idea. We decided to set a new goal to learn a new strategy and a new teaching idea.

Assessment Options

I observed students throughout the Guided Comprehension lesson in whole-class, small-group, and paired and individual settings. I observed the quality and frequency of their responses, their ability to work with others, and their ability to use strategies while reading. I also reviewed and commented on the work from Stage Two that was in the students' folders, and I provided feedback on their self-assessments.

Animals Aplenty: The Informational Text of Seymour Simon
Guided Comprehension Strategy: Monitoring
Teaching Idea: Say Something

STAGE ONE: Teacher-Directed Whole-Group Instruction

Text: *Dogs* (2009)

Explain: I began by explaining to the students the importance of monitoring our understanding while we are reading. I reminded them that our ultimate goal was to make sense of the text. I noted that while we were reading we should be asking ourselves if what we were reading was making sense. I described Say Something (see Appendix C, pages 240–241) as a technique we can use to help us examine what we were reading to see if it did make sense. I noted that Say Something would help us think about our reading and share our ideas with a partner. I explained that when using this technique, we would read a section of the text, stop and Say Something based on what we have read, and then continue reading, stopping periodically to Say Something to a partner.

Demonstrate: I demonstrated Say Something by using a read-aloud and a Think-Aloud. I also modeled with a student. (The student and I had planned the demonstration a few days before the lesson.) I introduced the text by sharing the cover and title. Madeline, my Say Something student partner, said "I see a dog on the cover, so I think the book will be about different types of dogs." Then we invited the other students to make connections to the title and cover. Most of the students' ideas focused on dogs they have had for pets, dogs they have read about, and dogs they know from movies and videos. Next, I explained that I would be reading text aloud, stopping periodically to Say Something to my partner, Madeline. Madeline would then Say Something, and I would continue reading. I read the first few pages, paused, and said, "Dogs developed from wolves." Madeline said, "Greyhounds can run far faster than people can." I continued to read aloud. When I paused, Madeline said, "Dogs see gray tones and some colors such as red." I said, "Dogs bark in different ways if they want to eat or go outside." Then we had a brief discussion.

Guide: I guided students to work with partners as I read the next few pages. I encouraged them to Say Something to their partners when I paused. Students' responses included the following:

- "Poodles can weigh up to 70 pounds."
- "Mutts are special."
- "Toy dogs are tiny dogs that used to have special jobs like warming people's feet."

Practice: I read the next section and stopped to provide the partners an opportunity to Say Something. I monitored student responses and offered support as necessary. We continued this process through the final section of the book. Students' responses included the following:

- "Puppies need a lot of care."
- "Dogs need someone to walk them and feed them."
- "Dogs are lifelong friends."

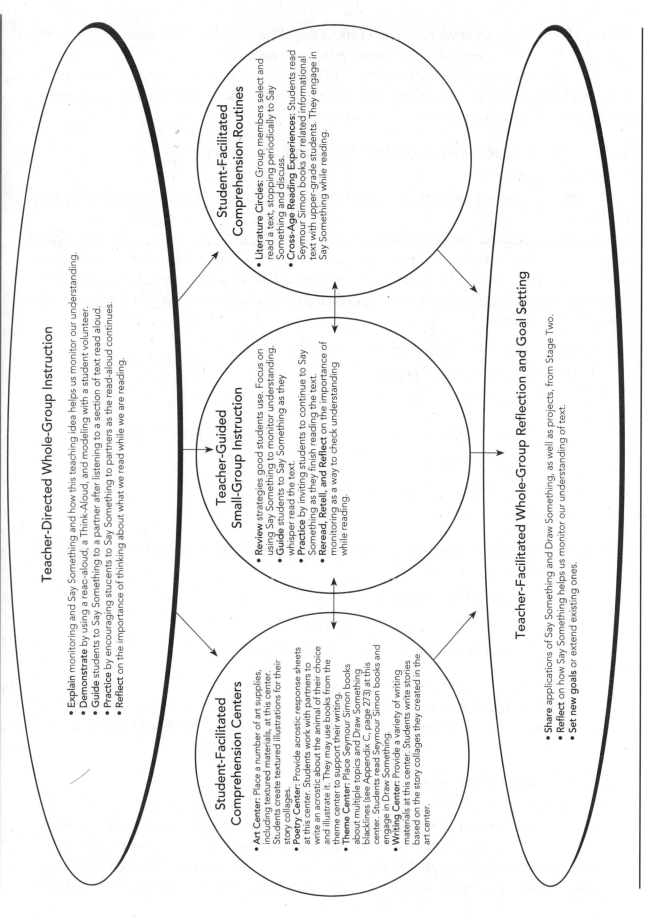

Teacher-Directed Whole-Group Instruction

- **Explain** monitoring and Say Something and how this teaching idea helps us monitor our understanding.
- **Demonstrate** by using a read-aloud, a Think-Aloud, and modeling with a student volunteer.
- **Guide** students to Say Something to a partner after listening to a section of text read aloud.
- **Practice** by encouraging students to Say Something to partners as the read-aloud continues.
- **Reflect** on the importance of thinking about what we read while we are reading.

Student-Facilitated Comprehension Routines

- **Literature Circles:** Group members select and read a text, stopping periodically to Say Something and discuss.
- **Cross-Age Reading Experiences:** Students read Seymour Simon books or related informational text with upper-grade students. They engage in Say Something while reading.

Teacher-Guided Small-Group Instruction

- **Review** strategies good students use. Focus on using Say Something to monitor understanding.
- **Guide** students to Say Something as they whisper read the text.
- **Practice** by inviting students to continue to Say Something as they finish reading the text.
- **Reread, Retell, and Reflect** on the importance of monitoring as a way to check understanding while reading.

Student-Facilitated Comprehension Centers

- **Art Center:** Place a number of art supplies, including textured materials, at this center. Students create textured illustrations for their story collages.
- **Poetry Center:** Provide acrostic response sheets at this center. Students work with partners to write an acrostic about the animal of their choice and illustrate it. They may use books from the theme center to support their writing.
- **Theme Center:** Place Seymour Simon books about multiple topics and Draw Something blacklines (see Appendix C, page 273) at this center. Students read Seymour Simon books and engage in Draw Something.
- **Writing Center:** Provide a variety of writing materials at this center. Students write stories based on the story collages they created in the art center.

Teacher-Facilitated Whole-Group Reflection and Goal Setting

- **Share** applications of Say Something and Draw Something, as well as projects, from Stage Two.
- **Reflect** on how Say Something helps us monitor our understanding of text.
- **Set new goals** or extend existing ones.

Next, we summarized what we had learned about dogs. The book contained interesting facts about dogs, and the students seemed highly motivated to learn about them.

Reflect: We reflected on the importance of thinking about what we are reading and how using Say Something helped us monitor our understanding. Angelo said, "When we use Say Something, we think about something we understood in the book."

STAGE TWO: Teacher-Guided Small-Group Instruction

Text: *Cats* (2009)

Review: I reviewed the strategies good readers use and then I focused on monitoring using Say Something.

Guide: I suggested that the students use the title and cover to predict what this text might be about. They quickly noted its similarity to *Dogs*, which we had used in Stage One, and suggested this book would be about different kinds of cats. I guided the students to read silently and stop at predetermined points to Say Something to their partners. At the first stop, students' responses included the following:

- "Cats use claws and teeth to hunt."
- "There are cat mummies in Egypt."
- "Cats live all over the world."

They continued to read, and at the second stop, their responses included the following:

- "Cats are great climbers."
- "Cats can land on all four paws when they fall."
- "Cats can see in color."

Practice: Students finished reading *Cats*, using Say Something at predetermined stops. Their final responses included the following:

- "There are 100 different breeds of cats."
- "Persian cats are the most popular kind of cats."
- "A feral cat is a pet cat that has gone back to being wild."

Then we discussed *Cats* and the interesting facts we had learned.

Reread, Retell, and Reflect: We did a choral rereading of selected sections of text and summarized what we had learned. Next, we reflected on how Say Something helped us understand what we read.

Student-Facilitated Comprehension Centers

Art Center: Students used a variety of textured materials, including pine cone pieces, felt, sand, and cotton balls, to create the collage part of their Story Collages. They created textured illustrations at this center and then wrote stories based on their collages at the writing center.

Poetry Center: Students used acrostic response sheets at this center. The sheets included the names of various animals, such as dogs, cats, and wolves, listed vertically. Students and their partners wrote acrostics about the animal of their choice and illustrated it. They were able to use books from the theme center to support their writing. They hung their illustrated poems in our Poetry Corner.

Theme Center: Students read Seymour Simon books about multiple topics at this center. As they read, they completed Draw Something blacklines before, during, and after reading (see Appendix C, page 273). After reading, they shared their strategy applications with a peer.

Writing Center: Students wrote stories to complete their Story Collages at this center. They combined their work from the art center with their writing to complete this project. When finished, they hung their Story Collages on our theme wall.

Student-Facilitated Comprehension Routines

Literature Circles: Group members prepared for Literature Circles by engaging in Patterned Partner Reading, using the Read–Pause–Say Something pattern. Then they met with their group to discuss the book. As an extension activity, some groups created definition poem posters that featured group-created definition poems and illustrations.

Cross-Age Reading Experiences: Students met with their cross-age partners and read Seymour Simon books or related informational text. While reading, they engaged in Say Something at least three times. Then they orally summarized what they had read.

STAGE THREE: Teacher-Facilitated Whole-Group Reflection and Goal Setting

Share: Students shared and discussed their applications of Say Something and related projects in small groups. These included Draw Something, their Story Collages, and their poetry projects. Then each group shared with the whole class.

Reflect: We reflected on how using Say Something helped us monitor our understanding when we are reading. Students appeared to enjoy that this technique could be used orally and through sketching.

Set New Goals: We decided to extend our goal and learn to use Say Something when reading narrative text. We discussed how what we would say when reading stories would be different from the facts we shared while reading Seymour Simon's books. For example, we discussed that while reading stories, we could use Say Something to share narrative elements: characters, setting, problem, attempts to resolve, and resolution.

Assessment Options

I observed students in multiple instructional settings: whole group, small group, paired, and individual. I reviewed and commented on students' strategy applications and projects. I also engaged students in fluency checks during teacher-guided small groups and completed running records with students who appeared ready to move to another group in teacher-guided instruction.

Animals Aplenty: The Informational Text of Seymour Simon
Guided Comprehension Strategy: Summarizing
Teaching Idea: Questions Into Paragraphs (QuIP)

STAGE ONE: Teacher-Directed Whole-Group Instruction

Texts: *Wolves* (2009) and D4KIDS—Dialogue for Kids (Idaho Public Television; see idahoptv.org/dialogue4kids/season8/wolves/facts.cfm)

Explain: I began by explaining summarizing to the students. I pointed out that summarizing informational text is very different from summarizing or retelling stories. Then I explained Questions Into Paragraphs (see Appendix C, pages 245–246) and noted that it was a technique that helped us to summarize. I reminded the students that we would be using the different levels of questioning we had recently learned when completing QuIPs. (For more information about generating questions, see Chapter 2, pages 21–23.) I further explained that when completing QuIPs we would use two sources to answer the questions we developed and that one source would be a book and one would be a website.

Demonstrate: I demonstrated QuIP by reading aloud the title and showing the students the cover of *Wolves* by Seymour Simon. As I did this, I said,

> This is the first Seymour Simon book I ever read. When I first saw the cover, I remember thinking how beautiful the photograph was. What do you think when you look at the photo? What connections can you make to it?

Students readily provided a variety of responses, including "I have an Akita dog. Her fur looks like that wolf's when snow is falling on her" and "Seeing the snowflakes on the wolf's fur reminds me of how my jacket looks when snow is falling on me." Then I shared the QuIP blacklines (see Appendix C, page 284) with the students. I also used an overhead projector to share an enlarged version of the blackline that I would be using to record information. I wrote the word *wolves* at the top of the blackline and explained that would be the focus of the QuIP we would be creating. Next, I showed the students where we would write three questions about wolves in the spaces provided on the blackline. I reminded students that the questions should be meaningful and that we would need to research our answers to them in *Wolves* and on a website. Then I said,

> When I think of things I would like to know about wolves, I wonder about how they are like dogs and how they are different. So, I think my first question is going to be, "How are wolves and dogs similar and how are they different?"

Then I read aloud the first few pages of *Wolves.* Some of the things we learned included the following:

- Wolves are loyal to their families
- Dogs are friendly and intelligent, and they got those traits from wolves.

We added both of these statements to our QuIP.

I continued to read aloud to the end of the book, stopping periodically for students to make connections and for us to discuss the text. Next, we visited the Dialogue for Kids website.

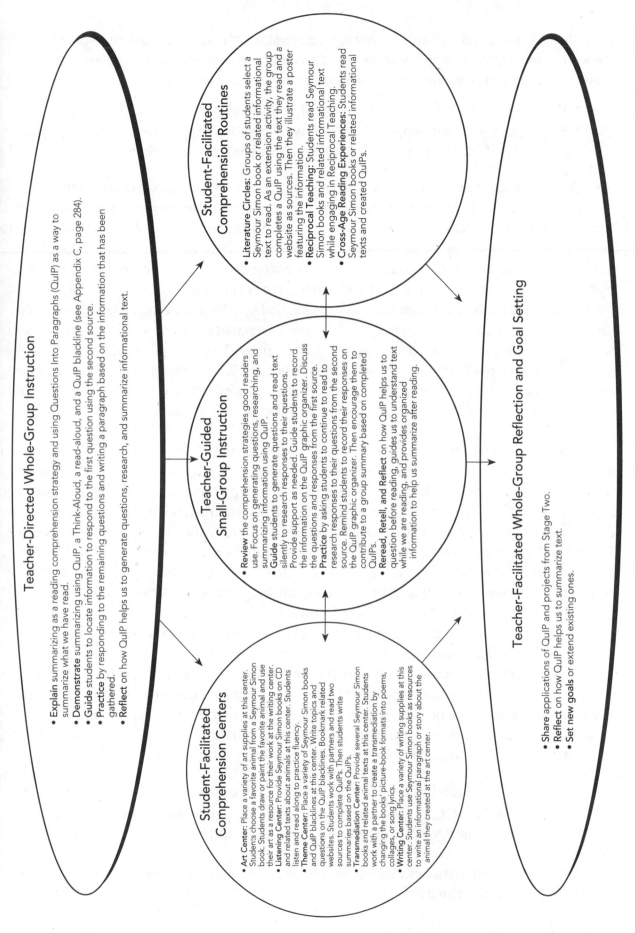

Teacher-Directed Whole-Group Instruction

- **Explain** summarizing as a reading comprehension strategy and using Questions Into Paragraphs (QuIP) as a way to summarize what we have read.
- **Demonstrate** summarizing using QuIP, a Think-Aloud, a read-aloud, and a QuIP blackline (see Appendix C, page 284).
- **Guide** students to locate information to respond to the first question using the second source.
- **Practice** by responding to the remaining questions and writing a paragraph based on the information that has been gathered.
- **Reflect** on how QuIP helps us to generate questions, research, and summarize informational text.

Student-Facilitated Comprehension Routines

- **Literature Circles:** Groups of students select a Seymour Simon book or related informational text to read. As an extension activity, the group completes a QuIP using the text they read and a website as sources. Then they illustrate a poster featuring the information.
- **Reciprocal Teaching:** Students read Seymour Simon books and related informational text while engaging in Reciprocal Teaching.
- **Cross-Age Reading Experiences:** Students read Seymour Simon books or related informational texts and created QuIPs.

Teacher-Guided Small-Group Instruction

- **Review** the comprehension strategies good readers use. Focus on generating questions, researching, and summarizing information using QuIP.
- **Guide** students to generate questions and read text silently to research responses to their questions. Provide support as needed. Guide students to record the information on the QuIP graphic organizer. Discuss the questions and responses from the first source.
- **Practice** by asking students to continue to read to research responses to their questions from the second source. Remind students to record their responses on the QuIP graphic organizer. Then encourage them to contribute to a group summary based on completed QuIPs.
- **Reread, Retell, and Reflect** on how QuIP helps us to question before reading, guides us to understand text while we are reading, and provides organized information to help us summarize after reading.

Student-Facilitated Comprehension Centers

- **Art Center:** Place a variety of art supplies at this center. Students choose a favorite animal from a Seymour Simon book. Students draw or paint the favorite animal and use their art as a resource for their work at the writing center.
- **Listening Center:** Provide Seymour Simon books on CD and related texts about animals at this center. Students listen and read along to practice fluency.
- **Theme Center:** Place a variety of Seymour Simon books and QuIP blacklines at this center. Write topics and questions on the QuIP blacklines. Bookmark related websites. Students work with partners and read two sources to complete QuIPs. Then students write summaries based on the QuIPs.
- **Transmediation Center:** Provide several Seymour Simon books and related animal texts at this center. Students work with a partner to create a transmediation by changing the books' picture-book formats into poems, collages, or song lyrics.
- **Writing Center:** Place a variety of writing supplies at this center. Students use Seymour Simon books as resources to write an informational paragraph or story about the animal they created at the art center.

Teacher-Facilitated Whole-Group Reflection and Goal Setting

- **Share** applications of QuIP and projects from Stage Two.
- **Reflect** on how QuIP helps us to summarize text.
- **Set new goals** or extend existing ones.

I introduced the site and explained how it was designed. Then I raised the same question: "How are wolves and dogs similar and how are they different?" I read aloud a section about connections between wolves and dogs. Information we learned included the following:

- Wolves and dogs are loyal, affectionate, and very intelligent.
- Dog puppies and wolf puppies like to play with toys. Dog puppies' toys are usually squeaky toys and rawhide bones, but wolf puppies play with bones and feathers.

We decided to add "*Wolves and dogs are loyal, affectionate, and very intelligent*" to our QuIP.

Guide: I guided the students to think of a question they and their partners could contribute to our QuIP. The students generated a variety of questions and we decided to add a few of them to our QuIP graphic organizer: What are some types of wolves? Why do wolves howl? I added them to the QuIP on the overhead projector, and the students added the questions to their copies of the blackline. I guided the students to work with partners to begin seeking responses to question two from source one, *Wolves*, and then from source two, Dialogue for Kids. When students reported the answers to question two, they had learned from *Wolves* that there are several different kinds of wolves. These included tundra (arctic) wolves, gray (or timber) wolves, red wolves, Mexican wolves, Rocky Mountain wolves, and Great Plains wolves (lobo). On Dialogue for Kids, the students learned that wolves come in a variety of colors, including white, gray, brown, and black. They also learned that arctic wolves are white so they can blend into the snow. We added our responses to the spaces provided.

Practice: Students practiced by responding to question three, first from *Wolves* and then from the website. We discussed the responses and then I modeled how to write a summary paragraph based on a completed QuIP. The students then worked with partners to write paragraphs based on their QuIP blacklines. When they finished, they shared their summaries with another pair. Next, we discussed the book and compared and contrasted it to the information we located on the website. Then I invited students to relax as I shared some photos of wolves, audio of howling wolves, and video of wolves running in the mountains. This resulted in a lively discussion. Figure 15 shows our completed QuIP Research Grid and the resulting QuIP Paragraph about wolves based on the three questions we generated and the two sources we used.

Reflect: We reflected on how much we could learn when summarizing information using QuIP. We began by discussing how important good questions are when we need to find information. Then we discussed using more than one research source and how that helped us write summaries based on our completed QuIPs. Shelly said that the completed QuIP had all the important information we needed to write our paragraphs and that made writing the summaries easy. Students agreed that using QuIP helped us organize and learn information. They also liked that they had input into creating questions for QuIP.

STAGE TWO: Teacher-Guided Small-Group Instruction

Texts: *Killer Whales* (2002) (Texts varied according to students' abilities.) and National Geographic: Killer Whale (Orca; see animals.nationalgeographic.com/animals/mammals/killer-whale.html)

Review: I reminded students about the strategies good readers use and focused on questioning and summarizing using QuIP.

Figure 15. QuIP Research Grid and QuIP Paragraph About Wolves

Topic: Wolves

Questions	Answers	
	Source A: *Wolves* by Seymour Simon	Source B: D4KIDS (idahoptv.org/Dialogue4kids/season8/wolves/facts.cfm)
1. How are wolves and dogs alike?	• Wolves are loyal to their families. • Dogs are friendly and intelligent and they get those traits from wolves.	• Wolves and dogs are loyal, affectionate, and intelligent.
2. What are some types of wolves?	• Some types of wolves are tundra, gray, red, Mexican, Rocky Mountain, and Great Plains.	• Wolves can be white, gray, brown, and black. Arctic wolves are white so they can blend into the snow.
3. Why do wolves howl?	• Wolves howl to find each other when separated from the pack, to warn other wolves to stay away from their territory, and they howl for pleasure.	• Howls keep a pack of wolves physically together. • Howls can be used to separate rival packs from each other.

Wolves and dogs are alike because they are loyal, affectionate, and intelligent. Some types of wolves are tundra, gray, red, Mexican, Rocky, and Great Plains. Wolves howl to find each other, to warn other wolves to stay away, and for pleasure.

Guide: I introduced *Killer Whales* by Seymour Simon by sharing the cover and title and inviting students to make connections. A few students made connections between the whale pictured on the cover and dolphins, and several made connections to the ocean. A few also discussed the killer whale's teeth. Then I guided the students to whisper read the short text, stopping periodically to make connections. We discussed the book and then I introduced the website, National Geographic: Killer Whale. Next pairs of students generated our three questions: (1) How do killer (orca) whale families work? (2) How do killer whales communicate? (3) What do killer whales eat?

Practice: Students practiced by responding to each question from two sources. They provided the information and I recorded it on a QuIP on my laptop computer. When our small-group QuIP was completed, I printed copies of it for the students. We discussed it and then they moved to the writing center and wrote QuIP paragraphs. Our completed QuIP Research Grid and the resulting QuIP Paragraph are presented in Figure 16.

Reread, Retell, and Reflect: We reread sections of the text and orally summarized what we read. We discussed what we had learned about killer (orca) whales from our two sources and reflected on the importance of using good questions in our QuIPs. Next, we talked about how recording the responses to the questions on a graphic organizer helped us to learn. Then students moved on to the writing center to write summary paragraphs based on their completed QuIPs.

Figure 16. QuIP Research Grid and QuIP Paragraph About Killer Whales

Topic: Killer Whales

Questions	Answers	
	Source A: *Killer Whales* by Seymour Simon	Source B: animals.nationalgeographic .com/animals/mammals/killer-whale.html
1. How do killer (orca) whales' family groups work?	• Killer whales live in family groups called pods. They hunt, eat, and protect one another.	• Orcas hunt in pods. • Each pod makes its own distinctive communicative sound, which every member of the pod recognizes.
2. How do killer (orca) whales communicate?	• In dark or cloudy waters, orcas make special clicking sounds. Then they listen to the way the sounds echo back. This lets the orcas know what is around them.	• Whales use echolocation to communicate and hunt, making sounds that travel underwater and then bounce back, revealing objects' location, size, and shape.
3. What do killer (orca) whales eat?	• Orcas eat fish, squid, seal, and penguins. They also hunt dolphins and other whales.	• Killer whales eat sea lions, seals, and whales.

Killer whales live in family groups called pods. They hunt, eat, and protect one another. Whales use echolocation to communicate and hunt. They make sounds that travel underwater and then bounce back, revealing objects' location, size, and shape. Orcas eat fish, squid, seal, sea lions, and penguins. They also hunt dolphins and other whales.

Student-Facilitated Comprehension Centers

Art Center: Using a wide variety of art supplies, students drew or painted their favorite animal. Then they used their art as a resource at the writing center.

Listening Center: Students listened to Seymour Simon books on CD or related texts about animals at this center. Students engaged in whisper read-alongs to practice fluency. At the end of the book, they discussed it with another student at the center.

Theme Center: Students read Seymour Simon books and completed QuIP blacklines at this center. When the students selected the books they wanted to read, they found QuIP blacklines complete with topics and questions tucked inside the cover. I had also bookmarked related websites for students to use as second sources. Students worked with partners and read from two sources—the book and the website—to complete QuIPs. Then they wrote summaries based on the QuIPs.

Transmediation Center: I provided a checklist at this center for students to follow as they created their transmediations. Students worked with partners to select a Seymour Simon book and change it into a poem, collage, or song lyrics. If time permitted, students illustrated their transmediations.

Writing Center: Students used their animal drawing or painting from the art center as a resource in their writing. Students wrote an informational paragraph or story about the animal they had illustrated.

Student-Facilitated Comprehension Routines

Literature Circles: The students read Seymour Simon books or related informational text and some groups created QuIP informational posters as an extension activity. They discussed their completed QuIPs and wrote their summary paragraphs in their Guided Comprehension Journals.

Reciprocal Teaching: The students used their ability to generate questions and summarize during the portions of the routine that focus on these strategies.

Cross-Age Reading Experiences: Students read Seymour Simon books or related informational texts with their cross-age partners. Then they generated questions for their QuIP and researched responses using their book and a bookmarked website.

STAGE THREE: Teacher-Facilitated Whole-Group Reflection and Goal Setting

Share: Students shared their QuIPs, transmediations, and other projects from Stage Two in small groups. Then we discussed examples as a whole class.

Reflect: We reflected on how QuIP questions guide our research and reading and how the organizer makes it easier to write a summary.

Set New Goals: Students felt confident with their ability to use QuIP to question and summarize research, so we created a new goal of learning how to summarize using Lyric Retellings and Summaries (see Appendix C, pages 243–244 and 278).

Assessment Options

I used observation throughout the lesson. In the QuIPs, I listened carefully to the questions students generated, and I reviewed their responses and paragraphs. I used checklists, which I provided at the center, when assessing students' transmediations. I reviewed and commented on students' projects and read and provided feedback on their center self-assessments. I also completed several fluency checks by inviting students to whisper read in teacher-guided small groups.

Final Thoughts About the Seymour Simon Theme

Whether reading about house pets, jungle animals, or sea creatures, the primary students who engaged in the Seymour Simon theme delighted in learning about animals. They were fascinated by the facts and reveled in sharing the new information they learned.

As noted in previous chapters, lessons on a variety of skills that underpin comprehension strategies were also taught during this theme. For example, aspects of language development, such as phonemic awareness and phonics, and skills such as sequencing, generating questions, and distinguishing important from less important ideas were embedded in the theme. (For ideas about how to use text to teach phonemic awareness, phonics, and fluency, see Appendix B.) For example, many of Seymour Simon's books were used to teach text structures and how to generate questions at a variety of levels. In addition, students practiced their fluency by choosing short selections about particular animals and engaging in repeated readings. They also read along with books on CD and used narrative texts about animals to engage in Readers Theatre. Because students found this theme so interesting, they were highly motivated to learn and readily engaged in applying the comprehension strategies. Teachers also adapted lessons for prereaders and prewriters by engaging in read-alouds and encouraging response through a variety of modes, including discussion, drawing, painting, singing, dancing, and dramatizing.

Theme Resources

Books

Simon, S. (1988). *Jupiter*. New York: HarperTrophy.

Simon, S. (1988). *Saturn*. New York: HarperCollins.

Simon, S. (1989). *The sun*. New York: HarperCollins.

Simon, S. (1990). *Uranus*. New York: HarperCollins.

Simon, S. (1991). *Galaxies*. New York: HarperCollins.

Simon, S. (1992). *Storms*. New York: HarperCollins.

Simon, S. (1993). *Autumn across America*. New York: Hyperion.

Simon, S. (1993). *New questions and answers about dinosaurs*. New York: Mulberry.

Simon, S. (1994). *Big cats*. New York: HarperCollins.

Simon, S. (1995). *Sharks*. New York: HarperCollins.

Simon, S. (1995). *Volcanoes*. New York: HarperTrophy.

Simon, S. (1997). *Deserts*. New York: HarperCollins.

Simon, S. (1997). *Mountains*. New York: HarperCollins.

Simon, S. (1997). *Neptune*. New York: HarperCollins.

Simon, S. (1998). *Comets, meteors, and asteroids*. New York: HarperCollins.

Simon, S. (1998). *Icebergs and glaciers*. New York: HarperCollins.

Simon, S. (1998). *Now you see it now you don't: The amazing world of optical illusions*. New York: HarperCollins.

Simon, S. (1998). *Mercury*. New York: HarperCollins.

Simon, S. (1998). *The sun*. New York: HarperCollins.

Simon, S. (1998). *They swim the seas: The mystery of animal migration.* New York: Harcourt.

Simon, S. (1998). *Venus.* New York: HarperCollins.

Simon, S. (1998). *Wild babies.* New York: HarperCollins.

Simon, S. (2000). *Bones: Our skeletal system.* New York: HarperCollins.

Simon, S. (2000). *Destination Jupiter.* New York: HarperCollins.

Simon, S. (2000). *Muscles: Our muscular system.* New York: HarperCollins.

Simon, S. (2000). *Wildfires.* New York: HarperCollins.

Simon, S. (2001). *Crocodiles and alligators.* New York: HarperCollins.

Simon, S. (2001). *Tornadoes.* New York: HarperCollins.

Simon, S. (2002). *Animals nobody loves.* San Francisco: Chronicle.

Simon, S. (2002). *Baby animals.* San Francisco: Chronicle.

Simon, S. (2002). *Fighting fires.* San Francisco: Chronicle.

Simon, S. (2002). *Out of sight.* San Francisco: Chronicle.

Simon, S. (2002). *Planets around the sun.* San Francisco: Chronicle.

Simon, S. (2002). *Danger! Earthquakes* (See More Readers, level 2). San Francisco: Chronicle.

Simon, S. (2002). *Danger! Volcanoes* (See More Readers, level 2). San Francisco: Chronicle.

Simon, S. (2002). *Giant machines* (See More Readers, level 1). San Francisco: Chronicle.

Simon, S. (2002). *Killer whales* (See More Readers, level 1). San Francisco: Chronicle.

Simon, S. (2002). *Seymour Simon's book of trucks.* New York: HarperCollins.

Simon, S. (2002). *Super storms* (See More Readers, level 2). San Francisco: Chronicle.

Simon, S. (2003). *Earth: Our planet in space.* New York: Simon & Schuster.

Simon, S. (2003). *Hurricanes.* New York: HarperCollins.

Simon, S. (2003). *The moon.* New York: Simon & Schuster.

Simon, S. (2004). *Destination: Mars.* New York: HarperCollins.

Simon, S. (2004). *Incredible sharks* (See More Readers, level 1). San Francisco: Chronicle.

Simon, S. (2004). *Pyramids and mummies.* San Francisco: Chronicle.

Simon, S. (2004). *Seymour Simon's book of trains.* New York: HarperCollins.

Simon, S. (2004). *Space travelers.* San Francisco: Chronicle.

Simon, S. (2005). *Amazing bats* (See More Readers, level 1). San Francisco: Chronicle.

Simon, S. (2005). *Eyes and ears.* New York: HarperCollins.

Simon, S. (2005). *Guts: Our digestive system.* New York: HarperCollins.

Simon, S. (2005). *Big bugs* (See More Readers, level 1). San Francisco: Chronicle.

Simon, S. (2005). *Bridges* (See More Readers, level 2). San Francisco: Chronicle.

Simon, S. (2005). *Emergency vehicles* (See More Readers, level 1). San Francisco: Chronicle.

Simon, S. (2005). *Skyscrapers* (See More Readers, level 2). San Francisco: Chronicle.

Simon, S. (2006). *The brain: Our nervous system.* New York: Collins.

Simon, S. (2006). *Destination: Space.* New York: Collins.

Simon, S. (2006). *Earthquake.* New York: Collins.

Simon, S. (2006). *Giant snakes* (See More Readers, level 2). San Francisco: Chronicle.

Simon, S. (2006). *The heart: Our circulatory system.* New York: Collins.

Simon, S. (2006). *Horses.* New York: HarperCollins.

Simon, S. (2006). *Knights and castles* (See More Readers, level 3). San Francisco: Chronicle.

Simon, S. (2006). *Lightning.* New York: Collins.

Simon, S. (2006). *Oceans*. New York: Collins.

Simon, S. (2006). *Planet mars* (See More Readers, level 1). San Francisco: Chronicle.

Simon, S. (2006). *Stars*. New York: Collins.

Simon, S. (2006). *The universe*. New York: Collins.

Simon, S. (2006). *Weather*. New York: Collins.

Simon, S. (2006). *Whales*. New York: Collins.

Simon, S. (2007). *Hurricanes*. New York: Collins.

Simon, S. (2007). *Lungs: Your respiratory system*. New York: Collins.

Simon, S. (2007). *Our solar system*. New York: Collins.

Simon, S. (2007). *Penguins*. New York: Collins.

Simon, S. (2007). *Snakes*. New York: Collins.

Simon, S. (2007). *Spiders*. New York: Collins.

Simon, S. (2008). *Gorillas*. New York: Collins.

Simon, S. (2008). *The human body*. New York: Collins.

Simon, S. (2009). *Cats*. New York: Collins.

Simon, S. (2009). *Dogs*. New York: Collins.

Simon, S. (2009). *Dolphins*. New York: Collins.

Simon, S. (2009). *The online space man and other cases: Einstein Anderson, science detective*. Bloomington, IN: iUniverse.

Simon, S. (2009). *Wolves*. New York: Collins.

Websites About Seymour Simon

Houghton Mifflin Reading: Meet the Author

> www.eduplace.com/kids/tnc/mtai/simon.html

Reading Rockets

> www.readingrockets.org/books/interviews/simon

Scholastic: Biography

> www2.scholastic.com/browse/contributor.jsp?id=2232

Seymour Science: Blog of Seymour Simon

> www.seymourscience.com

Seymour Simon

> www.seymoursimon.com

Related Websites

Killer Whales

Facts on Whales for Kids

> www.essortment.com/all/factsonwhalek_rsdn.htm

Kids Planet: Killer Whale

> www.kidsplanet.org/factsheets/orca.html

NASA Eclipse 99: *The Sun* Lesson Plan

> eclipse99.nasa.gov/pages/SunActiv.html

Wolves

International Wolf Center: Teaching the World About Wolves
    www.wolf.org/wolves/learn/justkids/kids.asp

KidsKonnect.com: Wolves
    www.kidskonnect.com/subject-index/13-animals/56-wolves.html

National Geographic Kids: Gray Wolves
    kids.nationalgeographic.com/Animals/CreatureFeature/Graywolf

Performance Extensions Across the Curriculum

Art

- On a trip to a local observatory, invite students to draw pictures and write about what they see through a telescope or when viewing the stars inside the observatory. Compile pictures and writing into a class book for everyone to enjoy.

- Create class art projects to support students' reading of Seymour Simon's books. For example, create a solar system or an ocean mural.

Math

- Engage in inquiry by brainstorming math-related questions about planets (e.g., How many moons does each planet have? What is the order of the planets from the sun?) with a partner. Explore various websites, such as Enchanted Learning: The Planets (www.enchantedlearning.com/subjects/astronomy/planets/) to find answers to the questions you raise.

- Read a Seymour Simon book on the topic of your choice (*Hurricanes, Penguins, Pyramids and Mummies, Stars*) and work with a partner to create math problems and solutions based on that topic. Use multiple mathematical operations, including the one you are currently studying.

Music

- Predict what kind of music we might one day find on other planets. Choose a planet and write a song about it in a small group. Sing the song for the class.

- Participate in a class talent show in which groups of students sing songs they have written related to Seymour Simon animal books and play rhythm instruments.

Science

- Work with a partner to read two of Seymour Simon's books on planets (*Earth: Our Planet in Space, Jupiter, Mercury, Neptune, Saturn, Uranus, Venus*). Compare and contrast characteristics of the two planets using a Venn Diagram. Explain their similarities and differences to the class by writing a song about them or creating a painting or sculpture of them.

- Bring a Seymour Simon science-themed book to life by creating a science project based on the topic of the book. For example, after reading *Volcanoes*, create an erupting volcano and explain it to the class.

Social Studies

- Read a book about natural disasters, such as *Earthquake* by Seymour Simon. As a class, discuss how these disasters impact people around the world. Work in a small group to brainstorm how to help people who are affected by these disasters. Make a poster or other type of presentation to share your ideas.

- Read Seymour Simon books and other informational texts about land formations: *Deserts*, *Mountains*, and *Icebergs and Glaciers*. Create projects such as Press Conferences, Illustrated Definition Poems, and Lyric Summaries to present what you have learned.

Culminating Activity

Animals Aplenty, Animals Galore! A Celebration of the Books of Seymour Simon. Students invite their families to participate in this theme celebration. Display Seymour Simon's animal books and students' related projects throughout the classroom. Invite students to narrate videos of selected animals in their natural habitats. Encourage others to serve as tour guides for different stations where student work is displayed. Post a class mural featuring photos of students working on projects throughout the theme. Invite visitors to provide feedback on the celebration by sending e-mails to the students on class computers. Students autograph copies of the class book, *Our Poems About Seymour Simon's Animals*, and give them as gifts to their families.

CHAPTER 9

Giggles Galore: The Humor of Dav Pilkey

There are always plenty of giggles in our classrooms when we and our students are reading Dav Pilkey's books. Whether writing picture books about a dog with bad breath that captures burglars or a dachshund that triumphs while wearing a mustard-covered hot dog bun Halloween costume, Pilkey makes connections to our lives, and humor ensues. Pilkey has also created such endearing characters as Dragon, a mouse named Ricky Ricotta, and Captain Underpants. These characters are featured in Pilkey's chapter book series, and, because of their humorous adventures, appeal to a wide range of student interests.

The sample Theme-Based Plan for Guided Comprehension: Giggles Galore: The Humor of Dav Pilkey (see Figure 17) offers an overview of the lessons and resources that support this theme. The plan begins by listing theme goals and making connections to state standards. The student goals for this theme include the following:

- Use appropriate comprehension skills and strategies
- Interpret and respond to text
- Communicate effectively

These goals support the following state standards:

- Learning to read independently
- Reading, analyzing, and interpreting text
- Types and quality of writing
- Speaking and listening

Sample assessments in this theme include observation, running records, retellings, student writing, skill and strategy applications, and student self-assessments. The Guided Comprehension lessons are based on the following strategies and corresponding teaching ideas:

- Previewing: Story Impressions
- Knowing How Words Work: Vocabulary Bookmark
- Making Connections: Draw and Write Connections
- Summarizing: Lyric Retelling

Figure 17. Theme-Based Plan for Guided Comprehension: Giggles Galore: The Humor of Dav Pilkey

Goals and Related State Standards | Students will

- Use appropriate comprehension skills and strategies. Standard: learning to read independently
- Interpret and respond to text. Standard: reading, analyzing, and interpreting text
- Communicate effectively. Standards: types and quality of writing; speaking and listening

Assessment

The following measures can be used for a variety of purposes, including diagnostic, formative, and summative assessment:

Draw and Write Connections	Story Impressions
Lyric Retelling	Student Self-Assessments
Observation	Student Writing
Running Records	Vocabulary Bookmark

Text	Title	Level
1. 'Twas the Night Before Thanksgiving		PreK–3
2. Dogzilla		PreK–3
3. Dragon Gets By		PreK–3
4. Dog Breath: The Horrible Trouble With Hally Tosis		PreK–3

Technology Resources

KidsReads.com: Bio and Author Talk
www.kidsreads.com/authors/au-pilkey-dav.asp

Official Dav Pilkey Website
www.pilkey.com

RIF Reading Planet: Meet the Author Interview
www.rif.org/kids/readingplanet/bookzone/pilkey.htm

Comprehension Strategies | Teaching Ideas

1. Previewing	1. Story Impressions
2. Knowing How Words Work	2. Vocabulary Bookmark
3. Making Connections	3. Draw and Write Connections
4. Summarizing	4. Lyric Retelling

Comprehension Centers

Students will apply the comprehension strategies and related teaching ideas in the following comprehension centers:

Art Center	Poetry Center
Listening Center	Teacher Center
Making and Writing Words Center	Theme Center
Making Books Center	Writing Center

Comprehension Routines

Students will apply the comprehension strategies and related teaching ideas in the following comprehension routines:

Literature Circles
Reciprocal Teaching
Cross-Age Reading Experiences

'Twas the Night Before Thanksgiving (2004), *Dogzilla* (2003), *Dragon Gets By* (1999), and *Dog Breath: The Horrible Trouble With Hally Tosis* (2004) are the texts used in Stage One for teacher-directed whole-group instruction. Numerous additional theme-related resources, including texts, websites, performances across the curriculum, and a culminating activity, are presented in the Theme Resources at the end of the chapter.

Examples of comprehension centers students use during Stage Two of Guided Comprehension include art, listening, making and writing words, making books, poetry, teacher, theme, and writing. Students also engage in strategy application in comprehension routines such as Literature Circles, Reciprocal Teaching, and Cross-Age Reading Experiences. Sample websites complete the overview.

In this chapter, all the lessons focus on books authored by Dav Pilkey. The lessons are appropriate for all learners, including English learners, struggling readers, and students with special needs. To accommodate these learners, the lessons include multiple modes of response (such as singing, sketching, and dramatizing), working with partners, books on CD, cross-age experiences, and extra guided instruction. Ideas used to differentiate instruction in these lessons include the following:

- Content—the information being taught

  - Using leveled text to accommodate students' abilities in teacher-guided small groups, centers, and routines

  - Providing leveled texts that accommodate student interest and help motivate them to read

- Process—the way in which the information is taught

  - Activating prior knowledge and/or providing background information

  - Scaffolding student learning by using the Guided Comprehension Model

  - Reading the text aloud during Stage One to make it accessible to all students

  - Using visuals to support students' construction of meaning

  - Adapting graphic organizers; providing paragraph frames

  - Encouraging students to work with peers in pairs and small groups to provide additional support

  - Preteaching students who may need additional support to use the strategies and skills such as sequencing and generating questions at multiple levels

- Product—how the students demonstrate their learning

  - Integrating alternative modes of representation, such as art, drama, poetry, or music

  - Providing opportunities for students to use computers when creating projects

Guided Comprehension Lessons

Giggles Galore: The Humor of Dav Pilkey
Guided Comprehension Strategy: Previewing
Teaching Idea: Story Impressions

STAGE ONE: Teacher-Directed Whole-Group Instruction

Text: *'Twas the Night Before Thanksgiving* (2004)

Explain: I began by explaining the importance of previewing a text before reading. I said, "When we preview, we activate prior knowledge, make predictions, and set purposes for reading." I explained that Story Impressions (see Appendix C, pages 217–218) provide a way for us to think about what we know about stories, predict what might happen in a story, and read the story to learn how it is similar to and different from what we write. I explained that we use clues about published stories to write Story Impressions—what we predict the story is about. I made clear to the students that the clues we use in Story Impressions include the same narrative elements— characters, setting, problem, attempts to resolve, and resolution—that we use when we complete Story Maps. Then I explained that writing Story Impressions about books we read helps get our minds ready to read and understand the text. I explained that we would use a list of clues that would help us predict what we would read about. Then we would write our impression or prediction of what would happen in the story.

Demonstrate: I shared the title and showed the students the cover of *'Twas the Night Before Thanksgiving.* I asked the students what connections they could make to the book. Rosie said, "I know a book called *'Twas the Night Before Christmas.*" Nannan said, "It reminds me of Thanksgiving when my family eats a big turkey." Javier said, "It reminds me of Thanksgiving at my grandma's house." We discussed the students' connections and then I showed students the clues—words and phrases from the story—that we would use to preview the text and create a Story Impression. I reminded students that we would need to use the clues in the order in which they appeared in the list. The clues, which represented the narrative elements in *'Twas the Night Before Thanksgiving*, were as follows:

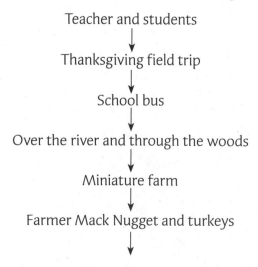

Teacher and students

↓

Thanksgiving field trip

↓

School bus

↓

Over the river and through the woods

↓

Miniature farm

↓

Farmer Mack Nugget and turkeys

↓

Guided Comprehension: Giggles Galore: The Humor of Dav Pilkey
Previewing: Story Impressions

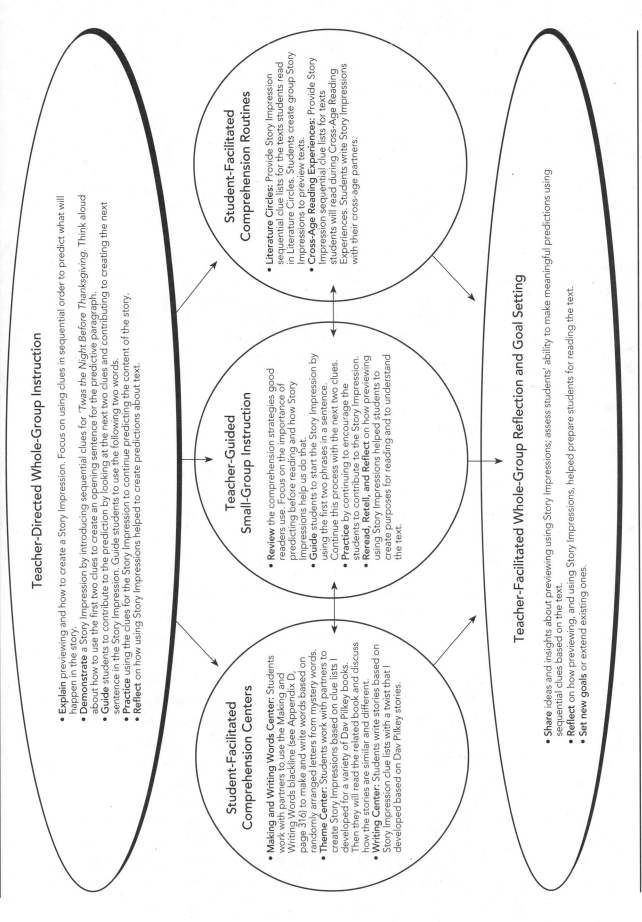

Teacher-Directed Whole-Group Instruction

- **Explain** previewing and how to create a Story Impression. Focus on using clues in sequential order to predict what will happen in the story.
- **Demonstrate** a Story Impression by introducing sequential clues for 'Twas the Night Before Thanksgiving. Think aloud about how to use the first two clues to create an opening sentence for the predictive paragraph.
- **Guide** students to contribute to the prediction by looking at the next two clues and contributing to creating the next sentence in the Story Impression. Guide students to use the following two words.
- **Practice** using the clues for the Story Impression to continue predicting the content of the story.
- **Reflect** on how using Story Impressions helped to create predictions about text.

Student-Facilitated Comprehension Centers

- **Making and Writing Words Center:** Students work with partners to use the Making and Writing Words blackline (see Appendix D, page 316) to make and write words based on randomly arranged letters from mystery words.
- **Theme Center:** Students work with partners to create Story Impressions based on clue lists I developed for a variety of Dav Pilkey books. Then they will read the related book and discuss how the stories are similar and different.
- **Writing Center:** Students write stories based on Story Impression clue lists with a twist that I developed based on Dav Pilkey stories.

Teacher-Guided Small-Group Instruction

- **Review** the comprehension strategies good readers use. Focus on the importance of predicting before reading and how Story Impressions help us do that.
- **Guide** students to start the Story Impression by using the first two phrases in a sentence. Continue this process with the next two clues.
- **Practice** by continuing to encourage the students to contribute to the Story Impression.
- **Reread, Retell, and Reflect** on how previewing using Story Impressions helped students to create purposes for reading and to understand the text.

Student-Facilitated Comprehension Routines

- **Literature Circles:** Provide Story Impression sequential clue lists for the texts students read in Literature Circles. Students create group Story Impressions to preview texts.
- **Cross-Age Reading Experiences:** Provide Story Impression sequential clue lists for texts students will read during Cross-Age Reading Experiences. Students write Story Impressions with their cross-age partners.

Teacher-Facilitated Whole-Group Reflection and Goal Setting

- **Share** ideas and insights about previewing using Story Impressions; assess students' ability to make meaningful predictions using sequential clues based on the text.
- **Reflect** on how previewing, and using Story Impressions, helped prepare students for reading the text.
- **Set new goals** or extend existing ones.

An ax

↓

Students cried and yelled

↓

Trip home

↓

Happy Thanksgiving

I read each of the clues and discussed them with the students. I paid special attention to words I thought the students may not know. For example, we focused on the meaning of *miniature* in the fifth clue. Many of the students were familiar with the term and cited examples of its use in the Christmas version of the story as well as in descriptions of certain types of dogs. Next, I modeled how to start our written prediction. I thought aloud and said,

> I see that *teachers and students* is the first clue and *Thanksgiving field trip* is the second clue. I think that the teachers and students are characters in the story and the Thanksgiving field trip is the setting—where the story takes place. So I am going to write, "*A teacher and her students went on a Thanksgiving field trip*" to begin our Story Impression.

The students and I discussed the first sentence and agreed that it was a good idea. Then I read the next two clues: *school bus* and *over the river and through the woods*. I asked the students how they thought these clues might fit into our Story Impression. They suggested that the students in the story had ridden in a school bus on the way to their field trip. I agreed. Then they said that over the river and through the woods is probably where the bus took the students and their teacher. So, I said, "Let's include your ideas in our second sentence." Then I wrote, "*The students and teacher rode in a school bus, and the bus went over the river and through the woods.*" The students agreed that our Story Impression sounded fine to this point, but they were starting to wonder what the story in the book would say.

Guide: I guided the students to work with partners to help me write the next two sentences. I read the next two clues: *miniature farm* and *Farmer Mack Nugget and turkeys*. I encouraged each pair to think about how these clues might fit into our story. After the students had time to discuss some possibilities, a few shared their ideas. They thought that the miniature farm was where the students went on their field trip and that Farmer Mack Nugget and the turkeys lived there. Then I said, "I will write the next sentence based on your ideas." I wrote, "*Then the bus arrived at a miniature farm where Farmer Mack Nugget and the turkeys lived.*" Next, I encouraged students to work with their partners to think about how we might use the next two clues: *an ax* and *students cried and yelled*. After discussing the clues, we agreed that I should write, "*The students saw an ax and they cried and yelled, because they thought the farmer was going to kill the turkeys and sell them for Thanksgiving dinners.*"

Practice: We practiced by writing the conclusion for our Story Impression, reading *'Twas the Night Before Thanksgiving*, and discussing how the book was similar to and different from our Story Impression. I guided the pairs as needed while they thought about how to use the final two clues: *trip home* and *happy Thanksgiving*. They suggested that I write, "*Before the students got on the bus for their trip home, they set the turkeys free, and everyone had a happy Thanksgiving.*" Then I read Dav Pilkey's *'Twas the Night Before Thanksgiving* and we talked about how it was similar to and different from our Story Impression. First, the students noted that our story was every bit as good as Dav Pilkey's. They thought the stories were alike because they started with some of the same ideas, and the students saved the turkeys in both stories. They also thought Pilkey's story was different in several ways. For example, it was written in rhyme just like *'Twas the Night Before Christmas*. The students also thought there were differences in what happened between Farmer Mack Nugget and the turkeys in the published story. They thought Pilkey's story was different because the farmer called the turkeys like Santa calls the reindeer, and they thought the turkey names were funny. We concluded our discussion by imagining what it would be like to have turkeys as holiday dinner guests. We agreed it would be very funny indeed.

Reflect: We reflected by discussing how the clues helped us predict what would happen in the story. Then we talked about how previewing a text this way helped prepare us for reading and made us want to read to find out if our predictions were accurate. We also talked about how previewing vocabulary ahead of time helped make the words easier to know when we encountered them in the text.

STAGE TWO: Teacher-Guided Small-Group Instruction

Text: *Kat Kong* (2003) (Texts varied according to students' abilities.)

Review: I reviewed with students that as good readers we can preview a text to get our minds ready to read. I also reviewed how we could use sequential clues from a text to create a prediction called a Story Impression. I introduced the book and asked the students what they noticed on the cover. We discussed and made connections to the skyline, the huge cat, and the small mouse. Then I shared the list of sequential clues—words and phrases from the book—that we would use to write our small-group Story Impression and reviewed them with the students. As we discussed the clues, we paid special attention to the words *explorers*, *trembles*, *Mousopolis*, and *curiosity*. For example, we talked about what happens when the ground "trembles," and several students suggested that it meant that the ground would shake. When we talked about *curiosity*, the students observed that it sounded like *curious*. That prompted Maria to say,

> Sometimes my Mom says being curious is a good thing, like when I ask questions about something I want to learn more about. But other times she says I am too curious, like when I snoop for my birthday presents before my birthday comes.

Discussing words with which the students may not be familiar helps them to recognize the words while they are reading the text. I also reminded the students that the clues are often related to the story elements: characters, setting, problem, attempts to resolve the problem, and resolution.

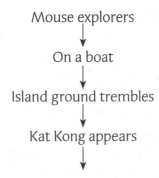

Mouse explorers

↓

On a boat

↓

Island ground trembles

↓

Kat Kong appears

↓

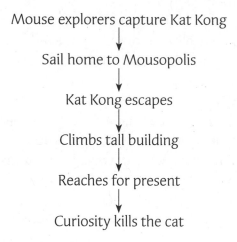

Mouse explorers capture Kat Kong

↓

Sail home to Mousopolis

↓

Kat Kong escapes

↓

Climbs tall building

↓

Reaches for present

↓

Curiosity kills the cat

Guide: I guided the students to look at the first two phrases—*mouse explorers* and *on a boat*—and think of the first sentence of our prediction. I reminded the students that the first two clues often provide possible information about the characters and the setting. They suggested that our first sentence should be, "*Mouse explorers were on a boat out on the ocean.*" Then I asked the students to consider the next two clues. They suggested that I write, "*The ground trembled when Kat Kong started running because Kat Kong was so big.*"

Practice: The students continued to suggest ideas and I continued to record them as we used the remaining clues. This is the rest of our Story Impression:

> The mouse explorers captured Kat Kong and brought him back to Mouseopolis, the town where they lived. Then Kat Kong escaped and climbed a tall building. The mice couldn't get him to come down, so they gave him a present – a box all wrapped up and filled with cat treats. Kat Kong couldn't wait to see what was in the box, so he fell and curiosity killed the cat.

Next, the students read the book silently in segments, and, when they paused, we made connections and discussed the story. Then we talked about how Dav Pilkey's story was similar to and different from our story.

Reread, Retell, and Reflect: We began by engaging in a group retelling of *Kat Kong*. Then I asked the students how using the Story Impression helped them to preview. They said they could use what they saw on the cover of the book and the list of clues to get ideas for the Story Impression. Rachel said, "It's like having some clues about what happens and using them to tell what we think happened in the story." Sophia and Michael also remarked that making connections helped them to contribute to the Story Impression. For example, the name Kat Kong reminded them of King Kong and his adventures. Robert said it was fun to read Dav Pilkey's story to see if our prediction was close to what the author was thinking when he wrote his story.

Student-Facilitated Comprehension Centers

Making and Writing Words Center: I placed a variety of Dav Pilkey-related mystery words at this center. I also left copies of the Making and Writing Words blackline (see Appendix D, page 316) with the letters of each mystery word randomly positioned at the top of the page. When students visited this center, they worked with a partner to create two-, three-, four-, five-, six-, and seven-letter words until they created the mystery word.

Theme Center: I provided Story Impression clues for several Dav Pilkey books at this center. I put each set of clues inside the cover of the appropriate book. Pairs of students used the clues to create Story Impressions. Then they read the related Dav Pilkey book, and they discussed how that story was similar to and different from their story. Finally, they put their Story Impression in their Guided Comprehension Profile.

Writing Center: Students used Story Impression clue lists that I left at this center as prompts to write their own stories. The Story Impression clues I left were based on Dav Pilkey's book, but each had a bit of a twist. For example, Suzy used clues based on *Moo Moo Kong*, the story of a very large and very scary cow. Here is her story:

> One day Moo Moo Kong poped out of a milk botle. Moo Moo Kong was a giant cow. She was so big and strong that when she walkd the earth trenbuled. She came to soccer practis one day and everybody who saw her was really, really scard. Everyone startd to run. Then Moo Moo Cow walkd onto the feld. She walkd up to the soccer ball and kickd it. It flew across the feld and landd in the school trash on the other side of the bilding. Everybody stoppd runing and lookd at Moo Moo Cow. She was just standing there eating the grass on the soccer feld. Everyone came back to the feld and the prinsapal hird Moo Moo Cow to be our soccer team's new coch.

Student-Facilitated Comprehension Routines

Literature Circles: Before each group began reading their Dav Pilkey book, I provided a list of Story Impression clues and observed as the students used the clues to complete a Story Impression based on their book. When each group finished reading its book, group members discussed how their Story Impression and Pilkey's story were similar and how they were different. As Literature Circle extension activities, the groups wrote a sequel to the Pilkey book they had read. Student titles included *Kat Kong and the Kittens*, *'Twas the Night Before the Fourth of July*, and *The Return of Dogzilla*.

Cross-Age Reading Experiences: Students and their cross-age partners completed Story Impressions and then read Dav Pilkey books. They stopped at predetermined points to discuss what they were reading.

STAGE THREE: Teacher-Facilitated Whole-Group Reflection and Goal Setting

Share: Students shared their work from Stage Two, first with partners and then with the class. They shared their Story Impressions and discussed examples of how their stories differed and how they were similar to Dav Pilkey's. They also shared their projects and their reflections from centers and routines.

Reflect: We discussed why previewing is important and how it helps us prepare to read and understand. The students thought it was great to be able to use clues to predict what might happen in a story. They all felt like authors and thoroughly enjoyed reading Dav Pilkey's books and becoming familiar with his author style.

Set New Goals: Everyone agreed that they were comfortable using Story Impressions on their own. So, we decided to create a new goal to learn other ways of previewing.

Assessment Options

I observed students in many settings throughout the lesson. For example, in whole-group instruction I focused on students' interactions with their partners, and in teacher-guided small-group instruction I observed the students' contributions to our Story Impression, as well as their contributions to the discussion. I reviewed students' completed Story Impressions to see if they wrote reasonable predictions. I also read and provided feedback on students' Literature Circle extension projects and self-assessments. In addition, I engaged several students in fluency checks by inviting them to whisper read during small-group instruction and others in running records if they were ready to move to another level in small-group guided instruction. I used what I learned from these assessments when planning future lessons.

Giggles Galore: The Humor of Dav Pilkey
Guided Comprehension Strategy: Knowing How Words Work
Teaching Idea: Vocabulary Bookmark

Stage One: Teacher-Directed Whole-Group Instruction

Text: *Dogzilla* (2003)

Explain: I began by explaining to my students that knowing how words work is a strategy good readers use while reading. I explained that using a Vocabulary Bookmark (see Appendix C, page 237) is one way that we can learn about how words work. Then I focused on how Vocabulary Bookmarks allow us to choose a word we want to learn and help us understand what we are reading. I explained that to complete a Vocabulary Bookmark, we would need to choose a word we would like to share with the whole class and write it on the bookmark. I also noted that we would need to write what we thought the word meant and the page number on which we found it.

Demonstrate: I used a read-aloud, a Think-Aloud, and the Vocabulary Bookmark blackline (see Appendix C, page 259) to model for students. I began by introducing *Dogzilla*. I held up the cover of the book and asked the students what connections they could make to the title. Several students said that they had dogs. Several others made connections between Dogzilla and Godzilla, a monster they knew about from movies and toys. Then we discussed the illustration on the cover and the students suggested that Dogzilla was a huge monster like Godzilla. Before I began reading aloud, I reminded students that as I was reading, I should be thinking about a word to choose for the Vocabulary Bookmark. Next, I read aloud the first few pages. When I stopped, I discussed that section with the students. We made connections and then I thought aloud about which word I might choose. I said,

> The word I am choosing is *barbecue*. I am going to write it on my Vocabulary Bookmark. I think it means to have a "cookout." I am also going to write the page number where I read the word. It appears twice—on page 2 and again on page 3.

I wrote *barbecue* on my Vocabulary Bookmark. Then I wrote what I thought it meant and the pages on which I had read it. After the students saw me write the information on a Vocabulary Bookmark I had placed on the overhead projector, I stopped to discuss my bookmark with them. I told them that I thought *barbecue* meant "cookout." Then I directed them to the pages on which the word appeared and I reread the sentences in context. After I read the sentence on page 2, I said, "Let's see if my meaning of the word fits into this sentence." Then I substituted *cookout* for *barbecue* in that sentence. The students and I decided the word worked well and that *barbecue* means "cookout." Then I read the sentence on page 3, but when we tried to substitute the words, it did not work. I thought aloud and said, "I have never heard of 'cookout sauce,' so I think "barbecue" may have another meaning. Let's talk with partners and see if we can think of a different meaning for *barbecue*." I monitored the students, providing support as necessary, as they discussed possibilities. Several of the students suggested *barbecue sauce* was a red sauce that they had tasted on chicken and ribs. They thought ketchup was one of the ingredients. Their thoughts described the meaning of *barbecue* on page 3 very well. We used dictionaries to verify the two meanings of *barbecue*. We knew they were correct, but I wanted to demonstrate for the students how to verify meanings.

Guided Comprehension: Giggles Galore: The Humor of Dav Pilkey
Knowing How Words Work: Vocabulary Bookmark

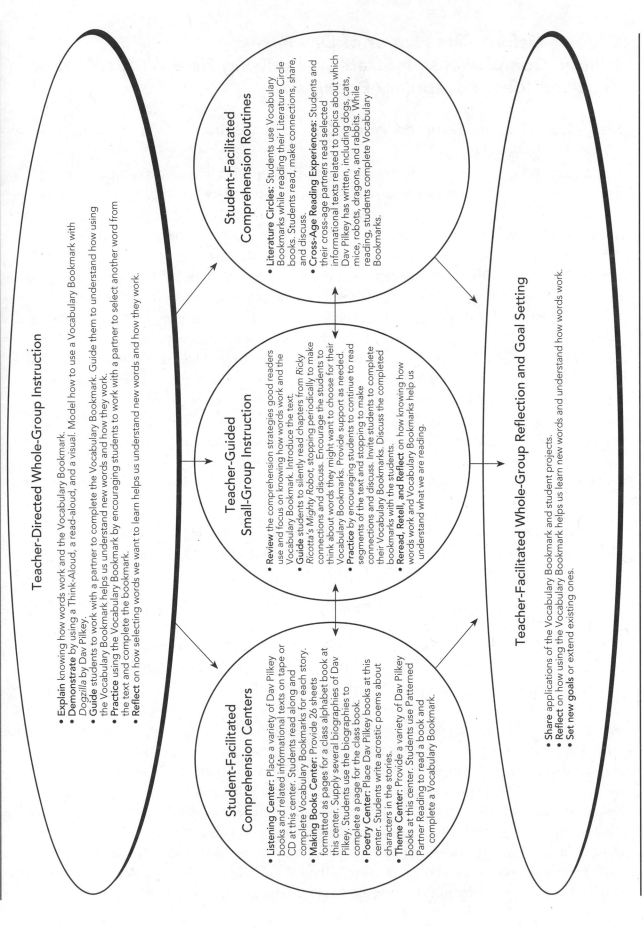

Teacher-Directed Whole-Group Instruction

- **Explain** knowing how words work and the Vocabulary Bookmark.
- **Demonstrate** by using a Think-Aloud, a read-aloud, and a visual. Model how to use a Vocabulary Bookmark with *Dogzilla* by Dav Pilkey.
- **Guide** students to work with a partner to complete the Vocabulary Bookmark. Guide them to understand how using the Vocabulary Bookmark helps us understand new words and how they work.
- **Practice** using the Vocabulary Bookmark by encouraging students to work with a partner to select another word from the text and complete the bookmark.
- **Reflect** on how selecting words we want to learn helps us understand new words and how they work.

Student-Facilitated Comprehension Centers

- **Listening Center:** Place a variety of Dav Pilkey books and related informational texts on tape or CD at this center. Students read along and complete Vocabulary Bookmarks for each story.
- **Making Books Center:** Provide 26 sheets formatted as pages for a class alphabet book at this center. Supply several biographies of Dav Pilkey. Students use the biographies of Dav Pilkey to complete a page for the class book.
- **Poetry Center:** Place Dav Pilkey books at this center. Students write acrostic poems about characters in the stories.
- **Theme Center:** Provide a variety of Dav Pilkey books at this center. Students use Patterned Partner Reading to read a book and complete a Vocabulary Bookmark.

Teacher-Guided Small-Group Instruction

- **Review** the comprehension strategies good readers use and focus on knowing how words work and the Vocabulary Bookmark. Introduce the text.
- **Guide** students to silently read chapters from *Ricky Ricotta's Mighty Robot*, stopping periodically to make connections and discuss. Encourage the students to think about words they might want to choose for their Vocabulary Bookmarks. Provide support as needed.
- **Practice** by encouraging students to continue to read segments of the text and stopping to make connections and discuss. Invite students to complete their Vocabulary Bookmarks. Discuss the completed bookmarks with the students.
- **Reread, Retell, and Reflect** on how knowing how words work and Vocabulary Bookmarks help us understand what we are reading.

Student-Facilitated Comprehension Routines

- **Literature Circles:** Students use Vocabulary Bookmarks while reading their Literature Circle books. Students read, make connections, share, and discuss.
- **Cross-Age Reading Experiences:** Students and their cross-age partners read selected informational texts related to topics about which Dav Pilkey has written, including dogs, cats, mice, robots, dragons, and rabbits. While reading, students complete Vocabulary Bookmarks.

Teacher-Facilitated Whole-Group Reflection and Goal Setting

- **Share** applications of the Vocabulary Bookmark and student projects.
- **Reflect** on how using the Vocabulary Bookmark helps us learn new words and understand how words work.
- **Set new goals** or extend existing ones.

Guided Comprehension in the Primary Grades (Second Edition) by Maureen McLaughlin. © 2010 by the International Reading Association. May be copied for classroom use.

Guide: As I continued to read aloud the next two sections of the book, I guided students to work with partners to choose words for the Vocabulary Bookmark. *Heroic, colossal,* and *tremendous* were some of the words they chose.

Practice: I read aloud to the end of the book and once again the students selected words for their Vocabulary Bookmarks. Words they chose this time included *confident* and *etched.* Then we listened as students presented their words and told us what they thought the words meant. Next, we visited the pages on which the words appeared and listened as the students read the sentences that contained their words. After that step, we discussed the word's suggested meaning and whether we thought it was correct. On a few occasions we verified meanings with dictionaries. Figure 18 shows Nick and Venetta's Vocabulary Bookmark.

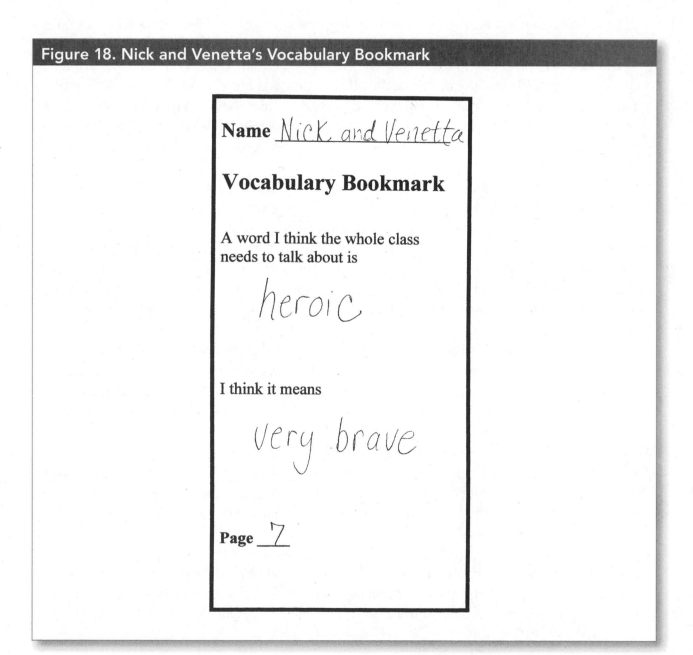

Figure 18. Nick and Venetta's Vocabulary Bookmark

Name *Nick and Venetta*

Vocabulary Bookmark

A word I think the whole class needs to talk about is

heroic

I think it means

very brave

Page *7*

Reflect: We began our reflection by discussing how the Vocabulary Bookmark helped us to read and to understand how words work. During our discussions, the students made many connections to their own lives and offered examples from their own experiences. For example, Andy said that he thought *colossal* meant "really really big," because when he was on vacation last summer he had ordered a "colossal soda" and it was the biggest he had ever seen. Paul said he liked using Vocabulary Bookmark, because it was fun to choose the words. Stephanie said she liked it because she got to think about what she thought a word meant. Everyone agreed that we could use a Vocabulary Bookmark whenever we were reading.

STAGE TWO: Teacher-Guided Small-Group Instruction

Text: *Ricky Ricotta's Mighty Robot vs. the Mecha-Monkeys From Mars* (2002) (Texts varied according to students' abilities.)

Review: I reminded students about the reading strategies good readers use and I reviewed how to complete and use a Vocabulary Bookmark.

Guide: I introduced *Ricky Ricotta's Mighty Robot vs. the Mecha-Monkeys From Mars*, a chapter book written by Dav Pilkey. We discussed the title and the cover illustration. The students were familiar with Ricky Ricotta from the author study we did on Dav Pilkey, and they recognized Ricky as the tiny mouse on the cover. Then we discussed the mighty robot. The students thought that he looked like a superhero made from metal parts and they wondered what he would do in the book to help Ricky.

Practice: I explained that we would be reading the first three chapters because the chapters were very short. The students read the chapters silently and after each one we made connections and discussed the story. For example, in Chapter 2, Gina made a connection to the flattened minivan. She said that it reminded her of when her family had passed a car that had been in an accident with a truck. When the students had read all three chapters, they completed Vocabulary Bookmarks. Examples of words they chose included *irresponsible* and *villains*. We discussed the words, revisited them in context, and verified with a dictionary as needed. Mike's Vocabulary Bookmark is featured in Figure 19.

Reread, Retell, and Reflect: We engaged in a group retelling of the first three chapters and predicted what might happen in the next chapter. Next, we talked about how using a Vocabulary Bookmark helped us understand what we read and how we could use it in centers and routines. We all looked forward to our next small-group session when we would continue reading the book.

Student-Facilitated Comprehension Centers

Listening Center: I provided a variety of Dav Pilkey books and related informational texts on tape or CD at this center. Students read along to practice fluency and demonstrate comprehension by retelling the story to a partner. Students completed Vocabulary Bookmarks for each story and included them in their Guided Comprehension Profiles.

Making Books Center: I placed 26 sheets formatted as pages for a class alphabet book at this center. I also provided several biographies of Dav Pilkey and a model page for the class book. Students created pages for the book that each featured a different fact about Pilkey. For example, Lindy created a *d* page that read "*Dav wrote Dogzilla.*" Students also illustrated their book pages and completed Center Reflections.

Figure 19. Mike's Vocabulary Bookmark

Name _Mike_

Vocabulary Bookmark

**A word I think the whole class
needs to talk about is**

Villains

I think it means

bad people

Page 26

Poetry Center: I provided a variety of Dav Pilkey books at this center. I also provided acrostic formats for a variety of Dav Pilkey characters, including *Dogzilla* and *Kat Kong*. I placed the formats within the related books. Students worked with partners to write acrostics about one of Pilkey's characters. Here is the acrostic that Dylan and Rosie wrote for Hally, the main character in *Dog Breath: The Horrible Trouble With Hally Tosis*:

H orrible trouble

A lways had stinky breath

L oved the Tosis family

L anded the burglars on the floor

Y ou would be lucky to have this dog

Theme Center: I placed a variety of Dav Pilkey books at this center. Students worked with partners and used Patterned Partner Reading to read the books. The pattern students used was Read–Pause–Make a Connection. They also discussed the books and completed Vocabulary Bookmarks. When they finished, students completed Center Reflections (see Appendix D, page 301) and included them and their Vocabulary Bookmarks in their Guided Comprehension Profiles.

Student-Facilitated Comprehension Routines

Literature Circles: Students selected the Dav Pilkey books they would read in their Literature Circles. After reading a segment, each student completed a Vocabulary Bookmark and shared it with the group in the course of the discussion. As an extension activity, groups created collages of pictures and words about the books they had read and presented them to the class.

Cross-Age Reading Experiences: Students and their cross-age partners read selected informational texts related to topics in Dav Pilkey's books. The topics included dogs, cats, mice, robots, dragons, and rabbits. When they finished reading, students and their partners completed Vocabulary Bookmarks, made connections, and discussed the books.

STAGE THREE: Teacher-Facilitated Whole-Group Reflection and Goal Setting

Share: Students shared their Vocabulary Bookmarks and projects from Stage Two in small groups. Then we discussed their applications as a whole class.

Reflect: We reflected on how using Vocabulary Bookmarks helps us understand how words work and what we read. We also talked about how we can use Vocabulary Bookmarks with stories and informational text. Then students reflected on how self-selecting the words motivated them to learn. Tommy said he liked using Vocabulary Bookmarks because he got to choose the words. Alicia said that choosing the words helped her to remember what they meant.

Set New Goals: Students felt confident in their ability to complete and use Vocabulary Bookmarks with stories and informational texts, so we decided to learn how to use mapping to learn more about how words work. We decided to begin by learning how to use a Semantic Map.

Assessment Options

I observed students and listened carefully as they discussed texts throughout this lesson and as they completed their Vocabulary Bookmarks and shared them with the class. I also observed how they worked with their partners and in small groups. I read and commented on the work students completed in centers and routines, as well as their self-assessments. I completed running records with students who appeared to be ready to move to a different level in small-group guided instruction, and I did fluency checks with several students by inviting them to whisper read during small-group instruction. On occasion, when I thought a student might struggle with a skill or strategy, I would preteach the concept to him, so he would have prior knowledge and an initial understanding when I taught the concept to the whole class. Overall, the students did very well during our Dav Pilkey theme. They seemed to be especially motivated by his humorous writing and ability to relate to students at their age level.

Giggles Galore: The Humor of Dav Pilkey
Guided Comprehension Strategy: Making Connections
Teaching Idea: Draw and Write Connections

STAGE ONE: Teacher-Directed Whole-Group Instruction

Text: *Dragon Gets By* (1999)

Explain: I explained to the students that good readers make connections to the text before reading, during reading, and after reading. We read or we see illustrations and we think about what we already know about the topic. I explained that we would be learning about a kind of connection called "text–self." Then I said, "For example, if we are reading about cats, we think about what we know about cats and make connections to what we are reading about cats." I provided several examples, including making connections between cats we may have read about, cats we may have as pets, or cats we have seen with friends or neighbors. I further explained that we can say our connections, write about them, and draw and write them, and that our focus today would be Draw and Write Connections.

Demonstrate: I introduced the book by asking students what they already knew about dragons. Their responses included that dragons were animals that lived long ago, that some dragons can breathe fire, and that they know about dragons from reading or listening to books. Then I showed the cover of *Dragon Gets By*, and the students said that dragon looked happy. Then I explained that we would be reading about a mixed-up day in Dragon's life and making connections between what happens to Dragon and things that have happened to us. Then I distributed the Draw and Write Connections blacklines for text–self connections (see Appendix C, page 267). I also placed a transparency of the blackline on the overhead projector. Then I read aloud, stopping at predetermined points. When I stopped, I thought aloud about connections I could make to Dragon's mixed-up day. Then I sketched myself when I am the way Dragon was on his mixed-up day. I sketched myself standing next to my bed in my pajamas. I was dropping a glass, because I woke up groggy. Then I wrote, "*When I wake up groggy, I make mistakes. Sometimes I even drop things on the floor.*" I reminded the students that we can use simple lines and shapes to draw our ideas, and that when we write about our connections, we should use complete sentences. Figure 20 shows my Draw and Write Connections to the beginning of *Dragon Gets By*.

Guide: I continued reading aloud and stopping at additional points during the story to use Draw and Write Connections. I guided students to work with partners to complete their Draw and Write Connections. We shared and discussed their sketches and sentences, noting they had made text–self connections. Then I shared my Draw and Write Connection and discussed it with the students and we discussed the story.

Practice: I finished reading the story, and we discussed the ending. The students thought it was funny that Dragon had watered his bed and gone to sleep in his plants. This time students engaged in Draw and Write Connections on their own. Then we discussed their responses.

Reflect: We reflected on how important it is to make connections while we are reading and how it helps us understand what we read. James said that he liked Draw and Write Connections because they made him think about what he already knew. Amy said she thought that drawing first was a good idea, because to draw, she really needed to think about it a lot. Then we talked about how we could use Draw and Write Connections with other texts.

Guided Comprehension: Giggles Galore: The Humor of Dav Pilkey
Making Connections: Draw and Write Connections

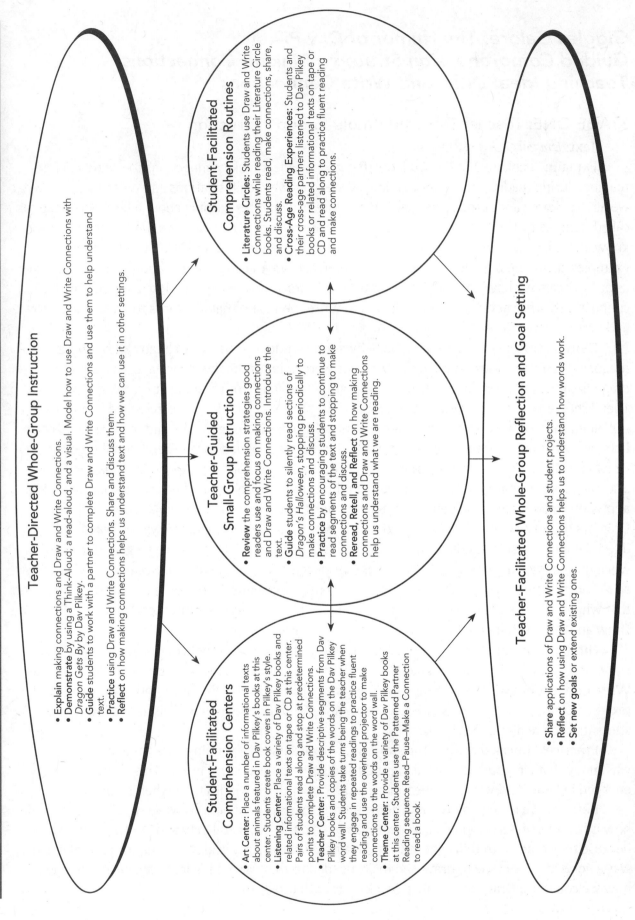

Teacher-Directed Whole-Group Instruction

- **Explain** making connections and Draw and Write Connections.
- **Demonstrate** by using a Think-Aloud, a read-aloud, and a visual. Model how to use Draw and Write Connections with *Dragon Gets By* by Dav Pilkey.
- **Guide** students to work with a partner to complete Draw and Write Connections and use them to help understand text.
- **Practice** using Draw and Write Connections. Share and discuss them.
- **Reflect** on how making connections helps us understand text and how we can use it in other settings.

Student-Facilitated Comprehension Centers

- **Art Center:** Place a number of informational texts about animals featured in Dav Pilkey's books at this center. Students create book covers in Pilkey's style.
- **Listening Center:** Place a variety of Dav Pilkey books and related informational texts on tape or CD at this center. Pairs of students read along and stop at predetermined points to complete Draw and Write Connections.
- **Teacher Center:** Provide descriptive segments from Dav Pilkey books and copies of the words on the Dav Pilkey word wall. Students take turns being the teacher when they engage in repeated readings to practice fluent reading and use the overhead projector to make connections to the words on the word wall.
- **Theme Center:** Provide a variety of Dav Pilkey books at this center. Students use the Patterned Partner Reading sequence Read-Pause-Make a Connection to read a book.

Student-Facilitated Comprehension Routines

- **Literature Circles:** Students use Draw and Write Connections while reading their Literature Circle books. Students read, make connections, share, and discuss.
- **Cross-Age Reading Experiences:** Students and their cross-age partners listened to Dav Pilkey books or related informational texts on tape or CD and read along to practice fluent reading and make connections.

Teacher-Guided Small-Group Instruction

- **Review** the comprehension strategies good readers use and focus on making connections and Draw and Write Connections. Introduce the text.
- **Guide** students to silently read sections of *Dragon's Halloween*, stopping periodically to make connections and discuss.
- **Practice** by encouraging students to continue to read segments of the text and stopping to make connections and discuss.
- **Reread, Retell, and Reflect** on how making connections and Draw and Write Connections help us understand what we are reading.

Teacher-Facilitated Whole-Group Reflection and Goal Setting

- **Share** applications of Draw and Write Connections and student projects.
- **Reflect** on how using Draw and Write Connections helps us to understand how words work.
- **Set new goals** or extend existing ones.

Figure 20. Teacher's Draw and Write Connection for *Dragon Gets By*

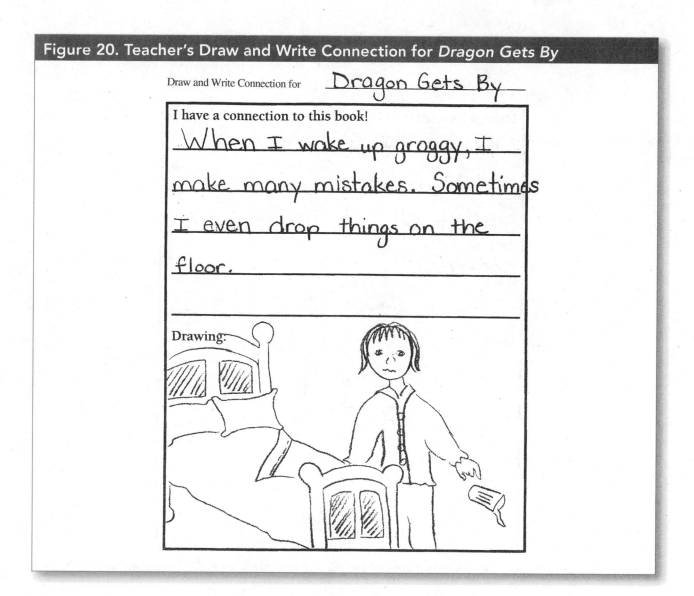

Draw and Write Connection for <u>Dragon Gets By</u>

I have a connection to this book!

When I wake up groggy, I make many mistakes. Sometimes I even drop things on the floor.

Drawing:

STAGE TWO: Teacher-Guided Small-Group Instruction

Text: *Dragon's Halloween* (2003) (Texts varied according to students' abilities.)

Review: I reviewed the comprehension strategies good readers use and focused on making connections using Draw and Write Connections.

Guide: I introduced *Dragon's Halloween* and, after sharing the title and cover, I guided students use Draw and Write Connections by sharing the prompt "I have a connection to this book...." The students' responses were connections they were able to make to Halloween. Then the students silently read the first section of the text and shared their ideas through Draw and Write Connections. Figure 21 shows Christina's Draw and Write Connection to *Dragon's Halloween*.

Practice: Students continued to read silently and share connections at designated points. When they had finished reading the story, the students shared their final connections and we discussed the story.

Reread, Retell, and Reflect: Students whisper read selected sections of the story and engaged in Patterned Partner Retelling. I used that time to complete a running record with a student who seemed to be ready to move to the next level. Next, we reflected on the importance of making

Figure 21. Christina's Draw and Write Connection for *Dragon's Halloween*

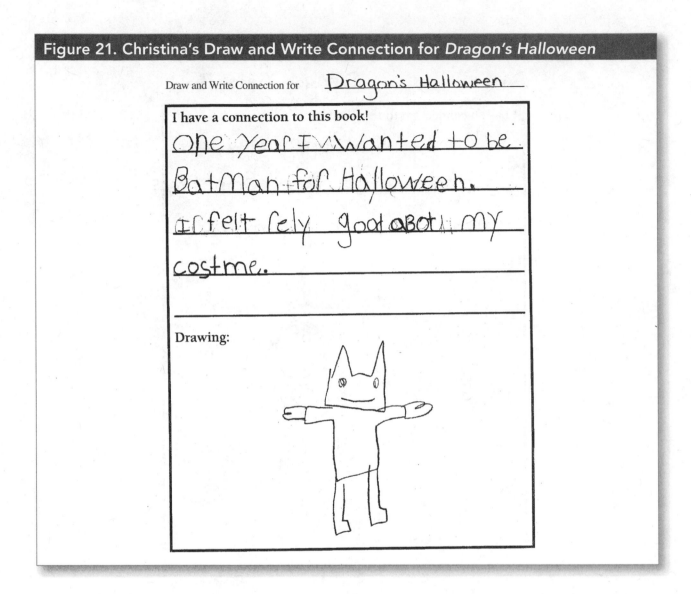

Draw and Write Connection for ___Dragon's Halloween___

I have a connection to this book!

one year I wanted to be Batman for Halloween. I felt rely good about my costme.

Drawing:

connections and how Draw and Write Connections helped us to better understand the text. Aliya said that everything that she reads and everything that happens in her life every day helps her to make better connections.

Student-Facilitated Comprehension Centers

Art Center: A variety of informational books about animals Dav Pilkey had written about were available at this center, along with a wide range of art supplies. Students chose a book to read and used bright-colored markers to create a Pilkey-style book cover for that animal. Students made connections between Pilkey's books and the animals they read about.

Listening Center: I placed a variety of Dav Pilkey books and related informational texts on tape or CD at this center. Students worked with partners to listen, read along, and stop at predetermined points to Draw and Write Connections.

Teacher Center: Pairs of students took turns being the "teacher" as they "read the room." This included reading the word wall, bulletin boards, and posters in the classroom. They also took turns being the "teacher" as they practiced their oral reading fluency by reading excerpts from Dav Pilkey books. The students completed Center Reflections (see Appendix D, page 301) and included them in their center folders.

Theme Center: I provided a variety of Dav Pilkey books at this center. Students worked with a partner to read the books using the Patterned Partner Reading pattern Read–Pause–Make Connections (see Appendix C, pages 239–240).

Student-Facilitated Comprehension Routines

Literature Circles: The students selected Dav Pilkey books to read in Literature Circles. As they read, they completed Draw and Write Connections. They shared their connections while discussing the book. When they finished reading the book, the students created puppets and retold the story to the class.

Cross-Age Reading Experiences: Students and their cross-age partners listened to Dav Pilkey books or related informational texts on tape or CD and read along to practice fluent reading. While reading, students made connections using Connection Stems such as "That reminds me of..." and "I can make a connection to that..." (character, animal, or story).

STAGE THREE: Teacher-Facilitated Whole-Group Reflection and Goal Setting

Share: Students shared and discussed their Draw and Label Connections, their projects, and their center and routine reflections in small groups. Then they shared selected applications with the whole class.

Reflect: We reflected on how using Draw and Write Connections helped us to make connections with the texts we read. The students also shared their thoughts about how making connections helped us to understand what we read and how we can make connections in other subjects, such as science and social studies.

Set New Goals: The students decided to set a goal to use Draw and Write Connections in our other classes. They also decided to extend their goal of making connections by learning about Double-Entry Journals.

Assessment Options

I observed students as they read, as they engaged in Draw and Write Connections, and as they worked with partners. I reviewed students' completed connections to assess their ability to make connections. I also read and commented on students' center and routine self-assessments. During small-group instruction, I completed running records with students who seemed ready to move to the next level. I also completed fluency checks with students throughout the theme. I pretaught a small group of students that I thought might need some additional background knowledge and practice using strategies. I also made adaptations to the blacklines we used when teaching English-language learners, struggling readers, and students with special needs. In addition, I ensured that students had accessible text when they were involved in teacher-guided small-group instruction and when they worked independently in centers and routines.

Giggles Galore: The Humor of Dav Pilkey
Guided Comprehension Strategy: Summarizing
Teaching Idea: Lyric Retelling

STAGE ONE: Teacher-Directed Whole-Group Instruction

Text: *Dog Breath: The Horrible Trouble With Hally Tosis* (2004)

Explain: I began by reminding students that we had already learned that when we summarize, we should include the important information from the text. Next, I focused on retelling and reviewed the narrative elements. I shared the Lyric Retelling blackline (see Appendix C, page 278) and noted that when we wrote our Lyric Retellings, we would need to include the important points from the story—the characters, setting, problem, attempts to resolve the problem, and resolution. I also reminded students that we would need to retell what happened in the story in the correct sequence. Next, I explained that our Lyric Retellings would be different from other retellings because we would be choosing a song that everyone knew and writing our retelling as new lyrics— or words—for that song.

Demonstrate: I demonstrated by using a Think-Aloud and an overhead projector. I explained that we would be writing our Lyric Retelling about *Bad Breath: The Horrible Trouble With Hally Tosis*, which we had read earlier in the day. To help focus our retelling, we completed a Story Map (see Appendix C, pages 247–248 and 289) that included characters, setting, problem, attempts to resolve the problem, and resolution. Then we read the map to help us retell the story. I said,

> I can see on the Story Map that we think the characters are Hally Tosis, the Tosis family, and the burglars. The map also reminds me that the setting is the Tosis family's house and the town they live in.

Next, I said, "I can tell by looking at the Story Map that we think the problem is Hally Tosis's bad breath." Then I asked the students to share one of the attempts to resolve the problem. The students quickly responded with the three attempts: the mountain with the breathtaking view, the movie, and the roller coaster. Then they told me that the problem was resolved when Hally Tosis caught the burglars and got to stay with the Tosis family.

Guide: I guided the students to choose a song we could use to create our Lyric Retelling. I explained to the students that everyone needed to know the song the class chose. After a brief discussion, we decided to use the children's song "Are You Sleeping?" Everyone knew it, so I suggested that we all sing that song with its original lyrics, and the students were happy to do so. Next, we began writing our Lyric Retelling. I said, "I think I will repeat phrases like we did when we sang, 'Are You Sleeping?'" Then I wrote, "*Hally Tosis, Hally Tosis, you have bad breath, you have bad breath.*" I sang those two lines and the students sang with me. I wrote two more lines: "*Will the children save you? Will the children save you? We don't know. We don't know.*" Then the children and I sang the chorus together. Next, I guided the students to work with partners to suggest ideas for subsequent lines, and we completed four more verses.

Practice: We practiced by continuing to write the next four verses of our Lyric Retelling. I recorded the lyrics on the overhead transparency. Then we were ready to sing it. This is our completed Lyric Retelling:

Guided Comprehension: Giggles Galore: The Humor of Dav Pilkey
Summarizing: Lyric Retelling

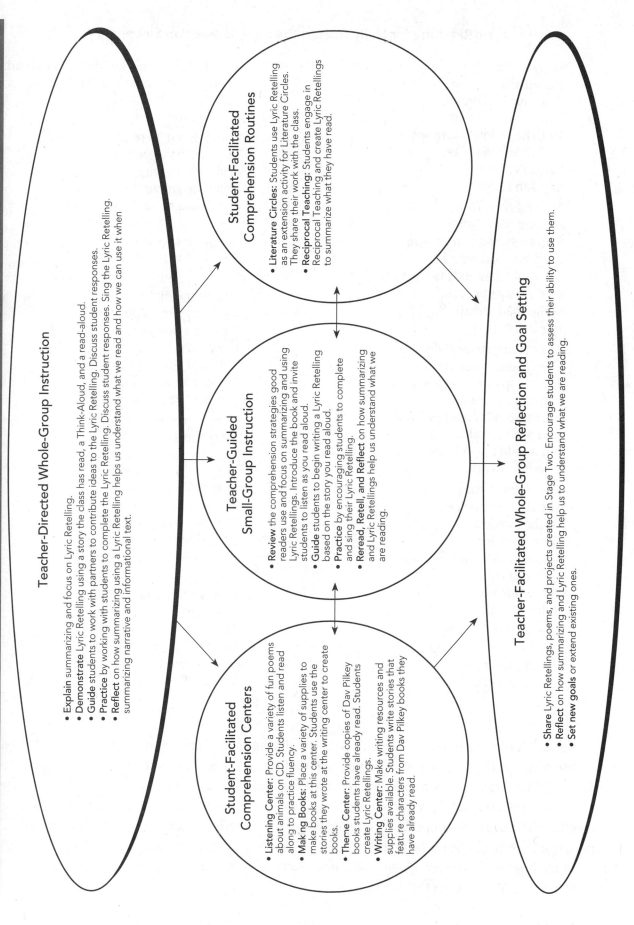

Teacher-Directed Whole-Group Instruction

- **Explain** summarizing and focus on Lyric Retelling.
- **Demonstrate** Lyric Retelling using a story the class has read, a Think-Aloud, and a read-aloud.
- **Guide** students to work with partners to contribute ideas to the Lyric Retelling. Discuss student responses.
- **Practice** by working with students to complete the Lyric Retelling. Discuss student responses. Sing the Lyric Retelling.
- **Reflect** on how summarizing using a Lyric Retelling helps us understand what we read and how we can use it when summarizing narrative and informational text.

Student-Facilitated Comprehension Centers

- **Listening Center:** Provide a variety of fun poems about animals on CD. Students listen and read along to practice fluency.
- **Making Books:** Place a variety of supplies to make books at this center. Students use the stories they wrote at the writing center to create books.
- **Theme Center:** Provide copies of Dav Pilkey books students have already read. Students create Lyric Retellings.
- **Writing Center:** Make writing resources and supplies available. Students write stories that feature characters from Dav Pilkey books they have already read.

Teacher-Guided Small-Group Instruction

- **Review** the comprehension strategies good readers use and focus on summarizing and using Lyric Retellings. Introduce the book and invite students to listen as you read aloud.
- **Guide** students to begin writing a Lyric Retelling based on the story you read aloud.
- **Practice** by encouraging students to complete and sing their Lyric Retelling.
- **Reread, Retell, and Reflect** on how summarizing and Lyric Retellings help us understand what we are reading.

Student-Facilitated Comprehension Routines

- **Literature Circles:** Students use Lyric Retelling as an extension activity for Literature Circles. They share their work with the class.
- **Reciprocal Teaching:** Students engage in Reciprocal Teaching and create Lyric Retellings to summarize what they have read.

Teacher-Facilitated Whole-Group Reflection and Goal Setting

- **Share** Lyric Retellings, poems, and projects created in Stage Two. Encourage students to assess their ability to use them.
- **Reflect** on how summarizing and Lyric Retelling help us to understand what we are reading.
- **Set new goals** or extend existing ones.

Lyric Retelling for Hally Tosis to the tune of "Are You Sleeping?"

Hally Tosis,
Hally Tosis,
You have bad breath.
You have bad breath.
Will the children save you?
Will the children save you?
We don't know.
We don't know.

Mr. and Mrs. Tosis,
Mr. and Mrs. Tosis,
Said Hally had bad breath,
Hally had bad breath.
They told their kids to help her,
Find a way to get rid
Of her bad breath,
Her bad breath.

The children took Hally,
The children took Hally
To the top of a mountain,
Top of a mountain.
It had a breathtaking view,
Had a breathtaking view,
But it didn't help Hally
Lose her breath.

The children took Hally,
The children took Hally,
To the movies,
To the movies,
To see *Breath of a Salesman*,
To see *Breath of a Salesman*,
But it didn't help,
It didn't help.

The children took Hally,
The children took Hally,
On a roller coaster,
On a roller coaster.

They thought she would lose her breath,
Thought she would lose her breath,
But she didn't,
But she didn't.

The children were sad,
The parents were sad,
Hally was moving out,
Hally was moving out.
She would leave the next day,
She would leave the next day.
Everyone was sad,
Everyone was sad.

During the night,
During the night,
Two burglars crept in,
Two burglars crept in.
Hally did not bark,
Hally did not bite.
She just kissed them,
She just kissed them.

Now everyone loves Hally,
Everyone loves Hally.
The burglars passed out,
The burglars passed out.
Now Hally is a famous,
Very, very famous
Crime-fighting dog,
Crime-fighting dog.

Hally Tosis,
Hally Tosis,
Lives with her family,
Lives with her family.
They say she is a wonderful,
Say she is a wonderful,
Wonderful watchdog,
Wonderful watchdog.

Reflect: We reflected on how using Lyric Retellings to summarize helped us understand what we were reading. The students also learned that writing Lyric Retellings is a lot of fun. They enjoyed trying to fit their ideas into a particular line of a song, and had a good time working with classmates to complete the retelling. They also enjoyed singing each line as we wrote it and singing the song to the point where we had stopped, so we could easily add more lyrics. It was a great learning experience. As Pietro, one of the students, said, "It is singing what we read about, and Hally's story was funny, but we were really giggling when we were writing and singing about it. It was fun and I remember everything about the story."

STAGE TWO: Teacher-Guided Small-Group Instruction

Text: *The Hallo-Wiener* (1999) (Texts varied according to students' abilities.)

Review: I began by reviewing the strategies good readers use and focusing on summarizing. Next, I reviewed how to create Lyric Retellings. I reminded students of the Lyric Retelling we had completed in Stage One, and that everyone in the small group would be working together to create a Lyric Retelling.

Guide: I introduced *The Hallo-Wiener* by discussing the title and cover with the students. They made connections to the holiday, the dogs, and the mustard-covered bun the dachshund was wearing for a Halloween costume. I guided the students to silently read the book. We stopped at predetermined points to discuss and make connections. While the students were reading, I invited a student to whisper read so I could complete a fluency check.

Practice: We practiced by writing a Lyric Retelling for *The Hallo-Wiener*. The students suggested our song should be "Jingle Bells," and we began by singing the song with its original lyrics. Then I invited students to contribute ideas and we wrote the following Lyric Retelling:

The Hallo-Wiener: A Lyric Retelling to the Tune of "Jingle Bells"

Halloween, Halloween,
Halloween's on its way
Oscar and his friends can't
Wait for Halloween day!
Halloween, Halloween,
Halloween's on its way
Oscar and his friends can't
Wait for Halloween day!

As soon as school is out
Oscar will hurry home
And make his very scary costume
To trick or treat tonight

Oscar's mother had a gift
And much to his surprise
When he opened it up
He couldn't believe his eyes

Halloween, Halloween,
Halloween's on its way
Oscar and his friends can't
Wait for Halloween day
Halloween, Halloween,
Halloween's on its way
Oscar and his friends can't
Wait for Halloween day!

A giant hot dog bun
Complete with yellow mustard
His mother wanted him to wear
But Oscar wouldn't dare

But to please his mom
Oscar put the costume on
His friends made fun of him
But later they'd be in a pond

Halloween, Halloween,
Halloween's on its way
Oscar and his friends can't
Wait for Halloween day!
Halloween, Halloween,
Halloween's on its way
Oscar and his friends can't
Wait for Halloween day!

A monster chased them into
The water oh so cold
But Oscar could see that it was
Just two cats on a pole

Oscar came to the rescue
And scared the cats away
And floated out to his friends
And saved the day. Hurray!

Halloween, Halloween,
Halloween's on its way
Oscar and his friends can't
Wait for Halloween day
Halloween Halloween
Halloween's on its way
Oscar and his friends can't
Wait for Halloween day!

Then all the dogs were pals
And Oscar got some treats
They said he was a hero
And Oscar was happy.

Everyone had fun
And ate lots of sweets
Even though it was a scary Halloween
It was a special treat!

Reread, Retell, and Reflect: We sang our Lyric Retelling and then we reflected on how summarizing using Lyric Retellings helped us understand what we read. Betsy said, "It's like the book is a song in my head now," and everyone agreed it was fun to sing our summary.

Student-Facilitated Comprehension Centers

Listening Center: I provided a wide variety of fun animal poems on CD at this center. Sources I used included *Poetry for Young People: Animal Poems* by John Hollander and Simona Mulazzani (2004); *Eric Carle's Animals, Animals* by Lauren Whipple (compiler) and Eric Carle (illustrator) (1999); and *Animal Poems* by Valerie Worth (2007). Students listened and read along to practice their fluency.

Making Books Center: After students wrote their stories in the writing center, they created covers for them at this center and placed them in a special section in our classroom library. Students shared their books with the class in Stage Three of Guided Comprehension.

Theme Center: Students worked in groups of four to create Lyric Retellings for story poems or Dav Pilkey books. They selected music, wrote lyrics, and practiced performing their Lyric Retelling. They sang their Lyric Retelling for the class during Stage Three.

Writing Center: I placed many different writing resources and supplies at this center. Students worked with partners to write new stories that featured Dav Pilkey characters. Titles of the students' stories included *Kat Kong Comes to School*, *Dogzilla Is Really Our Dog*, and *Ricky Ricotta Is Our Friend*.

Student-Facilitated Comprehension Routines

Literature Circles: Students used their Lyric Retellings as extension activities for the books they had just finished reading. They revisited the narrative elements of the story by completing a Story Map. Then they wrote their Lyric Retelling, practiced it, and sang it for the class during Stage Three.

Reciprocal Teaching: Students engaged in Reciprocal Teaching and then recorded the narrative elements on the Story Map blackline. They wrote their Lyric Retellings and shared them with the class in Stage Three.

STAGE THREE: Teacher-Facilitated Whole-Group Reflection and Goal Setting

Share: Students shared their work in small groups and then with the whole class. They sang their Lyric Retellings from Stage Two and shared projects such as the books they created. It was a fun sharing session because of all the singing. The students enjoyed singing and being audience members. They also enjoyed sharing their books and received a lot of positive feedback from the other students.

Reflect: We reflected on our understanding of summarizing and our ability to create Lyric Retellings. The students noted that writing the retelling as words to songs helped them to remember the stories.

Set New Goals: We decided that we all felt confident creating Lyric Retellings for story poems and stories. So, we extended our goal to learn how to summarize using Lyric Summaries with informational text.

Assessment Options

I observed students throughout the Guided Comprehension process and reviewed and commented on their Lyric Retellings, cinquains, and story poems. I also reviewed the students' self-assessments and completed fluency checks and running records as needed.

Final Thoughts About the Dav Pilkey Theme

Dav Pilkey's humor and writing style were wonderfully welcomed by all the primary classes I observed using this theme. Students delighted in reading about every character from Hally Tosis to Ricky Ricotta, and students and teachers alike celebrated Pilkey's amazing ability to write from such humorous perspectives.

As noted earlier in this book, lessons on a variety of skills that underpin comprehension strategies were taught during this theme. For example, aspects of language development, such as phonemic awareness and phonics, and skills such as sequencing, generating questions, and distinguishing important from less important ideas were embedded in the theme. (For ideas about how to use literature to teach phonemic awareness, phonics, and fluency, see Appendix B.) For example, Dav Pilkey titles such as *Dogzilla* and *'Twas the Night Before Thanksgiving* were used to teach sequencing. *Dogbreath: The Horrible Trouble With Hally Tosis* and *The Hallo-Wiener* served as the bases of lessons about text structures such as cause and effect and problem and solution. To improve fluency, students read along with books on CD and used a variety of Dav Pilkey books in Readers Theatre. Because many of Pilkey's stories have such clearly defined dilemmas, they sparked question generation and reflection. Students' abilities to make connections to the author, his characters, and his illustrations motivated them to read and promoted their engagement in learning. In addition, teachers adapted lessons for prereaders and prewriters by engaging in read-alouds and encouraging response through a variety of modes, including discussion, drawing, painting, singing, dancing, and dramatizing.

Theme Resources

Books

Pilkey, D. (1987). *World war won.* Kansas City, MO: Landmark Editions.

Pilkey, D. (1994). *The dumb bunnies.* New York: Scholastic.

Pilkey, D. (1994). *A friend for dragon.* New York: Scholastic.

Pilkey, D. (1995). *Dragon's fat cat.* New York: Orchard.

Pilkey, D. (1995). *The dumb bunnies' Easter.* New York: Scholastic.

Pilkey, D. (1995). *The Moonglow Roll-o-Rama.* New York: Scholastic.

Pilkey, D. (1996). *Make way for dumb bunnies.* New York: Scholastic.

Pilkey, D. (1996). *When cats dream.* New York: Orchard.

Pilkey, D. (1997). *The adventures of Captain Underpants.* New York: Scholastic.

Pilkey, D. (1997). *Big Dog and Little Dog getting in trouble.* New York: Red Wagon.

Pilkey, D. (1997). *Big Dog and Little Dog going for a walk.* New York: Red Wagon.

Pilkey, D. (1998). *Big Dog and Little Dog wearing sweaters.* New York: Red Wagon.

Pilkey, D. (1999). *Big Dog and Little Dog making a mistake.* New York: Red Wagon.

Pilkey, D. (1999). *Captain Underpants and the attack of the talking toilets.* New York: Scholastic.

Pilkey, D. (1999). *Dragon gets by.* New York: Orchard.

Pilkey, D. (1999). *God bless the gargoyles.* New York: Voyager.

Pilkey, D. (1999). *The Hallo-wiener.* New York: Scholastic.

Pilkey, D. (1999). *The paperboy.* New York: Scholastic.

Pilkey, D. (2000). *Captain Underpants and the perilous plot of Professor Poopypants*. New York: Scholastic.

Pilkey, D. (2000). *Ricky Ricotta's mighty robot vs. the mutant mosquitoes from Mercury*. New York: Scholastic.

Pilkey, D. (2000). *The silly gooses*. New York: Scholastic.

Pilkey, D. (2001). *Captain Underpants and the wrath of the wicked wedgie woman*. New York: Scholastic.

Pilkey, D. (2001). *The Captain Underpants extra-crunchy book o' fun*. New York: Blue Sky Press.

Pilkey, D. (2001). *Ricky Ricotta's mighty robot vs. the voodoo vultures from Venus*. New York: Scholastic.

Pilkey, D. (2002). *The all new Captain Underpants extra-crunchy book o' fun 2*. New York: Blue Sky Press.

Pilkey, D. (2002). *Ricky Ricotta's mighty robot vs. the Jurassic jackrabbits from Jupiter*. New York: Scholastic.

Pilkey, D. (2002). *Ricky Ricotta's mighty robot vs. the mecha-monkeys from Mars*. New York: Scholastic.

Pilkey, D. (2003). *Captain Underpants and the big, bad battle of the bionic booger boy Part 1: The night of the nasty nostril nuggets*. New York: Scholastic.

Pilkey, D. (2003). *Captain Underpants and the big, bad battle of the bionic booger boy Part 2: The revenge of the ridiculous robo-boogers*. New York: Scholastic.

Pilkey, D. (2003). *The complete adventures of Big Dog and Little Dog*. New York: Harcourt.

Pilkey, D. (2003). *Dogzilla*. New York: Harcourt.

Pilkey, D. (2003). *Dragon's Halloween*. New York: Orchard.

Pilkey, D. (2003). *Dragon's merry Christmas*. New York: Orchard.

Pilkey, D. (2003). *Kat Kong*. New York: Harcourt.

Pilkey, D. (2003). *Ricky Ricotta's mighty robot vs. the stupid stinkbugs from Saturn*. New York: Blue Sky Press.

Pilkey, D. (2004). *Dog breath: The horrible trouble with Hally Tosis*. New York: Scholastic.

Pilkey, D. (2004). *'Twas the night before Thanksgiving*. New York: Scholastic.

Pilkey, D. (2005). *Ricky Ricotta's mighty robot vs. the uranium unicorns from Uranus*. New York: Blue Sky Press.

Pilkey, D. (2006). *Captain Underpants: Three more wedgie-powered adventures*. New York: Scholastic.

Pilkey, D. (2006). *Ricky Ricotta's mighty robot*. New York: Blue Sky Press.

Pilkey, D. (2008). *Captain Underpants and the invasion of the incredibly naughty cafeteria ladies from outer space*. New York: Blue Sky Press.

Pilkey, D. (2009). *The dumb bunnies go to the zoo*. New York: Blue Sky Press.

Websites About Dav Pilkey

Dav Pilkey
> www.pilkey.com

Educational Book & Media Association: Biographical Essay
> www.edupaperback.org/showauth.cfm?authid=245

Houghton Mifflin Reading: Meet the Author/Illustrator
> www.eduplace.com/kids/hmr/mtai/pilkey.html

Kidsreads.com: Bio and Author Talk
> www.kidsreads.com/authors/au-pilkey-dav.asp

Reading Is Fundamental Reading Planet: Meet the Authors and Illustrators, Interview, and Book List
www.rif.org/kids/readingplanet/bookzone/pilkey.htm

Scholastic: Biography
www2.scholastic.com/browse/contributor.jsp?id=3499

Scholastic: The Online Adventures of Captain Underpants
www.scholastic.com/captainunderpants/index.htm

ThinkQuest: Biography
library.thinkquest.org/J001156/author%20reviews/sl_pilkey_bio.htm

Performance Extensions Across the Curriculum

Art

- Encourage students to use washable watercolors to paint their favorite type of animal. Compile the pictures to make a class book. Be sure to invite the artists to sign their work.

- Design a classroom mural based on Dav Pilkey's books. Students can draw Kat Kong, Dogzilla, Oscar, Hally Tosis, Ricky Ricotta, and other characters from his books, and write words to describe them.

Math

- Cut pet supply store ads from newspapers or print them from the Internet. Choose two or three things to buy. Write a list of these things, and work with a partner to determine how much your order would cost. Student cashiers add the costs and student customers check the bills and pay them. Using play money, cashiers and customers learn how to count money and make change.

- Brainstorm types of dogs with your class (such as bulldog, poodle, Akita, or dachshund). Invite each student to select his or her favorite dog. Survey the students and show their preferences on a pie chart. Perform various math operations using the figures in the chart. Determine which dog type is the most popular and the least popular.

Music

- As a class, read a fun book, such as *Ricky Ricotta's Mighty Robot* by Dav Pilkey. Make a list of interesting facts about the book. Select a simple, popular song the entire class knows. Create a Lyric Retelling written to the tune of the selected song.

- Create a class transmediation by turning information from a book, such as *Kat Kong* by Dav Pilkey, into a song, or by turning a song into a picture book or form poem.

Science

- After reading a book about robots, such as Dav Pilkey's *Ricky Ricotta's Mighty Robot vs. the Jurassic Jackrabbits From Jupiter*, invite students to build their own robots and write a sentence or paragraph telling about them. Students can only use parts they find around their homes, such as empty tissue boxes, shoe boxes, cardboard rolls from paper towels, straws, and aluminum foil, to build their robots.

- Encourage students to imagine that they are preparing to visit the Jurassic Jackrabbits on Jupiter, the Mecha-Monkeys on Mars, or the Mutant Mosquitoes on Mercury. Invite the students to work with partners to locate interesting facts about the planet of their choice to prepare for their trip.

Bookmark relevant websites on class computers for students to use. Then invite the pairs of students to create a page for the class book *Fun Facts About Jupiter, Mars, and Mercury.*

Social Studies

- Invite the class to engage in inquiry about animals. Make a list of the types of dogs that help people (such police dogs and guide dogs). Brainstorm questions the class has about the dogs. Place a picture of each dog on a separate poster board. Divide the class into small groups and invite groups to find answers to their questions using teacher-selected online articles and informational books. Small groups will share their discoveries with the class. This can also be completed as a whole-class activity.

- Engage in an inquiry activity to stimulate interest and questioning about various types of dogs around the world. Either the whole class or several small groups will choose a dog that represents a country or territory (such as a German shepherd, Siberian husky, or Irish setter). Questions Into Paragraphs (QuIP; see Appendix C, pages 245–246 and 284) can be used to organize questions and responses. Either the whole class can display and discuss the information that was learned, or each small group can take turns presenting its information to the class.

Culminating Activity

Giggles and More: A Celebration of Favorite Author Dav Pilkey. Invite parents and community members to participate in this theme celebration. Display students' projects from the Dav Pilkey theme. Invite students to dramatize scenes from selected books, display their acrostics, and share the sequels they wrote based on Pilkey's characters. Create a variety of stations where students can explain their other theme-based projects. Provide visitors with interactive opportunities for feedback on the celebration, such as writing comments on a class mural or e-mailing comments to students on class computers. Students will autograph copies of the class book *Dav Pilkey ABC* and give them as gifts to their families.

CHAPTER 10

Oceans Alive: Sea Creatures, Coral Reefs, Ecology, and More!

Oceans fascinate us. Whether we are swimming in them or learning about them, they are sources of wonder and amazement for us and our students. We are in awe of the sheer presence of whales and dolphins and find ourselves mesmerized by underwater worlds of colorful fish and coral reefs. Oceans provide habitats for sea creatures, food for people, valuable ecological information, venues for recreation and commerce, and a home for one of Earth's most precious resources: water.

The sample Theme-Based Plan for Guided Comprehension: Oceans Alive: Sea Creatures, Coral Reefs, Ecology, and More! (see Figure 22) offers an overview of the lessons and resources that support this theme. The plan begins by listing theme goals and making connections to state standards. The student goals for this theme include the following:

- Use appropriate comprehension skills and strategies
- Interpret and respond to text
- Communicate effectively

These goals support the following state standards:

- Learning to read independently
- Reading, analyzing, and interpreting text
- Types and quality of writing
- Speaking and listening

Sample assessments in this theme include observation, running records, student writing, skill and strategy applications, and student self-assessments. The Guided Comprehension lessons are based on the following strategies and corresponding teaching ideas:

- Previewing: Anticipation/Reaction Guide
- Knowing How Words Work: Concept of Definition Map
- Self-Questioning: Paired Questioning
- Visualizing: Draw and Write Visualizations

First Encyclopedia of Seas and Oceans (Denne, 2001), *Coral Reef* (Davis, 1997), *Flotsam* (Wiesner, 2006), and *What Do Sharks Eat for Dinner? Questions and Answers About Sharks* (Berger & Berger,

Figure 22. Theme-Based Plan for Guided Comprehension: Oceans Alive: Sea Creatures, Coral Reefs, Ecology, and More!

Goals and Related State Standards

Students will

- Use appropriate comprehension skills and strategies. Standard: learning to read independently
- Interpret and respond to text. Standard: reading, analyzing, and interpreting text
- Communicate effectively. Standards: types and quality of writing; speaking and listening

Assessment

The following measures can be used for a variety of purposes, including diagnostic, formative, and summative assessment:

Anticipation/Reaction Guide	Paired Questioning
Concept of Definition Map	Running Records
Draw and Write Visualizations	Student Self-Assessments
Observation	Student Writing

Comprehension Strategies

1. Previewing
2. Knowing How Words Work
3. Self-Questioning
4. Visualizing

Teaching Ideas

1. Anticipation/Reaction Guide
2. Concept of Definition Map
3. Paired Questioning
4. Draw and Write Visualizations

Comprehension Centers

Students will apply the comprehension strategies and related teaching ideas in the following comprehension centers:

ABC Center	Making Books Center
Art Center	Poetry Center
Drama Center	Theme Center
Making and Writing Words Center	Writing Center

Comprehension Routines

Students will apply the comprehension strategies and related teaching ideas in the following comprehension routines:

Literature Circles
Reciprocal Teaching
Cross-Age Reading Experiences

	Title	Level
1.	*First Encyclopedia of Seas and Oceans*	PreK–3
2.	*Coral Reef*	4–7
3.	*Flotsam*	PreK–3
4.	*What Do Sharks Eat for Dinner?*	PreK–3

Technology Resources

All About Oceans and Seas
www.enchantedlearning.com/subjects/ocean/
Oceans Field Trip
www.field-trips.org/tours/sci/oceank/_tourlaunch1.htm
Planet Ocean
school.discoveryeducation.com/schooladventures/
planetocean

2001) are the texts used in Stage One for teacher-directed whole-group instruction. Numerous additional theme-related resources, including texts, websites, performances across the curriculum, and a culminating activity, are presented in the Theme Resources at the end of the chapter.

Examples of comprehension centers students use during Stage Two of Guided Comprehension include ABC, art, drama, making and writing words, making books, poetry, theme, and writing. Students also engage in strategy application in comprehension routines such as Literature Circles, Reciprocal Teaching, and Cross-Age Reading Experiences. Sample websites complete the overview.

In this chapter, all the lessons focus on books about oceans. The lessons are appropriate for all learners, including English learners, struggling readers, and students with special needs. To accommodate these learners, the lessons include multiple modes of response (such as singing, sketching, and dramatizing), working with partners, books on CD, cross-age experiences, and extra guided instruction. Ideas used to differentiate instruction in these lessons include the following:

- Content—the information being taught

  - Using leveled text to accommodate students' abilities in teacher-guided small groups, centers, and routines
  - Providing leveled texts that accommodate student interest and help motivate them to read

- Process—the way in which the information is taught

  - Activating prior knowledge and/or providing background information
  - Scaffolding student learning by using the Guided Comprehension Model
  - Reading the text aloud during Stage One to make it accessible to all students
  - Using visuals to support students' construction of meaning
  - Adapting graphic organizers; providing paragraph frames
  - Encouraging students to work with peers in pairs and small groups to provide additional support
  - Preteaching students who may need additional support to use the strategies and skills such as sequencing and generating questions at multiple levels

- Product—how the students demonstrate their learning

  - Integrating alternative modes of representation, such as art, drama, poetry, or music
  - Providing opportunities for students to use computers when creating projects

Guided Comprehension Lessons

Oceans Alive: Sea Creatures, Coral Reefs, Ecology, and More!
Guided Comprehension Strategy: Previewing
Teaching Idea: Anticipation/Reaction Guide

STAGE ONE: Teacher-Directed Whole-Group Instruction

Text: *First Encyclopedia of Seas and Oceans* (Denne, 2001)

Explain: I began by explaining previewing and focusing on the Anticipation/Reaction Guide (see Appendix C, page 214). I said,

> Previewing is a reading comprehension strategy that involves activating background knowledge, predicting, and setting purposes for reading. That means we need to think about what we already know about the topic, make predictions, and then read to confirm or disconfirm our predictions.

Then I said,

> One way we can preview text is to use an Anticipation/Reaction Guide. We use this technique when we are reading informational text. Anticipation/Reaction Guides help us to activate our prior knowledge, make connections to text, set purposes for reading, and develop more accurate understandings of informational text.

Next, I showed students the Anticipation/Reaction Guide we would be using during Stage One. I pointed out that the guide consisted of three statements that related to an informational text about oceans. I explained that the statements may be true, or they may not be true. I said,

> Before reading the text, we read the statements and indicate whether we agree or disagree with each one of them by placing a check in that column. Then we discuss our responses. Next, we read the text. After reading, we revisit the statements and decide whether our thinking has changed. If it has, we place an "X" in that column to indicate that reading the text changed our thinking. After that, we discuss again and explain any changes that may have occurred in our thinking. We use Anticipation/Reaction Guides before and after reading informational texts.

Demonstrate: I demonstrated by using a Think-Aloud, a read-aloud, an Anticipation/Reaction Guide, and an overhead projector. I began by reading the statements that appeared on the guide and showing where we place a check mark to indicate whether we agreed or disagreed with each statement. I read the first statement: "*Some fish travel in schools.*" Then I said, "I know that fish sometimes travel in groups and I know those groups are called schools, so I am going to agree with this statement." Then I placed a check in the agree column for statement one, and discussed my response with the students. I asked them to discuss with a partner whether they agreed or disagreed with statement one. When we discussed their responses, they said that they also agreed with the statement, because we learned that fish travel in schools several times throughout our theme, and we had seen some travel in schools during theme-related field trips. I encouraged the students to place a check in the agree column for statement one on our Anticipation/Reaction Guide.

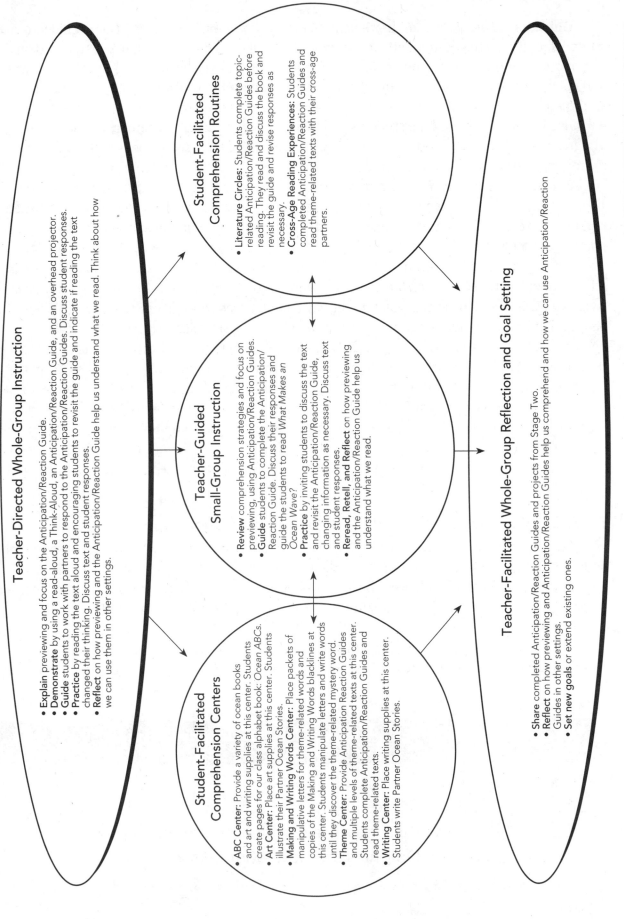

Teacher-Directed Whole-Group Instruction

- **Explain** previewing and focus on the Anticipation/Reaction Guide.
- **Demonstrate** by using a read-aloud, a Think-Aloud, an Anticipation/Reaction Guide, and an overhead projector.
- **Guide** students to work with partners to respond to the Anticipation/Reaction Guides. Discuss student responses.
- **Practice** by reading the text aloud and encouraging students to revisit the guide and indicate if reading the text changed their thinking. Discuss text and student responses.
- **Reflect** on how previewing and the Anticipation/Reaction Guide help us understand what we read. Think about how we can use them in other settings.

Student-Facilitated Comprehension Routines

- **Literature Circles:** Students complete topic-related Anticipation/Reaction Guides before reading. They read and discuss the book and revisit the guide and revise responses as necessary.
- **Cross-Age Reading Experiences:** Students completed Anticipation/Reaction Guides and read theme-related texts with their cross-age partners.

Teacher-Guided Small-Group Instruction

- **Review** comprehension strategies and focus on previewing, using Anticipation/Reaction Guides.
- **Guide** students to complete the Anticipation/Reaction Guide. Discuss their responses and guide the students to read *What Makes an Ocean Wave?*
- **Practice** by inviting students to discuss the text and revisit the Anticipation/Reaction Guide, changing information as necessary. Discuss text and student responses.
- **Reread, Retell, and Reflect** on how previewing and the Anticipation/Reaction Guide help us understand what we read.

Student-Facilitated Comprehension Centers

- **ABC Center:** Provide a variety of ocean books and art and writing supplies at this center. Students create pages for our class alphabet book: *Ocean ABCs.*
- **Art Center:** Place art supplies at this center. Students illustrate their Partner Ocean Stories.
- **Making and Writing Words Center:** Place packets of manipulative letters for theme-related words and copies of the Making and Writing Words blacklines at this center. Students manipulate letters and write words until they discover the theme-related mystery word.
- **Theme Center:** Provide Anticipation Reaction Guides and multiple levels of theme-related texts at this center. Students complete Anticipation/Reaction Guides and read theme-related texts.
- **Writing Center:** Place writing supplies at this center. Students write Partner Ocean Stories.

Teacher-Facilitated Whole-Group Reflection and Goal Setting

- **Share** completed Anticipation/Reaction Guides and projects from Stage Two.
- **Reflect** on how previewing and Anticipation/Reaction Guides help us comprehend and how we can use Anticipation/Reaction Guides in other settings.
- **Set new goals** or extend existing ones.

Guide: I read aloud the next statement: *"All sharks are harmful to people."* Then I guided the students to discuss this statement with partners. They all agreed with the statement, based on information they had read or heard about shark attacks. I said, "I have also read about shark attacks and I don't ever recall hearing about sharks that are not harmful, so I am going to agree with statement two." Then I placed a check in the agree column. Then I read statement three: *"Dolphins are slow swimmers."* I invited the students and their partners to discuss whether they agreed or disagreed with it. Most of them disagreed with it, because we had seen videos about dolphins swimming and they were moving quickly.

Practice: I introduced *First Encyclopedia of Seas and Oceans* and students made connections. Then they practiced by listening as I read selected segments from the book. When I had finished reading, we revisited the three statements and the responses we had made before reading. After I read statement one, the students pointed out that the text supported our belief that some fish travel in schools. Andy, one of my students, also noted that the book said that some fish travel in schools to protect themselves from other fish who try to eat them. Then we revisited statement two. We were all smiling at this point, because we had learned through our reading that scientists believe that sharks do not intentionally attack people. Scientists believe the sharks mistake the people for other sea animals. This provided a great opportunity to show the students how our reading can change our thinking. To show that our thinking had changed, we placed an "X" in the disagree column in front of statement two. Then we reviewed statement three. We noted that once again our reading had confirmed what we thought to be true: Dolphins are fast swimmers. Figure 23 shows the Anticipation/Reaction Guide Maria and Kyle completed during Stage One.

Reflect: We reflected on how we used the Anticipation/Reaction Guide to help us to preview text and how important it is to have background knowledge and be able to activate it when we are thinking about different topics.

STAGE TWO: Teacher-Guided Small-Group Instruction

Text: *What Makes an Ocean Wave? Questions and Answers About Oceans and Ocean Life* (Berger & Berger, 2001) (Texts varied according to students' abilities.)

Review: I reminded students about comprehension strategies active readers use and focused on previewing and using Anticipation/Reaction Guides. I also referenced the guide we had completed in Stage One.

Guide: I explained to the students that we would be completing an Anticipation/Reaction Guide about *What Makes an Ocean Wave?* I introduced the book by sharing the title and cover and

Figure 23. Anticipation/Reaction Guide for *First Encyclopedia of Seas and Oceans*

Agree	Disagree	
✓		1. Some fish travel in schools.
✓	X	2. All sharks are harmful to people.
	✓	3. Dolphins are slow swimmers.

inviting students to make connections. They made text–self connections and noted that the cover reminded them of being at the beach for vacation and jumping into ocean waves. Then I guided the students to complete the Anticipation/Reaction Guide I had created previously. I suggested that we read the statements silently and indicate whether we agree or disagree. When we completed the guides, we discussed each statement. The first said, "*Whales breathe underwater.*" Some students agreed with this and others did not. The second statement said, "*There is little food at the bottom of the ocean.*" The students weren't sure about this statement, but some disagreed, because they thought they had seen pictures of the ocean floor that were very colorful and filled with plants. The third statement said, "*Some fish can make their own light.*" Many of the students disagreed with this statement. After we discussed our responses, I guided the students to silently read selected sections of the book. Then we briefly discussed them.

Practice: Students practiced by revisiting their Anticipation/Reaction Guides. They had learned from their reading that whales do not breathe underwater. Rather, they come to the surface and breathe air like we do. Students also learned from the text that the bottom of the ocean is a cold, dark place and that food is hard to find there. Students were surprised to learn from their reading that anglerfish, also known as flashlight fish, make their own light. As we discussed each statement, the students put an "X" in the agree or disagree column to indicate when their reading had changed their thinking. Beth's Anticipation/Reaction Guide for *What Makes an Ocean Wave?* is shown in Figure 24.

Reread, Retell, and Reflect: We reflected on how previewing and Anticipation/Reaction Guides help us to understand text and make connections between what know and what we read. Then we discussed how we could use the guides in our science and social studies classes.

Student-Facilitated Comprehension Centers

ABC Center: While at this center, students created pages for our class alphabet book *Ocean ABCs*. They used a model page I had completed as a guide and a variety of supplies I had left at the center.

Art Center: Students visited the art center after they had written Partner Ocean Stories at the writing center. Each partner created an illustration for their stories at this center.

Making and Writing Words Center: Students used packets of manipulative letters that made up theme-related words to create two-, three-, four-, and five-letter words until they used all the letters to create the mystery word. As they created the words, they wrote them on the Making and Writing Words blackline (see Appendix D, page 316).

Theme Center: Students completed Anticipation/Reaction Guides and read theme-related narrative and informational texts. After reading, students revisited the guides and revised as necessary.

Figure 24. Anticipation/Reaction Guide for *What Makes an Ocean Wave?*		
Agree	Disagree	
_____	✓	1. Whales breathe underwater.
X	✓	2. There is little food at the bottom of the ocean.
✓	_____	3. Some fish can make their own light.

Writing Center: Students selected partners and wrote Partner Ocean Stories. Throughout the stories, students took turns writing sentences to contribute narrative elements and details.

Student-Facilitated Comprehension Routines

Literature Circles: Students completed topic-related Anticipation/Reaction Guides before reading. They read and discussed the book and revisited the Guide and revised responses as necessary.

Cross-Age Reading Experiences: Students read theme-related narrative and informational texts with their cross-age partners. They completed Anticipation/Reaction Guides before reading and revisited them after reading to revise and discuss.

STAGE THREE: Teacher-Facilitated Whole-Group Reflection and Goal Setting

Share: Students shared their Anticipation/Reaction Guides and stories in small groups. Then we discussed selected examples as a whole class. Students also shared and discussed the pages they created for our class book *Oceans ABCs*. We applauded for the authors as they presented their pages. We were all very proud of our book and placed it in our classroom library.

Reflect: We reflected on how previewing and using Anticipation/Reaction Guides helped us to understand what we read. We also talked about how well we could use the guides in other subject areas.

Set New Goals: Students felt good about using Anticipation/Reaction Guides, and we decided to extend our use of them to informational text in science and social studies.

Assessment Options

In this lesson, I observed students working with peers, contributing to discussion, reading in small groups, and completing Anticipation/Reaction Guides. I reviewed and commented on the students' Anticipation/Reaction Guides, writing, and projects, as well as their self-assessments. I also conducted a few fluency checks in teacher-guided small groups and completed a running record with a student who appeared ready to move to another level.

Oceans Alive: Sea Creatures, Coral Reefs, Ecology, and More!
Guided Comprehension Strategy: Knowing How Words Work
Teaching Idea: Concept of Definition Map

STAGE ONE: Teacher-Directed Whole-Group Instruction

Text: *Coral Reef* (Davis, 1997)

Explain: I began by explaining knowing how words work and focusing on the Concept of Definition Map. I said, "Knowing how words work is a reading comprehension strategy that involves understanding words. The Concept of Definition Map provides us with a way to learn about word meanings. This is a Concept of Definition Map" (see Appendix C, pages 232 and 261). Then I showed the students the blackline on the overhead projector and distributed copies. I continued to explain. I said,

> As we can see on the organizer, the focus word appears in the center. This is the word we are going to be learning. The other parts of the map provide information about this word—a definition, a description, examples, and a comparison.

I also noted that we can add what we already know about the topic to the Concept of Definition Map before reading, and we can verify the information and add other facts after reading. Next, I explained that when the map is complete, we can use it to write a definition or summary of the focus word.

Demonstrate: I demonstrated by using a Think-Aloud, a read-aloud, the graphic organizer, and an overhead projector. I showed the students the Concept of Definition Map blackline and explained that I had numbered each section, so we could find each area more easily. I read aloud the various categories of information we would need to complete it. I wrote *coral reef*, the topic for our Concept of Definition Map, in the center oval (which I had labeled *1*) and explained that we would need to provide information about coral reefs for each category on the map. I read aloud the next category of information, "What is it?" I thought aloud and said, "When I think about a coral reef, I think of an underwater community that provides food and shelter. So, that is what I am going to write in section 2 of the map." Next, I pointed at sections 1 and 2 and said, "A coral reef is an underwater community that provides food and shelter."

Guide: I introduced the book, and students made connections to it. This book was written at a slightly higher level than most of our texts, but I knew it would work well with my students because I was reading to them and focusing only on the section that dealt with coral reefs as habitats. We had already been studying coral reefs for a while, so the students were very familiar with the vocabulary. When they made connections to the book cover, they referenced a short video about coral reefs that we had watched together. The students thought that the cover photograph reminded them of coral reefs they had seen in the video. I suggested that I read aloud the first section of the book and then we would continue completing our map. I guided the students to listen as I read, and to think about the remaining questions on our Concept of Definition Map: *What is it like? What are some types of coral? What is a comparison?* As I read, students followed along in their copies of *Coral Reef*. When I finished reading the opening section, I revisited our Concept of Definition Map and asked pairs of students how we might answer question 3: *What is it like?* I said, "Let's think about how we will describe a coral reef." The partners discussed this, and

Guided Comprehension: Oceans Alive: Sea Creatures, Coral Reefs, Ecology, and More! Knowing How Words Work: Concept of Definition Map

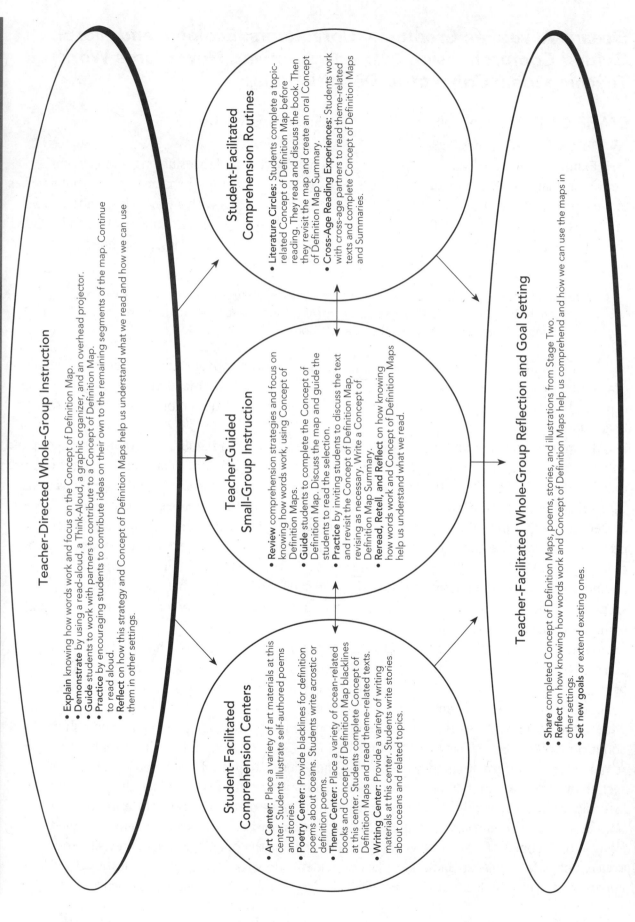

Teacher-Directed Whole-Group Instruction

- **Explain** knowing how words work and focus on the Concept of Definition Map.
- **Demonstrate** by using a read-aloud, a Think-Aloud, a graphic organizer, and an overhead projector.
- **Guide** students to work with partners to contribute to a Concept of Definition Map.
- **Practice** by encouraging students to contribute ideas on their own to the remaining segments of the map. Continue to read aloud.
- **Reflect** on how this strategy and Concept of Definition Maps help us understand what we read and how we can use them in other settings.

Student-Facilitated Comprehension Routines

- **Literature Circles:** Students complete a topic-related Concept of Definition Map before reading. They read and discuss the book. Then they revisit the map and create an oral Concept of Definition Map Summary.
- **Cross-Age Reading Experiences:** Students work with cross-age partners to read theme-related texts and complete Concept of Definition Maps and Summaries.

Teacher-Guided Small-Group Instruction

- **Review** comprehension strategies and focus on knowing how words work, using Concept of Definition Maps.
- **Guide** students to complete the Concept of Definition Map. Discuss the map and guide the students to read the selection.
- **Practice** by inviting students to discuss the text and revisit the Concept of Definition Map, revising as necessary. Write a Concept of Definition Map Summary.
- **Reread, Retell, and Reflect** on how knowing how words work and Concept of Definition Maps help us understand what we read.

Student-Facilitated Comprehension Centers

- **Art Center:** Place a variety of art materials at this center. Students illustrate self-authored poems and stories.
- **Poetry Center:** Provide blacklines for definition poems about oceans. Students write acrostic or definition poems.
- **Theme Center:** Place a variety of ocean-related books and Concept of Definition Map blacklines at this center. Students complete Concept of Definition Maps and read theme-related texts.
- **Writing Center:** Provide a variety of writing materials at this center. Students write stories about oceans and related topics.

Teacher-Facilitated Whole-Group Reflection and Goal Setting

- **Share** completed Concept of Definition Maps, poems, stories, and illustrations from Stage Two.
- **Reflect** on how knowing how words work and Concept of Definition Maps help us comprehend and how we can use the maps in other settings.
- **Set new goals** or extend existing ones.

Guided Comprehension in the Primary Grades (Second Edition) by Maureen McLaughlin. © 2010 by the International Reading Association. May be copied for classroom use.

then they suggested several words to describe coral reefs, including *colony, crowded, busy,* and *food supply.* Because we had mentioned food in our definition, I included the first three descriptors on the map. Next, I prompted students to complete the next part of the Concept of Definition Map. I said, "Section 4 of the map asks us to provide three examples of coral reefs. What information do you think we should include in this section?" The students immediately turned to page 6 of the book. Pictures of four different types of coral appeared there: Elkhorn, brain, fire, and pillar. I chose three of the types and students did the same. Next, I asked what we might include in section 5, a comparison. I reminded the students that when we look for comparisons, we are looking for topics that are similar. Because our definition included the word *community,* Joseph and Eddie suggested that *rainforest* would be a good comparison. They said, "Rainforests are a lot like the coral reefs. They provide shelter and food for the animals that live there." We followed their suggestion and included *rainforest* as a comparison. I went back to the center oval (section 1) and read the information we had on our completed Concept of Definition Map.

Practice: I continued reading the book aloud. When I finished, we discussed it. Then we revisited our Concept of Definition Map. We decided that the information included in all sections of the map was accurate, so we used it to write a Concept of Definition Map Summary. Our completed Concept of Definition Map and Summary appear in Figure 25.

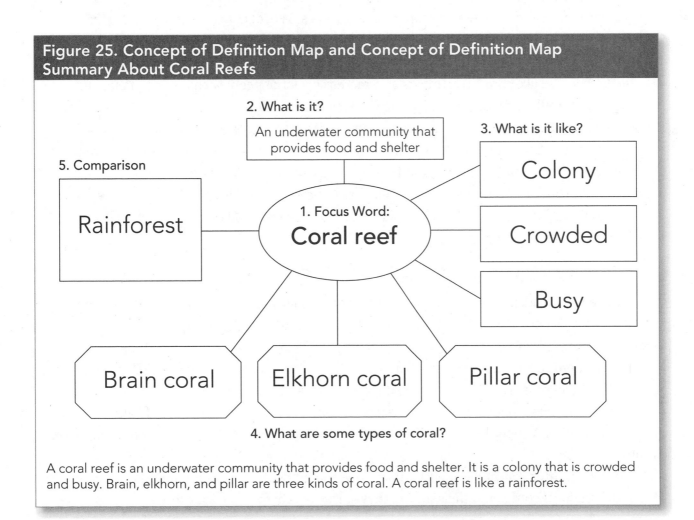

Figure 25. Concept of Definition Map and Concept of Definition Map Summary About Coral Reefs

2. What is it?
An underwater community that provides food and shelter

3. What is it like?
Colony
Crowded
Busy

5. Comparison
Rainforest

1. Focus Word:
Coral reef

Brain coral   Elkhorn coral   Pillar coral

4. What are some types of coral?

A coral reef is an underwater community that provides food and shelter. It is a colony that is crowded and busy. Brain, elkhorn, and pillar are three kinds of coral. A coral reef is like a rainforest.

Reflect: We reflected on how we used the Concept of Definition Map to help us understand how words work and to understand what we read. The students were genuinely engaged in learning about this underwater habitat.

STAGE TWO: Teacher-Guided Small-Group Instruction

Text: *What Is a Coral Reef?* (Kranking, 1996) (Texts varied according to students' abilities.)

Review: I reminded students about comprehension strategies active readers use and focused on knowing how words work and using Concept of Definition Maps. I also referenced the map we had completed in Stage One.

Guide: I gave the small group of students Concept of Definition Map blacklines (see Appendix C, page 261) and explained that our focus word (section 1) this time would be *coral*. We briefly discussed some things we knew about coral, then I introduced *What Is a Coral Reef?* After we made a few connections, I guided the students to silently read the short text, stopping midway to make connections and discuss. Next, we discussed the students' suggestions for what we should include in section 2: *What is it?* The students' responses focused on small sea animals that combine to make a coral reef, so we wrote that on our maps. Then we discussed section 3, *How would you describe it?* Students' responses included *colorful*, *stony houses*, and *building blocks*.

Practice: Students practiced by completing section 4: *What kinds of places can coral grow into?* They thought about this question and decided to suggest ideas from the book's subheadings. These included *lunchroom*, *hiding place*, and *bedroom*. For section 5: *Comparison*, students suggested *apartment*, because like coral, apartments are stacked so a lot of people can live in the building.

Reread, Retell, and Reflect: We wrote Concept of Definition Map Summaries based on our completed map. Then we reflected on how Concept of Definition Maps and Summaries help us understand how words work and how to make connections between what we know and what we have read. Theresa said, "This is a good way to write summaries. Everything we need is right in front of us." Finally, we discussed how we could use Concept of Definition Maps and Concept Map Summaries to help us understand texts in other settings. A completed Concept of Definition Map and Summary is featured in Figure 26.

Student-Facilitated Comprehension Centers

Art Center: Students used a variety of art supplies to illustrate the poems and stories they wrote at other centers. When they finished the illustrations, the students displayed their work in our Class Gallery.

Poetry Center: At this center, students wrote definition poems (see Appendix D, page 327) or acrostics about oceans. They later illustrated their poems at the art center.

Theme Center: Students read ocean-related books and completed Concept of Definition Maps at this center. When the maps were completed, students wrote Concept of Definition Map Summaries.

Writing Center: Pairs of students wrote stories about oceans and related topics at this center. When the students completed their stories, they illustrated them in the art center.

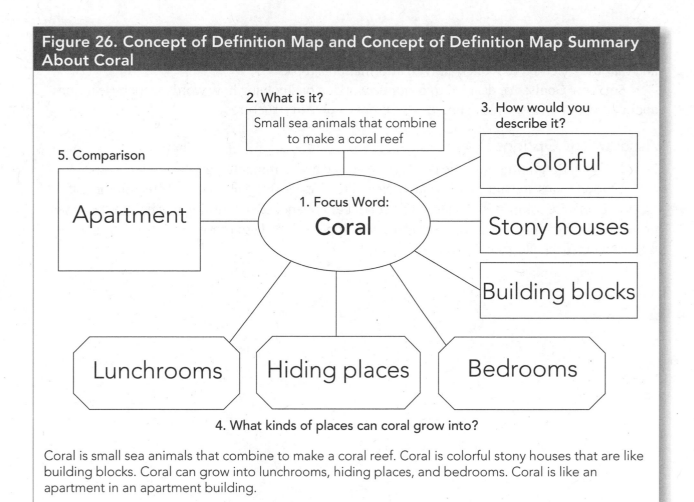

Figure 26. Concept of Definition Map and Concept of Definition Map Summary About Coral

2. What is it?
Small sea animals that combine to make a coral reef

3. How would you describe it?
Colorful
Stony houses
Building blocks

5. Comparison
Apartment

1. Focus Word:
Coral

Lunchrooms Hiding places Bedrooms

4. What kinds of places can coral grow into?

Coral is small sea animals that combine to make a coral reef. Coral is colorful stony houses that are like building blocks. Coral can grow into lunchrooms, hiding places, and bedrooms. Coral is like an apartment in an apartment building.

Student-Facilitated Comprehension Routines

Literature Circles: Students in each Literature Circle completed a Concept of Definition Map before reading. Then they read and discussed the book. After reading, they revisited the map and wrote Concept of Definition Map Summaries. As an extension activity, some groups created new book covers for the books they read. The poster-sized book covers included the title, illustrations, and the author's name on the front, and a book summary and book reviews written by the students on the back.

Cross-Age Reading Experiences: Students worked with cross-age partners to read theme-related texts and complete Concept of Definition Maps. After reading, they revisited their maps and wrote Concept of Definition Map Summaries.

STAGE THREE: Teacher Facilitated Whole-Group Reflection and Goal Setting

Share: Students shared their Concept of Definition Maps and Summaries from Stage Two in small groups. Then we discussed selected examples as a whole class. Next, the small groups walked through our Class Gallery, stopping to hear each group member read his or her acrostic or definition poem. They also viewed the students' stories.

Reflect: We reflected on how knowing how words work and using Concept of Definition Maps helped us to understand what we read. We also talked about how well we could use the maps and that they seemed to work best with informational topics.

Set New Goals: We decided to continue working on knowing how words work by learning about Semantic Maps, which I noted were more flexible in structure.

Assessment Options

I used observation throughout the lessons. I reviewed and commented on the students' Concept of Definition Maps and Summaries and projects from Stage Two. I also commented on the self-assessments they completed. In addition, I conducted fluency checks during teacher-guided small groups and a running record with a student who appeared ready to move to another group in teacher-guided small-group instruction.

Oceans Alive: Sea Creatures, Coral Reefs, Ecology, and More!
Guided Comprehension Strategy: Self-Questioning
Teaching Idea: Paired Questioning

STAGE ONE: Teacher-Directed Whole-Group Instruction

Text: *Flotsam* (Wiesner, 2006)

Explain: I began by explaining self-questioning as a comprehension strategy that involves generating questions to guide our reading. Next, I explained Paired Questioning (see Appendix C, page 222):

> When we use Paired Questioning, we work with partners to generate and respond to questions after we have read a segment of text silently. When we finish reading the text, we take turns explaining what we believe to be the important information in the story. We agree or disagree about what we think is important. After that, we have a class discussion about the story and talk about how we used Paired Questioning.

Demonstrate: I began demonstrating Paired Questioning by introducing *Flotsam*, a wordless picture book by David Wiesner. I read aloud the title and showed the students the cover of the book. I said,

> I know that flotsam is something that floats, and the cover illustration looks as if things are floating in the ocean. I can see the smaller fish, but I am not sure what the eye is. I wonder if it is the eye of a very big fish.

Then I asked students if they had ever seen things floating in the ocean. Several said they had seen fish and seaweed. Others said they had seen trash, such as plastic bottles. After the students had made connections, I focused on the word *flotsam* to ensure students understood it. I used it in several sentences, referring to what the students had seen floating on the ocean, and discussed it further with them. I reminded the students that this book had been created by David Wiesner and asked them what that meant. They readily noted that Wiesner writes wordless picture books, so we would need to read the pictures in this book. They knew about Wiesner because we had recently completed an author study about him. Then I reminded the students that we would engage in Paired Questioning as we "read" the text. Next, Melanie, a student I had previously asked to help me demonstrate, joined me at the front of the room. Melanie and I each had our own copies of the book—as did the students—and we "read" the first segment of the wordless picture book. Then I said, "This illustration shows a family at the beach. Why do you think the parents brought their son to the beach?" Melanie replied, "I think they brought their son to the beach so he could explore. It looks like he brought a magnifying glass and a microscope to examine the things he might find." Then Melanie asked me, "What kinds of things have you found at the beach?" I told her that I have often found seashells on the beach. I turned a few pages and showed the students the pages on which the boy is sitting on the sand and a camera and crab are at the edge of the ocean. Then I asked Melanie, "What do you think the boy will do with the camera?" She replied, "I think he will examine the camera with his magnifying glass." Then she asked me, "Did you notice anything unusual about the camera?" I said that I had noticed that it was an old underwater camera and it looked as if it had been in the water

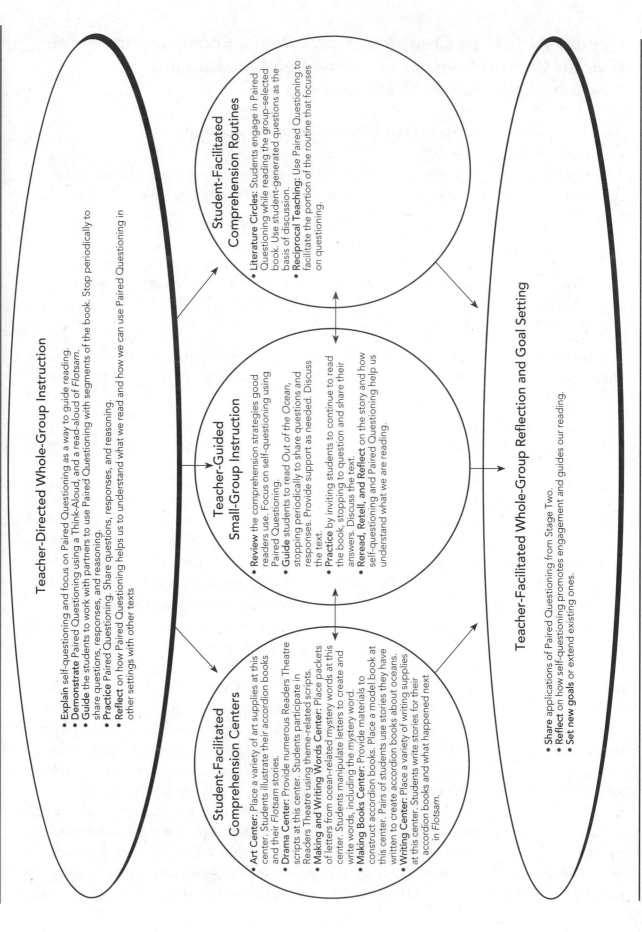

Teacher-Directed Whole-Group Instruction

- **Explain** self-questioning and focus on Paired Questioning as a way to guide reading.
- **Demonstrate** Paired Questioning using a Think-Aloud, and a read-aloud of *Flotsam*.
- **Guide** the students to work with partners to use Paired Questioning with segments of the book. Stop periodically to share questions, responses, and reasoning.
- **Practice** Paired Questioning. Share questions, responses, and reasoning.
- **Reflect** on how Paired Questioning helps us to understand what we read and how we can use Paired Questioning in other settings with other texts

Student-Facilitated Comprehension Routines

- **Literature Circles:** Students engage in Paired Questioning while reading the group-selected book. Use student-generated questions as the basis of discussion.
- **Reciprocal Teaching:** Use Paired Questioning to facilitate the portion of the routine that focuses on questioning.

Teacher-Guided Small-Group Instruction

- **Review** the comprehension strategies good readers use. Focus on self-questioning using Paired Questioning.
- **Guide** students to read *Out of the Ocean*, stopping periodically to share questions and responses. Provide support as needed. Discuss the text.
- **Practice** by inviting students to continue to read the book, stopping to question and share their answers. Discuss the text.
- **Reread, Retell, and Reflect** on the story and how self-questioning and Paired Questioning help us understand what we are reading.

Student-Facilitated Comprehension Centers

- **Art Center:** Place a variety of art supplies at this center. Students illustrate their accordion books and their *Flotsam* stories.
- **Drama Center:** Provide numerous Readers Theatre scripts at this center. Students participate in Readers Theatre using theme-related scripts.
- **Making and Writing Words Center:** Place packets of letters from ocean-related mystery words at this center. Students manipulate letters to create and write words, including the mystery word.
- **Making Books Center:** Provide materials to construct accordion books. Place a model book at this center. Pairs of students use stories they have written to create accordion books about oceans.
- **Writing Center:** Place a variety of writing supplies at this center. Students write stories for their accordion books and what happened next in *Flotsam*.

Teacher-Facilitated Whole-Group Reflection and Goal Setting

- **Share** applications of Paired Questioning from Stage Two.
- **Reflect** on how self-questioning promotes engagement and guides our reading.
- **Set new goals** or extend existing ones.

for a long time. Then we discussed the book to that point as a class, noting what we thought was important.

Guide: I invited the students to work with partners to generate and respond to Paired Questions as they "read" the text. We repeated the process with another segment of text. Then we briefly discussed the text and Paired Questioning. Pairs of questions the students generated included the following:

"Why do you think one fish has a wind-up key in his side?"
"It looks like he is a toy fish in the middle of a school of real fish."

"What does the octopus family and fish reading in the living room remind you of?"
"It reminds me of a coral reef because we learned the reef could be a lunchroom and a bedroom, so I think it could also be a living room."

Practice: Students continued "reading" segments silently and practiced creating Paired Questions independently. Students asked questions and responded to their partners' questions. Examples of their Paired Questions included the following:

"Who do you think the children were who were in the pictures?"
"I think they were other children from around the world who had found the old camera and put it back in the water after they took pictures."

"Why do you think the boy threw the camera back into the ocean?"
"I think he made a lot of discoveries while he had the camera and he wanted someone else to find it and enjoy it."

Then we discussed the book and students' Paired Questions. Next, Melanie and I discussed what we thought was important in the book. Melanie said, "I think it is important that the boy thought about going to the beach as an opportunity to explore. He came prepared with his magnifying glass, microscope, and binoculars." I said, "I agree with what you said, Melanie," and added, "I also think it was important that he got the film developed and returned the camera to the sea so others could find it." Melanie said that she agreed with me. Then we invited the students to think about what was important and share it with their partners. We discussed their ideas and I reminded the students that when we engage in Paired Questioning, we do not always need to agree with each other about what is important in the text.

Reflect: We began our reflection by thinking about the outcome of the story and what might happen next with the camera. I invited the students to visit the writing center, working in pairs to write a story about what happens to the camera next, and then to visit the art center to illustrate their stories. The students found it interesting that we were reading pictures instead of words this time. They thought that was fun because their ideas, which were based on David Wiesner's illustrations, became the text. Then we reflected on how using Paired Questioning kept us interested in what we were reading and helped us understand the story.

STAGE TWO: Teacher-Guided Small-Group Instruction

Text: *Out of the Ocean* (Frasier, 2002) (Texts varied according to students' abilities.)

Review: I reminded students about the strategies good readers use and then focused on self-questioning. I briefly recalled an example of Paired Questioning from Stage One.

Guide: I introduced the story *Out of the Ocean*, which is about a mother and her child appreciating nature—the ocean, the sun, and the beach. I showed the cover of the book, read the title, and invited students to engage in Paired Questioning. We stopped periodically for students to share their Paired Questions. Examples of their questions and responses included the following:

"Why do you think the mother brought her child to the beach?"
"I think she brought her child to the beach so the child would learn to appreciate the ocean and the beach.

"Where do you think the seashells came from?"
"I think waves brought them onto the shore from the ocean."

"Why do you think the mother said it is easy to forget big things?"
"She said that because we see big things—like the sky—every day and we can forget about them because they are always there."

Practice: Students practiced by sharing what they thought was important in the text. Then we discussed their ideas.

Reread, Retell, and Reflect: The students did a paired rereading of the book and we did an oral retelling. Then we discussed how Paired Questioning helped us understand what we read.

Student-Facilitated Comprehension Centers

Art Center: Students illustrated their *Flotsam* stories and their accordion books. When they finished their stories, they hung them in our Writing Gallery.

Drama Center: Students practiced fluency by engaging in Readers Theatre with classmates. The students read Readers Theatre scripts about theme-related stories.

Making and Writing Words Center: Students used packets of letters from ocean-related mystery words to create and write multiple-letter words. Their goal was to increase the length of the words until they used all the letters to create the theme-related mystery word. They wrote the words they created on the Making and Writing Words blackline (see Appendix D, page 316).

Making Books Center: Pairs of students used the stories they wrote in the writing center to create accordion books about oceans.

Writing Center: Pairs of students wrote stories to use in their accordion books, which they completed in the making books center. Students worked individually to write stories about what happened next to the camera in *Flotsam*, which they later illustrated in the art center.

Student-Facilitated Comprehension Routines

Literature Circles: Students engaged in Paired Questioning while reading their group-selected book. Then they used their questions to generate group discussion.

Reciprocal Teaching: The students used Paired Questioning in the portion of the routine that focuses on questioning. Then they discussed their responses and ideas to support their thinking.

STAGE THREE: Teacher-Facilitated Whole-Group Reflection and Goal Setting

Share: Students shared their Paired Questionings from Stage Two in small groups and then we discussed their applications as a whole class. Then they shared their illustrated stories. Next, students presented their accordion books. Students' stories and illustrations were very creative, and we applauded as they were shared.

Reflect: We reflected on how self-questioning can promote engagement and guide our reading. We also reflected on how working with partners helped to support our thinking and how well we could use Paired Questioning in other settings.

Set New Goals: Students felt confident using Paired Questioning with books, so we decided to use it while reading about particular topics on theme-related websites I had bookmarked.

Assessment Options

I observed students in multiple settings and listened carefully to their Paired Questions and responses throughout the lesson. I reviewed and commented on students' poems, books, and self-assessments from Stage Two. During teacher-guided small groups, I also periodically administered running records and fluency checks.

Oceans Alive: Sea Creatures, Coral Reefs, Ecology, and More!
Guided Comprehension Strategy: Visualizing
Teaching Idea: Draw and Write Visualizations

STAGE ONE: Teacher-Directed Whole-Group Instruction

Text: *What Do Sharks Eat for Dinner? Questions and Answers About Sharks* (Berger & Berger, 2001)

Explain: I explained that visualizing, one of the comprehension strategies good readers use, involves our creating pictures in our minds based on what we are reading. Next, I introduced and explained Draw and Write Visualizations (see Appendix C, pages 227–228 and 271). I explained to the students that we would be using simple sketching—lines and shapes—to draw the images that we were creating in our minds as I read aloud. I modeled some simple lines and shapes and reminded the students that what was important was to sketch the images and that we did not need to be great artists to do that.

Demonstrate: I demonstrated Draw and Write Visualizations using a Think-Aloud, large chart paper, Draw and Write Visualization blacklines, and a read-aloud of *What Do Sharks Eat for Dinner?* I introduced the book by sharing the title and cover. I encouraged students to make connections, and then I began reading the first few pages aloud. I thought aloud about the mental images I was creating based on the information I read. I said, "Great white sharks eat a lot, so I am going to draw a great white shark with its mouth open looking for food." I sketched the great white shark in the ocean and then I wrote, "*Great white sharks eat seals, sea lions, dolphins, whales, and other sharks.*" I explained that great white sharks also eat lots of other things, but I wanted to share just a few examples. Then I read another segment and engaged in Draw and Write Visualizations a second time. Figure 27 shows my first Draw and Write Visualization.

Guide: I read aloud the next four pages and guided pairs of students to create pictures in their minds and sketch what they were thinking about the text while listening to the read-aloud. I monitored this activity, prompting as necessary. The students used paper and pencils I had provided. They used Think-Alouds to share their reasoning with their partners, as they individually sketched the images they pictured in their minds and wrote about them. When they had finished, I thought aloud and sketched the mental image I had created as I was reading. I waited to do my sketch because I wanted the students to focus on creating their visualizations and not copy mine. Then the students and I shared our sketches and our thinking with partners. After we had discussed our ideas, we wrote about our sketch in the space provided on the blackline. Although each sketch was unique, most of us had visualized something about the world of sharks. Once again, we shared with a partner, and selected students shared with the class. I drew attention to the individual nature of the visualizations and reinforced the roles text and prior knowledge play in the personal construction of meaning. I repeated this process with subsequent pages.

Practice: The students practiced by continuing to create Draw and Write Visualizations and share with partners, as I continued to read aloud selected sections of the book. When I finished reading the book, the students shared their final application of Draw and Write Visualizations with the class. Then we discussed what I had read. For example, we talked about how sharks are at the top of the food chain and how they react to people.

Guided Comprehension: Oceans Alive: Sea Creatures, Coral Reefs, Ecology, and More! Visualizing: Draw and Write Visualizations

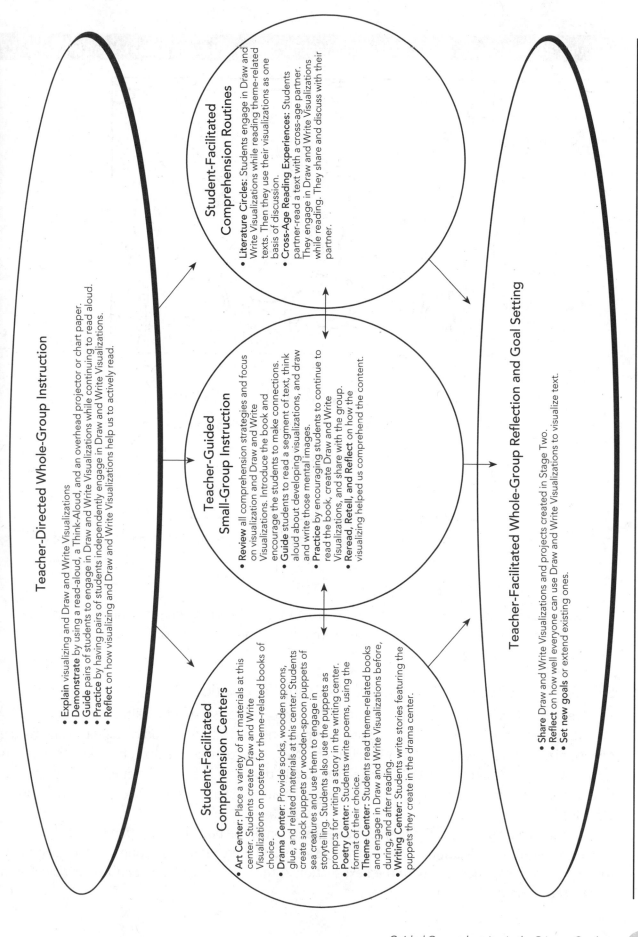

Teacher-Directed Whole-Group Instruction

- **Explain** visualizing and Draw and Write Visualizations
- **Demonstrate** by using a read-aloud, a Think-Aloud, and an overhead projector or chart paper.
- **Guide** pairs of students to engage in Draw and Write Visualizations while continuing to read aloud.
- **Practice** by having pairs of students independently engage in Draw and Write Visualizations.
- **Reflect** on how visualizing and Draw and Write Visualizations help us to actively read.

Student-Facilitated Comprehension Routines

- **Literature Circles:** Students engage in Draw and Write Visualizations while reading theme-related texts. Then they use their visualizations as one basis of discussion.
- **Cross-Age Reading Experiences:** Students partner-read a text with a cross-age partner. They engage in Draw and Write Visualizations while reading. They share and discuss with their partner.

Teacher-Guided Small-Group Instruction

- **Review** all comprehension strategies and focus on visualization and Draw and Write Visualizations. Introduce the book and encourage the students to make connections.
- **Guide** students to read a segment of text, think aloud about developing visualizations, and draw and write those mental images.
- **Practice** by encouraging students to continue to read the book, create Draw and Write Visualizations, and share with the group.
- **Reread, Retell, and Reflect** on how the visualizing helped us comprehend the content.

Student-Facilitated Comprehension Centers

- **Art Center:** Place a variety of art materials at this center. Students create Draw and Write Visualizations on posters for theme-related books of choice.
- **Drama Center:** Provide socks, wooden spoons, glue, and related materials at this center. Students create sock puppets or wooden-spoon puppets of sea creatures and use them to engage in storytelling. Students also use the puppets as prompts for writing a story in the writing center.
- **Poetry Center:** Students write poems, using the format of their choice.
- **Theme Center:** Students read theme-related books and engage in Draw and Write Visualizations before, during, and after reading.
- **Writing Center:** Students write stories featuring the puppets they create in the drama center.

Teacher-Facilitated Whole-Group Reflection and Goal Setting

- **Share** Draw and Write Visualizations and projects created in Stage Two.
- **Reflect** on how well everyone can use Draw and Write Visualizations to visualize text.
- **Set new goals** or extend existing ones.

Draw:

Write:
Great white sharks eat seals, sea lions, dolphins, whales, and other sharks.

Reflect: We discussed how Draw and Write Visualizations helped us to think about the text and understand what we were reading. Then we talked about how we could use visualizing when reading different types of text.

STAGE TWO: Teacher-Guided Small-Group Instruction

Text: *Sea Turtles* (Rhodes, 2006) (Texts varied according to students' abilities.)

Review: I briefly reviewed the reading comprehension strategies good readers use and focused on visualizing and Draw and Write Visualizations. Next, I introduced the text and asked the students to sketch and write about what they were picturing in their minds as they listened to me share the title and read the first page. I also drew and wrote about my mental image. Then we shared and discussed.

Guide: The students whisper read the next section of the book and stopped to engage in Draw and Write Visualizations. I guided their reading and sketching, prompting as necessary. We followed the same procedure with the next section of the text. Layla's Draw and Write Visualization is featured in Figure 28.

Figure 28. Layla's Draw and Write Visualization About Sea Turtles

Draw:

Write: the Turtle Lay Three egg on the Sand andthy also can Miygrat.

Practice: The students practiced by independently reading the remaining sections of the book. They stopped twice at designated points to draw and write about the pictures they created in their minds. I monitored their discussion, prompting when necessary.

Reread, Retell, and Reflect: We engaged in a second reading of the text, and I used that as an opportunity to complete a running record with one of the students. Then we created an oral summary. Finally, we discussed how the visualized images belonged to each reader, and how they were sometimes similar and sometimes very different from the images of others in our group. We also talked about how Draw and Write Visualizations helped us understand the information about sea turtles. Nate said, "Having pictures in my head helps me remember," and Tanya said, "At first, I thought we would all have the same pictures, but we didn't. Everyone had a picture in their mind that was just theirs."

Student-Facilitated Comprehension Centers

Art Center: Students created Draw and Write Visualizations on poster board for theme-related books of their choice. Then they hung them in our Ocean Gallery.

Drama Center: Students created sock puppets or wooden-spoon puppets of sea creatures and used them to initiate storytelling. Later, they used the puppets as prompts for writing stories in the writing center.

Poetry Center: Students wrote poems about sea creatures. They selected formats from acrostics, definition poems, or cinquains. Students included their poems in our class book *Sea Creature Poems.*

Theme Center: Students worked in pairs to read ocean and theme-related books. They engaged in Draw and Write Visualizations before, during, and after reading and shared and discussed with their partners.

Writing Center: Students wrote stories featuring the puppets they created in the drama center. Then they displayed the puppets and their stories in our Ocean Gallery.

Student-Facilitated Comprehension Routines

Literature Circles: While reading, students stopped at designated points and engaged in Draw and Write Visualizations. When the group members had finished reading, they met in circle and used their drawings and writings as the basis of discussion. At the conclusion of the discussion, students used the Literature Circle Self-Evaluation (see Appendix D, page 315) to comment on their participation and how well the group worked.

Cross-Age Reading Experiences: Students engaged in Patterned Partner Reading (see Appendix C, pages 239–240) with their cross-age partners. The pattern they used was Read–Pause–Draw and Write Visualization. They shared their responses with their partners.

STAGE THREE: Teacher-Facilitated Whole-Group Reflection and Goal Setting

Share: The students shared and discussed their applications of Draw and Write Visualizations from Stage Two in small groups. This included visiting our Ocean Gallery and sharing the sea creature poems they wrote for our class book. Then students shared and discussed selected applications with the whole class.

Reflect: We reflected on how visualizing and techniques such as Draw and Write Visualizations can help us understand what we read. Hannah said, "When I think about the pictures in my mind, it's like a movie. The more I read, the more pictures there are." Kyle said, "Picturing what I am reading helps me. I see the picture in my mind and then I write about what I see."

Set New Goals: We decided that we could all use Draw and Write Visualizations effectively, so we decided to extend our understanding of visualization by learning how to use Guided Imagery.

Assessment Options

I observed students in each stage of Guided Comprehension. I also carefully reviewed and commented on students' applications of Draw and Write Visualizations, their projects from Stage Two, and their self-assessments. I also completed two running records and multiple fluency checks.

Final Thoughts About the Ocean Theme

As I observed the lessons in the ocean theme being taught by a number of primary-grade teachers, it became abundantly clear that oceans were a topic of fascination for all involved. Whether learning about the sea or its creatures, students were enthusiastically engaged and could not wait to learn the next incredibly interesting fact.

As noted in previous chapters, it is important to acknowledge that lessons about a variety of skills that underpin comprehension strategies were taught during this theme. For example, aspects of language development, such as phonemic awareness and phonics, and skills such as sequencing, generating questions, and distinguishing important from less important ideas were embedded in the theme. (For ideas about how to use literature to teach phonemic awareness, phonics, and fluency, see Appendix B.) A variety of informational texts such as *Sea Turtles* and *Oceans* were used to teach text frames and generate questions at a variety of levels. Students improved fluency by engaging in repeated readings of short sections of texts from titles such as *Out of the Ocean* and *First Encyclopedia of Seas and Oceans*. They also eagerly participated in Readers Theatre based on ocean-related narrative texts such as *Three Little Fish and the Big Bad Shark* (Geist & Gorton, 2007). Students' keen interest in the ocean theme motivated them to read and promoted their engagement in learning. In addition, teachers adapted lessons for prereaders and prewriters by engaging in read-alouds and encouraging response through a variety of modes—including discussion, drawing, singing, dancing, and dramatizing.

Theme Resources

Books

Andreae, G. (2002). *The pop-up commotion in the ocean*. Wilton, CT: Tiger Tales.

Arnosky, J. (2008). *All about sharks*. New York: Scholastic.

Berger, M., & Berger, G. (2001). *What do sharks eat for dinner? Questions and answers about sharks*. New York: Scholastic.

Berkes, M.C., & Canyon, J. (2004). *Over in the ocean: In a coral reef*. Nevada City, CA: Dawn.

Bramwell, M. (2001). *Ocean watch*. New York: Dorling Kindersley.

Bright, M. (2002). *The encyclopedia of awesome oceans*. Brookfield, CT: Copper Beech.

Bright, M. (2002). *People and the sea*. Brookfield, CT: Copper Beech.

Brooke, S. (2008). *Coral reefs: In danger*. New York: Grosset & Dunlap.

Bryan, A. (2000). *Salting the ocean: 100 poems by young poets*. New York: HarperCollins.

Cole, J. (1994). *The magic school bus on the ocean floor*. New York: Scholastic.

Cole, J. (1998). *The magic school bus takes a dive: A book about coral reefs*. New York: Scholastic.

Davies, N. (2008). *Surprising sharks*. London: Walker.

Dawson, S. (2001). *Sea and land animals*. Washington, DC: National Geographic.

Denne, B. (2001). *First encyclopedia of seas and oceans*. Tulsa, OK: EDC.

Douglas, L.G. (2005). *Coral reef*. Danbury, CT: Children's Press.

Dorling Kindersley (DK Publishing). (2001). *Ocean*. New York: Author.

Dorling Kindersley (DK Publishing). (2005). *Coral reef*. New York: Author.

Dorling Kindersley (DK Publishing). (2008). *Shark* (Eyewitness expert). New York: Author.

Dunphy, M. (2006). *Here is the coral reef.* Berkeley, CA: Web of Life Children's Books.

Earle, S.A. (2001). *Hello, fish! Visiting the coral reef.* Washington, DC: National Geographic.

Editors of Time for Kids. (2005). *Sharks!* (Time for Kids science scoops). New York: HarperCollins.

Frasier, D. (2002). *Out of the ocean.* New York: HarperCollins.

Gaarder-Juntti, O. (2008). *What lives in coral reefs?* Edina, MN: Super Sandcastle.

Galko, F. (2002). *Coral reef animals.* Chicago: Heinemann.

Galloway, R. (2005). *Smiley shark.* Wilton, CT: Tiger Tales.

Geist, K., & Gorton, J. (2007). *Three little fish and the big bad shark.* New York: Cartwheel.

Gibbons, G. (2002). *Exploring the deep, dark sea.* Boston: Little, Brown.

Gordon, D.G. (2004). *Uncover a shark.* Berkeley, CA: Silver Dolphin.

Guiberson, B.Z. (2002). *Ocean life.* New York: Scholastic.

Holden-Bloone, A. (1998). *Coral reef eye to eye.* Markham, ON: Fairmount.

Lensch, C. (2005). *Coral reef hide and seek.* Atlanta, GA: Piggy Toes Press.

Llewellyn, C. (2005). *The best book of sharks.* London: Kingfisher.

Macaulay, K., & Kalman, B. (2005). *Coral reef food chains.* New York: Crabtree.

MacQuitty, M. (2008). *Ocean.* London: Dorling Kindersley.

Mara, W. (2005). *The four oceans.* Danbury, CT: Children's Press.

Nyquist, K.B. (2002). *The oceans around us.* Washington, DC: National Geographic.

Patent, D.H. (2003). *Colorful, captivating coral reefs.* New York: Walker.

Pfeffer, W. (2009). *Life in a coral reef.* New York: HarperCollins.

Priddy, R. (2005). *Sharks.* New York: Priddy.

Rhodes, M.J. (2006). *Sea turtles.* Danbury, CT: Children's Press.

Rhodes, M.J., & Hall, D. (2007). *Life on a coral reef.* Danbury, CT: Children's Press.

Ryan, P.M. (2001). *Hello ocean.* Watertown, MA: Charlesbridge.

Sherry, K. (2007). *I'm the biggest thing in the ocean.* New York: Penguin.

Simon, S. (2006). *Oceans.* New York: HarperCollins.

Sommers, J. (2007). *The coral reef tunnel book: Take a peek under the sea!* Chicago: Tunnel Vision.

Stewart, M. (2008). *Extreme coral reef! Q & A.* New York: HarperCollins.

Stierle, C., & Crawley, A. (2007). *Ocean life from A to Z* (book and DVD). Pleasantville, NY: Reader's Digest.

Taylor-Butler, C. (2006). *A home in the coral reefs.* Danbury, CT: Children's Press.

Thomson, S. (2006). *Amazing sharks!* New York: HarperCollins.

Troll, R. (2002). *Sharkabet: A sea of sharks from A to Z.* Portland, OR: Westwinds.

Wagner, K., & Wagner, O. (2005). *Everything kids' sharks book: Dive into fun-infested waters!* Cincinnati, OH: Adams Media.

Ward, J. (2000). *Somewhere in the ocean.* Flagstaff, AZ: Rising Moon.

Wojahn, R.H., & Wojahn, D. (2009). *A coral reef food chain: A who-eats-what adventure in the Caribbean Sea.* Minneapolis, MN: Lerner.

Wood, A.J. (2001). *In the ocean.* Berkeley, CA: Silver Dolphin.

Websites

Discovery Education: Planet Ocean
school.discoveryeducation.com/schooladventures/planetocean/

Enchanted Learning: All About Oceans and Seas
www.enchantedlearning.com/subjects/ocean/

Enchanted Learning: Coral Reef Animal Printouts
www.enchantedlearning.com/biomes/coralreef/coralreef.shtml

Enchanted Learning: What Is a Shark?
www.enchantedlearning.com/subjects/sharks/

Kidzone: Sharks
www.kidzone.ws/sharks/index.htm

Ocean Collection for Kids
www.calstatela.edu/faculty/eviau/edit557/oceans/

Ocean Songs and Fingerplays
www.angelfire.com/la/kinderthemes/ofingerplays.html

Ocean World: Coral Reefs
oceanworld.tamu.edu/students/coral/index.html

Oceans Field Trip
www.field-trips.org/tours/sci/oceank/_tourlaunch1.htm

Oceans for Youth
www.oceansforyouth.com

Planet Ocean
school.discoveryeducation.com/schooladventures/planetocean

Research/Informational Websites About Oceans
edtech.kennesaw.edu/web/oceans.html

Performance Extensions Across the Curriculum

Art

- Create a class mural of an ocean ecosystem. Draw various types of ocean animals, coral reefs, and plant life.

- Invent a new kind of ocean animal. Design and create it. Then suspend it from the ceiling in the Class Gallery.

Math

- Use theme-related books and bookmarked websites to list six types of ocean animals. Record the size of each animal and arrange them on a chart from smallest to largest.

- Participate in a class field trip to a local aquarium and take pictures. Observe the type of shapes and lines you see in ocean animals. Sketch a few of the ones you see using simple lines and shapes. Use your photos and sketches as visuals when you talk to your class about the field trip.

Music

- In small groups, write Lyric Summaries (see Appendix C, page 278) about an ocean animal of your choice. Use bookmarked websites and theme-related books as sources and sing your Lyric Summary when it is completed.

- Work with partners to create ocean life dances like "The Octopus Rock," "The Turtle Twist," and "The Whale Wiggle." Perform the dances for classmates and teach them how to do the dances.

Science

- Use bookmarked websites and theme-related books to explore how the ocean impacts our lives. Share at least three ideas that you learn through the medium of your choice, such as a poster or skit.

- Investigate undersea plant life and create posters to represent the various types of plants.

Social Studies

- Create a class wall map that illustrates the locations of oceans around the world. Choose an ocean and use bookmarked websites to research it. Share at least three new facts you learn about the ocean with the class.

- As a class, discuss problems our oceans face, such as pollution and overfishing. Work with a partner to discover ways to protect our oceans using bookmarked websites. Create a poster explaining an idea you discover. Illustrate your poster.

Culminating Activity

Somewhere Under the Sea. Invite students to create sea creature masks in art class and wear them as they greet their guests at an end-of-theme celebration. Hang sheared blue cellophane from the hall and classroom ceilings to create an underwater effect. Display students' performances in the corridors and at various stations in the classroom. Encourage students to engage in a variety of performances, including singing original ocean songs, dramatizing an original ocean play, playing a fact or fiction ocean game show, and discussing the ocean as a habitat for animals and plants. Serve refreshments, including a wide variety of theme-related desserts. Invite participants to write their comments about the celebration on poster board sailboats and hang them on the ocean mural. Give autographed copies of the class book *Sea Creature Poems* to the guests as the celebration concludes.

Guided Comprehension Resources

Focus: Resources that underpin the Guided Comprehension Model and facilitate its use in the primary grades.

Developmental Continuum: Appendix A contains the Continuum of Children's Development in Early Reading and Writing, from *Learning to Read and Write: Developmentally Appropriate Practices for Young Children* (IRA & NAEYC, 1998), which suggests skills students should be able to use at various points in the primary grades.

The Five Building Blocks of Literacy: Appendix B contains teaching ideas and booklists focused on phonemic awareness, phonics, fluency, vocabulary, and comprehension—the emphases of the National Reading Panel report (NICHD, 2000) and other U.S. government publications and legislation. The topics are presented in terms of their definitions, what research can tell us about them, and how we can teach them. A list of suggested readings appears at the close of each section. An extensive bibliography of trade books to use when teaching phonemic awareness, phonics, and fluency completes this appendix.

Comprehension Strategies, Teaching Ideas, and Blacklines: Appendix C offers a wide variety of ideas for teaching comprehension strategies that can be used before, during, and after reading. Organized by comprehension strategy, the teaching ideas are presented in a step-by-step instructional format. Teaching examples and reproducible blackline masters complete this appendix.

Resources for Organizing and Managing Comprehension Centers and Routines: A wide variety of reproducible blackline masters to facilitate classroom organization and management, as well as graphic organizers that support a number of comprehension centers and comprehension routines, are presented in Appendix D.

Informal Assessments and Sources of Leveled Texts: Informal assessments, ranging from attitude and motivation surveys to observation guides, are featured in Appendix E. Sources of leveled texts, including websites and publishers' materials, are presented in Appendix F.

Ideas for Creating Home–School Connections: A variety of activities that are easily adaptable to the themes presented in Chapters 7–10 are described in Appendix G.

Guided Comprehension Planning Forms: Reproducible forms for planning Guided Comprehension themes and lessons are included in Appendix H. A sample schedule form for Guided Comprehension lessons is also included in this section.

Primary-Level Developmental Continuum for Reading and Writing

Note: This list is intended to be illustrative, not exhaustive. Children at any grade level will function at a variety of phases along the reading/writing continuum.

Phase 1: Awareness and Exploration (Goals for Preschool)

Children explore their environment and build the foundations for learning to read and write.

Children can

- Enjoy listening to and discussing storybooks
- Understand that print carries a message
- Engage in reading and writing attempts
- Identify labels and signs in their environment
- Participate in rhyming games
- Identify some letters and make some letter-sound matches
- Use known letters or approximations of letters to represent written language (especially meaningful words like their name and phrases such as "I love you")

What teachers do

- Share books with children, including Big Books, and model reading behaviors
- Talk about letters by name and sounds
- Establish a literacy-rich environment
- Reread favorite stories
- Engage children in language games
- Promote literacy-related play activities
- Encourage children to experiment with writing

What parents and family members can do

- Talk with children, engage them in conversation, give names of things, show interest in what a child says
- Read and reread stories with predictable texts to children
- Encourage children to recount experiences and describe ideas and events that are important to them
- Visit the library regularly
- Provide opportunities for children to draw and print, using markers, crayons, and pencils

Phase 2: Experimental Reading and Writing (Goals for Kindergarten)

Children develop basic concepts of print and begin to engage in and experiment with reading and writing.

Kindergartners can

- Enjoy being read to and retelling simple narrative stories or informational texts
- Use descriptive language to explain and explore
- Recognize letters and letter-sound matches
- Show familiarity with rhyming and beginning sounds
- Understand left-to-right and top-to-bottom orientation and familiar concepts of print
- Match spoken words with written ones
- Begin to write letters of the alphabet and some high-frequency words

What teachers do

- Encourage children to talk about reading and writing experiences
- Provide many opportunities for children to explore and identify sound-symbol relationships in meaningful contexts
- Help children to segment spoken words into individual sounds and blend the sounds into whole words (for example, by slowly writing a word and saying its sound)
- Frequently read interesting and conceptually rich stories to children
- Provide daily opportunities for children to write
- Help children build a sight vocabulary
- Create a literacy-rich environment for children to engage independently in reading and writing

What parents and family members can do

- Daily read and reread narrative and informational stories to children
- Encourage children's attempts at reading and writing

- Allow children to participate in activities that involve writing and reading (for example, cooking, making grocery lists)
- Play games that involve specific directions (such as "Simon Says")
- Have conversations with children during mealtimes and throughout the day

Phase 3: Early Reading and Writing (Goals for First Grade)

Children begin to read simple stories and can write about a topic that is meaningful to them.

First graders can

- Read and retell familiar stories
- Use strategies (rereading, predicting, questioning, contextualizing) when comprehension breaks down
- Use reading and writing for various purposes on their own initiative
- Orally read with reasonable fluency
- Use letter-sound associations, word parts, and context to identify new words
- Identify an increasing number of words by sight
- Sound out and represent all substantial sounds in spelling a word
- Write about topics that are personally meaningful
- Attempt to use some punctuation and capitalization

What teachers do

- Support the development of vocabulary by reading daily to the children, transcribing their language, and selecting materials that expand children's knowledge and language development
- Model strategies and provide practice for identifying unknown words
- Give children opportunities for independent reading and writing practice
- Read, write, and discuss a range of different text types (poems, informational books)
- Introduce new words and teach strategies for learning to spell new words
- Demonstrate and model strategies to use when comprehension breaks down
- Help children build lists of commonly used words from their writing

What parents and family members can do

- Talk about favorite storybooks
- Read to children and encourage them to read to you
- Suggest that children write to friends and relatives
- Bring to a parent–teacher conference evidence of what your child can do in writing and reading
- Encourage children to share what they have learned about their writing and reading

Phase 4: Transitional Reading and Writing
(Goals for Second Grade)

Children begin to read more fluently and write various text forms using simple and more complex sentences.

Second graders can

- Read with greater fluency
- Use strategies more efficiently (rereading, questioning, and so on) when comprehension breaks down
- Use word identification strategies with greater facility to unlock unknown words
- Identify an increasing number of words by sight
- Write about a range of topics to suit different audiences
- Use common letter patterns and critical features to spell words
- Punctuate simple sentences correctly and proofread their own work
- Spend time reading daily and use reading to research topics

What teachers do

- Create a climate that fosters analytic, evaluative, and reflective thinking
- Teach children to write in multiple forms (stories, information, poems)
- Ensure that children read a range of texts for a variety of purposes
- Teach revising, editing, and proofreading skills
- Teach strategies for spelling new and difficult words
- Model enjoyment of reading

What parents and family members can do

- Continue to read to children and encourage them to read to you
- Engage children in activities that require reading and writing
- Become involved in school activities
- Show children your interest in their learning by displaying their written work
- Visit the library regularly
- Support your child's specific hobby or interest with reading materials and references

Phase 5: Independent and Productive Reading and Writing
(Goals for Third Grade)

Children continue to extend and refine their reading and writing to suit varying purposes and audiences.

Third graders can

- Read fluently and enjoy reading
- Use a range of strategies when drawing meaning from the text
- Use word identification strategies appropriately and automatically when encountering unknown words
- Recognize and discuss elements of different text structures
- Make critical connections between texts
- Write expressively in many different forms (stories, poems, reports)
- Use a rich variety of vocabulary and sentences appropriate to text forms
- Revise and edit their own writing during and after composing
- Spell words correctly in final writing drafts

What teachers do

- Provide opportunities daily for children to read, examine, and critically evaluate narrative and expository texts
- Continue to create a climate that fosters critical reading and personal response
- Teach children to examine ideas in texts
- Encourage children to use writing as a tool for thinking and learning
- Extend children's knowledge of the correct use of writing conventions
- Emphasize the importance of correct spelling in finished written products
- Create a climate that engages all children as a community of literacy learners

What parents and family members can do

- Continue to support children's learning and interest by visiting the library and bookstores with them
- Find ways to highlight children's progress in reading and writing
- Stay in regular contact with your children's teachers about activities and progress in reading and writing
- Encourage children to use and enjoy print for many purposes (such as recipes, directions, games, and sports)
- Build a love of language in all its forms and engage children in conversation

Research-Based Resources for Teaching Phonemic Awareness, Phonics, Fluency, Vocabulary, and Comprehension

Research-based ideas for teaching phonemic awareness, phonics, fluency, vocabulary, and comprehension are presented in this appendix. Each term's definition is followed by a summary of its research base, practical ideas for teaching it, and suggestions for further reading. A list of books to use when teaching phonemic awareness, phonics, and fluency—titles that emphasize particular sounds or contain repeated patterns—completes the appendix.

Phonemic Awareness

What Is It?

> Phonemic awareness is the awareness that the speech stream consists of a sequence of sounds—specifically phonemes, the smallest unit of sound that makes a difference in communication. It is a phoneme that determines the difference between the words *dog* and *hog*, for instance, and between *look* and *lick*. These differences influence meaning. (Yopp & Yopp, 2000, p. 130)

Harris and Hodges (1995) concur, noting, "Phonemic awareness is the awareness of the sounds (phonemes) that make up spoken words" (p. 185). Note the distinction between phonemic awareness and phonics: Phonics correlates phonemes (the smallest units of sound) with graphemes (written letters). Ehri and Nunes (2002) elaborate on this distinction by observing, "Whereas phonemic awareness is a specific skill that involves manipulating sounds in speech, phonics is a method of teaching reading" (p. 113).

What Does the Research Tell Us?

Researchers agree that phonemic awareness is a powerful predictor of reading and spelling acquisition (Ball & Blachman, 1991; Ehri & Nunes, 2002; IRA, 1998). We also know that phonemic awareness can be taught, but Yopp and Yopp (2000) caution that its instruction needs to be situated in a broader reading program to be effective. The National Reading Panel (NICHD, 2000) presents similar conclusions, noting that teaching children to manipulate phonemes in words was highly effective under a variety of teaching conditions with a variety of learners.

What Are Some Practical Ideas for Teaching Phonemic Awareness?

There are numerous practical, motivational, and fun ways to teach different aspects of phonemic awareness. Frequently hearing, saying, and creating rhymes; manipulating sounds; and singing songs adapted to promote phonemic awareness are among many found to be effective. According to Ehri and Nunes (2002), phonemic awareness tasks include the following:

1. Phoneme isolation, which requires recognizing individual sounds in words, for example, "Tell me the first sound in *paste*." (/p/)

2. Phoneme identity, which requires recognizing the common sound in different words, for example, "Tell me the sound that is the same in *bike*, *boy*, and *bell*." (/b/)

3. Phoneme categorization, which requires recognizing the word with the odd sound in a sequence of three or four words, for example, "Which word does not belong? *Bus*, *bun*, or *rug*." (*rug*)

4. Phonemic blending, which requires listening to a sequence of separately spoken sounds and combining them to form a recognizable word, for example, "What word is /s/ /k/ /u/ /l/?" (*school*)

5. Phoneme segmentation, which requires breaking a word into its sounds by tapping out or counting the sounds, or by pronouncing and positioning a marker for each sound, for example, "How many phonemes in *ship*?" (three: /š/ /i/ /p/)

6. Phoneme deletion, which requires stating the word that remains when a specified phoneme is removed, for example, "What is smile without the /s/?" (*mile*) (pp. 111–112)

Yopp and Yopp (2000) note that "phonemic awareness supports reading development only if it is part of a broader program that includes—among other things—development of students' vocabulary, syntax, comprehension, strategic reading abilities, decoding strategies, and writing across all content areas" (p. 142). What follows is a sampling of ideas for teaching phonemic awareness. For a more extensive list of classroom resources, see the articles cited at the conclusion of this section. For fun and engaging literature to use when teaching phonemic awareness, see the booklist at the conclusion of this appendix.

Rhyme. Read a variety of rhymes to students and encourage them to say or sing them along with you. *Read-Aloud Rhymes for the Very Young*, compiled by Jack Prelutsky (1986) and illustrated by Marc Brown, is one example of a book that provides a wide variety of rhymes to share. The students will also enjoy developing their understanding of rhyme by frequently saying classic nursery rhymes such as "Jack and Jill" and "Humpty Dumpty."

Read books with rhyming texts to the students. After the students become familiar with the rhyme scheme, pause and encourage them to predict the next rhyming word. Nancy Shaw's sheep books—*Sheep in a Jeep* (1986), *Sheep in a Shop* (1991), *Sheep Out to Eat* (1995), *Sheep Trick or Treat* (1997)—are examples of texts that would work well. See the booklist at the end of this appendix for other suggestions. To access a wide variety of rhyming words to use in phonemic awareness activities, visit the Rhyme Zone at www.rhymezone.com.

Syllable manipulation.
The song "Clap, Clap, Clap Your Hands" can be adapted for language manipulation (Yopp, 1992). The following version of the song encourages blending syllables; the first two verses are part of the original song, and the last two verses are an adaptation (Yopp & Yopp, 2000).

Clap, clap, clap your hands,
Clap your hands together.
Clap, clap, clap your hands,
Clap your hands together.

Snap, snap, snap your fingers.
Snap your fingers together.
Snap, snap, snap your fingers.
Snap your fingers together.

Say, say, say these parts.
Say these parts together.
Say, say, say these parts,
Say these parts together:

Teacher: *moun* (pause) *tain* (children respond, "mountain!")
Teacher: *love* (pause) *ly* (children respond, "lovely!")
Teacher: *un* (pause) *der* (children respond, "under!")
Teacher: *tea* (pause) *cher* (children respond, "teacher!")

Phoneme manipulation.
Singing traditional songs with lyrics revised to promote phonemic awareness can be used to promote a variety of aspects of phonemic awareness, including sound isolation, sound addition or deletion, and full segmentation.

Sound Isolation Activities: Yopp (1992) suggests that children may be given a word and asked to tell what sound occurs at the beginning, middle, or end of the word. In this activity, students sing new lyrics to the well-known children's song "Old MacDonald Had a Farm." The following lyrics focus on isolating beginning sounds:

What's the sound that starts these words:
Turtle, time, and *teeth*?
/t/ is the sound that starts these words:
Turtle, time, and *teeth*.
With a /t/, /t/ here, and a /t/, /t/ there,
Here a /t/, there a /t/, everywhere a /t/, /t/.
/t/ is the sound that starts these words:
Turtle, time, and *teeth*.
(*Chicken, chin*, and *cheek* would be another option for the song.)

Sound Isolation Activity: Bear et al. (2007) created Beginning-Middle-End, an activity that involves three steps. First, the teacher places the letters of a three- or four-letter word face down in a pocket chart so that the students cannot see them. Then the teacher says the word for the students (e.g., "hat"). Next, the teacher and students sing the following brief song to the tune of "Are You

Sleeping, Brother John?": "Beginning, middle, end; beginning, middle, end / Where is the sound? Where is the sound? / Where's the /t/ in *hat*? Where's the /t/ in *hat*? / Let's find out. Let's find out." After the song, one student comes forward, picks the sound position (beginning, middle, or end), and turns around the letter card.

Sound Addition or Deletion Activity: Students may add or substitute sounds in words in familiar songs. In this activity, students sing the traditional verses of the well-known children's song "Row, Row, Row Your Boat," but they sing different beginning sounds in the repeated words in the chorus. For example, the traditional chorus is "merrily, merrily, merrily, merrily, life is but a dream." In alternate versions of the song designed to promote phonemic awareness, the beginning sound of *merrily* may be replaced by any consonant. It doesn't matter if the word created is a nonsense word. The lyrics to "Row, Row, Row Your Boat" that follow focus on substituting beginning sounds:

> Row, row, row your boat
> Gently down the stream
> Merrily, merrily, merrily, merrily
> Life is but a dream
> (Berrily, berrily, berrily, berrily)
> (Terrily, terrily, terrily, terrily)

Full Segmentation: In full segmentation, the word is segmented or separated into individual sounds. In this activity, students sing new lyrics to the classic children's song "Twinkle, Twinkle, Little Star." The lyrics that follow focus on presenting a word—in this case *face*—and then segmenting or separating the individual sounds that make up the word:

> Listen, listen to my word,
> Then tell me the sounds you heard: *face*
> /f/ is one sound
> /a/ is two,
> /s/ is the last sound it's true.
> Thanks for listening to my words,
> And telling me the sounds you heard.

Scavenger Hunt (letters) (Yopp & Yopp, 2000): Children work in teams of three. Each team has a bag. The outside of the bag has a letter and a picture of an object that begins with that letter. For instance, one team receives a bag with letter *M* on it and a picture of a monkey; another team receives a bag with letter *S* on it and a picture of a snake. Next, children set off on a scavenger hunt to find objects in the classroom that begin with their target sound. Provide enough time for the children to be successful and then bring them together to share their target sound and the objects they found.

What Can We Read to Learn More About Teaching Phonemic Awareness?

Ehri, L.C., & Nunes, S.R. (2002). The role of phonemic awareness in learning to read. In A.E. Farstrup & S.J. Samuels (Eds.), *What research has to say about reading instruction* (3rd ed., pp. 110–139). Newark, DE: International Reading Association.

Yopp, H.K. (1992). Developing phonemic awareness in young children. *The Reading Teacher, 45,* 696–703.

Yopp, H.K., & Yopp, R.H. (2000). Supporting phonemic awareness development in the classroom. *The Reading Teacher, 54,* 130–143.

Phonics

What Is It?

Phonics is "a way of teaching reading and spelling that stresses symbol-sound relationships, used especially in beginning instruction" (Harris & Hodges, 1995, p. 186).

What Does the Research Tell Us?

According to Norman and Calfee (2004),

> The goal of early reading instruction is to help students move as quickly as possible toward independent comprehension of a broad range of texts. Phonics instruction is one gateway toward this goal by providing students with the skills to decode unfamiliar words encountered in new and challenging passages. (p. 42)

Stahl, Duffy-Hester, and Stahl (1998) report that good phonics instruction

- Develops the alphabetic principle
- Develops phonological awareness
- Provides a thorough grounding in the letters
- Does not teach rules, need not use worksheets, should not dominate instruction, and does not need to be boring
- Provides sufficient practice in reading words
- Leads to automatic word recognition
- Is one part of reading instruction

Researchers also note that students differ in their needs for phonics instruction and concur with Stahl and colleagues' belief that phonics is just one component of a balanced reading program (Cunningham & Cunningham, 2002; NICHD, 2000). The National Reading Panel (NICHD, 2000) reports that systematic phonics instruction produces significant benefits for students in kindergarten through grade 6 and for children having difficulty learning to read.

What Are Some Practical Ideas for Teaching Phonics?

Cunningham and Cunningham (2002) suggest that children should spend a majority of their time reading and writing and that phonics instruction should be taught through a variety of multilevel activities that emphasize transfer. Numerous teaching ideas support this thinking. *Words Their Way: Word Study for Phonics, Vocabulary, and Spelling* (Bear et al., 2007) and *Phonics They Use: Words for*

Reading and Writing (Cunningham, 2008) are bursting with engaging suggestions. What follows is a sampling of activities that have proven to be effective.

Alphabet Scrapbook. For Alphabet Scrapbook (Bear et al., 2007), prepare a blank dictionary for each child by stapling together sheets of paper. (Seven sheets of paper folded and stapled in the middle is enough for one letter per page.) Children can use this book in a variety of ways.

1. Practice writing uppercase and lowercase forms of the letter on each page.
2. Cut out letters in different fonts or styles from magazines and newspapers and paste them into their scrapbooks.
3. Draw and label pictures and other things that begin with that letter sound.
4. Cut and paste magazine pictures onto the corresponding letter page. These pictures, too, can be labeled.
5. Add sight words as they become known to create a personal dictionary.

Making Words. In Making Words (adapted from Cunningham, 2008), students manipulate a group of letters to create words of varying lengths. They may create the words based on clues or just list as many words as possible. Then they guess the mystery word—the source of the random letters. When creating the words, students may manipulate plastic letters or arrange magnetic letters on a cookie sheet.

Making and Writing Words. In Making and Writing Words (Rasinski, 1999a), students follow the same procedure as in Making Words, but instead of manipulating the letters, they write them. An adaptation is to encourage the students to manipulate the letters and then record them on the Making and Writing Words chart (see Appendix D, page 316).

Making and Writing Words Using Letter Patterns. In Making and Writing Words Using Letter Patterns (Rasinski, 1999b), students use rimes (word families) and other patterns, as well as individual letters, to write words. Then the students transfer their knowledge to create new words. Finally, they cut up the organizer to create word cards, which they can use to practice the words in games and sorts.

Onset and Rime Word Wall and Portable Word Wall. Use the 37 common rimes and onsets of your choice to create a word wall. Use the word wall as a resource for students' reading and writing.

-ack	-an	-aw	-ick	-ing	-op	
-unk	-ain	-ank	-ay	-ide	-ink	
-or	-ake	-ap	-eat	-ight	-ip	
-ore	-ale	-ash	-ell	-ill	-ir	
-uck	-all	-at	-est	-in	-ock	
-ug	-ame	-ate	-ice	-ine	-oke	-ump

Extend this idea, or any word wall, by having students create Portable Word Walls that they can use in other instructional settings or at home. This is easily accomplished by using manila folders to house the word wall and having students use markers to copy the words onto the inside of the folder.

What Can We Read to Learn More About Teaching Phonics?

Bear, D.R., Invernizzi, M., Templeton, S., & Johnston, F. (2007). *Words their way: Word study for phonics, vocabulary, and spelling instruction* (4th ed.). Upper Saddle River, NJ: Prentice Hall.

Cunningham, P.M. (2008). *Phonics they use: Words for reading and writing* (5th ed.). New York: HarperCollins.

Stahl, S.A., Duffy-Hester, A.M., & Stahl, K.A.D. (1998). Everything you wanted to know about phonics (but were afraid to ask). *Reading Research Quarterly, 33,* 338–355.

Fluency

What Is It?

According to Rasinski (2010), fluency is "the ability to read quickly, effortlessly, and efficiently with good, meaningful expression" (p. 26). Harris and Hodges (1995) note that fluency is "(1) the clear, easy, written or spoken expression of ideas; (2) freedom from word-identification problems that might hinder comprehension in silent reading or the expression of ideas in oral reading; automaticity" (p. 85). The National Reading Panel (NICHD, 2000) reports that fluent readers read orally with speed, accuracy, and expression.

What Does the Research Tell Us?

Rasinski (2010, 2011) stresses fluency's connection to reading comprehension. Other researchers agree that oral reading fluency contributes to comprehension (Nathan & Stanovich, 1991; NICHD, 2000; Zutell & Rasinski, 1991). The National Reading Panel (NICHD, 2000) reports also that repeated oral reading procedures that include guidance from teachers, peers, or parents have significant and positive impacts on the word recognition, fluency, and comprehension of both good and poor readers.

What Are Some Practical Ideas for Teaching Fluency?

To be fluent readers, students need to have good models, access to text, and time to read. To practice fluency, students engage in techniques such as choral reading and repeated readings. To do this independently, students need to have access to text they can read without teacher assistance. A list of trade books that promote phonemic awareness, phonics, and fluency can be found at the end of this appendix.

Fluent reading models. Providing fluent reading models for students helps them become fluent readers. Teachers, parents, cross-age volunteers, and audio books all can provide good fluency models for students.

Choral reading. In choral reading, the teacher and the students read together. When engaging in choral reading, the pressure is off the individual reader, so there is more of a tendency to focus on the fluent manner in which the poem or text segment is being read. Engaging in choral reading also provides everyone engaged with good fluency models.

Echo reading. To engage in echo reading, the teacher reads a short selection (such as a poem) segment by segment (e.g. line by line). As the teacher reads, the students "echo" or repeat what the teacher has read. In this activity, the teacher's reading provides a fluent model for the students.

Repeated reading. Repeated reading of text helps students read more fluently (Samuels, 1979, 2002). In this process, students work with partners; pairing a strong reader with a less-able reader is preferable. In each pair, students take turns assuming the role of teacher and student. The teacher looks at the words in the text while listening to the student read orally. The passage is read four times, with students changing roles after each reading. This improves comprehension, because as the reading becomes more fluent, less emphasis is placed on decoding and more on constructing meaning.

Readers Theatre. Readers Theatre does not involve producing a class play; it is like a read-through of a script. A narrator often introduces the work, sets the scene, and provides transitional information during the performance. The readers use their voices to create the scene and bring the characters to life. Books that have a lot of dialogue can be used for Readers Theatre. A number of websites also provide scripts for this technique.

Fluency-oriented reading instruction. Fluency-oriented reading instruction (Stahl, Heubach, & Cramond, 1997; Stahl & Kuhn, 2002) helps children become fluent readers so they can focus on text comprehension. To achieve this objective, the program focuses on five goals: (1) to keep the focus of reading lessons on students' comprehension of text, (2) to have students read material on their instructional reading levels, (3) to support students in their reading of instructional level text through repeated readings, (4) to provide opportunities for children to engage in text-based social interactions through partner reading, and (5) to expand the amount of time children spend reading at home and school. To accomplish these goals, students engage in a reading program that has three main components: a redesigned basal lesson, home reading, and a free-choice reading period.

What Can We Read to Learn More About Teaching Fluency?

Rasinski, T.V. (2010). *The fluent reader: Oral & silent reading strategies for building fluency, word recognition & comprehension* (2nd ed.). New York: Scholastic.

Richards, M. (2000). Be a good detective: Solve the case of oral reading fluency. *The Reading Teacher,* *53,* 534–539.

Samuels, S.J., & Farstrup, A.E. (Eds.). (2006). *What research has to say about fluency instruction.* Newark, DE: International Reading Association.

Vocabulary

What Is It?

Vocabulary development is "(1) the growth of a person's stock of known words and meanings; (2) the teaching-learning principles and practices that lead to such growth, as comparing and classifying word meanings, using context, analyzing root words and affixes, etc." (Harris & Hodges, 1995, p. 275). Pearson, Hiebert, and Kamil (2007) note that vocabulary may seem simple, but it is complex. Words relate to our experiences and knowledge, and their meanings change depending on the context in which they are used.

What Does the Research Tell Us?

Researchers agree that if our students do not know the words in a given context, they will have difficulty comprehending what they are reading (Dixon-Krauss, 2001; Duke, 2007; McLaughlin & Allen, 2002a; NICHD, 2000; Richek, 2005). Vocabulary instruction leads to gains in comprehension, but the methods must be appropriate to the age and ability of the reader (NICHD, 2000). Baumann and Kame'enui (1991) report that direct instruction of vocabulary and learning from context should be balanced. Blachowicz and Fisher (2000) note that the following four guidelines emerge from existing research about vocabulary instruction:

> Students should be active in developing their understanding of words and ways to learn them; students should personalize word learning; students should be immersed in words; students should build on multiple sources of information to learn words through repeated exposures. (p. 504)

A number of researchers conclude that reading widely is an effective way to promote vocabulary growth (Baumann & Kame'enui, 1991; Beck & McKeown, 1991; Hiebert et al., 1998; Snow et al., 1998).

What Are Some Practical Ideas for Teaching Vocabulary?

Descriptions of a variety of ideas for teaching vocabulary and related blackline masters can be found in Appendix C of this book. These include Concept of Definition Maps, Context Clues, List–Group–Label, RIVET, Semantic Feature Analysis, Semantic Maps, Semantic Question Maps, and Text Transformations. In addition, poem forms for cinquains, which work well when teaching synonyms, and diamantes, which work well when teaching antonyms, can be found in Appendix D.

Numerous other ideas for teaching vocabulary can be found in current academic journals and professional books. "Fun With Vocabulary" (Towell, 1997), which is summarized on the next page, is an example of the former; *Content Area Reading: Teaching and Learning in an Age of Multiple Literacies* (McLaughlin, 2010) is an example of the latter.

V Vocabulary Self-Collection Strategy: After locating a new word in their environment, students are asked to share (a) where they found the word, (b) the context, and (c) the importance of the word and why they selected it.

Visual-Auditory-Kinesthetic-Tactile: A multisensory technique in which students trace the target word with a finger while pronouncing each syllable until it can be written from memory.

O Onsets and rimes: The onset is the part of the word before the vowel; the rime includes the vowel and the rest of the letters in the word.

C Color shock: A color shock is a technique originally designed for right-brained learning disabled students to help them remember sight words. Each word is written in a different color beginning with the color green for "go" to designate the beginning of the word.

Clusters: For vocabulary instruction to be meaningful, words should be presented in semantic frameworks through categories or clusters. A cluster is a set of words that relate to a single concept.

A ABC books and anagrams: Students create their own alphabet books and discover words through illustrations on the basis of their prior knowledge or schemata. Anagrams are another fun and interesting way to learn vocabulary or spelling words.

B Book boxes: Boxes for related reading materials.

Boxes for visual configuration: This visual discrimination technique involves drawing around words to emphasize their length and shape.

Word banks: Students should have personal word banks for storing and remembering their self-selected and teacher-selected words, such as spelling words.

U Unknown words: A strategy for primary grades is beep it, frame it, begin it, split it, and find it in the dictionary.

L List–Group–Label: Working in cooperative groups, students list as many words as possible that begin with a specific letter on a piece of chart paper. Students sort and label the words according to different categories.

Language Experience Approach: A student tells a story, the teacher creates a book using the student's words, and the student reads the book.

A Active involvement: Students must be actively involved in learning and using vocabulary.

R Repetition, rhymes, riddles, roots: Encountering the words they have learned in multiple settings, engaging in word play (using books by Fred Gwynne or Marvin Terban), and engaging in structural analysis support vocabulary development.

Y Yarns: Using their vocabulary to spin yarns or tall tales is a fun way for students to use words they have learned. The stories can be shared through storytelling or writing.

What Can We Read to Learn More About Teaching Vocabulary?

Blachowicz, C.L.Z., & Fisher, P. (2000). Vocabulary instruction. In M.L. Kamil, P.B. Mosenthal, P.D. Pearson, & R. Barr (Eds.), *Handbook of reading research* (Vol. 3, pp. 503–523). Mahwah, NJ: Erlbaum.

Blachowicz, C.L.Z., Fisher, P., Ogle, D.M., & Watts-Taffe, S. (2006). Vocabulary: Questions from the classroom. *Reading Research Quarterly*, 41, 524–539.

Graves, M.F., & Watts-Taffe, S.M. (2002). The place of word consciousness in a research-based vocabulary program. In A.E. Farstrup & S.J. Samuels (Eds.), *What research has to say about reading instruction* (pp. 140–165). Newark, DE: International Reading Association.

Comprehension

What Is It?

Duke and Pearson (2002) note that "Comprehension is a consuming, continuous, and complex activity, but one that, for good readers, is both satisfying and productive" (p. 206). According to Harris and Hodges (1995), comprehension is

> the construction of the meaning of a written or spoken communication through a reciprocal, holistic interchange of ideas between the interpreter and the message in a particular communicative context. *Note:* The presumption here is that meaning resides in the intentional problem-solving, thinking processes of the interpreter during such an interchange, that the content of meaning is influenced by that person's prior knowledge and experience, and that the message so constructed by the receiver may or may not be congruent with the message sent. (p. 39)

What Does the Research Tell Us?

Much of what we know about comprehension is based on studies of good readers—readers who are actively engaged in the reading process, who have set clear goals, and who constantly monitor the relation between their goals and the text they are reading (Duke & Pearson, 2002; Pearson, 2001a; Pressley, 2000). Good readers use a repertoire of comprehension strategies to facilitate the construction of meaning (Duke & Pearson, 2002; McLaughlin, 2010; NICHD, 2000; Palincsar & Brown, 1984; Roehler & Duffy, 1984).

Researchers including Duke and Pearson (2002), Pressley (2001), and Hilden and Pressley (2002) note that reading comprehension strategies can be taught in the primary grades. Pressley (2001) suggests that students begin learning comprehension skills and a few strategies as early as kindergarten.

What Are Some Practical Ideas for Teaching Comprehension?

Comprehension skills and strategies can be taught at the primary level, and a variety of teaching ideas and related blacklines that support the comprehension strategies can be found in Appendix C of this book. In addition, Reciprocal Teaching, a technique that involves multiple comprehension strategies, is fully delineated in Chapter 4 and summarized in Appendix C.

What Can We Read to Learn More About Teaching Comprehension?

Duke, N.K., & Pearson, P.D. (2002). Effective practices for developing comprehension. In A.E. Farstrup & S.J. Samuels (Eds.), *What research has to say about reading instruction* (3rd ed., pp. 205–242). Newark, DE: International Reading Association.

Greene, K., Guthrie, L., Kotinopoulos, C., Mellos, S., Sullivan, J., & Trim, J. (Eds.). (2009). *Teaching comprehension strategies that develop oral language, vocabulary, and fluency.* New York: Guilford.

Rasinski, T.V. (Ed.). (2011). *Developing reading instruction that works.* Bloomington, IN: Solution Tree.

Books to Use When Teaching Phonemic Awareness, Phonics, and Fluency

Ashman, L. (2002). *Can you make a piggy giggle?* New York: Dutton.

Axtell, D. (1999). *We're going on a lion hunt.* New York: Scholastic.

Bennett, J. (1987). *Noisy poems.* Hong Kong: Oxford University Press.

Brown, A. (1984). *Willy the wimp.* New York: Knopf.

Brown, M.W. (1993). *Four fur feet.* New York: Doubleday.

Bruss, D. (2001). *Book! Book! Book!* New York: Arthur A. Levine.

Bynum, J. (1999). *Altoona baboona.* New York: Harcourt.

Calmenson, S. (1998). *The teeny tiny teacher.* New York: Scholastic.

Carle, E. (2002). *Does a kangaroo have a mother, too?* New York: HarperCollins.

Carle, E. (2002). *"Slowly, slowly, slowly," said the sloth.* New York: Penguin Putnam.

Christelow, E. (1989). *Five little monkeys jumping on the bed.* New York: Clarion.

Christelow, E. (1991). *Five little monkeys sitting in a tree.* New York: Trumpet Club.

Colandro, L. (2002). *There was an old lady who swallowed a bat!* New York: Scholastic.

Cronin, D. (2008). *Thump, quack, moo: A whacky adventure.* New York: Atheneum.

Dewdney, A. (2009). *Llama Llama misses mama.* New York: Viking.

Dunrea, O. (1985). *Mogwogs on the march!* New York: Holiday House.

Edwards, P. (1995). *Four famished foxes and Fosdyke.* New York: HarperTrophy.

Ehlert, L. (1989). *Eating the alphabet: Fruits and vegetables from A to Z.* San Diego: Harcourt Brace Jovanovich.

Fajerman, D. (2002). *How to speak moo!* Hauppauge, NY: Barron's Educational Series.

Freedman, C. (2001). *Where's your smile, crocodile?* Atlanta, GA: Peachtree.

Fuge, C. (2002). *I know a rhino.* New York: Sterling.

Galdone, P. (1968). *Henny Penny.* New York: Scholastic.

Galdone, P. (1979). *The little red hen.* New York: Scholastic.

Gordon, J. (1991). *Six sleepy sheep.* New York: Puffin.

Hawkins, C., & Hawkins, J. (1986). *Tog the dog.* New York: G.P. Putnam's Sons.

Hicks, B.J. (2005). *Jitterbug jam.* New York: Farrar, Straus and Giroux.

Hymes, L., & Hymes, J. (1964). *Oodles of noodles.* New York: Young Scott.

Jackson, A. (1997). *I know an old lady who swallowed a pie.* New York: Penguin Group.

Kuskin, K. (1990). *Roar and more.* New York: HarperTrophy.

Martin, B. Jr. (1967). *Brown bear, brown bear, what do you see?* New York: Henry Holt.

Martin, B. Jr. (1997). *Polar bear, polar bear, what do you hear?* New York: Henry Holt.

Martin, B. Jr. (2007). *Baby bear, baby bear, what do you see?* New York: Henry Holt.

Martin, B. Jr., & Sampson, M. (2008). *The Bill Martin Jr. big book of poetry.* New York: Simon & Schuster.

Martin, B. Jr., Sampson, M., & Bryant, L.J. (2008). *Kitty cat, kitty cat, are you waking up?* Tarrytown, NY: Marshall Cavendish.

Miranda, A. (1998). *To market to market.* New York: Scholastic.

Numeroff, L. (1999). *Sometimes I wonder if poodles like noodles.* New York: Simon & Schuster.

Numeroff, L. (2006). *Mouse cookies & more: A treasury.* New York: HarperCollins.

Numeroff, L. (2008). *If you give a cat a cupcake.* New York: HarperCollins.

Numeroff, L. (2008). *Time for school, mouse!* New York: HarperFestival.

Obligado, L. (1983). *Faint frogs feeling feverish and other terrifically tantalizing tongue twisters.* New York: Viking.

Ochs, C.P. (1991). *Moose on the loose.* Minneapolis, MN: Carolrhoda.

Otto, C. (1991). *Dinosaur chase.* New York: HarperTrophy.

Parry, C. (1991). *Zoomerang-a-boomerang: Poems to make your belly laugh.* New York: Puffin.

Patz, N. (1983). *Moses supposes his toeses are roses.* San Diego: Harcourt Brace Jovanovich.

Prelutsky, J. (1982). *The baby uggs are hatching.* New York: Mulberry.

Prelutsky, J. (1986). *Read-aloud rhymes for the very young.* New York: Knopf.

Prelutsky, J. (1989). *Poems of a nonny mouse.* New York: Knopf.

Prelutsky, J. (2009). *The swamps of Sleethe: Poems from beyond the solar system.* New York: Knopf.

Raschka, C. (2008). *Peter and the wolf.* New York: Atheneum.

Rosen, M. (1997). *We're going on a bear hunt.* New York: Little Simon.

Roth, C. (2002). *The little school bus.* New York: North-South.

Rovetch, L. (2001). *Ook the book.* San Francisco: Chronicle.

Segal, L. (1977). *Tell me a Trudy.* New York: Farrar, Straus & Giroux.

Sendak, M. (1990). *Alligators all around: An alphabet.* New York: HarperTrophy.

Seuss, Dr. (1965). *Fox in socks.* New York: Random House.

Seuss, Dr. (1974). *There's a wocket in my pocket.* New York: Random House.

Seuss, Dr. (1976). *One fish, two fish, red fish, blue fish.* New York: Random House.

Seuss, Dr. (1996). *Dr. Seuss's ABC.* New York: Random House.

Seuss, Dr. (1996). *Mr. Brown can moo! Can you? Dr. Seuss's book of wonderful noises.* New York: Random House.

Shange, N. (2009). *Coretta Scott.* New York: Amistad/Tegen.

Shaw, N. (1986). *Sheep in a Jeep.* Boston: Houghton Mifflin.

Shaw, N. (1991). *Sheep in a shop.* Boston: Houghton Mifflin.

Shaw, N. (1995). *Sheep out to eat.* Boston: Houghton Mifflin.

Shaw, N. (1997). *Sheep trick or treat.* Boston: Houghton Mifflin.

Shulman, L. (2002). *Old MacDonald had a woodshop.* New York: G.P. Putnam's Sons.

Silverstein, S. (1964). *A giraffe and a half.* New York: HarperCollins.

Slate, J. (1996). *Miss Bindergarten gets ready for kindergarten.* New York: Dutton.

Slate, J. (1998). *Miss Bindergarten celebrates the 100th day.* New York: Puffin.

Slate, J. (2001). *Miss Bindergarten takes a field trip*. New York: Dutton.

Taback, S. (1997). *There was an old lady who swallowed a fly*. New York: Viking.

Tallon, R. (1979). *Zoophabets*. New York: Scholastic.

Weeks, S. (1998). *Mrs. McNosh hangs up her wash*. New York: HarperTrophy.

Wood, A. (1984). *The napping house*. Orlando, FL: Harcourt.

Yolen, J. (1997). *The three bears rhyme book*. San Diego, CA: Harcourt.

Yolen, J. (2000). *Color me a rhyme*. Honesdale, PA: Boyds Mills.

Comprehension Skill- and Strategy-Based Teaching Ideas and Blackline Masters

TEACHING IDEAS AT A GLANCE

Teaching Idea	When to Use	Comprehension Strategy	Text
Previewing			
Anticipation/Reaction Guide	Before After	Previewing Monitoring	Narrative Informational
Predict-o-Gram	Before After	Previewing Summarizing	Narrative
Probable Passages	Before	Previewing Making Connections	Narrative
Semantic Map	Before After	Previewing Knowing How Words Work Summarizing	Narrative Informational
Semantic Question Map	Before After	Previewing Knowing How Words Work Summarizing	Informational
Story Impressions	Before	Previewing Making Connections	Narrative
Storybook Introductions	Before	Previewing Making Connections Knowing How Words Work	Narrative
Self-Questioning			
"I Wonder" Statements	Before During After	Self-Questioning Previewing Making Connections	Narrative Informational
K–W–L and K–W–L–S	Before During After	Self-Questioning Previewing Making Connections	Informational
Paired Questioning	During After	Self-Questioning Making Connections Monitoring	Narrative Informational
Question–Answer Relationships (QAR)	During After	Self-Questioning Making Connections Monitoring	Narrative Informational
Thick and Thin Questions	Before During After	Self-Questioning Making Connections	Narrative Informational
Making Connections			
Coding the Text	During	Making Connections	Narrative Informational
Connection Stems	After	Making Connections	Narrative Informational
Double-Entry Journal	Before During After	Making Connections Monitoring Summarizing	Narrative Informational
Draw and Write Connections	During After	Making Connections Visualizing	Narrative Informational

TEACHING IDEAS AT A GLANCE

Teaching Idea	When to Use	Comprehension Strategy	Text
Visualizing			
Draw and Write Visualizations	During After	Visualizing Making Connections Summarizing	Narrative Informational
Graphic Organizers/ Visual Organizers	Before During After	Visualizing Making Connections Summarizing	Narrative Informational
Guided Imagery	Before After	Visualizing Making Connections	Narrative Informational
Open-Mind Portrait	After	Visualizing Making Connections	Narrative Informational
Sketch to Stretch	After	Visualizing Making Connections	Narrative Informational
Knowing How Words Work			
Concept of Definition Map	Before After	Knowing How Words Work	Narrative Informational
Context Clues	During	Knowing How Words Work	Narrative Informational
List–Group–Label	Before After	Knowing How Words Work Previewing Making Connections	Informational
RIVET	Before	Knowing How Words Work Previewing	Informational
Semantic Feature Analysis	Before After	Knowing How Words Work Making Connections	Narrative Informational
Text Transformations	During	Knowing How Words Work	Narrative
Vocabulary Bookmark	During After	Knowing How Words Work Monitoring	Narrative Informational
Monitoring			
Bookmark Technique	During After	Monitoring Knowing How Words Work Making Connections	Narrative Informational
Cueing Systems Check	During	Monitoring Knowing How Words Work Evaluating	Narrative Informational
Patterned Partner Reading	During	Monitoring Making Connections Evaluating	Narrative Informational
Say Something	During	Monitoring Making Connections	Narrative Informational
Think-Alouds	Before During After	All	Narrative Informational

Guided Comprehension in the Primary Grades (Second Edition) by Maureen McLaughlin.
© 2010 by the International Reading Association. May be copied for classroom use.

TEACHING IDEAS AT A GLANCE

Teaching Idea	When to Use	Comprehension Strategy	Text
Summarizing			
Bio-Pyramid	After	Summarizing Making Connections Monitoring	Informational
Lyric Retelling	After	Summarizing	Narrative Informational
Paired Summarizing	Before During After	Summarizing Making Connections Monitoring	Narrative Informational
QuIP (Questions Into Paragraphs)	After	Summarizing Self-Questioning	Informational
Retelling	After	Summarizing	Narrative
Story Map	After	Summarizing Monitoring	Narrative
Story Pyramid	After	Summarizing Making Connections Monitoring	Narrative
Summary Cube	Before During After	Summarizing	Narrative Informational
Evaluating			
Evaluative Questioning	During After	Evaluating Self-Questioning	Narrative Informational
Journal Responses	During After	Evaluating Making Connections Summarizing	Narrative Informational
Mind and Alternative Mind Portraits	During After	Evaluating	Narrative Informational
Persuasive Writing	Before During After	Evaluating	Narrative Informational
Venn Diagram	During After	Evaluating Making Connections Summarizing	Informational
Comprehension Routines			
Cross-Age Reading Experiences	Before During After	All	Narrative Informational
Directed Reading–Thinking Activity/Directed Listening–Thinking Activity	Before During After	Previewing Making Connections Monitoring	Narrative Informational
Literature Circles	Before During After	All	Narrative Informational
Reciprocal Teaching	Before During After	Previewing Self-Questioning Monitoring Summarizing	Narrative Informational

TEACHING IDEAS

Anticipation/Reaction Guide

Purposes: To set purposes for reading texts; to activate prior knowledge and help make connections with the text.

Comprehension Strategies: Previewing, Monitoring

Text: Narrative, Informational   **Use:** Before and After Reading

Procedure: (Begin by explaining and demonstrating Anticipation/Reaction Guides.)

1. Select a text for the students to read.

2. Create three to five general statements for the students to respond to with "agree" or "disagree." Create statements that are intuitively sound but may be disconfirmed by reading the text, or that appear intuitively incorrect but may be proven true by reading the text.

3. Ask students to read the statements and indicate agreement or disagreement by placing a check in the appropriate "agree" or "disagree" column.

4. Introduce the text to the students.

5. Ask students to read the text to confirm or disconfirm their original responses.

6. After reading, encourage students to revisit their predictions and modify, if necessary.

Example: Bauer, M.D. (2003). *Wind*. New York: Scholastic.

Agree   Disagree

_____   _____ 1. Plants use wind to carry their seeds.

_____   _____ 2. Warm air rises, but cool air falls.

_____   _____ 3. Wind can move clouds.

Source: Readence, J.E., Bean, T.W., & Baldwin, R. (2004). *Content area reading: An integrated approach* (8th ed.). Dubuque, IA: Kendall/Hunt.

Predict-o-Gram

(See blackline, page 281.)

Purposes: To make predictions about a story using narrative elements; to introduce vocabulary.

Comprehension Strategies: Previewing, Summarizing

Text: Narrative   **Use:** Before and After Reading

Procedure: (Begin by explaining and demonstrating Predict-o-Grams.)

1. Select vocabulary from the story to stimulate predictions. Vocabulary should represent the story elements: characters, setting, problem, action, solution.

2. Ask students to work with partners to decide which story element the word tells about and write each word on the Predict-o-Gram in the appropriate place.

3. Introduce the story and invite students to read it.

TEACHING IDEAS

4. Revisit the original predictions with students and make changes as necessary. Use the resulting information to summarize or retell the story.

Example: Carle, E. (1984). *The very busy spider*. New York: Philomel.

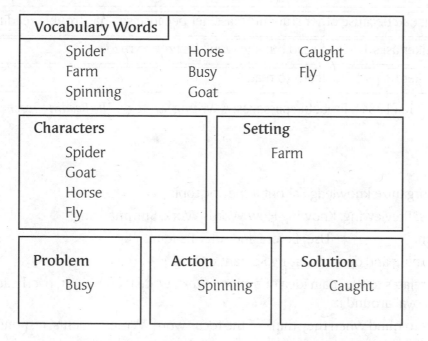

Source: Blachowicz, C.L.Z. (1986). Making connections: Alternatives to the vocabulary notebook. *Journal of Reading*, 29, 643–649.

Probable Passages

(See blackline, page 282.)

Purposes: To make predictions using story elements; to introduce vocabulary; to use story vocabulary to make connections with story structure.

Comprehension Strategies: Previewing, Making Connections

Text: Narrative   **Use:** Before Reading

Procedure: (Begin by explaining and demonstrating Probable Passages.)

1. Introduce key vocabulary from the story to students. (Choose vocabulary that represents the elements of the story: characters, setting, problem, attempts to resolve the problem, and resolution.)

2. Invite students to use the key vocabulary to create probable sentences to predict each element in the story. (Providing a story frame/story map facilitates this process.)

3. Encourage students to use their probable sentences to create a story and share it with the class.

4. Introduce the story and read it.

5. Compare and contrast Probable Passages with the story. Confirm or modify original predictions.

TEACHING IDEAS

Example: Polacco, P. (1998). *Thank you, Mr. Falker*. New York: Scholastic.

Setting:	The story takes place in a school.
Characters:	The characters' names are Mr. Falker and Tricia.
Problem:	Tricia is sad because other students tease her because she has trouble reading.
Events:	Mr. Falker asks Tricia to read but she won't be able to read.
Solution:	Mr. Falker helps Tricia learn to read.

Source: Adapted from Wood, K. (1984). Probable passages: A writing strategy. *The Reading Teacher, 37,* 496–499.

Semantic Map

Purposes: To activate and organize knowledge about a specific topic.

Comprehension Strategies: Previewing, Knowing How Words Work, Summarizing

Text: Narrative, Informational   **Use:** Before and After Reading

Procedure: (Begin by explaining and demonstrating Semantic Maps.)

1. Select a focus word that relates to the main idea or topic of a text; write it on a chart, overhead, or chalkboard; and draw an oval around it.

2. Ask students what comes to mind when they think of the focus word. Write students' responses.

3. Invite students to review the list of responses and suggest subtopics that emerge.

4. Add the subtopics to the Semantic Map, draw ovals around them, and use lines to connect them to the focus word.

5. Visit each subtopic and ask students which of their original responses support each subtopic. Record these ideas beneath each subtopic.

6. Read the text and revise the Semantic Map to reflect new knowledge.

Example: Scholastic First Discovery. (1989). *Ladybugs and other insects*. New York: Scholastic.

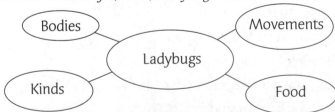

Source: Johnson, D.D., & Pearson, P.D. (1984). *Teaching reading vocabulary* (2nd ed.). New York: Holt, Rinehart and Winston.

TEACHING IDEAS

Semantic Question Map

Purposes: To use specific questions to activate and organize knowledge about a particular topic.

Comprehension Strategies: Previewing, Knowing How Words Work, Summarizing

Text: Narrative, Informational   **Use:** Before and After Reading

Procedure: (Begin by explaining and modeling Semantic Question Maps.)

1. Select the main idea or topic of the passage; write it on a chart, overhead, or chalkboard; and draw an oval around it.

2. Draw four arms that extend from the oval. At the end of each arm, draw another oval. Write a specific question about the topic in each of the four ovals. Number the questions.

3. Discuss the topic with the students and share the four questions. Then, beginning with question one, invite the students to share whatever information they may already know to respond to the question. Record student responses beneath each question.

4. Read the text and revise the Semantic Question Map to reflect new knowledge.

5. Use the questions and responses to summarize what students know about the topic.

Example: Scholastic First Discovery. (1989). *Ladybugs and other insects*. New York: Scholastic.

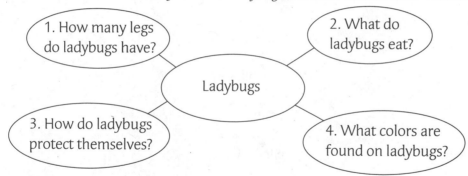

Source: McLaughlin, M. (2003). *Guided Comprehension in the primary grades*. Newark, DE: International Reading Association.

Story Impressions

(See blackline, page 288.)

Purposes: To provide a framework for narrative writing; to encourage predictions about the story; to make connections between story vocabulary and story structure.

Comprehension Strategies: Previewing, Making Connections

Text: Narrative   **Use:** Before Reading

Procedure: (Begin by explaining and demonstrating Story Impressions.)

1. Provide students with a list of words that provide clues about the story. Choose words that relate to the narrative elements—characters, setting, problem, attempts to resolve, and resolution. Clues may be up to 5 words long. The maximum number of clues is 10.

TEACHING IDEAS

2. List the clues in the order in which they appear in the story. Connect them with downward arrows. Share the list of sequential clues with the students.

3. Ask students to work in small groups to use the sequential clues to write Story Impressions.

4. Invite small groups to share their Story Impressions with the class and discuss them.

5. Read the original story to the class and ask students to compare and contrast their Story Impressions with the original story.

Example: Wild, M., & Argent, K. (2000). *Nighty night!* Atlanta, GA: Peachtree.

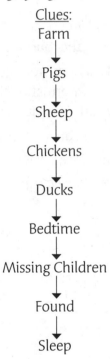

Clues:
Farm
↓
Pigs
↓
Sheep
↓
Chickens
↓
Ducks
↓
Bedtime
↓
Missing Children
↓
Found
↓
Sleep

Story Impression: Once there was a farm. Pigs, sheep, chickens, and ducks lived there. When the animals went to tuck in their children at bedtime they found them missing. They searched all over the farm and found the children playing a game of hide and seek. The animals took their children home to get some sleep.

Adaptations: Create Poem Impressions using story poems. Create Bio-Impressions or Text Impressions using informational text.

Source: McGinley, W., & Denner, P. (1987). Story impressions: A prereading/prewriting activity. *Journal of Reading, 31*, 248–253.

Storybook Introductions

Purposes: To introduce story, characters, vocabulary, and style of a book prior to reading; to promote prediction and anticipation of a story; to make new texts accessible to readers.

Comprehension Strategies: Previewing, Making Connections, Knowing How Words Work

Text: Narrative   **Use:** Before Reading

TEACHING IDEAS

Procedure: (Begin by explaining and modeling Storybook Introductions.)

1. Preview the text and prepare the introduction. Focus on those points that will help make the text accessible to students. These may include text structure, specific vocabulary, language patterns, plot, or difficult parts.

2. Introduce the text (topic, title, and characters).

3. Encourage students to respond to the cover and text illustrations by making connections to personal experiences or other texts.

4. Do a picture walk with the text. While browsing through the illustrations, introduce the plot up to the climax (if possible, not giving away the ending). Throughout this process, encourage students to make connections to personal experiences or other texts, and make predictions about what will happen next.

5. Choose to introduce some literary language, vocabulary, or repetitive sentence patterns that will be helpful to the readers.

6. Invite students to read the text, or a section of the text. Then engage in discussion and other activities, such as retelling.

Note: It is important to make decisions about the introduction based on the text and the students' competency and familiarity with the text type.

Adaptation: Use with informational texts, focusing on text elements.

Example: Numeroff, L. (1998). *If you give a pig a pancake*. New York: HarperCollins.

- <u>Introduce the text (topic, title, and characters)</u>: For example, "The title of this book is *If You Give a Pig a Pancake*. The characters are a pig and a young girl. This book is about giving a pig a pancake and what happens to that pig."

- <u>Ask the students to make connections</u>: Encourage students to respond to the cover and text illustrations by making connections to personal experiences or other text.
  Student One: "The cover and title remind me of when my dad made pancakes and we gave one to my dog. He ate the pancake so fast, and I could tell he wanted another one. I think that after the pig eats a pancake he will want to eat another one, just like my dog." (Text–Self Connection)

- <u>Do a Picture Walk and invite students to make connections and predictions</u>: Browse the text and illustrations with the students, and introduce the plot up to the climax (if possible without giving away the ending). Browse the text up until the last three pages, encourage students to make connections to personal experiences or other texts, and make predictions about what they think will happen next.
  Student Two: "I think that the pig is going to turn the house into a mess and get syrup from the pancakes everywhere. The whole house will be sticky." (Prediction)

- <u>Choose to introduce some literacy language or repetitive sentence patterns</u> that will be helpful to the readers. For this text you may bring up the repetitive fashion of giving the pig something, which builds on the pig wanting something else.

TEACHING IDEAS

- <u>Invite students to read the text</u> or a section of the text. For example, "Now it is time for us to read the story. Let's remember the connections and predictions we made. We'll discuss *If You Give a Pig a Pancake* when we finish reading."

Source: Clay, M.M. (1991). Introducing a new storybook to young readers. *The Reading Teacher, 45,* 264–273.

"I Wonder" Statements

Purposes: To encourage self-questioning; to provide a model for active thinking during the reading process.

Comprehension Strategies: Self-Questioning, Previewing, Making Connections

Text: Narrative, Informational   **Use:** Before, During, and After Reading

Procedure: (Begin by explaining and demonstrating "I Wonder" Statements.)

1. Model for students how to wonder. Do this orally and in writing, beginning your thoughts with "I wonder...." Wonder about life experiences or the world, as well as events in stories or facts presented in texts.

2. Guide students to wonder about the world, their lives, story events, and ideas presented in texts.

3. Provide students with a format for sharing their wonderings orally or in writing, including "I Wonder" Bookmarks.

4. Share wonders and discuss them with text support, if possible.

5. Encourage students to wonder throughout the reading of a story or informational text. Use students' "I Wonder" Statements to provide structure for further reading or research.

Example: Carle, E. (1977). *The grouchy ladybug.* New York: HarperTrophy.

Before Reading:	• I wonder why the ladybug is so grouchy.
	• I wonder if someone made the ladybug grouchy.
	• I wonder if the ladybug will cheer up.
During Reading:	• I wonder why the grouchy ladybug won't share with the friendly ladybug.
	• I wonder why the ladybug wants to fight everyone.
	• I wonder why the whale doesn't answer the ladybug.
After Reading:	• I wonder why the friendly ladybug was still so nice to the grouchy ladybug.
	• I wonder if the grouchy ladybug will still be grouchy in the morning.
	• I wonder if the grouchy ladybug will still want to fight with everyone.

Alternative Formats: Draw and Write Wonders and "I Wonder" Bookmarks (See blacklines, pages 272 and 274.)

Source: Harvey, S., & Goudvis, A. (2000). *Strategies that work: Teaching comprehension to enhance understanding.* York, ME: Stenhouse.

Guided Comprehension in the Primary Grades (Second Edition) by Maureen McLaughlin.
© 2010 by the International Reading Association. May be copied for classroom use.

TEACHING IDEAS

Know–Want to Know–Learn (K–W–L)

(See blacklines, pages 276–277.)

Purposes: To activate students' prior knowledge about a topic; to set purposes for reading; to confirm, revise, or expand original understandings related to a topic.

Comprehension Strategies: Self-Questioning, Previewing, Making Connections

Text: Informational   **Use:** Before, During, and After Reading

Procedure: (Begin by explaining and demonstrating K–W–L.)

1. Ask students to brainstorm everything they know, or think they know, about a specific topic. Write, or ask students to write, these ideas in the *K* column of the K–W–L chart.

2. Next, invite students to write or tell some things they want to know about the topic. List these in the *W* column.

3. Encourage students to read the text. (As they read, they can jot down new ideas, facts, or concepts they learn in the *L* column.)

4. List or have students list what they learned in the *L* column.

5. Revisit the *K* column to modify or confirm original understandings.

6. Revisit the *W* column to check if all questions have been answered.

7. Discuss the completed K–W–L chart. Use it to summarize the topic.

Example: Berger, M., & Berger, G. (2004). *Earth*. New York: Scholastic.

TOPIC: Earth

K (what I know or think I know)	W (what I want to know)	L (what I learned)
• It is a planet. • It is the third planet from the sun. • Earth has four seasons.	• How long does it take Earth to circle the sun? • What causes night and day?	• It takes the Earth one year to circle the sun. • The spinning of the Earth causes night and day.

Source: Ogle, D. (1986). K-W-L: A teaching model that develops active reading of expository text. *The Reading Teacher, 39*, 564–570.

Adaptation: Know–Want to Know–Learned–Still Want to Know (K–W–L–S)

Extend K–W–L by inviting students to list what they *still* want to know in a fourth column. Develop a plan to help them find answers to these questions.

Source: Sippola, A.E. (1995). K-W-L-S. *The Reading Teacher, 48*, 542–543.

TEACHING IDEAS

Paired Questioning

Purpose: To engage in questioning and active decision making during the reading of a narrative or informational text.

Comprehension Strategies: Self-Questioning, Making Connections, Monitoring

Text: Narrative, Informational   **Use:** During and After Reading

Procedure: (Begin by explaining and demonstrating Paired Questioning.)

1. Introduce a text and encourage students to read the title or subtitle of a manageable section, put the reading material aside, and ask a question related to the title or subtitle. Each partner provides a reasonable answer to the question.

2. Encourage students to silently read a predetermined (by teacher or students) section of text and take turns asking a question about the reading. If needed, they can use the text when asking or responding to the question. Students reverse roles and continue reading and asking questions until the text is finished.

3. After the text is read, invite each partner to explain what he or she believes to be the important and unimportant ideas in the text. Encourage the students to share their reasoning. Then the partner agrees or disagrees with the choices and offers support for his or her thinking.

Example: Shaw, N. (1986). *Sheep in a jeep*. Boston: Houghton Mifflin.

Student 1: Do you think the sheep are going for a ride in the jeep?
Student 2: It looks that way, but sheep are animals. They can't drive.

Student 2: Do you think the jeep is broken?
Student 1: I think it is broken because they had to push it.

Student 1: Do you think anyone will buy the jeep?
Student 2: Yes, I think they will because the jeep is for sale cheap.

Student 2: I think the important idea in this book is that sheep don't know how to drive, so they shouldn't drive.
Student 1: I agree with you. I think it means that people shouldn't do something if they don't know how to do it.

Source: Vaughn, J., & Estes, T. (1986). *Reading and reasoning beyond the primary grades*. Boston: Allyn & Bacon.

Question–Answer Relationships (QAR)

(See blackline, page 283.)

Purposes: To promote self-questioning; to answer comprehension questions by focusing on the information source needed to answer the question.

Comprehension Strategies: Self-Questioning, Making Connections, Monitoring

Text: Narrative, Informational   **Use:** During and After Reading

TEACHING IDEAS

Procedure: (Begin by explaining and demonstrating QAR.)

1. Introduce the QAR concept and terminology. Explain that there are two kinds of information:

   In the Book: The answer is found in the text.

   In My Head: The answer requires input from the student's understandings and background knowledge.

   Explain that there are two kinds of QARs for each kind of information:

   In the Book

   Right There: The answer is stated in the passage.

   Think and Search: The answer is derived from more than one sentence or paragraph but is stated in the text.

   In My Head

   On My Own: The answer is contingent on information the reader already possesses in his or her background knowledge.

   Author and Me: The answer is inferred in the text, but the reader must make the connections with his or her own prior knowledge.

2. Use a Think-Aloud to practice using QAR with a text. Model choosing the appropriate QAR, giving the answer from the source, and writing or speaking the answer.

3. Introduce a short passage and related questions. Ask groups or individuals to work through the passages and the questions. Students answer the questions and tell the QAR strategy they used. Any justifiable answer should be accepted.

4. Practice QAR with additional texts.

Principles of Teaching QAR: Give immediate feedback; progress from shorter to longer texts; guide students from group to independent activities; provide transitions from easier to more difficult tasks.

Example: Johnson, D. (2002). *Substitute teacher plans*. New York: Henry Holt.

In the Book

Right There: What did Miss Huff forget to write on the top of her list?
Substitute Teacher Plans

Think and Search: Why did Miss Huff stay up all night writing a list of fun things to do instead of going to bed?
She had to write her substitute teacher plans and then her list of fun things to do. She was having so much fun thinking of fun things to do that she lost track of time.

In My Head

Author and Me: Did Miss Huff really dislike her job?
No, she was happy doing all the things she had planned for her class to do. She didn't even know that she had mixed up her lists.

On My Own: Why does Miss Huff invite the principal to join the class on tomorrow's trip?
She invites him because he needs a day away from school, too.

Source: Raphael, T. (1986). Teaching Question Answer Relationships, revisited. *The Reading Teacher, 39*, 516–522.

TEACHING IDEAS

Thick and Thin Questions

(See blackline, page 293.)

Purposes: To create questions pertaining to a text; to help students discern the depth of the questions they ask and are asked; to use questions to facilitate understanding a text.

Comprehension Strategies: Self-Questioning, Making Connections

Text: Narrative, Informational   **Use:** Before, During, and After Reading

Procedure: (Begin by explaining and demonstrating Thick and Thin Questions.)

1. Teach the students the difference between thick questions and thin questions. Thick questions deal with the big picture and large concepts. Answers to thick questions are involved, complex, and open-ended. Thin questions deal with specific content or words. Answers to thin questions are short (often one, two, or three words) and close-ended. Thick questions usually require higher order thinking; thin questions require literal responses.

2. Guide students to work with partners to create Thick and Thin Questions. Read a portion of text and prompt students with stems such as "Why..." or "What if..." for thick questions and "How far..." and "When..." for thin questions.

3. Encourage students to create Thick and Thin Questions for the texts they are reading. They can use the blackline master, write the questions in their Guided Comprehension Journals, or write their thick questions on larger sticky notes and their thin questions on smaller sticky notes.

4. Share questions and answers in small and large groups.

Example: Carle, E. (2002). *"Slowly, slowly, slowly," said the sloth*. New York: Philomel.

Before Reading

> Thick Question: Why is the sloth moving so slowly?
> Thin Question: When will the sloth accomplish its task?

During Reading

> Thick Question: Why won't the sloth speak with the other animals?
> Thin Question: When will the other animals tire of asking the sloth questions?

After Reading

> Thick Question: Why does the sloth like to move so slowly?
> Thin Question: When did the sloth answer the jaguar's questions?

Source: Lewin, L. (1998). *Great performances: Creating classroom-based assessment tasks*. Alexandria, VA: Association for Supervision and Curriculum Development.

Coding the Text

Purposes: To make connections while reading; to actively engage in reading.

Comprehension Strategy: Making Connections

Text: Narrative, Informational   **Use:** During Reading

TEACHING IDEAS

Procedure: (Begin by explaining and demonstrating Coding the Text.)

1. Explain that we can make three different kinds of connections: text–self, text–text, and text–world.

2. Think aloud as you model examples of each type of connection.

3. Read aloud while demonstrating how to code a section of text that elicits a connection. Use a sticky note, a code (T–S = text–self, T–T = text–text, T–W = text–world), and a few words to describe the connection.

4. Invite students to work with partners, read additional sections, and code the text. Ask them to share their connections with the class.

5. Encourage students to code the text using sticky notes to record their ideas.

Example: Cronin, D. (2004). *Duck for president.* New York: Simon & Schuster.

Text-to-Self	Text-to-Text	Text-to-World
This story reminds of when my mom had to leave my father, brother, and me to visit a sick relative. We had to do all the chores and cook for ourselves. It was hard work, and I learned just how much my mom does for us.	This book reminds me of *Substitute Teacher Plans* because the duck doesn't realize how much he liked his life until he spent time doing other things. The teacher realized she liked her life just like the duck in this story.	This book makes me think that we may not always think about how good our lives are.

Source: Harvey, S., & Goudvis, A. (2000). *Strategies that work: Teaching comprehension to enhance understanding.* York, ME: Stenhouse.

Connection Stems

Purposes: To provide a structure to make connections while reading; to encourage reflection during reading.

Comprehension Strategy: Making Connections

Text: Narrative, Informational   **Use:** After Reading

Procedure: (Begin by explaining and demonstrating Connection Stems.)

1. After reading a section of text aloud, show students a sentence stem, and think aloud about the process you use for completing it. Use text support and personal experiences to explain the text–self, text–text, or text–world connection.

2. Read another section of text aloud and guide the students to complete the stem orally with a partner.

3. Invite students to read a short text in pairs and work together to complete Connection Stems.

4. Discuss the completed stems.

> Connection Stems
> - That reminds me of…
> - I remember when…
> - I have a connection to…

- An experience I have had like that...
- I felt like that character when...
- If I were that character, I would...

Example: Mitton, T. (2002). *Dinosaurumpus!* New York: Orchard.

This book reminds me of my sleepover. The dinosaurs stayed up late and danced until they were really tired. At my sleepover, my friends and I stayed up late dancing and watching movies. We ended up falling asleep watching a movie on the living room floor.

Source: Adapted from Harvey, S., & Goudvis, A. (2000). *Strategies that work: Teaching comprehension to enhance understanding.* York, ME: Stenhouse.

Double-Entry Journal

(See blacklines, pages 265–266.)

Purposes: To provide a structure for reading response; to make decisions about significant aspects of text and reflect on personal connections to the text.

Comprehension Strategies: Making Connections, Monitoring, Summarizing

Text: Narrative, Informational   **Use:** Before, During, and After Reading

Procedure: (Begin by explaining and demonstrating Double-Entry Journals.)

1. Provide students with a Double-Entry Journal blackline.

2. Model the procedure by writing a quote, phrase, or idea in the left column and providing corresponding examples of reflective comments in the right column. (Encourage text–self, text–text, or text–world connections.)

3. Invite students to read (or listen to) a text or part of a text.

4. Ask students to select a key event, idea, word, quote, or concept from the text and write it in the left column.

5. In the right column, ask students write their response or connection to the item in the left column.

6. Use Double-Entry Journals as a springboard for discussion of text.

Adaptation: Use a different Double-Entry Journal format and ask students to create a summary and reflection.

Example: Polacco, P. (2001). *Mr. Lincoln's way.* New York: Scholastic.

Idea/Text From Story	My Connection
Eugene's love for birds.	My cousin also loves birds. Whenever I see him, he likes to talk about birds and teach the rest of the family what he knows. I like to watch birds with my cousin.

Source: Tompkins, G.E. (2006). *Literacy for the 21st century: A balanced approach* (4th ed.). Upper Saddle River, NJ: Prentice Hall.

TEACHING IDEAS

Draw and Write Connections

(See blacklines, pages 267–269.)

Purposes: To provide a structure to make connections while reading; to use visual representations to express connections.

Comprehension Strategies: Making Connections, Visualizing

Text: Narrative, Informational   **Use:** During and After Reading

Procedure: (Begin by explaining and modeling Drawing Connections.)

1. Demonstrate how to draw visual representations (pictures, shapes, lines) to communicate connections with text.

2. Read a section of text and think aloud about a connection you can make. Demonstrate sketching a visual representation of your thoughts. Then think aloud as you write a sentence explaining the connection you made.

3. Read another section of text to the students and ask them to create visual representations of their connections to the text. Next, ask students to write a sentence explaining their connections. Finally, invite students to share their drawings and explain their connections in small groups.

4. Encourage students to create visual representations of texts they are reading on their own and write a sentence explaining their connection.

Example: Laverde, A. (2000). *Alaska's three little pigs.* Seattle, WA: Sasquatch.

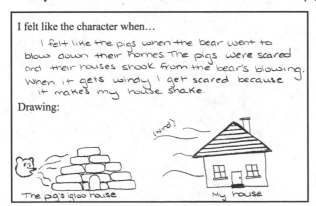
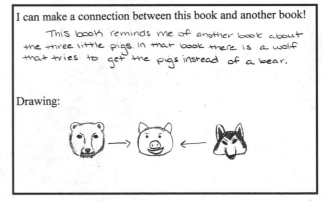

Source: McLaughlin, M., & Allen, M.B. (2009). *Guided Comprehension in grades 3–8* (2nd ed.). Newark, DE: International Reading Association.

Draw and Write Visualizations

(See blackline, page 271.)

Purposes: To provide a structure to encourage students to create mental images while reading; to encourage students to use artistic representations to express visualizations.

Comprehension Strategy: Visualizing, Making Connections, Summarizing

Text: Narrative, Informational   **Use:** During and After Reading

TEACHING IDEAS

Procedure: (Begin by explaining and modeling Draw and Write Visualizations.)

1. Demonstrate how to use visual representations (pictures, shapes, lines) to express the pictures made in your head while reading.

2. Think aloud about the visualization and the sketch. Then write a sentence about it.

3. Invite students to listen to a selection and ask them to draw their visualizations. Next, encourage students to write a sentence about their drawing. Then ask them to share their drawings in small groups, explaining how their drawings show the pictures they created in their heads.

4. Encourage students to create visual representations of texts they are reading on their own. Remind them to write sentences explaining their visualizations.

Example: Silverstein, S. (1974). "Sarah Cynthia Sylvia Stout" in *Where the sidewalk ends*. New York: HarperCollins.

Source: McLaughlin, M., & Allen, M.B. (2009). *Guided Comprehension in grades 3–8* (2nd ed.). Newark, DE: International Reading Association.

Graphic Organizers/Visual Organizers

Purposes: To provide a visual model of the structure of text; to provide a format for organizing information and concepts.

Comprehension Strategies: Visualizing, Making Connections, Summarizing

Text: Narrative, Informational   **Use:** Before, During, and After Reading

TEACHING IDEAS

Procedure: (Begin by explaining and demonstrating Graphic Organizers/Visual Organizers.)

1. Introduce the Graphic Organizer to students. Demonstrate how it works by reading a piece of text and noting key concepts and ideas on the organizer.

2. Ask students to work with partners to practice using the Graphic Organizer with ideas from an independently read text. Share ideas with the class.

3. Choose organizers that match text structures and thinking processes.

4. Encourage students to use graphic organizers to help them think through text.

Examples: Concept of Definition Map and K–W–L–S

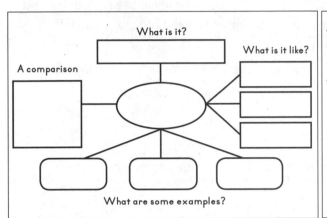

Guided Imagery

Purposes: To create mental images; to provide opportunities to discuss visualizations.

Comprehension Strategies: Visualizing, Making Connections

Text: Narrative, Informational   **Use:** Before and After Reading

Procedure: (Begin by explaining and demonstrating Guided Imagery.)

1. Ask students to turn to partners and describe to each other the mental images they create when you provide a verbal stimulus of things with which the students are familiar—a birthday party, a favorite pet, or a fireworks display. Provide time for students to elaborate on their mental pictures.

2. Introduce the text students will be reading next. Invite them to preview the text by focusing on illustrations, charts, or any other graphics.

3. Explain to students that they should close their eyes, breathe deeply, and relax. Guide the students to think more deeply about the topic they will read about. Provide a detailed description of the setting, the action, sensory images, emotions, and so on.

4. Ask students to open their eyes and work with partners to share the pictures they made in their minds. Monitor and respond to any questions.

TEACHING IDEAS

5. Invite students to write or draw information gleaned from Guided Imagery.

6. Finally, ask students to read the text and modify or enhance their writing or sketching as necessary.

Example: Shaw, N. (1995). *Sheep out to eat.* Mooloolaba, QLD, Australia: Sandpiper.

I think the book tells a story about sheep who go out to eat in a restaurant. I pictured them in Friendly's, my favorite restaurant. I could see the people in the restaurant staring at the sheep, because you don't usually see sheep in a restaurant. I could see the sheep. They were wearing clothes because they were going out to eat. They were sitting in chairs at a table. I could picture them trying to do what people do in a restaurant. I could see them trying to read a menu and adding strange things to what they ordered. The funny part was when they were asked to leave the restaurant and wound up on the front lawn. It was funny because the sheep enjoyed eating the grass and left money to pay their check.

Source: Lasear, D. (1991). *Seven ways of teaching: The artistry of teaching with multiple intelligences.* Palatine, IL: Skylight.

Open-Mind Portrait

Purposes: To create and represent personal meanings for a story; to understand a character's perspective or point of view.

Comprehension Strategies: Visualizing, Making Connections

Text: Narrative, Informational　　　　　**Use:** After Reading

Procedure: (Begin by explaining and demonstrating Open-Mind Portraits.)

1. Invite students to draw and color a portrait of a character from a story or a famous person from a biography.

2. Ask students to cut out the portrait and use it to trace on one or several sheets of paper to create one or more blank head shapes.

3. Staple the color portrait and the blank sheets together.

4. On the blank pages, students should draw or write about the person's thoughts and feelings throughout the text.

5. Share Open-Mind Portraits in book clubs, Literature Circles, or class meeting time.

Adaptation: Students fold a large sheet of paper (11" × 17") in half. On one half, they draw a portrait of a character from the book. On the other half, they draw the same shape of the portrait but do not fill in facial features. Instead, they fill the head with words and pictures to represent the thoughts and feelings of the character.

TEACHING IDEAS

Example: Stevens, J., & Crummel, S.S. (2005). *The great fuzz frenzy*. New York: Scholastic.

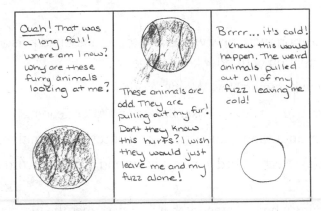

Source: Tompkins, G.E. (2006). *Literacy for the 21st century: A balanced approach* (4th ed.). Upper Saddle River, NJ: Prentice Hall.

Sketch to Stretch

Purposes: To create, represent, and share personal meanings for a narrative or informational text; to summarize understandings through sketches.

Comprehension Strategies: Visualizing, Making Connections

Text: Narrative, Informational   **Use:** After Reading

Procedure: (Begin by explaining and demonstrating Sketch to Stretch.)

1. After reading or listening to text, ask students to sketch what the text means to them.

2. Encourage students to experiment, and assure them there are many ways to represent personal meanings.

3. Organize students in groups of three to five.

4. Each person in the group shares his or her sketch. As the sketch is shared, all other group members give their interpretation of the sketch. Once everyone has shared, the artist tells his or her interpretation.

5. Repeat Step 4 until everyone in the group has had a chance to share.

Example: Johnson, A. (2007). *Lily Brown's paintings*. New York: Orchard.

I drew a picture of my family—my mother, my sister, and me. When Lily was finished painting, it was her family that meant the most to her, and it is my family that means the most to me.

Source: Short, K.G., Harste, J.C., & Burke, C. (1996). *Creating classrooms for authors and inquirers*. Portsmouth, NH: Heinemann.

TEACHING IDEAS

Concept of Definition Map

(See blackline, page 261.)

Purposes: To make connections with new words and topics and build personal meanings by connecting the new information with prior knowledge.

Comprehension Strategy: Knowing How Words Work

Text: Informational, Narrative   **Use:** Before and After Reading

Procedure: (Begin by explaining and demonstrating a Concept of Definition Map.)

1. Select or have student(s) select a word to be explored and place the word in the center of the map. (Example: *wolf*)

2. Ask students to determine a broad category that best describes the word and write it in the *What is it?* section. (Example: *animal*)

3. Encourage student(s) to provide some words that describe the focus word in the *What is it like?* section. (Examples: *furry, fast, big teeth*)

4. Have students provide some specific examples of the word in the *What are some examples?* section. (Examples: *gray, red, arctic*)

5. Ask students to determine a comparison. (Example: *German Shepherd* or *Husky dog*)

6. Discuss the Concept of Definition Map.

7. Read the text. Revisit the map. Make modifications or additions.

8. Encourage students to write a Concept of Definition Map Summary after completing the map.

Example: Simon, S. (1993). *Wolves*. New York: HarperCollins.

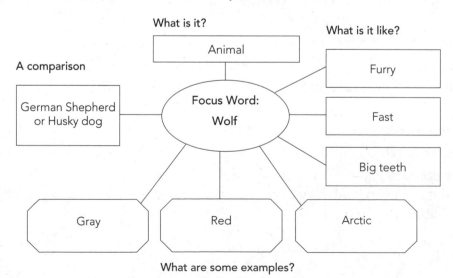

Source: Schwartz, R., & Raphael, T. (1985). Concept of definition: A key to improving students' vocabulary. *The Reading Teacher, 39*, 198–205.

TEACHING IDEAS

Context Clues

Purposes: To use semantics and syntax to figure out unknown words; to use a variety of cueing systems to make sense of text.

Comprehension Strategy: Knowing How Words Work

Text: Narrative, Informational   **Use:** During Reading

Procedure: (Begin by demonstrating how to use Context Clues to figure out word meanings.)

1. Explain to students the eight types of Context Clues and give examples of each:

    <u>Definition</u>: provides a definition that often connects the unknown word to a known word
    <u>Example/Illustration</u>: provides an example or illustration to describe the word
    <u>Compare/Contrast</u>: provides a comparison or contrast to the word
    <u>Logic</u>: provides a connection (such as a simile) to the word
    <u>Root Words and Affixes</u>: provides meaningful roots and affixes that the reader uses to determine meaning
    <u>Grammar</u>: provides syntactical cues that allow for reader interpretation
    <u>Cause and Effect</u>: cause and effect example allows the reader to hypothesize meaning
    <u>Mood and Tone</u>: description of mood related to the word allows readers to hypothesize meaning

2. Read aloud and think aloud to demonstrate using one or more of the clues to determine the meaning of a difficult or unfamiliar word in the text. (Use a Think-Aloud to demonstrate the most effective type of clue based on the context of the sentence.) Readers use several of the clues to figure out unknown words.

3. If the context does not provide enough information, demonstrate other strategies for figuring out the meaning of the word.

Example: Nash, S. (2004). *Tuff fluff*. Cambridge, MA: Candlewick.

Example/Illustration Clue: Bag of garbage

<u>Cause and Effect Clue</u>: Duckie's brain being stolen (the cause) led to the case being solved by Tuff Fluff, Private Investigator (effect). He found Duckie's brain (flattened fluff) between two pages in a book.

Source: McLaughlin, M. (2010). *Content area reading: Teaching and learning in an age of multiple literacies*. Boston: Allyn & Bacon.

TEACHING IDEAS

List–Group–Label

Purposes: To activate prior knowledge about a topic; to develop clearer understandings about concepts.

Comprehension Strategies: Knowing How Words Work, Previewing, Making Connections

Text: Informational   **Use:** Before and After Reading

Procedure: (Begin by explaining and demonstrating List–Group–Label.)

1. Write a cue word or phrase on the board or overhead.

2. Ask students to brainstorm words or concepts related to the topic. Write down all ideas.

3. Lead a discussion about whether any words should be eliminated, and if so, why?

4. Divide the class into groups of three or four. Invite groups to cluster the words and give each cluster a descriptive term.

5. Encourage groups to share their clusters and give reasons for their choices. (There are no wrong answers if clusters and labels can be justified.)

6. Introduce the text and ask students to read it. Afterward, invite students to revisit their clusters and modify, if necessary.

Example: Simon, S. (1998). *Icebergs and glaciers*. New York: Scholastic.

Cue word: Glaciers

Locations	Characteristics	Movement
Greenland	Frozen rivers	Melt
Alaska	Sheets of ice	Slide
Iceland		Creep

Source: Maring, G., Furman, G., & Blum-Anderson, J. (1985). Five cooperative learning strategies for mainstreamed youngsters in content area classrooms. *The Reading Teacher, 39*, 310–313.

RIVET

Purposes: To activate prior knowledge of a topic; to make predictions; to introduce vocabulary; to model spelling of specific vocabulary words.

Comprehension Strategies: Knowing How Words Work, Previewing

Text: Informational   **Use:** Before Reading

Procedure: (Begin by explaining and demonstrating RIVET.)

1. Choose six to eight interesting and important words from the selection to be read.

2. Create a visual representation of the words in a numbered list, leaving lines for each letter in the words. (You may want to provide students with a copy of this.)

3. Fill in the letters of the first word, one by one. Ask students to fill in their sheets or copy the words along with you. Ask students to predict what the word might be.

4. Continue this process for each word on the list.

TEACHING IDEAS

5. Make sure students understand word meanings. Encourage them to share.

6. Invite students to make predictions about the text, using the lists of words. Record the predictions.

7. Encourage students to ask questions prompted by the list of words. Record the questions.

8. Read the text. Revisit predictions to confirm or modify. Answer questions on the list.

Example: Polacco, P. (2004). *An orange for Frankie.* New York: Philomel.

1. __ __ __ __ __ __ (orange)
   O R

2. __ __ __ __ __ __ __ (sweater)
   S W

3. __ __ __ __ __ __ __ (miracle)
   M I R

4. __ __ __ __ __ (share)
   S H

5. __ __ __ __ __ __ (ribbon)
   R I

Source: Cunningham, P.M. (2008). *Phonics they use: Words for reading and writing* (5th ed.). New York: HarperCollins.

Semantic Feature Analysis

(See blackline, page 285.)

Purposes: To make predictions about attributes related to specific vocabulary words or concepts; to set a purpose for reading or researching; to confirm predictions.

Comprehension Strategies: Knowing How Words Work, Making Connections

Text: Narrative, Informational   **Use:** Before and After Reading

Procedure: (Begin by explaining and demonstrating Semantic Feature Analysis.)

1. Select a topic and some words or categories that relate to that topic. List the words in the left-hand column of the Semantic Feature Analysis chart.

2. Choose characteristics that relate to one or more of the related words. List those across the top row of the chart.

3. Ask students to make predictions about which characteristics relate to each word by placing a + if it is a characteristic, a − if it is not, and a ? if they are not sure.

4. Discuss students' predictions. Have them explain why they chose the characteristics.

5. Introduce the text and ask students to read about the topic and modify their charts as necessary.

6. Encourage students to share completed charts in small groups and then discuss as a class.

TEACHING IDEAS

Example: Vogt, G. (2001). *Solar system*. New York: Scholastic.

Categories	Characteristics			
	Has its own moon	Has rings	Has clouds	Is a planet
Mercury	–	–	–	+
Venus	–	–	+	+
Earth	+	–	+	+
Mars	+	–	+	+
Jupiter	+	+	+	+

Source: Johnson, D.D., & Pearson, P.D. (1984). *Teaching reading vocabulary* (2nd ed.). New York: Holt, Rinehart and Winston.

Text Transformations

(See blackline, page 292.)

Purposes: To develop vocabulary by using synonyms in engaging ways.

Comprehension Strategy: Knowing How Words Work

Text: Narrative   **Use:** During Reading

Procedure: (Begin by explaining and modeling Text Transformations.)

1. Choose original nursery rhymes or poems. Underline words students will need to replace with synonyms. Share the rhymes or poems with the class. Discuss and use these as the models for transformations.

2. Read the nursery rhyme or poem, emphasizing words that you had underlined.

3. Invite the students to brainstorm synonyms to replace the underlined words. Use dictionaries and thesauruses as necessary to help find new words.

4. Share new rhymes and poems.

Adaptations:

• Use the structure of the original nursery rhyme or poem to create new rhymes or poems.

• Rewrite nursery rhymes with new characters or events.

Example: Jack and Jill

> Jack and Jill (ran) up a hill
> To (get) a pail of water
> Jack fell down and broke his (head)
> And Jill came (somersaulting) after.

Source: McLaughlin, M., & Allen, M.B. (2009). *Guided Comprehension in grades 3–8* (2nd ed.). Newark, DE: International Reading Association.

TEACHING IDEAS

Vocabulary Bookmark

(See blackline, page 259.)

Purposes: To expand vocabularies; to motivate students to learn new words.

Comprehension Strategy: Knowing How Words Work, Monitoring

Text: Narrative, Informational   **Use:** During and After Reading

Procedure: (Begin by explaining and demonstrating Vocabulary Bookmark.)

1. Select a word from a current narrative or informational text that you think the whole class needs to discuss.

2. Write the word, what you think it means, and the page number on which it appears on the Vocabulary Bookmark.

3. Read the word in context. Then share what you think the word means and discuss the word and its meaning with the students. Verify the meaning in a dictionary if needed.

4. Invite the students to work with a partner to choose a word from a current narrative or informational text that they think the whole class needs to discuss.

5. Guide the students to write the word, what they think the word means, and the page on which it is located.

6. Invite the pairs of students to share their word choices, read them in context, explain what they think the words mean, and discuss them with the class. Verify word meanings in a dictionary as needed.

7. Invite students to complete their own Vocabulary Bookmarks when they have had sufficient practice working with a partner.

Example: Slonim, D. (2003). *Oh, Ducky!* San Francisco: Chronicle.

Vocabulary Bookmark

A word I think the whole class needs to talk about is...

timpani

I think it is a kind of drum.

Page number _7_

TEACHING IDEAS

Bookmark Technique

(See blacklines, pages 259–260.)

Purposes: To monitor comprehension while reading; to make evaluative judgments about aspects of text.

Comprehension Strategies: Monitoring, Knowing How Words Work, Making Connections

Text: Narrative, Informational   **Use:** During and After Reading

Procedure: (Begin by explaining and demonstrating the Bookmark Technique.)

1. As students read, ask them to make decisions and record specific information on each bookmark, including the page and paragraph where the information is located.

> Bookmark 1: Write and/or sketch about the part of the text that you found most interesting.
> Bookmark 2: Write a word you think the whole class needs to discuss.
> Bookmark 3: Write and/or sketch something you found confusing.
> Bookmark 4: Choose a chart, map, graph, or illustration that helped you to understand what you were reading.

2. Use the completed bookmarks to promote discussion about the text.

Example: Cronin, D. (2000). *Click, clack, moo: Cows that type.* New York: Scholastic.

Bookmark 1	Bookmark 2	Bookmark 3	Bookmark 4
The part I found most interesting was when the duck used the typewriter to get something he wanted. He did what the cows did. p. 24	*Impossible* I think it means it can't be done. p. 6	I am confused about what a typewriter is. Is it like a computer? p. 10	The picture of the chickens holding up the sign that reads, "Closed. No milk. No eggs" helped me understand. p. 16

Source: McLaughlin, M., & Allen, M.B. (2009). *Guided Comprehension in grades 3–8* (2nd ed.). Newark, DE: International Reading Association.

Cueing Systems Check

Purposes: To promote strategic reading; to promote independent reading.

Comprehension Strategies: Monitoring, Knowing How Words Work, Making Connections

Text: Narrative, Informational   **Use:** During Reading

Procedure: (Begin by explaining and modeling Cueing Systems Check.)

1. Teach students that cues offer us information while we are reading. For example, the graphophonic cueing system helps us to pronounce words, the syntactic cueing system helps us to choose correct

parts of speech, and the semantic cueing system helps us to determine if the word(s) makes sense. Explain that all three cueing systems function when we are reading. Demonstrate the need to have all three cueing systems interacting by introducing a word in isolation that students don't know. Ask them what they know about the word. They may be able to pronounce it, but they will not be able to determine how it functions in a sentence or what it means without more information.

2. Model cross-checking responses for the students by using a Think-Aloud. Associating questions with the cues facilitates this process:

> <u>Graphophonic Cues</u>: Does that look right? Does what you say match what you see?
> <u>Syntactic Cues</u>: Does that sound right? Is that the way we talk?
> <u>Semantic Cues</u>: Does that make sense?

3. Monitor as students partner read and think aloud about cross-checking.

Example: Appelt, K. (1993). *Elephants aloft*. New York: Harcourt Brace.

<u>Graphophonic Cues</u>: Does that look right? Did what you said match what you saw?
Yes, what I said matched what I saw. I know how to say the words and what they mean in the story.

<u>Syntactic Cues</u>: Does that sound right? Is that the way we talk?
Yes, it sounds like we talk. It is telling me information about the baby elephants and their travels.

<u>Semantic Cues</u>: Does it make sense?
Yes, I know who is doing what and why. I can also tell the story makes sense. I know that the baby elephants flew over cities and mountains in a hot air balloon. At the end of the story, the two elephants run into a larger elephant's arms. I read that the lady elephant is their aunt.

Source: Adapted from Clay, M.M. (1993b). *Reading Recovery: A guidebook for teachers in training*. Portsmouth, NH: Heinemann.

Patterned Partner Reading

Purposes: To provide a structure for reading interactively with another; to promote strategic reading.

Comprehension Strategies: Monitoring, Making Connections, Evaluating

Text: Narrative, Informational   **Use:** During Reading

Procedure: (Begin by explaining and demonstrating Patterned Partner Reading.)

1. Invite students to select a text and a partner with whom they will read, or assign partners yourself.

2. Partners should determine the amount of text to be read and choose a pattern such as the following to use as they engage in the reading:

> <u>Read–Pause–Ask Questions</u>: partners read a page silently and then ask each other a question about that page before moving on
> <u>Predict–Read–Discuss</u>: partners make predictions about material, read to confirm or disconfirm their predictions, discuss the outcome, and renew the cycle

TEACHING IDEAS

<u>Read–Pause–Retell</u>: partners read, stop to think, and take turns retelling what they have read to a given point

<u>Read–Pause–Make Connections</u>: partners read a predetermined amount and then tell the text–self, text–text, or text–world connections they have made

<u>Read–Pause–Visualize</u>: partners read a portion of the text and describe the pictures they have created in their minds

<u>You Choose Days</u>: partners select which pattern to use

Example: Waber, B. (1965). *Lyle, Lyle, crocodile.* Boston: Houghton Mifflin.

<u>Read–Pause–Retell</u>:

pp. 1–8

Lyle the crocodile lives with the Primm family. Lyle likes to help Joshua with his homework. Lyle is liked by everyone but Loretta, Mr. Grump's cat.

<u>Read–Pause–Ask Questions</u>:

p. 9

How did Lyle attempt to win over Loretta? He smiled at her.

Why was Loretta afraid of Lyle? The sight of his sharp teeth scared her.

Source: Adapted from Cunningham, P., & Allington, R. (1999). *Classrooms that work: They can all read and write* (2nd ed.). New York: Addison-Wesley.

Say Something

Purposes: To make connections with texts during reading; to enhance comprehension of written material through short readings and oral discussion.

Comprehension Strategies: Monitoring, Making Connections

Text: Narrative, Informational **Use:** During Reading

Procedure: (Begin by explaining and demonstrating Say Something.)

1. Instruct pairs of students to select text to read.

2. Designate a stopping point for reading.

3. Ask students to read to the stopping point and then "Say Something" about the text to their partner.

4. Allow pairs to choose the next stopping point. (If the text has subheadings, these make good stopping points.)

5. Students repeat Steps 3 and 4 until they have finished reading the text.

TEACHING IDEAS

Example: Polacco, P. (1996). *Aunt Chip and the great Triple Creek Dam affair.* New York: Philomel.

Student 1: I like to watch TV, but I do other things besides watch TV. These townspeople do nothing but watch TV.

Student 2: Aunt Chip doesn't watch TV at all. I don't think I could give TV up entirely, but I don't need to watch it all the time. pp. 1–8

Student 1: That town is in bad shape. It's hard to believe a town would get so run down just because people are watching TV.

Student 2: I guess if you watch nothing but TV you will forget how to read and ride a bike. You won't care about the things you should. pp. 9–18

Student 1: Aunt Chip was the librarian. She couldn't stop the townspeople from taking the books before, but now she is setting things right.

Student 2: The adults were mad when the TVs were turned off. They didn't even realize their children had been missing because they were so caught up in watching the TV. pp. 19–30

Student 1: I think it is great that the kids get to teach their parents to read.

Student 2: I am glad that the townspeople realized how much their town needed to be changed. pp. 31–39

Source: Adapted from Short, K.G., Harste, J.C., & Burke, C. (1996). *Creating classrooms for authors and inquirers.* Portsmouth, NH: Heinemann.

Think-Alouds

Purpose: To provide a model for active thinking during the reading process.

Comprehension Strategies: Previewing, Visualizing, Monitoring, Self-Questioning, Making Connections, Knowing How Words Work, Summarizing, Evaluating

Text: Narrative, Informational   **Use:** Before, During, and After Reading

Procedure: (Begin by explaining and demonstrating Think-Alouds.)

1. Introduce the text. Select a passage to read aloud to the students. The passage should require some strategic thinking in order to clarify understandings.

2. Before reading, encourage students to work with partners to make predictions for the story or chapter and explain their reasoning. (For example, "From the title [or cover], we can predict... because....")

3. During reading, encourage students to think aloud to demonstrate strategies such as the following:

TEACHING IDEAS

- Making/confirming/modifying predictions ("We were thinking _____, but now we predict _____."; "We thought that was what was going to happen because _____.")
- Visualizing—making pictures in our minds ("What we are seeing in our minds right now is _____.")
- Making connections ("This reminds us of _____."; This is like a _____.")
- Monitoring ("This is confusing. We need to reread or read on or ask someone for help."; "This is not what we expected.")
- Figuring out unknown words ("We don't know that word, but it looks like _____."; "That word must mean _____ because _____.")

4. After guiding them to practice with partners several times, encourage students to use this technique on their own.

Example: Simon, S. (1998). *The universe.* New York: Scholastic.

<u>Visualizing</u>: After reading this passage, what are you seeing in your mind right now?
What I am seeing in my mind right now is the creation of our solar system. I see a big ball of dust and gases swirling around together like a tornado. In the center of the swirling disk I see the sun. As things slow down, the particles and gases form planets and that is how our solar system came to be.

Source: Davey, B. (1983). Think-aloud—Modeling the cognitive processes of reading comprehension. *Journal of Reading, 27,* 44–47.

Bio-Pyramid

(See blackline, page 258.)

Purposes: To summarize a person's life; to provide a format for summary writing.

Comprehension Strategies: Summarizing, Making Connections, Monitoring

Text: Informational   **Use:** After Reading

Procedure: (Begin by explaining and demonstrating the Bio-Pyramid.)

1. After reading about a person's life, show students the format for writing Bio-Pyramids.

Line 1—person's name
Line 2—two words describing the person
Line 3—three words describing the person's childhood
Line 4—four words indicating a problem the person had to overcome
Line 5—five words stating one of his or her accomplishments
Line 6—six words stating a second accomplishment
Line 7—seven words stating a third accomplishment
Line 8—eight words stating how mankind benefited from the accomplishments

TEACHING IDEAS

2. Create a Bio-Pyramid as a class.

3. Invite students to create Bio-Pyramids in pairs or small groups.

4. Use the completed Bio-Pyramids to promote discussion and summarize the person's life.

Example: Baker, C. (2004). *Rosa Parks*. New York: Scholastic.

1.   Rosa
Person's name

2.   Brave,   inspirational
Two words describing the person

3.   Worked   for   education
Three words describing the person's childhood

4.   Segregating   blacks   and   whites
Four words indicating a problem the person had to overcome

5.   Refused   to   give   up   seat
Five words stating one of his/her accomplishments

6.   She   helped   people   pass   voting   tests
Six words stating a second accomplishment

7.   Her   actions   inspired   the   Montgomery   bus   boycott
Seven words stating a third accomplishment

8.   She   inspired   a   world   where   everyone   is   equal
Eight words stating how mankind benefited from his/her accomplishments

Source: Macon, J.M. (1991). *Literature response*. Paper presented at the Annual Literacy Workshop, Anaheim, CA.

Lyric Retelling/Lyric Summary

(See blackline, page 278.)

Purposes: To provide an alternative format for narrative text retellings or informational text summaries; to provide opportunities to use multiple modalities when creating summaries; to link content learning and the arts.

Comprehension Strategy: Summarizing

Text: Narrative and Informational   **Use:** After Reading

Procedure: (Begin by explaining and demonstrating Lyric Retellings/Lyric Summaries.)

1. Review summarizing with the students. Ask them to note the types of information that make up narrative or informational summaries. Choose a topic and brainstorm a list of related information.

2. Introduce the musical aspect of Lyric Retellings/Lyric Summaries by explaining to students that summaries can also be written as song lyrics to familiar tunes (rock, easy listening, children's songs).

TEACHING IDEAS

3. Choose a melody with which students are familiar and use the brainstormed list to write lyrics. Write the first line and then encourage pairs of students to suggest subsequent lines. When the Lyric Retelling/Lyric Summary is completed, sing it with the class.

4. Ask small groups of students to brainstorm a list of facts they know about a story they have read or a content area topic they have studied. Invite them to choose a melody everyone in the group knows and create their own Lyric Retellings/Lyric Summaries.

5. Invite the students to sing their completed summaries for the class.

Example: Simon, S. (1996). *The heart: Our circulatory system.* New York: Morrow Junior Books.

> Sung to the tune of "Twinkle Twinkle Little Star"
>
> The heart pumps blood through our bodies.
> It is a muscle that works very hard.
> The heart, blood, and blood vessels
> Provide our cells with food and oxygen.
> The heart pumps blood through our bodies.
> It is a muscle that works very hard.

Source: McLaughlin, M. & Allen, M.B. (2009). *Guided Comprehension in grades 3–8* (2nd ed.). Newark, DE: International Reading Association.

Paired Summarizing

Purposes: To provide a format for pairs to summarize narrative or informational text and to articulate understandings and confusions.

Comprehension Strategies: Making Connections, Monitoring, Summarizing

Text: Narrative, Informational   **Use:** After Reading

Procedure: (Begin by explaining and demonstrating Paired Summarizing.)

1. Ask pairs of students to read a selection, and invite each student to write a summary or retelling. They may refer to the text to help cue their memory, but they should not write while they are looking at the text.

2. Ask partners to trade the retellings or summaries that they wrote and read each other's work. Encourage each student to write a summary of the other partner's paper.

3. Encourage students to compare and contrast their summaries. The discussion should focus on
   - Articulating what each reader understands
   - Identifying what they collectively cannot come to understand
   - Formulating clarification questions for classmates and the teacher

4. Invite students to share understandings and questions in a small-group or whole-class discussion.

TEACHING IDEAS

Example: Harris, J. (1999). *The three little dinosaurs*. Gretna, LA: Pelican.

<u>Student 1 Summary</u>: In this story the three dinosaurs are afraid of the T-Rex because he keeps blowing their houses down. Then the three dinosaurs decide to build a house of rocks and the T-Rex cannot blow it down. The three dinosaurs were able to stay safe in that house for a long time, while the T-Rex made new plans to destroy it. Then when the T-Rex finally destroys their house, he meets the three dinosaurs and finds out that they grew up to be really big dinosaurs. He runs away because he is so scared.

<u>Student 2 Summary of First Summary</u>: The three little dinosaurs can't keep the T-Rex from knocking down their houses, sol they go to the house that is built of rocks. They were safe there and a very long time went by. Then the T-Rex figured out a way to destroy the rock house. After he did, he met the three dinosaurs who had grown into really big dinosaurs. He runs away because he is really scared.

Source: Vaughn, J., & Estes, T. (1986). *Reading and reasoning beyond the primary grades*. Boston: Allyn & Bacon.

QuIP (Questions Into Paragraphs)

(See blackline, page 284.)

Purpose: To provide a framework for initiating research and structuring writing.

Comprehension Strategies: Summarizing, Self-Questioning

Text: Informational   **Use:** Before, During, and After Reading

Procedure: (Begin by explaining and demonstrating QuIP.)

1. Invite students to choose a topic to explore and write the topic at the top of the QuIP grid.

2. Ask students to generate and write on the grid three broad questions related to the topic.

3. Students should locate and read two sources to find the answers to their questions. They write the titles of the sources in spaces provided on the grid.

4. Students record answers to the questions in the spaces provided on the grid.

5. Students synthesize information into a paragraph. (Demonstrating synthesizing and paragraph writing facilitates this process.)

6. Students share their paragraphs in pairs or small groups.

TEACHING IDEAS

Examples: Berger, M., & Berger, G. (2003). *Whales*. New York: Scholastic.

Milton, J. (1989). *Whales: The gentle giants*. New York: Random House.

TOPIC: Whale

Questions	Answers	
	Source 1: Berger, M., & Berger, G. (2003). *Whales*. New York: Scholastic.	Source 2: Milton, J. (1989). *Whales: The gentle giants*. New York: Random House.
A. What is the biggest animal in the world?	The blue whale is the biggest animal ever to live on land or sea.	The blue whale is the biggest animal in the world.
B. How does a whale breathe?	A whale breathes through its blowhole.	A whale breathes through a hole in its head called a blowhole.
C. How does a whale catch its dinner?	A whale catches tiny sea plants and animals using its baleen.	A whale uses its baleen to catch food. It grows in long strips and works like a strainer.

The biggest animal on land and sea is a type of whale called a blue whale. Whales breathe through a small hole on their heads called a blowhole. Whales catch their food by capturing small plants and animals with their baleen. Baleen grows in long strands and works like a big strainer for capturing food.

Source: McLaughlin, E.M. (1987). QuIP: A writing strategy to improve comprehension of informational structure. *The Reading Teacher, 40*, 650–654.

Retelling

(See blackline, page 270.)

Purposes: To promote reflection about narrative text; to provide a format for summarizing narrative text structure.

Comprehension Strategy: Summarizing

Text: Narrative   **Use:** After Reading

Procedure: (Begin by explaining and demonstrating Retelling.)

1. Explain to the students the purpose of retelling a story and the major elements that are included (characters, setting, problem, attempts to resolve the problem, resolution).

2. Demonstrate a Retelling after reading a story aloud. Discuss the components you included. (A story map or other graphic organizer may help.)

3. Read another story to the students, and then ask them to form groups and retell the story. (You may want to give each student in the group a card listing a specific story element, such as characters, setting, problem, attempts to resolve the problem, resolution.)

4. Share information with the class and record it on a chart or overhead. Review the Retellings to ensure all elements are addressed.

TEACHING IDEAS

5. Encourage students to do Retellings orally, in writing, or through sketching or dramatization to demonstrate understanding of a narrative text.

Adaptation: Invite students to complete Draw and Write Retellings.

Example: Polacco, P. (2005). *The Graves family goes camping.* New York: Penguin.

The Graves family and their neighbors decided to go camping at Lake Bleakmire. They must return home from camping on time because the town council asked Dr. Graves to create a show for the Fourth of July. The group goes exploring in the woods and falls into a hole, which turns out to be a Fire-breathing Dragon's foot print. The dragon finds the Grave's camp site and asks for food. The Graves feed him and when it is time to leave the dragon refuses to let them go. The Graves scold the dragon and find a forgotten boat that takes them home. The dragon follows the group home. Mr. Graves puts something in the Dragon's food that causes the dragon's fire to change color. The townspeople got a great show for the Fourth of July, and the dragon learned its lesson.

Source: Morrow, L.M. (1985). Retelling stories: A strategy for improving children's comprehension, concept of story, and oral language complexity. *The Elementary School Journal, 85*(5), 647–661.

Story Map

(See blackline, page 289.)

Purposes: To promote understanding of the narrative elements; to encourage summarizing using narrative text structure.

Comprehension Strategy: Monitoring, Summarizing

Text: Narrative   **Use:** After Reading

Procedure: (Begin by explaining and modeling a Story Map.)

1. Explain to the students the purpose of summarizing and the narrative (story) elements that are included (characters, setting, problem, attempts to resolve the problem, solution) when summarizing a story.

2. Demonstrate completing a Story Map after reading a story aloud. Think aloud about who was in the story, where the story took place, etc. Discuss the components as you complete each. (A story map or other visual cues may help.) Use the completed Story Map to briefly summarize the story.

3. Read another story to the students and in small groups, invite them to complete a Story Map. (Be sure students have the Story Map blackline master; it includes the narrative elements.) 4. Share and discuss the completed Story Maps. Use them to summarize the story.

   Ideas for using Story Maps
   - Summarize key events in a story.
   - Predict key events in a story.
   - Plan story elements when writing a story.
   - Increase students' understanding of story structure when reading and writing original stories.

TEACHING IDEAS

Example: Freedman, C. (2001). *Where's your smile, crocodile?* Atlanta, GA: Peachtree.

Title: *Where's Your Smile, Crocodile?*

Setting: Jungle	**Characters:** Kyle, Parrot, Monkey, Elephant, Lion Cub

Problem: Kyle loses his smile.

Events: • Kyle loses his smile. • The parrot, monkey, and elephant try to cheer him up. • Kyle finds a lost cub, and they search for his smile and the lion's home.

Solution: Kyle and the cub find the cub's home. That makes Kyle smile.

Story Pyramid

(See blackline, page 290.)

Purposes: To summarize a narrative or story text; to provide a format for summary writing.

Comprehension Strategies: Making Connections, Monitoring, Summarizing

Text: Narrative   **Use:** After Reading

Procedure:

1. After reading a story, show students the format for writing Story Pyramids.

>   Line 1—character's name
>   Line 2—two words describing the character
>   Line 3—three words describing the setting
>   Line 4—four words stating the problem
>   Line 5—five words describing one event
>   Line 6—six words describing another event
>   Line 7—seven words describing a third event
>   Line 8—eight words describing the solution to the problem

2. Create a Story Pyramid as a class.

3. Have students create Story Pyramids in pairs or small groups for a story they have read.

4. Use the completed pyramids as the basis for discussion.

TEACHING IDEAS

Example: Minters, F. (1994). *Cinder-Elly*. New York: Viking.

1. <u>Cinder-Elly</u>
Character's name

2. <u>Kind</u> <u>Intelligent</u>
Two words describing the character

3. <u>New</u> <u>York</u> <u>City</u>
Three words describing the setting

4. <u>Wants</u> <u>to</u> <u>attend</u> <u>game</u>
Four words stating the problem

5. <u>Meets</u> <u>a</u> <u>helpful</u> <u>fairy</u> godmother
Five words describing one event

6. <u>Meets</u> <u>the</u> <u>prince</u> <u>at</u> <u>the</u> <u>dance</u>
Six words describing another event

7. <u>Loses</u> <u>a</u> <u>glass</u> <u>sneaker</u> <u>at</u> <u>the</u> <u>dance</u>
Seven words describing a third event

8. <u>Prince</u> <u>uses</u> <u>the</u> <u>glass</u> <u>sneaker</u> <u>to</u> <u>find</u> <u>Cinder-Elly</u>
Eight words describing a solution to the problem

Source: Waldo, B. (1991). Story pyramid. In J.M. Macon, D. Bewell, & M.E. Vogt (Eds.), *Responses to literature: Grades K–8* (pp. 23–24). Newark, DE: International Reading Association.

Summary Cube

(See blackline, page 291.)

Purpose: To provide a structure for summarizing factual information or retelling key points of a story.

Comprehension Strategy: Summarizing

Text: Narrative, Informational   **Use:** Before, During, and After Reading

Procedure: (Begin by explaining and demonstrating Summary Cubes.)

1. Explain the idea of cubing to the students. Describe the information that goes on each side of the cube.

2. Demonstrate through read-aloud and Think-Aloud the process of determining key ideas about either narrative or informational text to write on the cube. Show the students how to assemble the cube.

3. Guide the students to work with partners to read text and create Summary Cubes.

4. Share ideas with the class. Display Summary Cubes.

5. Encourage students to create their own cubes as follow-ups to reading narrative and informational texts.

TEACHING IDEAS

Information for cubes:

	Option 1	Option 2	Option 3	Option 4
Side 1	Who?	Title	Animal	State
Side 2	What?	Characters	Habitat	Capital
Side 3	Where?	Setting	Food	Weather
Side 4	When?	Problem	Physical description	Products
Side 5	Why?	Solution	Classification	Nickname
Side 6	How?	Theme	Illustration	Fun Fact

Adaptation: Complete the Bio-Cube detailed at the ReadWriteThink website: www.readwritethink.org/classroom-resources/student-interactives/cube-30057.html

Summary Cube Example: Gill, S. (2007). *Alaska*. Watertown, MA: Charlesbridge.

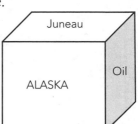

Side 1—State: Alaska
Side 2—Capital: Juneau
Side 3—Weather: 60 degrees below zero in winter to 100 degrees in summer
Side 4—Product: Oil
Side 5—Nickname: America's Last Frontier
Side 6—Fun Fact: Seward's Icebox

Source: McLaughlin, M., & Allen, M.B. (2009). *Guided Comprehension in grades 3–8* (2nd ed.). Newark, DE: International Reading Association.

Evaluative Questioning

Purpose: To promote self-questioning and evaluative thinking.

Comprehension Strategy: Evaluating, Self-Questioning

Text: Narrative, Informational   **Use:** During and After Reading

Procedure: (Begin by explaining and demonstrating Evaluative Questioning.)

1. Explain the importance of multiple levels of questioning, focusing on evaluative questions. (See Chapter 2.)

2. Model creating and responding to evaluative questions using a read-aloud and Think-Aloud. Explain the signal words and cognitive operations used to form and respond to evaluative questions.

    Signal words: *defend, judge, justify*
    Cognitive operations: valuing, judging, defending, justifying

3. Using a common text, guide small groups of students to read the text and create an evaluative question. One at a time, ask groups to share their question and encourage other students to respond. Discuss the cognitive processes students used to answer each question.

4. Provide opportunities for students to use evaluative questions to engage in reflection and conversations about the texts they read.

TEACHING IDEAS

Example: Gill, S. (2007). *Alaska.* Watertown, MA: Charlesbridge.

How do you think global warming will affect us in the future? How do you think it will affect Alaska in the future? Defend your responses.

Source: Ciardiello, A.V. (1998). Did you ask a good question today? Alternative cognitive and metacognitive strategies. *Journal of Adolescent & Adult Literacy, 42,* 210–219.

Journal Responses

Purposes: To provide opportunities for reflection and critical thinking; to encourage students to respond in writing to what they are reading.

Comprehension Strategies: Evaluating, Making Connections, Summarizing

Text: Narrative, Informational   **Use:** During and After Reading

Procedure: (Begin by explaining and demonstrating Journal Responses.)

1. Provide students with a journal or a system for keeping their responses.

2. Show students examples of good responses to texts. Help students identify aspects of thoughtful reading responses.

3. Read aloud a portion of text and think aloud through a thoughtful response. Discuss with students why it was thoughtful.

4. Read aloud another portion of text and encourage students to write a thoughtful response and share it with partners.

5. For independent reading, ask students to write the date and the title of the text or chapter at the top of the page or in the left margin.

6. After reading a text, or listening to one, use Journal Responses as one of many methods students use to respond to what they read. Journal Responses can include reactions, questions, wonderings, predictions, connections, or feelings.

    Possible Journal Response prompts
    • What was the most interesting part of what you read? Explain.
    • How did this make you feel? Explain.
    • What was important in the chapter? How do you know?
    • What is something new you learned? Explain.
    • What connection(s) did you make? Explain.

7. Encourage students to share responses in groups or with the whole class.

Example: Polacco, P. (1997). *In Enzo's splendid gardens.* New York: Philomel.

What was the most interesting part of the story? Why?

My favorite part of the story was when Enzo spills spaghetti on the cat. The cat is running around with a pot on its head. I like this part because it reminds me of the day my cat got stuck in a gym bag. She crawled in and couldn't get out. She meowed and meowed and I eventually had to rescue her. It was pretty funny for everyone except my cat.

TEACHING IDEAS

Mind and Alternative Mind Portraits

(See blackline, page 280.)

Purpose: To examine a topic or issue from two perspectives; to examine a story through two characters.

Comprehension Strategy: Evaluating

Text: Narrative, Informational   **Use:** During and After Reading

Procedure: (Begin by explaining and modeling Mind and Alternative Mind Portraits.)

1. Introduce, read, and discuss the text.

2. Work with the students to determine a perspective that is prevalent. Then contemplate a perspective that is not presented equally or is silenced or missing from the text.

> Mind Portrait: Encourage students to write about the portrait to represent the perspective of one person or character. Inside the portrait, encourage students to write, draw, or collage ideas and experiences that delineate that person's perspective.

> Alternative Mind Portrait: Encourage students to label the portrait to represent the alternative perspective of a person or character. Inside the portrait, encourage students to write, draw, or collage ideas and experiences that delineate that person's perspective.

3. Invite students to share and discuss portraits to compare and contrast perspectives.

Adaptations: Narratives and Alternative Narratives; Photographs and Alternative Photographs; Videos and Alternative Videos

Example: Adler, D.A. (2007). *Cam Jansen and the mystery writer mystery*. New York: Scholastic.

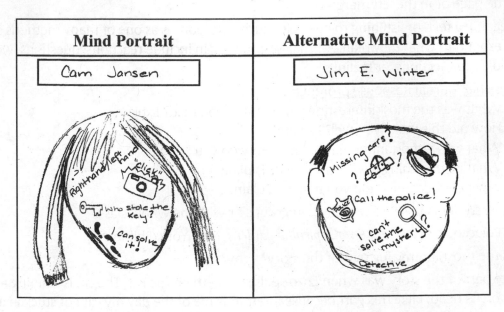

Source: McLaughlin, M., & Allen, M.B. (2009). *Guided Comprehension in grades 3–8* (2nd ed.). Newark, DE: International Reading Association.

TEACHING IDEAS

Persuasive Writing

Purposes: To express points of view with supporting ideas; to foster understanding of multiple perspectives on a topic.

Comprehension Strategy: Evaluating

Text: Narrative, Informational   **Use:** Before, During, and After Reading

Procedure: (Begin by explaining and demonstrating Persuasive Writing.)

1. Introduce a topic by reading an article that contains two points of view about the same issue.

2. Use a Think-Aloud to share the different perspectives about the topic.

3. Then choose a side and write persuasively to defend your choice. Think aloud throughout this process. Be certain to support your argument with facts.

4. Discuss your writing with the students and encourage them to express their ideas about the topic.

5. Then guide the students to engage in Persuasive Writing by sharing a different article and scaffolding their ability to write persuasively.

6. Provide additional opportunities for students to engage in practice by using current events, character choices, and historical events in other instructional settings.

Example: Van Allsburg, C. (1990). *Just a dream*. Boston: Houghton Mifflin.

This book reminds me that we need to take care of our planet. Everyone can do something to help. We can plant trees, recycle garbage, and save water. If everyone helps, the world will be a better place for all of us.

Source: McLaughlin, M., & Allen, M.B. (2009). *Guided Comprehension in grades 3–8* (2nd ed.). Newark, DE: International Reading Association.

Venn Diagram

(See blackline, page 294.)

Purposes: To compare and contrast two topics.

Comprehension Strategies: Making Connections, Summarizing, Evaluating

Text: Informational   **Use:** During and After Reading

Procedure: (Begin by explaining and modeling a Venn Diagram.)

1. Explain that we use Venn Diagrams to show what is similar and what is different about two topics.

2. Read aloud a brief text that includes information about two topics.

3. Demonstrate how to complete a Venn Diagram. Use the blackline and label the diagram with the topics to be discussed. Next, think aloud as you list the similarities the topics share in the section where the circles overlap. Then think aloud as you list what is unique about each topic in the section of the diagram directly below where that topic is listed. Use the completed Venn Diagram to summarize and discuss how the topics are similar and how they are different.

TEACHING IDEAS

4. Read aloud another brief text that includes information about two topics. Distribute copies of the Venn Diagram blackline to students.

5. Invite students to work with a partner to list similarities in the overlapped section of the circles. Discuss the ideas the students record.

6. Encourage students to write what is unique about each topic in the outer portion of the circle that appears below each topic. Discuss the ideas the students record.

7. Invite the students to use the completed Venn Diagram to summarize similarities and differences about the topics.

Example: Simon, S. (2008). *Gorillas*. New York: HarperCollins.

Western Lowland Gorilla   Mountain Gorilla

- Zoos have this type of gorilla.
- Hair is short and ranges in color from black to grayish brown.
- They live in tropical rainforests in western Africa.

- Live in Africa
- Larger than humans

- This gorilla is very rare.
- Hair is long and dark.
- They live in the Virunga Mountains.

COMPREHENSION ROUTINES

Cross-Age Reading Experiences

(See Chapter 4; blackline in Appendix D, page 306; and observation guide in Appendix E, page 348.)

Purposes: To provide a structure for reading strategically with a more experienced partner; to promote discussion and negotiation of meaning in a social setting.

Comprehension Strategies: All

Text: Narrative, Informational   **Use:** Before, During, and After Reading

Procedure: (Begin by explaining and modeling Cross-Age Reading Experiences.)

1. Meet with the coordinator of cross-age volunteers or the teacher of the partner class to discuss organizational issues such as meeting time, materials, and matching students with buddies.

2. Meet with the cross-age volunteers and discuss the goals of the Cross-Age Reading Experience. Focus on the students' needs and introduce or review the Guided Comprehension strategies and teaching ideas. Model cross-age reading—including fluency and strategy use—for the volunteers. Discuss the process.

3. Begin the Cross-Age Reading Experience with an introductory activity such as "Getting to Know You," in which the students and volunteers have time to learn about each other. Provide appropriate theme-related texts for reading. Respond to any questions participants may have.

4. Integrate Cross-Age Reading Experiences as a routine in Stage Two of Guided Comprehension. Remember to ensure that students have access to appropriate theme-related texts, that students and cross-age volunteers are aware of the strategy focus, and that they engage in reflection and sharing at the close of the experience.

5. Provide opportunities for students to engage in Cross-Age Reading Experiences in Stage Two of Guided Comprehension on a regular basis.

Directed Reading–Thinking Activity (DR–TA)/ Directed Listening–Thinking Activity (DL–TA)

Purposes: To encourage students to make predictions about a story or text; to use the author's clues to make meaningful connections and predictions; to foster active reading or listening of a text.

Comprehension Strategies: Previewing, Making Connections, Monitoring

Text: Narrative, Informational   **Use:** Before, During, and After Reading

Procedure: (Begin by explaining and demonstrating DR–TA or DL–TA.)

1. Invite students to look at the title and/or cover of a book and ask them, "What do you think this story (or book) is about? Explain your thinking." Students respond with predictions and reasons for their thinking. This helps activate prior knowledge.

2. Ask students to read to a designated stopping point in the text, review their predictions, make new predictions, and explain the reasons for the new predictions.

3. Repeat Step 2 until the text is finished.

4. Encourage students to reflect on their predictions, stating what was helpful, what was surprising, and what was confusing.

> Other ideas for using DR–TA:
> - Students can predict orally, in writing, or by illustrating.
> - For DL–TA, students listen to the story. The reader stops at various preselected places and asks students to review predictions, make new ones, and explain their reasoning.

Source: Stauffer, R. (1975). *Directing the reading–thinking process*. New York: Harper & Row.

Literature Circles

(See Chapter 2 and blacklines, pages 313–315 and 349.)

Purposes: To provide a structure for student talk about texts from a variety of perspectives; to provide opportunities for social learning.

Comprehension Strategies: All

Text: Narrative, Informational   **Use:** After Reading

Procedure: (Begin by explaining and demonstrating Literature Circles.)

1. Invite students to select books to read and to join groups based on their text selections.

2. Ask groups to meet to develop a schedule—how much they will read, when they will meet, and so on.

3. Encourage students to read the predetermined amount of text independently, taking notes as they read. Students can keep their notes in their Guided Comprehension Journals. The notes can reflect the students' role in the Literature Circle or their personal connections to the text. Roles within the Literature Circles should vary from meeting to meeting.

4. Encourage students to continue to meet according to the group schedule to discuss ideas about the text until the book is completed.

5. Provide opportunities for students to participate in Literature Circles in Stage Two of Guided Comprehension.

Source: Daniels, H. (2002). *Literature circles: Voice and choice in the student-centered classroom* (2nd ed.). York, ME: Stenhouse.

Reciprocal Teaching

(See Chapter 2 and blacklines, pages 330–332 and 350.)

Purposes: To provide a format for using comprehension strategies—predicting, self-questioning, monitoring, and summarizing—in a small-group setting; to facilitate a group effort to bring meaning to a text; to monitor thinking and learning.

Comprehension Strategies: Previewing, Self-Questioning, Monitoring, Summarizing

Text: Narrative, Informational   **Use:** Before, During, and After Reading

COMPREHENSION ROUTINES

Procedure: (Begin by explaining and demonstrating Reciprocal Teaching.)

1. Explain the procedure and each of the four reading comprehension strategies: predicting, self-questioning, monitoring, and summarizing.

2. Model thinking related to each of the four strategies by using an authentic text and thinking aloud.

3. With the whole class, guide students to engage in similar types of thinking by providing responses for each of the strategies. Sentence stems, such as the following, facilitate this

Predicting:	• I think...
	• I bet...
	• I imagine...
	• I suppose...
Questioning:	• What connections can I make?
	• How does this support my thinking?
Clarifying:	• I did not understand the part where...
	• I need to know more about...
Summarizing:	• The important ideas in what I read are...

4. Place students in groups of four and provide each group with copies of the same text to use as the basis for Reciprocal Teaching.

5. Assign each student one of the four strategies and the suggested prompts.

6. Invite students to engage in Reciprocal Teaching using the process that was modeled.

7. Ask students to reflect on the process and their comprehension of the text.

8. Provide opportunities for the students to engage in Reciprocal Teaching in Stage Two of Guided Comprehension as an independent comprehension routine.

Source: Palincsar, A.S., & Brown, A.L. (1986). Interactive teaching to promote independent learning from text. *The Reading Teacher, 39,* 771–777.

BIO-PYRAMID

Name: _____ Date: _____

1. _____
   Person's name

2. _____
   Two words describing the person

3. _____
   Three words describing the person's childhood

4. _____
   Four words indicating a problem the person had to overcome

5. _____
   Five words stating one of his or her accomplishments

6. _____
   Six words stating a second accomplishment

7. _____
   Seven words stating a third accomplishment

8. _____
   Eight words stating how mankind benefited from his or her accomplishments

BOOKMARK TECHNIQUE

BOOKMARK _____

Name: _____

Date: _____

The most interesting part was...

_____

_____

_____

_____

_____

_____

Page number: _____

BOOKMARK _____

Name: _____

Date: _____

A word I think the whole class needs to talk about is . . .

_____

_____

_____

_____

_____

_____

Page number: _____

BOOKMARK TECHNIQUE

BOOKMARK

Name: _____

Date: _____

Something that confused me was...

_____

_____

_____

_____

_____

_____

Page number: _____

BOOKMARK

Name: _____

Date: _____

My favorite illustration was...

_____

_____

_____

_____

_____

_____

Page number: _____

CONCEPT OF DEFINITION MAP

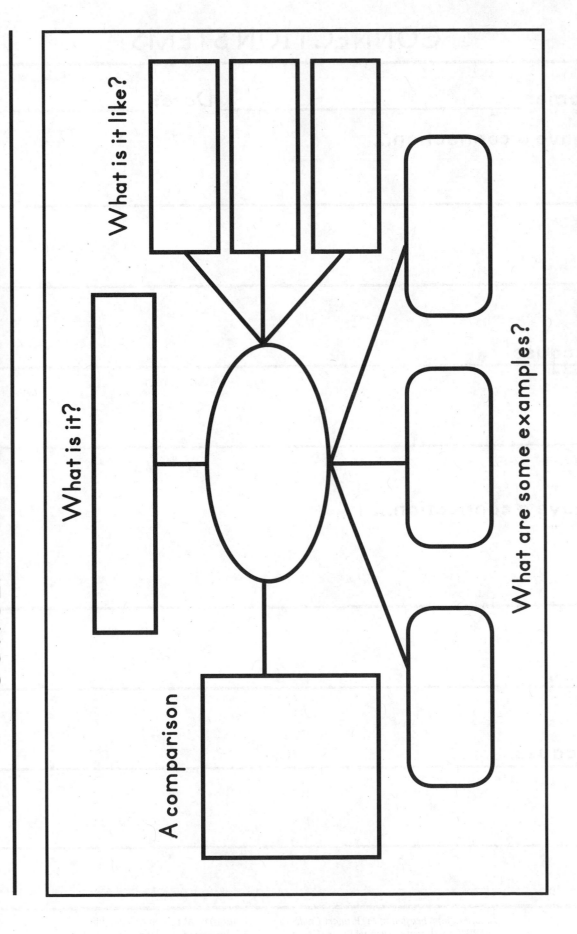

What is it?

What is it like?

A comparison

What are some examples?

Guided Comprehension in the Primary Grades (Second Edition) by Maureen McLaughlin. © 2010 by the International Reading Association. May be copied for classroom use.

CONNECTION STEMS

Name: _____ Date: _____

I have a connection...

to _____

_____

because _____

_____

I have a connection...

to _____

_____

because _____

_____

CONNECTION STEMS

Name: _____ Date: _____

That reminds me of...

_____

_____

because _____

_____

That reminds me of...

_____

_____

because _____

_____

CONTRAST CHART

Name: _____   Date: _____

```
┌─────────────────┐          ┌─────────────────┐
│                 │          │                 │
│                 │          │                 │
│                 │          │                 │
│                 │          │                 │
└─────────────────┘          └─────────────────┘
```

1. _____   1. _____

2. _____   2. _____

3. _____   3. _____

4. _____   4. _____

5. _____   5. _____

DOUBLE-ENTRY JOURNAL

Name: _____ Date: _____

Idea	Reflection/Reaction

DOUBLE-ENTRY JOURNAL

Name: _____ Date: _____

Idea/Text From Story	My Connection

DRAW AND WRITE CONNECTIONS

Name: _____ Date: _____

Book Title: _____

Drawing:

I have a connection to this book!

_____

_____

_____

_____

DRAW AND WRITE CONNECTIONS

Name: _____ Date: _____

Book Titles: _____

Drawing:

I can make a connection between this book and another book!

_____

_____

_____

_____

DRAW AND WRITE CONNECTIONS

Name: _____ Date: _____

Book Title: _____

Drawing:

I felt like the character when...

_____

_____

_____

_____

_____

DRAW AND WRITE RETELLING

Name: _____ Date: _____

DRAW AND WRITE RETELLING FOR _____

Who?	Where?
Draw:	Draw:
Write:	Write:

What happened?	How did it end?
Draw:	Draw:
Write:	Write:

DRAW AND WRITE VISUALIZATIONS

Name: _____ Date: _____

Draw:

Write:

DRAW AND WRITE WONDERS

Name: _____ Date: _____

"I WONDER" STATEMENTS

Drawing:

I wonder...

DRAW SOMETHING

Name: _____

Date: _____

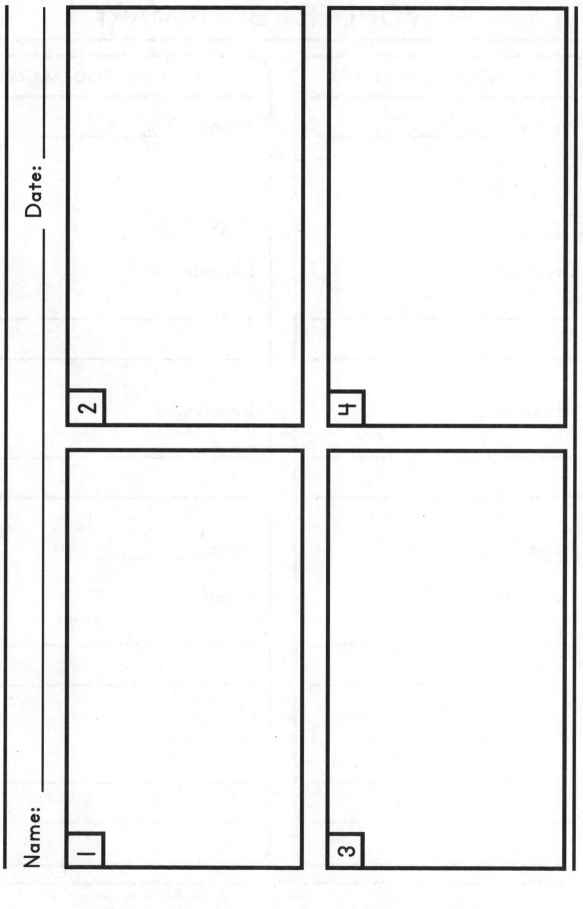

1

2

3

4

"I WONDER" BOOKMARK

"I WONDER" BOOKMARK	"I WONDER" BOOKMARK
Name: _____	Name: _____
Page _____	Page _____
I wonder...	I wonder...
_____	_____
_____	_____
because...	because...
_____	_____
_____	_____
Page _____	Page _____
I wonder...	I wonder...
_____	_____
_____	_____
because...	because...
_____	_____
_____	_____

IN MY HEAD...WHAT I READ

Name: _____ Date: _____

In My Head...	What I Read...

K–W–L

Name: _____ Date: _____

Topic: _____

K	W	L
(What I know or think I know)	(What I want to know)	(What I learned)

K–W–L–S

Name: _____ Date: _____

Topic: _____

K (What I know or think I know)	W (What I want to know)	L (What I learned)	S (What I still want to know)

LYRIC RETELLING/LYRIC SUMMARY

Name: _____ Date: _____

Text: _____

Tune: _____

Verse I:

_____

_____

_____

_____

Verse 2:

_____

_____

_____

_____

Refrain (or Verse 3):

_____

_____

_____

_____

MAIN IDEA TABLE

Name: _____ Date: _____

Main Idea			

Supporting Details

MIND AND ALTERNATIVE MIND PORTRAITS

Name: _____ Date: _____

Mind Portrait

Alternative Mind Portrait

PREDICT-O-GRAM

Vocabulary Words

Characters

Setting

Problem

Action

Solution

PROBABLE PASSAGES

Name: _____   Date: _____

Setting:

Characters:

Problem:

Events:

Solution:

QUESTION–ANSWER RELATIONSHIPS
(QAR)

Name:_____ Date: _____

- In the text

  - Right There—the answer is within one sentence in the text.

  - Think and Search—the answer is contained in more than one sentence from the text.

- In my head

  - Author and You—the answer needs information from the reader's background knowledge and the text.

  - On Your Own—the answer needs information from only the reader's background knowledge.

Guided Comprehension in the Primary Grades (Second Edition) by Maureen McLaughlin.
© 2010 by the International Reading Association. May be copied for classroom use.

QUIP RESEARCH GRID

Name: _____ Date: _____

Topic: _____

Questions	Answers	
	Source:	Source:
1.		
2.		
3.		

SEMANTIC FEATURE ANALYSIS

Name: _____

Date: _____

Categories	Characteristics								

Guided Comprehension in the Primary Grades (Second Edition) by Maureen McLaughlin. © 2010 by the International Reading Association. May be copied for classroom use.

SEMANTIC QUESTION MAP

Name: _____

Date: _____

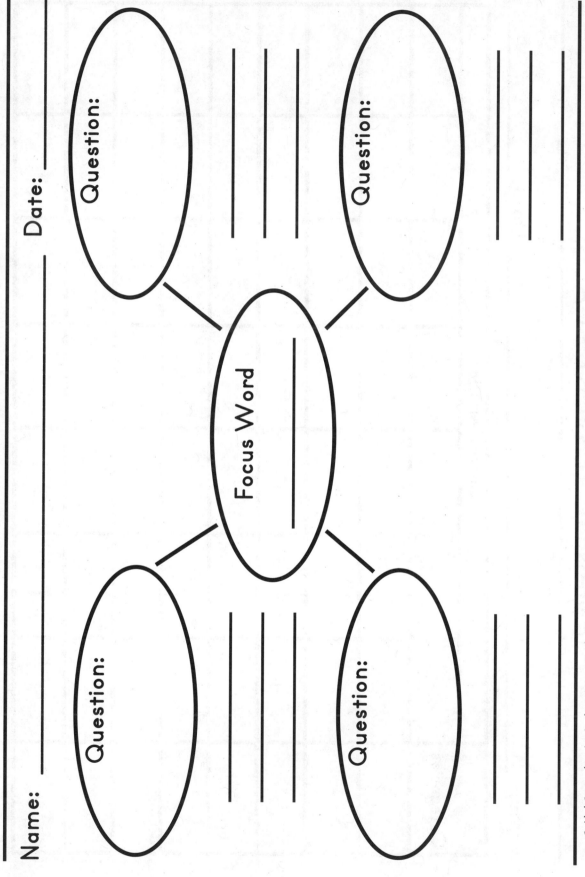

Question: _____
_____
_____

Question: _____
_____
_____

Focus Word
_____

Question: _____
_____
_____

Question: _____
_____
_____

SEQUENCE CHAIN

Name: _____ Date: _____

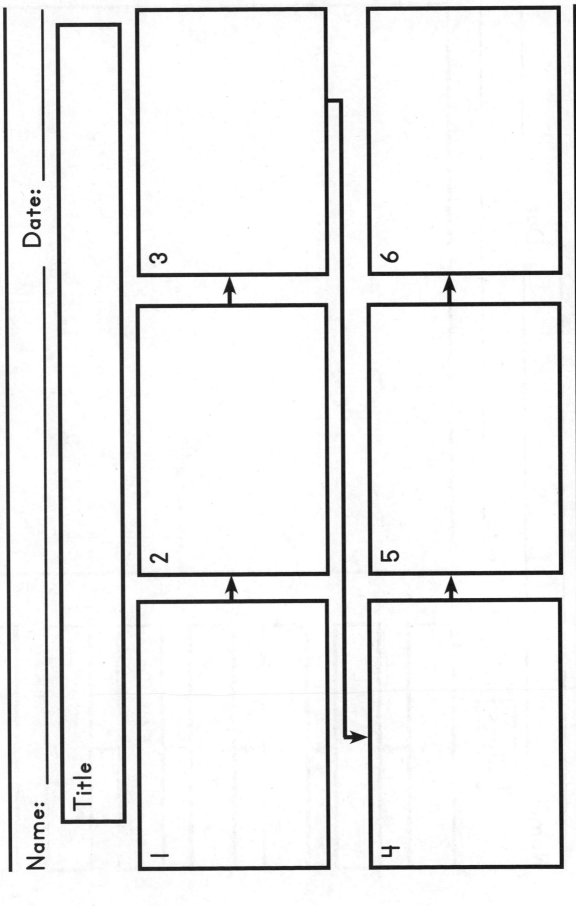

Title

| 1 | 2 | 3 |

| 4 | 5 | 6 |

STORY IMPRESSIONS

Name: _____

For: _____

Date: _____

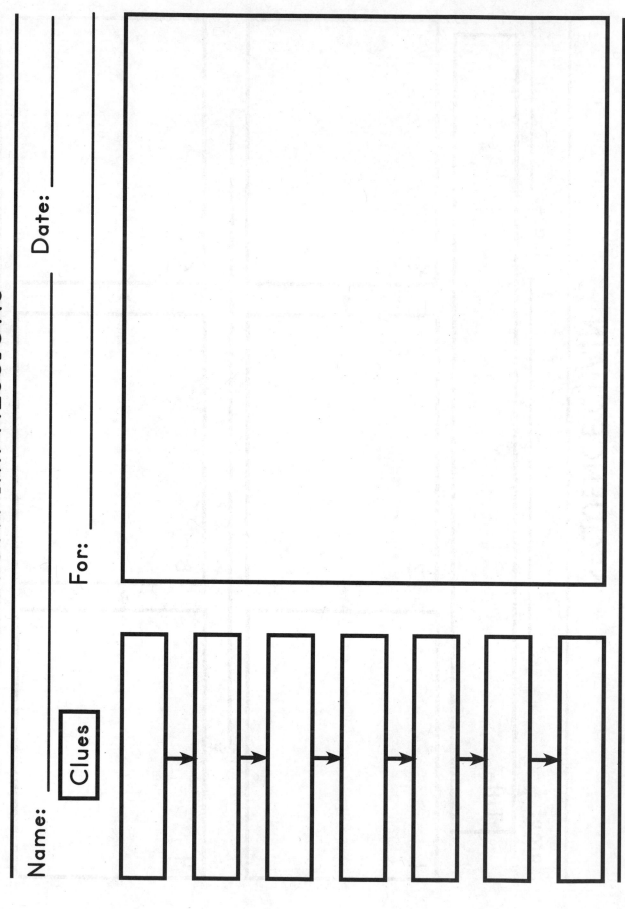

Clues

STORY MAP

Name:_____ Date: _____

Title/Chapter: _____

Setting	Characters

Problem

Event 1

Event 2

Event 3

Solution

STORY PYRAMID

Name: _____ Date: _____

1. _____
Character's name

2. _____
Two words describing the character

3. _____
Three words describing the setting

4. _____
Four words stating the problem

5. _____
Five words describing one event

6. _____
Six words describing another event

7. _____
Seven words describing a third event

8. _____
Eight words describing a solution to the problem

SUMMARY CUBE

Name: _____ Date: _____

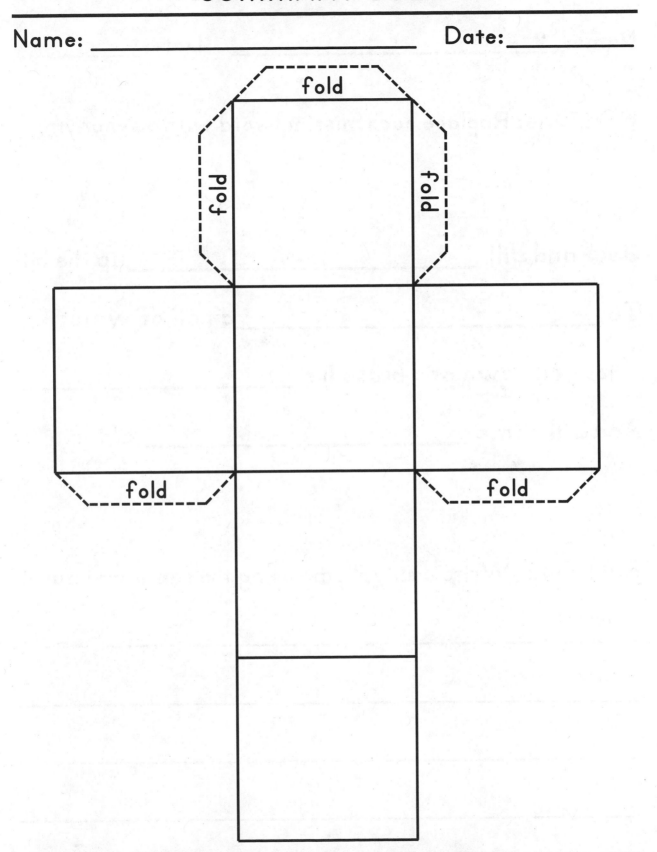

TEXT TRANSFORMATIONS

Name: _____   Date: _____

Part One: Replace each missing word with a synonym.

Jack and Jill _____ up the hill

To _____ a pail of water.

Jack fell down and broke his _____

And Jill came _____ after.

Part Two: Write a silly rhyme using the same structure.

_____

_____

_____

_____

THICK AND THIN QUESTIONS

Name: _____ Date: _____

Page	Thin Questions	Thick Questions

VENN DIAGRAM

Name: _____

Date: _____

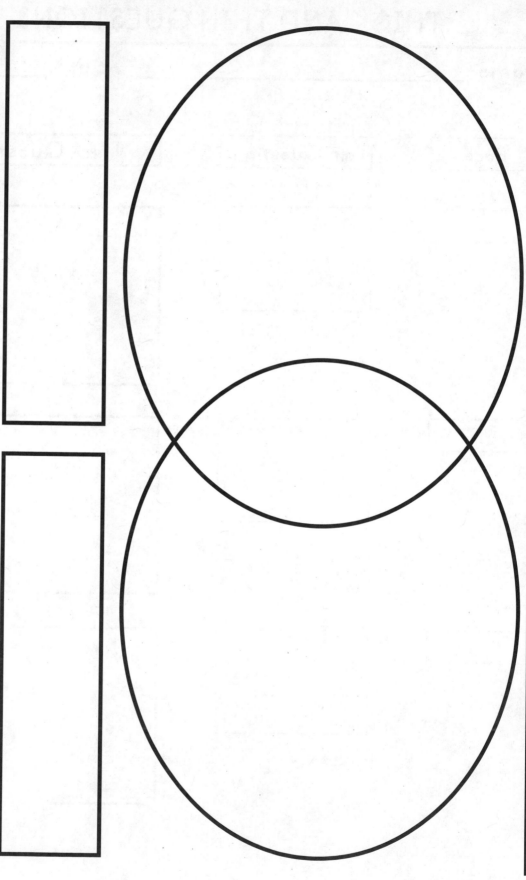

Resources for Organizing and Managing Comprehension Centers and Routines

Name: _____   Date: _____

ABC CENTER
SEQUENTIAL ROUNDTABLE ALPHABET

A		B		C	
D		E		F	
G		H		I	
J		K		L	
M		N		O	
P		Q		R	
S		T		U	
V		W		X	
Y		Z			

ALPHABET BOOKS

Ada, A.F. (1997). *Gathering the sun: An alphabet in Spanish and English*. New York: HarperCollins.

Azarian, M. (2000). *A gardener's alphabet*. Boston: Houghton Mifflin.

Blackwell, D. (1989). *An ABC bestiary*. New York: Farrar, Straus & Giroux.

Bronson, L. (2001). *The circus alphabet*. New York: Henry Holt.

Browne, P.A. (1995). *African animals ABC*. San Francisco: Sierra Club.

Carle, E. (2007). *Eric Carle's ABC*. New York: Grosset & Dunlap.

Cheney, L. (2002). *America: A patriotic primer*. New York: Simon & Schuster.

Crane, C. (2000). *S is for sunshine: A Florida alphabet*. Chelsea, MI: Sleeping Bear.

Crane, C. (2001). *L is for Lone Star: A Texas alphabet*. Chelsea, MI: Sleeping Bear.

Crosby, E.T. (2001). *A is for adopted*. Gilbert, AZ: SWAK PAK.

Demarest, C. (1999). *The cowboy ABC*. New York: Dorling/Kindersley.

Demarest, C. (2000). *Firefighters A to Z*. New York: Scholastic.

Ehlert, L. (1989). *Eating the alphabet: Fruits and vegetables from A to Z*. New York: Harcourt.

Ernst, L.C. (2004). *The turn-around, upside-down alphabet book*. New York: Simon & Schuster.

Fleming, D. (2002). *Alphabet under construction*. New York: Henry Holt.

Gagliano, E. (2003). *C is for cowboy: A Wyoming alphabet*. Chelsea, MI: Sleeping Bear.

Gowan, B. (2002). *G is for Grand Canyon: An Arizona alphabet*. Chelsea, MI: Sleeping Bear.

Hall, B. (2003). *A is for arches: A Utah alphabet book*. Chelsea, MI: Sleeping Bear.

Harley, A. (2001). *Leap into poetry: More ABC's of poetry*. Honesdale, PA: Boyds Mills.

Harris, J. (1997). *A is for artist: A Getty Museum alphabet*. Los Angeles: Getty.

Inkpen, M. (2001). *Kipper's A to Z*. New York: Harcourt.

Jordan, M., & Jordan, T. (1996). *Amazon alphabet*. New York: Kingfisher.

Kalman, M. (2001). *What Pete ate from A–Z*. New York: Penguin.

Kirk, D. (1998). *Miss Spider's ABC*. New York: Scholastic.

Martin, B. Jr (2000). *Chicka chicka boom boom*. New York: Aladdin.

Melmed, L.K. (2009). *Heart of Texas: A Lone Star ABC*. New York: Collins.

Murphy, C. (1997). *Alphabet magic*. New York: Simon & Schuster.

Nathan, C. (1995). *Bugs and beasties ABC*. Boca Raton, FL: Cool Kids.

Onyefulu, I. (1993). *A is for Africa*. New York: Puffin.

Pallotta, J. (1989). *The yucky reptile alphabet book*. Watertown, MA: Charlesbridge.

Pallotta, J. (1990). *The dinosaur alphabet book*. Watertown, MA: Charlesbridge.

Pallotta, J. (1990). *The furry animal alphabet book*. Watertown, MA: Charlesbridge.

Pallotta, J. (1990). *The icky bug alphabet book*. Watertown, MA: Charlesbridge.

Pallotta, J. (1991). *The bird alphabet book*. Watertown, MA: Charlesbridge.

Pallotta, J. (1991). *The frog alphabet book*. Watertown, MA: Charlesbridge.

Pallotta, J. (1991). *The ocean alphabet book*. Watertown, MA: Charlesbridge.

Pallotta, J. (1991). *The underwater alphabet book*. Watertown, MA: Charlesbridge.

Pallotta, J. (1992). *The Victory Garden vegetable alphabet book*. Watertown, MA: Charlesbridge.

Pallotta, J. (1993). *The extinct alphabet book*. Watertown, MA: Charlesbridge.

Pallotta, J. (1994). *The desert alphabet book*. Watertown, MA: Charlesbridge.

Pallotta, J. (1995). *The butterfly alphabet book*. Watertown, MA: Charlesbridge.

Pallotta, J. (1996). *The freshwater alphabet book*. Watertown, MA: Charlesbridge.

Pallotta, J. (1997). *The airplane alphabet book*. Minneapolis, MN: Econo-Clad.

Pallotta, J. (1997). *The flower alphabet book*. Watertown, MA: Charlesbridge.

Pallotta, J. (1999). *The jet alphabet book*. Watertown, MA: Charlesbridge.

Pallotta, J. (2003). *The boat alphabet book*. Watertown, MA: Charlesbridge.

Pallotta, J. (2004). *The beetle alphabet book*. Watertown, MA: Charlesbridge.

Pallotta, J. (2006). *The construction alphabet book*. Watertown, MA: Charlesbridge.

Picayo, M. (2007). *Caribbean journey from A to Y—Read and discover what happened to the Z*. New York: Campanita.

Pfister, M. (2002). *Rainbow fish A, B, C*. New York: North-South.

Reynolds, C.F. (2001). *H is for Hoosier: An Indiana alphabet*. Chelsea, MI: Sleeping Bear.

Reynolds, C.F. (2001). *L is for lobster: A Maine alphabet*. Chelsea, MI: Sleeping Bear.

Rose, D.L. (2000). *Into the A, B, sea: An ocean alphabet*. New York: Scholastic.

Schnur, S. (2002). *Winter: An alphabet acrostic*. New York: Houghton Mifflin.

Schonberg, M. (2000). *B is for buckeye: An Ohio alphabet*. Chelsea, MI: Sleeping Bear.

Scillian, D. (2001). *A is for America*. Chelsea, MI: Sleeping Bear.

Sendak, M. (1999). *Alligators all around: An alphabet*. New York: HarperCollins.

Shahan, S. (2002). *The jazzy alphabet*. New York: Penguin Putnam.

Shoulders, M. (2001). *V is for volunteer: A Tennessee alphabet*. Chelsea, MI: Sleeping Bear.

Sierra, J. (1998). *Antarctic antics*. New York: Harcourt Brace.

Slate, J. (1996). *Miss Bindergarten gets ready for kindergarten*. New York: Penguin.

Smith, R. M. (2008). *An A to Z walk in the park*. Alexandria, VA: Clarence-Henry.

Stutson, C. (1999). *Prairie primer*. New York: Puffin.

Tudor, T. (2001). *A is for Annabelle: A doll's alphabet*. New York: Simon & Schuster.

Ulmer, M. (2001). *M is for maple: A Canadian alphabet*. Chelsea, MI: Sleeping Bear.

Walton, R., & Miglio, P. (2002). *So many bunnies: A bedtime ABC and counting book*. New York: HarperTrophy.

Wargin, K. (2000). *L is for Lincoln: An Illinois alphabet*. Chelsea, MI: Sleeping Bear.

Wood, A. (2001). *Alphabet adventure*. New York: Scholastic.

Yolen, J. (1997). *All in the woodland early: An ABC book*. Honesdale, PA: Boyds Mills.

Young, J. (2001). *S is for show me: A Missouri alphabet*. Chelsea, MI: Sleeping Bear.

BOOK MOBILE ORGANIZER

Name:_____ Date: _____

Directions: Write or draw your ideas on the parts of the mobile. Remember to use both sides. Then cut out the six pieces and follow the directions in the folder.

CENTER CHART FOR STUDENTS

Center: _____ Week: _____

Directions: If you used this center, sign your name and place a check mark underneath the day you visited.

Students	Monday	Tuesday	Wednesday	Thursday	Friday

CENTER PLANNER

Theme: _____

Center Title: _____

Format: _____Display Board   _____Pizza Box   _____Folder

Schedule: _____Wall Chart   _____Rotation   _____Free Choice

Accountability:

    Assessment: _____Review Strategy Applications

                            _____Student Self-Assessments

                             _____Other: _____

    Recordkeeping: _____Guided Comprehension Profiles

                             _____Center Folders

                             _____Other: _____

Materials:

    Texts: _____

    _____

    Supplies: _____

    _____

Sample Activity: _____

_____

_____

_____

CENTER REFLECTIONS

Name: _____ Date: _____

Center: _____

While I was working at this center, I was able to

_____

_____

_____

I learned

_____

_____

_____

The next time I plan to

_____

_____

_____

CENTER RUBRIC

Name:_____ Date: _____

Center: _____

Directions: Think about what you did at the center today. Then use this rubric to describe your performance.

	Minimal	Satisfactory	Good	Excellent
	1	2	3	4
My work is complete.	1	2	3	4
I followed the directions.	1	2	3	4
I made personal interpretations.	1	2	3	4
My presentation is appealing.	1	2	3	4
I made connections that are supported by the text.	1	2	3	4
I used multiple modes of response.	1	2	3	4

Comments:

_____

_____

_____

CENTER STUDENT SELF-EVALUATION

Name: _____ Date: _____

Center: _____

My goal was

_____

_____

_____

I know I reached my goal because

_____

_____

_____

My new goal is

_____

_____

_____

CHOOSE YOUR OWN PROJECT

Name: _____

Date: _____

You may work with a partner to do this. Choose a project and follow the directions in the folder.

Write a new ending for the story.

Make a character puppet.

Make a story collage.

Make a picture collage.

Make a character mobile.

Put the characters in a new story.

Create an advertisement for a book.

Create a book jacket.

Write a trifold report.

Interview a classmate.

Survey the class about authors/books.

Write a Lyric Summary and sing it.

CLASS CENTER CHART FOR TEACHERS

Centers					
Students					

CROSS-AGE READING EXPERIENCE
SELF-EVALUATION

Name: _____ Date: _____

Text: _____

1. What is one thing you did to prepare for the Cross-Age Reading Experience that was helpful?

_____

_____

_____

2. What is something you learned in your Cross-Age Reading Experience?

_____

_____

_____

3. How would you rate your Cross-Age Reading Experience?
   great   good   poor

4. How helpful was today's Cross-Age Reading Experience?
   very helpful   somewhat helpful   not helpful

5. What will you do to improve your next Cross-Age Reading Experience time?

_____

_____

_____

DIRECTIONS FOR MAKING BOOKS

Slotted Book

STEP 1: Take at least two pieces of paper and hold them in a landscape (horizontal) position (Fig. 1). You can use more than two pages to create books with more than four pages.

STEP 2—MAKING THE SLOT: Separate one page from the pack of papers. Make sure the fold or SPINE is nice and flat. Measure 1-1/2 inches from the top of the spine and make a mark and the same at the bottom of the page of the spine.

Cut into the spine and carefully cut away the spine between the marks you have made. Only cut into the spine about 1/16 of an inch (Fig. 2). Open your page and you should see a SLOT (Fig. 3).

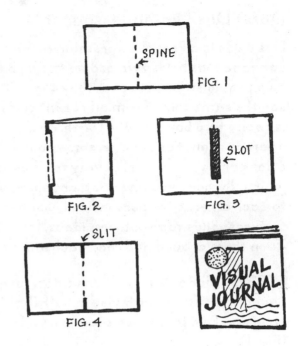

STEP 3—MAKING THE SLITS: Take the other page(s) and make sure the spine is nice and flat. Measure the same 1-1/2 inches from the top and bottom of the spine.

This time cut from the bottom of the page up to the mark to create a SLIT. Repeat the process at the top of the page. You should have a SLIT at the top and bottom of the page (Fig. 4).

STEP 4—SLIPPING THE BOOK TOGETHER: Open the slotted page. Take the other page(s) with slits and bend them in half horizontally. SLIP them through the slot until you have reached the center of the book. Carefully slip the slit and slot together and roll the pages open and fold it like a book.

Source: Pinciotti, P. (2001). *Book arts: The creation of beautiful books*. East Stroudsburg: East Stroudsburg University of Pennsylvania.

DIRECTIONS FOR MAKING BOOKS

Dos à Dos Dialogue Journals

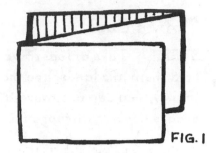

FIG. 1

Dos à dos is a French expression meaning a couch or a carriage that holds two people sitting back to back. When two people sit back to back they see different things or they see the same thing from different points of view. This book is really two books in one (or three or more — you decide). There is room for each person's point of view or story. Dos à dos can be a wonderful way to structure a dialogue journal where you and another person write back and forth to each other. Each person has his or her own book and in turn responds to the others' ideas, questions, and feelings. Turn them around and read each other's response!

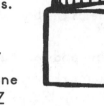

FIG. 2

STEP 1:   For a two-part dos à dos, take a piece of 11 x 17 paper and cut it lengthwise in half (5-1/2 inches). Take one strip and fold into three equal parts. It should look like a Z (Fig. 1).

STEP 2:   Cut all the text pages so they are 8 x 5-1/2 inches. Fold them in half and divide them to create two booklets or signatures with equal pages.

STEP 3:   Slip a signature into the first fold. The crease of the signature or booklet should be nested inside the crease of the cover. You can either staple the signature into the cover
or sew the signature into the cover. The simplest way is to staple the booklet in by using a book arm stapler that lets you staple deep into the center of the signature.

STEP 4:   Repeat step 3 for the other signature nesting it in the other crease.

STEP 5:   Fold the book back and forth so that you can open one signature from the front and one from the back.

STEP 6 — DECORATE THE COVERS: Consider these wild variations! As with any book, you can change the shape, size, and materials of this book. Make a dos à dos dialogue journal for three or four people (Fig. 2). Just make an extra long cover or paste together two of them. What an interesting conversation you could have!

Try different types of text pages. If you need some extra long pages, cut some text pages longer than the others, and make fold outs. Cut some pages taller than others and make fold downs. Add some pop-ups.

Source: Pinciotti, P. (2001). *Book arts: The creation of beautiful books.* East Stroudsburg: East Stroudsburg University of Pennsylvania.

DIRECTIONS FOR MAKING BOOKS

Basic Origami Book

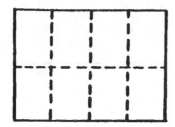

1. Fold an A4 piece of paper into eight equal parts. Lay flat on the landscape position.

2. Fold in half vertically and cut from the folded edge to the center with scissors.

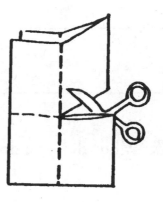

3. Open out then fold horizontally. Push left and right ends to center.

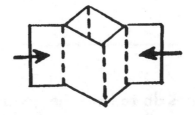

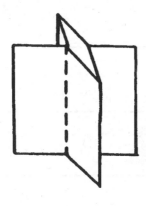

4. Fold around to form a book with six art/writing pages and a front and back cover.

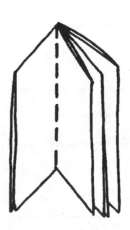

Source: Pinciotti, P. (2001). *Book arts: The creation of beautiful books*. East Stroudsburg: East Stroudsburg University of Pennsylvania.

GROUP WORK REFLECTION SHEET

Name: _____ Date: _____

1. How did your group do today? _____

_____

_____

2. What did you do to help your group? _____

_____

_____

3. What did the others do to help the group? _____

_____

_____

4. What will your group do to improve next time? _____

_____

_____

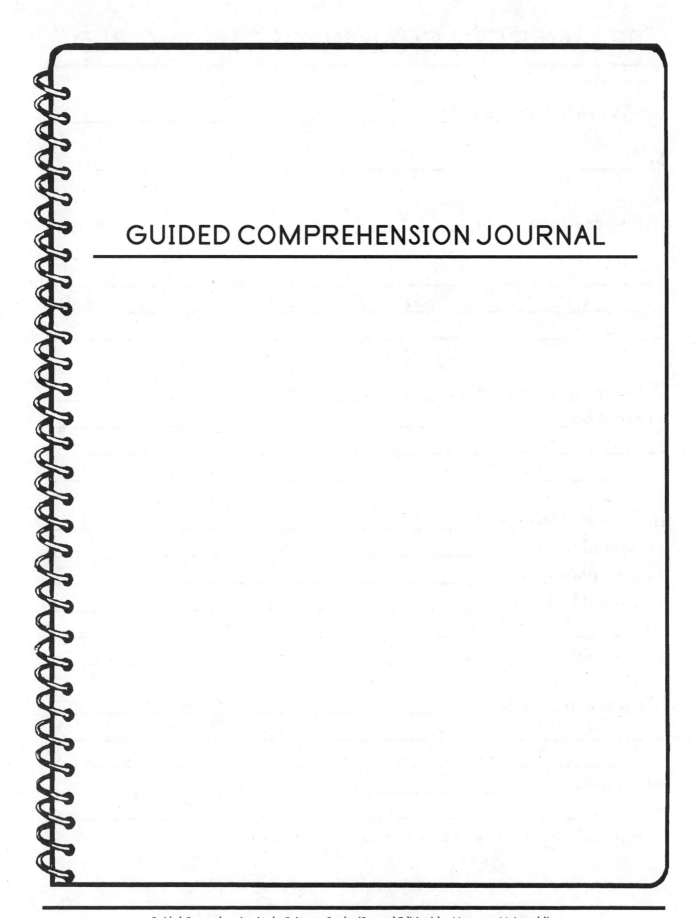

GUIDED COMPREHENSION JOURNAL

" IF I WERE IN CHARGE OF THE WORLD "

If I Were in Charge of _____

by _____

If I were in charge of _____ , I'd cancel
_____ ,
_____ ,
_____ , and also
_____ .

If I were in charge of _____ ,
There'd be _____ ,
_____ , and
_____ .

If I were in charge of _____ ,
You wouldn't have _____
You wouldn't have _____
You wouldn't have _____
Or _____
You wouldn't even have _____

If I were in charge of _____ ,
_____
_____

And a person _____
And _____
Would still be allowed to be in charge of the world.

Source: Adapted from Viorst, J. (1981). *If I were in charge of the world and other worries.* New York: Atheneum.

LITERATURE CIRCLE BOOKMARK

LITERATURE CIRCLE BOOKMARK

Name: _____

Date: _____

I will talk to my group about...

I will ask my group about...

My favorite part was...

LITERATURE CIRCLE BOOKMARK

Name: _____

Date: _____

I will talk to my group about...

I will ask my group about...

My favorite part was...

LITERATURE CIRCLE GROUP EVALUATION

Group Members

_____   _____

_____   _____

_____   _____

4 = Great   3 = Good   2 = Fair   1 = Poor

1. My group worked well together.   _____

2. My group used its time wisely.   _____

3. I did my best work.   _____

4. I think my group deserves a   _____

Student Comments:

Teacher Comments:

LITERATURE CIRCLE SELF-EVALUATION

Name: _____ Date: _____

Text: _____

1. What did you do to prepare for the Literature Circle that was helpful?

_____

_____

_____

2. What is something you learned in your Literature Circle?

_____

_____

_____

3. How would you rate your group's Literature Circle?

    great   good   poor

4. How helpful was today's discussion?

    very helpful   somewhat helpful   not helpful

5. What will you do to improve next time?

_____

_____

MAKING AND WRITING WORDS

Name: _____ Date: _____

How many words can you make from the word _____?

Two-letter words:

___ ___   ___ ___   ___ ___   ___ ___

Three-letter words:

_____   _____   _____   _____

_____   _____   _____   _____

_____   _____   _____   _____

Four-letter words:

_____   _____   _____   _____

_____   _____   _____   _____

_____   _____   _____   _____

Longer words:

_____   _____

_____   _____

_____   _____

Source: Adapted from Rasinski, T.V. (1999). Making and writing words using letter patterns. *Reading Online* [Online]. Available: www.readingonline.org/articles/words/rasinski_index.html.

MAKING AND WRITING WORDS

Name: _____ Date: _____

Directions: Use the vowels and consonants provided to make words based on the clues given by the teacher.

Vowels	Consonants

Directions: Listen carefully as your teacher or classmate provides clues to words that you will write in each box.

1	5
2	6
3	7
4	8

Source: Adapted from Rasinski, T.V. (1999). Making and writing words using letter patterns. *Reading Online* [Online]. Available: www.readingonline.org/articles/words/rasinski_index.html.

MANAGING STAGE TWO

OPTION I: Participation Chart

Student	Session I	Session 2

OPTION 2: Center Rotation Chart

Center _____ _____ _____ _____

Group				
Blue	1	2	3	4
Green	2	3	4	1
Red	3	4	1	2
Yellow	4	1	2	3

MYSTERY PYRAMID

Name: _____ Date: _____

1. ___
   (one word—detective's name)

2. ___ ___
   (two words—describe the detective)

3. ___ ___ ___
   (three words—describe the victim)

4. ___ ___ ___ ___
   (four words—describe the crime/crime scene)

5. ___ ___ ___ ___ ___
   (five words—explain the motive)

6. ___ ___ ___ ___ ___ ___
   (six words—clues that distract you from discovering the culprit)

7. ___ ___ ___ ___ ___ ___ ___
   (seven words—clues that help you discover the culprit)

8. ___ ___ ___ ___ ___ ___ ___ ___
   (eight words—how the case was solved)

MYSTERY SUSPECT ORGANIZER

Name: _____ Date: _____

Prediction
(Who do you think committed the crime?)

_____

_____

_____

Suspect _____   Suspect _____   Suspect _____

Clues: Clues: Clues:

_____   _____   _____

_____   _____   _____

_____   _____   _____

_____   _____   _____

_____   _____   _____

_____   _____   _____

Conclusion
(Who do you think committed the crime? Why do you think so?)

_____

_____

_____

_____

_____

_____

PATTERN BOOK ORGANIZER

Name: _____ Date: _____

Title:

FORTUNATELY _____

Unfortunately _____

FORTUNATELY _____

Unfortunately _____

FORTUNATELY _____

Unfortunately _____

FORTUNATELY _____

Unfortunately _____

FORTUNATELY _____

Unfortunately _____

FORTUNATELY _____

Unfortunately _____

Source: Charlip, R. (1993). *Fortunately.* New York: Aladdin.

PATTERN BOOK ORGANIZER

Name: _____ Date: _____

Fact or Fiction?

Fact or Fiction

_____

_____

_____

Answer_____

Support

_____

_____

_____

Fact or Fiction

_____

_____

_____

Answer_____

Support

_____

_____

_____

POETRY FORM

Name: _____ Date: _____

| Acrostic Poem |

_____   _____

_____   _____

_____   _____

_____   _____

_____   _____

_____   _____

_____   _____

_____   _____

_____   _____

_____   _____

POETRY FORM

Name: _____ Date: _____

Cinquain

_____

one word—noun

_____

two adjectives describing line one

_____ _____ _____

three -ing words telling actions of line one

_____ _____ _____ _____

four-word phrase describing a feeling related to line one

_____

one word—synonym or reference to line one

POETRY FORM

Name: _____ Date: _____

Diamante

_____
subject—one noun

_____ _____
two adjectives describing the subject

_____ _____ _____
three participles (–ing) telling about the subject

_____ _____ _____ _____
four nouns—first two relate to the subject;
last two relate to the opposite

_____ _____ _____
three participles (–ing) telling about the opposite

_____ _____
two adjectives describing the opposite

_____
opposite of subject—one noun

POETRY FORM

Name: _____ Date: _____

Bio-Poem

Line 1 — First name _____

Line 2 — Four traits that describe #1 _____

_____

Line 3 — Related to/sibling of _____

Line 4 — Cares about/likes _____

Line 5 — Who feels _____

Line 6 — Who needs _____

Line 7 — Who gives _____

Line 8 — Who fears _____

Line 9 — Who would like to see _____

Line 10 — Resident of _____

Line 11 — Last name _____

POETRY FORM

Name: _____ Date: _____

Definition Poem

What is _____? (topic)

_____

Description of topic

_____

Description of topic

_____

Description of topic

_____

Description of topic

_____

Description of topic

_____

Description of topic

_____

Description of topic

That is _____! (topic)

PRESS CONFERENCE SUMMARY

Name: _____ Date: _____

Topic: _____

_____

What I read: _____

_____

What I learned: _____

_____

_____

What I will tell the class: _____

_____

_____

_____

_____

_____

QUICK CLOUD

Name: _____ Date: _____

This is what I was thinking while I was reading.

RECIPROCAL TEACHING BOOKMARKS

Name: _____

Date: _____

Title: _____

Pages: _____

Make a prediction about what might happen next in the text.

My prediction is:

_____

_____

_____

I think this because:

_____

_____

_____

Prediction Prompts—

I think...   I predict...
I bet...   I anticipate...
I wonder...   I hypothesize...
I imagine...   Based on...I predict...
I suppose...

Name: _____

Date: _____

Title: _____

Pages: _____

Create questions that help to identify important information and connect prior knowledge with new ideas:

Questions:

1. _____

_____

2. _____

_____

3. _____

_____

Question Prompts—

Who is...?   What if...?
Where...?   I wonder how...?
When...?   Which is better...? Why?
What...?   Why did...?
How...?   What is your opinion...?
Why is...?   Why?

RECIPROCAL TEACHING BOOKMARKS

Name: _____

Date: _____

Title: _____

Pages: _____

Identify words or concepts that are difficult to understand. Share how you figured it out.

Word or concept:

_____

I figured it out by:

_____

_____

Word or concept:

_____

I figured it out by:

_____

_____

Clarifying Prompts —

I did not understand...

The confusing part was...

I need to know more about...

A difficult word/phrase is...

Name: _____

Date: _____

Title: _____

Pages: _____

Identify the key ideas and summarize them.

Key ideas:

1. _____

2. _____

3. _____

Summary:

_____

_____

Summary Prompts —

The important ideas so far...

New facts I have learned...

The main character(s) is...

The problem is...

The important story events are...

RECIPROCAL TEACHING
SELF-EVALUATION

Name: _____ Date: _____

Text: _____

1. How would you rate your participation in Reciprocal Teaching?

      just right   too much   too little   not at all

2. What is the main message of the text?

_____

_____

_____

3. How would you rate your group's Reciprocal Teaching?

    great   good   poor

4. How helpful was today's session?

    very helpful   somewhat helpful   not helpful

5. What will you do to improve next time?

_____

_____

_____

REQUIRED AND OPTIONAL CENTER AND ACTIVITY FORM

Name: _____   Date: _____

Centers	Monday	Tuesday	Wednesday	Thursday	Friday
D					
D					
W					
W					
W					
W					
W My Choice: _____					
W My Choice: _____					

Mark the day with an X when you visit that center.
D = visit center daily; W = visit center weekly

Guided Comprehension in the Primary Grades (Second Edition) by Maureen McLaughlin. © 2010 by the International Reading Association. May be copied for classroom use.

STORY TRIFOLD

Name: _____   Date: _____

Beginning	Middle	End

WORD DETECTIVE SEQUENTIAL ROUNDTABLE ORGANIZER

Name: _____

Date: _____

A	B	C
D	E	F
G	H	I
J	K	L
M	N	O
P	Q	R
S	T	U
V	W	X
Y	Z	

WRITE YOUR OWN MYSTERY

Name: _____ Date: _____

Draw, describe, or explain the crime scene.

Write two clues that are in your mystery.

_____

_____

_____

Choose the detective, a suspect, or a victim and write two words to describe that character.

Character: _____

1. Word: _____

2. Word: _____

Describe how the mystery was or will be solved.

_____

_____

_____

Assessment Blackline Masters

ATTITUDE SURVEY 1

Name: _____ Date: _____

1. I think reading is _____

   because _____ .

2. I think I am a _____ reader

   because _____ .

3. I think _____ is a good reader because

   _____ .

4. I think writing is _____

   because _____ .

5. I think I am a _____ writer because _____

   _____ . _____ .

6. I think _____ is a good writer because

   _____ .

ATTITUDE SURVEY 2

Name: _____ Date: _____

Directions: Please place a check under the category that best describes your response.

Y = Yes
N = No

	Y	N
1. I read in my free time.	____	____
2. I like to receive books as gifts.	____	____
3. I like to choose what I read.	____	____
4. Reading is a rainy-day activity I enjoy.	____	____
5. I would rather read than watch television.	____	____
6. I keep a journal.	____	____
7. I like to write to my friends.	____	____
8. I like to write in school.	____	____
9. I use my computer to write.	____	____
10. I often revise my writing to make it better.	____	____

CLASSROOM READING MISCUE ASSESSMENT

Reader's Name _____ Date _____

Grade Level _____ Teacher _____

Selection Read _____

I. What percent of the sentences read make sense?

Sentence by sentence tally   Total

_____ Number of semantically acceptable sentences

_____ Number of semantically unacceptable sentences

_____ % Comprehending score:

Number of semantically acceptable sentences
_____ × 100 TOTAL _____
Total number of sentences read

	Seldom	Sometimes	Often	Usually	Always
II. In what ways is reader constructing meaning?					
A. Recognizes when miscues have disrupted meaning	1	2	3	4	5
B. Logically substitutes	1	2	3	4	5
C. Self–corrects errors that disrupt meaning	1	2	3	4	5
D. Uses picture and/or other visual clues	1	2	3	4	5
In what ways is reader disrupting meaning?					
A. Substitutes words that don't make sense	1	2	3	4	5
B. Makes omissions that disrupt meaning	1	2	3	4	5
C. Relies too heavily on graphic clues	1	2	3	4	5

	No		Partial		Yes
III. If narrative text is used:					
A. Character recall	1	2	3	4	5
B. Character development	1	2	3	4	5
C. Setting	1	2	3	4	5
D. Relationship of events	1	2	3	4	5
E. Plot	1	2	3	4	5
F. Theme	1	2	3	4	5
G. Overall retelling	1	2	3	4	5
If expository text is used:	No		Partial		Yes
A. Major concepts	1	2	3	4	5
B. Generalizations	1	2	3	4	5
C. Specific information	1	2	3	4	5
D. Logical structuring	1	2	3	4	5
E. Overall retelling	1	2	3	4	5

Source: Adapted from Rhodes, L.K., Shanklin, N.L., & Valencia, S.W. (1990). Miscue analysis in the classroom. *The Reading Teacher, 44,* 252–254.

GUIDED COMPREHENSION PROFILE
SUMMARY SHEET

Student:_____ Grade:_____ School Year:_____

Summary of Background Information:

Student's Interests:

Reading Levels:	September	December	March	June
Independent				
Guided				
Strategy Use:				
Previewing				
Self-Questioning				
Making Connections				
Visualizing				
Knowing How Words Work				
Monitoring				
Summarizing				
Evaluating				

Not Observed (NO) — Student does not use the strategy.
Emerging (E) — Student attempts to use the strategy.
Developing (D) — Student is using the strategy on some occasions.
Consistent (C) — Student effectively uses the strategy to make meaning from text.

Comments:

INTEREST INVENTORY I

Name: _____ Date: _____

1. What is your favorite school subject? Why do you like it? _____
_____

2. What is your favorite book? Why do you like it?_____
_____

3. Do you go to the library? Do you have a library card? _____
_____

4. Who is your favorite author? Why? _____
_____

5. What is a dream or wish you have? _____
_____

6. What do you like to do after school? _____
_____

7. If you had a day off from school, how would you spend the day?
_____

8. What magazine do you like to read? _____
_____

9. If you could meet any famous person, whom would you choose?
What would you like to talk about? _____
_____

10. If you could receive any book as a gift, what kind of book would
you choose? _____

INTEREST INVENTORY 2

Name: _____ Date: _____

1. What is one of your hobbies? What do you like about it? _____
_____

2. If you could plan an afternoon to do anything you wanted to do,
   what would you do? _____
_____

3. What kinds of things do you like to draw?_____
_____

4. What is your favorite food? _____
_____

5. What is your favorite kind of music? Favorite song? Favorite
   group? What do you like about it (them)? _____
_____

6. What is your favorite television show? Why do you like it? _____
_____

7. Do you like to read to someone at home? Do you like it when
   someone reads to you? _____
_____

8. If you could choose a book about any topic that someone would read
   to you, what would it be? _____
_____

LITERACY HISTORY PROMPTS

To learn about your students' literacy experiences, you may wish to have them create their literacy histories. The following prompts will facilitate this process. Having the students illustrate their experiences or provide photos related to their experiences enhances their histories. Be sure to demonstrate this activity by sharing this part of your literacy history as a model for the class.

1. What was your favorite book before you came to school?

2. What was your favorite memory of having someone read to you when you were younger?

3. Can you remember a sign you could read at a young age (McDonald's, Burger King, Toys "R" Us, supermarket, etc.)? What do you remember about that experience?

4. Did you ever read to your stuffed animals, dolls, or younger brothers and sisters? What do you remember about those experiences?

5. What was the first thing you ever wrote (crayon scribbles on a wall, writing in a tablet, note to parents, thank-you note, etc.)? What do you remember about that experience?

6. What was the first book that you read? What do you remember about that experience?

7. What was the first thing you wrote that you were really proud of?

8. What book are you reading outside of school now? Why did you choose to read it?

9. What are some things you are writing outside of school now?

10. Do you and your friends talk about what you read? What is something you would tell them about a book you read recently?

11. Do you think you are a good reader now? Do you plan to continue reading as you get older?

12. Do you think you are a good writer now? Do you plan to continue writing as you get older?

Source: Gambrell, L.B., Palmer, B.M., Codling, R.M., & Mazzoni, S.A. (1996). Assessing motivation to read. *The Reading Teacher, 49,* 518–533.

MOTIVATION TO READ PROFILE
CONVERSATIONAL INTERVIEW

Student: _____ Date: _____

A. Emphasis: Narrative text

Suggested prompt (designed to engage student in a natural conversation): I have been reading a good book...I was talking with...about it last night. I enjoy talking about good stories and books that I've been reading. Today I'd like to hear about what you have been reading.

1. Tell me about the most interesting story or book you have read this week (or even last week). Take a few minutes to think about it. (Wait time.) Now, tell me about the book or story.

Probes: What else can you tell me? Is there anything else? _____

_____

_____

_____

2. How did you know or find out about this story? _____

_____

_____

☐ assigned   ☐ in school
☐ chosen   ☐ out of school

3. Why was this story interesting to you? _____

_____

_____

_____

(continued)

Source: Gambrell, L.B., Palmer, B.M., Codling, R.M., & Mazzoni, S.A. (1996). Assessing motivation to read. *The Reading Teacher, 49,* 518–533.

MOTIVATION TO READ PROFILE
CONVERSATIONAL INTERVIEW (continued)

B. Emphasis: Informational text

Suggested prompt (designed to engage student in a natural conversation): Often we read to find out about something or to learn about something. We read for information. For example, I remember a student of mine... who read a lot of books about...to find out as much as he/she could about.... Now, I'd like to hear about some of the informational reading you have been doing.

1. Think about something important that you learned recently, not from your teacher and not from television, but from a book or some other reading material. What did you read about? (Wait time.) Tell me about what you learned.

Probes: What else could you tell me? Is there anything else? _____

_____

_____

_____

2. How did you know or find out about this book/article? _____

_____

_____

☐ assigned   ☐ in school
☐ chosen   ☐ out of school

3. Why was this book (or article) important to you? _____

_____

_____

(continued)

Source: Gambrell, L.B., Palmer, B.M., Codling, R.M., & Mazzoni, S.A. (1996). Assessing motivation to read. *The Reading Teacher, 49,* 518–533.

MOTIVATION TO READ PROFILE
CONVERSATIONAL INTERVIEW (continued)

C. Emphasis: General reading

1. Did you read anything at home yesterday? _____ What?

_____

_____

2. Do you have any books at school (in your desk/storage area/locker/book bag) today that you are reading? _____ Tell me about them.

_____

_____

3. Tell me about your favorite author.

_____

_____

4. What do you think you have to learn to be a better reader?

_____

_____

5. Do you know about any books right now that you'd like to read? Tell me about them.

_____

_____

6. How did you find out about these books?

_____

_____

7. What are some things that get you really excited about reading books?

_____

_____

8. Tell me about...

_____

_____

9. Who gets you really interested and excited about reading books?

_____

_____

10. Tell me more about what they do.

_____

_____

Source: Gambrell, L.B., Palmer, B.M., Codling, R.M., & Mazzoni, S.A. (1996). Assessing motivation to read. *The Reading Teacher, 49,* 518–533.

CROSS-AGE READING EXPERIENCE OBSERVATION

Student:_____ Date: _____

Directions: Place a check if the behavior is observed.

Observation:

1. Student was prepared for the Cross-Age Reading Experience. _____
2. Student welcomed his or her cross-age reading buddy. _____
3. Student(s) self-selected an appropriate text from the book basket. _____
4. Student focused on the task. _____
5. Student actively engaged in reading. _____
6. Student successfully engaged in strategy application. _____
7. Student engaged in meaningful discussion. _____
8. Student was competent in his or her role. _____
9. Student's contributions demonstrated depth of understanding. _____
10. Student respected ideas of others involved in the experience. _____

Student's self-evaluation indicated _____

_____

_____

_____

Notes: _____

_____

_____

_____

LITERATURE CIRCLE OBSERVATION

Student: _____ Date: _____

Directions: Place a check if the behavior is observed.

Observation:

1. Student was prepared for the Literature Circle. _____
2. Student was focused on the group task. _____
3. Student engaged in discussion. _____
    Talk focused on the content of the book. _____
    Talk focused on the reading process. _____
    Talk focused on personal connections. _____
    Talk focused on the group process. _____
4. Student was competent in his or her discussion role. _____
5. Student's contributions demonstrated depth
    of understanding. _____
6. Student respected ideas of other group
    members. _____

Student's self-evaluation indicated _____

_____

_____

_____

_____

Notes: _____

_____

_____

_____

Guided Comprehension in the Primary Grades (Second Edition) by Maureen McLaughlin.
© 2010 by the International Reading Association. May be copied for classroom use.

RECIPROCAL TEACHING OBSERVATION

Student: _____ Date: _____

Directions: Place a check if the behavior is observed.

Observation:

    1. Student was prepared for Reciprocal Teaching.   _____

    2. Student was focused on the group task.   _____

    3. Student was actively engaged in Reciprocal Teaching.   _____

    4. Student successfully engaged in prediction.   _____

    5. Student successfully generated meaningful questions.   _____

    6. Student successfully clarified meaning.   _____

    7. Student successfully summarized text.   _____

    8. Student used strategy prompts.   _____

    9. Student's contributions demonstrated depth
        of understanding.   _____

   10. Student respected ideas of other group members.   _____

Student's self-evaluation indicated _____

_____

_____

_____

_____

Notes: _____

_____

_____

_____

Guided Comprehension in the Primary Grades (Second Edition) by Maureen McLaughlin.
© 2010 by the International Reading Association. May be copied for classroom use.

STUDENT SELF-REFLECTION
AND GOAL SETTING

Name: _____ Date: _____

Hobby or Special Interest

This activity is designed to help you reflect on one of your hobbies or special interests. Remember that self-reflection involves thinking about what you did, how well you did it, and what you can do to make it better next time. To begin your reflection, focus on your hobby or special interest. Then think about the last time you did it. How well did it go? What is one thing you can do to improve it next time? What is your new goal?

1. My hobby or special interest is _____
_____

2. Something I learned to do in my hobby or special interest is
_____
_____

3. The last time I did it _____
_____
_____

4. One thing I can do to improve it next time is _____
_____
_____

5. My new goal for my hobby or special interest is _____
_____
_____

STUDENT SELF-REFLECTION AND GOAL SETTING IN GUIDED COMPREHENSION

Name: _____ Date: _____

This activity is designed to help you create a self-reflection about your reading. Remember that self-reflection involves thinking about what you did, how well you did it, and what you can do to make it better next time. To begin your reflection, focus on something you have learned during Guided Comprehension. Then think about the last time you did it. How well did it go? What is one thing you can do to improve it next time? What is your new goal?

1. What I read _____

_____

2. What I learned _____

_____

3. The last time I did it _____

_____

4. One thing I can do to improve it next time is _____

_____

5. My new goal is _____

_____

REFLECTION AND GOAL SETTING

Name: _____ Date: _____

1. Today my goal was _____

_____

_____

2. What I did _____

_____

_____

3. What I learned _____

_____

_____

4. Questions I have _____

_____

_____

5. When I reflect on how well I achieved my goal, I think

_____

_____

6. Tomorrow my goal will be _____

_____

_____

TICKETS OUT

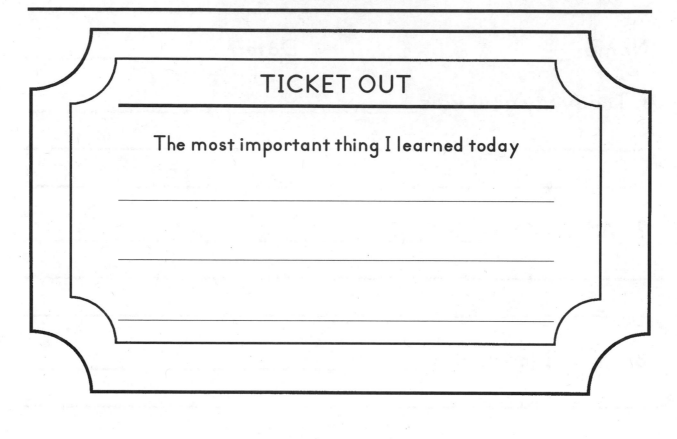

TICKET OUT

The most important thing I learned today

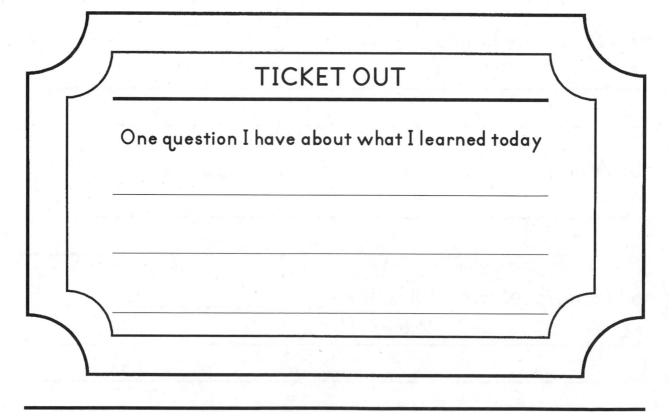

TICKET OUT

One question I have about what I learned today

Sources of Leveled Narrative and Expository Texts

Websites Maintained by Teachers or School Districts

Leveled Book Lists by Nancy Giansante

home.comcast.net/~ngiansante

This site features many titles of books easily sorted by title, author, or grade level. The information provided includes title, author, Guided Reading level, and grade level. For example, when you click on grade 2, you get a listing of titles spanning Guided Reading levels H through M. These are 10 examples from the second-grade lists:

Title	Author	Guided Reading	Grade Level
Bailey Goes Camping	Henkes, Kevin	H	1.70
We Are Best Friends	Aliki	H	1.70
Alligators All Around	Sendak, Maurice	I	1.94
Henny Penny	Galdone, Paul	I	1.94
Bear Shadow	Asch, Frank	J	2.00
The Cat in the Hat	Dr. Seuss	J	2.00
Arthur Babysits	Brown, Marc	K	2.25
Manatee Winter	Zoehfeld, Kathleen	K	2.25
Dolphins	Morris, Robert	L	2.50
The Dog That Stole Home	Christopher, Matt	L	2.50

Beaverton School District Leveled Books Database

registration.beaverton.k12.or.us/lbdb

This site includes a large collection of titles in English and Spanish that are classified by Guided Reading and Reading Recovery levels. You can search by title, publisher, author, keyword, or level. For example, if you want books that are at an H Guided Reading level, put H in that box and a list of 505 books is displayed. Following are the first 10 titles of that list:

Title	Author
Ben's Tooth	PM Story Books
Just This Once	Sunshine
Letters for Mr. James	Sunshine
Mrs. Spider's Beautiful Web	PM Story Books
Pepper's Adventure	PM Story Books
The Bag I'm Taking to Grandma's	Neitzel, Shirley
Island Picnic, The	PM Story Books
Water	Wonder World
Clean House for Mole and Mouse, A	Ziefert, Harriet
Animal Tricks	Wildsmith, Brian

If you search for Eric Carle, you will see the 9 titles displayed below. If you click on a book title, you will see the Reading Recovery and the Guided Reading levels. For example, if you click on *The Grouchy Ladybug*, you will learn the RR level is 22 and the Guided Reading level is L.

Title	Author
Grouchy Ladybug, The	Carle, Eric
Have You Seen My Cat?	Carle, Eric
Very Busy Spider, The	Carle, Eric
Very Hungry Caterpillar, The	Carle, Eric
Pancakes, Pancakes	Carle, Eric
Rooster's Off to See the World	Carle, Eric
What's for Lunch?	Carle, Eric
Do You Want to Be My Friend?	Carle, Eric
The Very Hungry Caterpillar/ Oruga Muy Hambrienta, La	Carle, Eric

Leveled Materials Available From Publishers

National Geographic School Publishing

www.ngsp.com

Windows on Literacy is 400 nonfiction readers in science and social studies. The titles are designed to meet the needs of young readers from "Step Up" to "Fluent Plus" levels. Titles featured in the emergent level include the following:

Watch the Sky	Who Lives Here?
Weather in the City	What Grows Here?
The Baby Shark	Who Works at the Zoo?
The Little Panda	Numbers in Our World
When the Rain Comes	What Shapes Do You See?

Scholastic Teacher Book Wizard

bookwizard.scholastic.com/tbw/homePage.do

This is a site where you can enter titles and get an approximate level, you can enter levels and get a list of books at that level, or you can enter a title and get other books that are written at that approximate level. For example, if you enter *Eric Carle* in the Quick Search box, the site will display 49 of Eric Carle's books. If you click on a title, such as *Dream Snow*, you can learn the interest level (K–2), grade-level equivalent (1.7), lexile measure (300L), DRA levels (18–20), Guided Reading level (J), genre/theme (fiction), and related topics (Christmas, farm and ranch life, winter). If you enter the title *We're Going on a Bear Hunt*, you will find more than 200 books that have similar approximate levels. Finally, you can search by putting in a range of grade-equivalent levels and choosing type, topic, and genre. Then a list of books meeting those criteria is displayed.

Lexiles and Readability Graphs

The Lexile Framework for Reading

www.lexile.com

The Lexile Framework levels books according to sentence length and word frequency and assigns each book a lexile based on this information. The site defines *lexile* as "a unit of measurement used when determining the difficulty of text and the reading level of readers." The site has a large book database that is easy to use. Books can be searched by author or by title, and a lexile level is displayed. For example, if you search the title *The Drinking Gourd*, a 370L suggests that this title is in the second-grade level range. (For a chart describing the range of lexiles for each grade, see www .lexile.com/m/uploads/maps/Lexile-Map.pdf.)

Kathy Schrock's Guide for Educators—Fry's Readability Graph: Directions for Use

school.discoveryeducation.com/schrockguide/fry/fry.html

This site offers a clear description of how to analyze a text using Fry's Readability Graph. The Fry Graph uses sentence length and vocabulary complexity for determining levels of reading materials. Although this tool gives an estimate of level, it will give you some ideas about the ease or difficulty of a particular text.

Home–School Connections

Creating and maintaining positive relationships with students' families is a valued component of the educational process. A variety of ideas for facilitating such relationships in the primary grades are presented in this appendix.

Alphabetize Environmentally
Foster the child's knowledge of the alphabet by providing environmental print (labels, advertisements, store bags, street names) to alphabetize (Rule, 2001).

Billboards, Street Signs, and Labels
Parents or older siblings walk with the student throughout the community, pointing out different types of environmental print. Students can notice street signs in their neighborhood and see billboard advertisements. If a stop is made at a local market or if a snack is served after the walk, the student can also make connections between the foods and their labels.

Book Backpacks
Fill a backpack with reading and writing materials and send it home with a student for a weekend. Have the family members use the materials together to read stories, write stories, or create illustrations for stories. You also can include a list of creative ways to respond to literature, and the families can choose what they would like to do. When the backpack is returned to school, the child shares how the family engaged in literacy.

It Happened Just This Way
After reading aloud to a child or having the child read to you, have the child retell the story orally, through drawings, through dramatization, or by writing.

Library Buddies
Send a list of popular book titles home to parents. Have a parent or older sibling become the student's library buddy. The buddies can check out the latest in children's literature, listen to an audio book, or attend a story hour together. When they return home, they can talk about their experience, draw pictures about it, or write about it in a special journal.

Read the Pictures
Take photographs during favorite family moments at home, on vacations, or in the community and use them as the basis of storytelling (Spielman, 2001).

Reading Time Just for You and Me
Parents should read aloud to their child every day in a special place and at a special time. As the child grows, he or she can read to the parents.

Storypals
Students practice reading storybooks with classmates or cross-age partners in school. They explore the narrative structure of stories and write retellings of familiar storybooks. Children read these same storybooks to younger siblings, cousins, and neighborhood children at home.

READING = SUCCESS...

...when parents or caregivers

R — Read aloud every day. Read old favorites and new books. Read different kinds of books. Talk when reading with the children. Ask them what pictures they liked or to tell what they think might happen next.

E — Ensure that the environment is literacy-rich, filled with books, magazines, and newspapers for reading as well as papers, cards, pens, and pencils for writing.

A — Allow children to see reading and writing for different purposes every day. Having positive role models will encourage children to read and write.

D — Develop an excitement and enthusiasm about reading when the teacher sends home the classroom's "reading suitcase." It is filled with books that can be shared with everyone in the family.

I — Invite children to talk, read, and write about their favorite experiences. They may even make a family book to which all members can contribute.

N — Nurture children's love of books by taking them to the library on a regular basis and allowing them to buy books that interest them.

G — Guide children's comprehension of a story through responding. You and the children can sketch or dramatize the events of the story.

S — Share stories with predictable texts that will encourage children to read along.

U — Use the Internet as a resource for ideas and materials. Some websites that are helpful include www.famlit.org, www.rif.org, www.ed.gov/pubs/SimpleThings.

C — Create opportunities that foster literacy development. Have the children act out television commercials or put new words to familiar songs.

C — Collect recipes together and make something special with the children. Cooking and eating is a shared bonding experience as well as a learning one.

E — Encourage the children to take risks when they attempt reading and writing. Praise them for their efforts. Leave notes in their lunchboxes.

S — Support the children's learning by reading the "book in the bag" sent home that day. This gives the children opportunities to practice, build confidence, and gain fluency.

S — Stay in regular contact with the children's teachers.

Source: Romano, S. (2002). *Reading = Success: Literacy activities that promote home-school connections* [Emergent Literacy Course Syllabus]. East Stroudsburg: East Stroudsburg University of Pennsylvania.

Books About Families and Communities: A List to Share!

Families

Braun, S. (2004). *I love my mommy*. New York: HarperCollins.

Bridwell, N. (1990). *Clifford's family*. New York: Scholastic.

Brown, M. (1995). *Arthur's family vacation* (Arthur adventures series). New York: Little, Brown.

Bunting, E. (1989). *The Wednesday surprise*. New York: Clarion.

Capdevila, R. (2003). *Grandparents!* La Jolla, CA: Kane/Miller.

Carlson, N.L. (2006). *My family is forever*. London: Puffin.

Carlson, N.S. (1989). *The family under the bridge*. New York: HarperCollins.

Christian, A.K. (2008). *Butterfly kisses for grandma and grandpa*. Raleigh, NC: Blue Whale.

Cleary, B. (1992). *Ramona Quimby, age 8*. New York: William Morrow.

Cole, J. (1997). *I'm a big sister*. New York: William Morrow.

Cosgrove, S. (2001). *Hucklebug*. New York: Penguin Putnam.

Evans, D. (2001). *The elevator family*. New York: Bantam Doubleday Dell.

Garza, C.L. (2000). *In my family*. Chicago: Children's Book Press.

Gutman, A., & Hallensleben, G. (2003). *Daddy kisses*. San Francisco: Chronicle.

Gutman, A., & Hallensleben, G. (2003). *Mommy hugs*. San Francisco: Chronicle.

Hoberman, M.A. (2001). *Fathers, mother, sisters, brothers: A collection of family poems*. New York: Little, Brown.

Hoberman, M.A. (2009). *All kinds of families!* New York: Little, Brown.

Isadora, R. (2006). *What a family!* New York: Putnam.

Leavitt, C. (2007). *The kids' family tree book*. New York: Sterling.

Mayer, G., & Mayer, M. (1992). *This is my family*. New York: Golden Books.

McBratney, S. (1999). *Guess how much I love you*. Cambridge, MA: Candlewick.

Moss, M. (2000). *Amelia's family ties*. Middleton, WI: Pleasant Company.

Munsch, R. (1988). *Love you forever*. Willowdale, ON: Firefly.

Munsch, R. (1991). *Good families don't*. New York: Bantam Doubleday Dell.

Murkoff, H.E. (2000). *What to expect when mommy's having a baby*. New York: HarperCollins.

Parr, T. (2003). *The family book*. New York: Little, Brown.

Parr, T. (2006). *The grandpa book*. New York: Little, Brown.

Parish, P. (1997). *Amelia Bedelia's family album*. New York: HarperCollins.

Pellegrini, N. (1991). *Families are different*. New York: Holiday House.

Polacco, P. (1994). *My rotten redheaded older brother*. New York: Simon & Schuster.

Rylant, C. (1998). *Henry and Mudge in the family trees: The fifteenth book of their adventures*. New York: Simon & Schuster.

Say, A. (1993). *Grandfather's journey*. Boston: Houghton Mifflin.

Sera, L. (2004). *Another tree in the yard*. Waterbury, CT: Vocalis.

Shemin, C., Capone, D., & McCoy, J. (2003). *Families are forever*. Southampton, NY: As Simple As That.

Shoulders, M. (2008). *Say daddy!* Farmington Hills, MI: Sleeping Bear Press.

Simon, N. (2003). *All families are special*. Morton Grove, IL: Albert Whitman.

Skutch, R. (1998). *Who's in a family?* Berkeley, CA: Tricycle Press.

Sklansky, A.E. (2005). *My daddy and me*. New York: Scholastic.

Sweeney, J. (2000). *Me and my family tree*. New York: Random House.

Viorst, J. (1976). *Alexander and the terrible, horrible, no good, very bad day.* New York: Simon & Schuster.

White, E.B. (1974). *Stuart Little.* New York: HarperCollins.

Wild, M., & Argent, K. (2000). *Nighty night!* Atlanta: Peachtree.

Wilder, L.I. (1976). *Little house in the big woods.* New York: HarperCollins.

Wyss, J. (1999). *The Swiss family Robinson.* New York: Random House.

Communities

Bauer, J. (2002). *Hope was here.* New York: Penguin Putnam.

Bunting, E. (1994). *Smoky night.* New York: Harcourt.

Caseley, J. (2002). *On the town: A community adventure.* New York: HarperCollins.

DiSalvo-Ryan, D. (1994). *City green.* New York: William Morrow.

Ditchfield, C. (2004). *Serving your community.* New York: Children's Press.

Flanagan, A.K. (2000). *Mr. Paul and Mr. Luecke build communities.* New York: Scholastic.

Greenfield, E. (1996). *Night on a neighborhood street.* New York: Penguin.

Hayward, L. (2001). *A day in the life of a police officer.* New York: Dorling/Kindersley.

Hollenbeck, K.M. (2003). *Neighborhood and community* (Early themes). New York: Scholastic.

Kalman, B.D. (1999). *What is a community? A to Z.* New York: Crabtree.

Kalman, B.D., & Walker, N. (1997). *Community helpers from A to Z.* New York: Crabtree.

Kottke, J. (2000). *A day with police officers.* New York: Scholastic.

Maass, R. (2002). *Fire fighters.* New York: Scholastic.

Mecca, J.T. (1999). *Multicultural plays: A many-splendored tapestry honoring our global community.* Nashville, TN: Incentive.

Parish, H.S. (2001). *Amelia Bedelia 4 mayor.* New York: HarperCollins.

Pellegrino, M.W. (1999). *My grandma's the mayor: A story for children about community spirit and pride.* Washington, DC: American Psychological Association.

Polacco, P. (1998). *Thank you, Mr. Falker.* New York: Philomel.

Rael, E.O. (2000). *What Zeesie saw on Delancey Street.* New York: Aladdin.

Rey, M. (1985). *Curious George at the fire station.* Boston: Houghton Mifflin.

Rey, M. (1998). *Curious George goes to a movie.* Boston: Houghton Mifflin.

Rey, M., & Rey, H.A. (1966). *Curious George goes to the hospital.* Boston: Houghton Mifflin.

Rathmann, P. (1995). *Officer Buckle and Gloria.* New York: Putnam.

Rondeau, A. (2004). *Do something in your community.* South Pasadena, CA: SandCastle.

Saunders-Smith, G. (1997). *Communities.* Mankato, MN: Capstone.

Sommer, C. (2001). *Mayor for a day.* Houston, TX: Advance.

Soto, G. (1992). *Neighborhood odes.* New York: Harcourt.

Steiner, S.F., & Ada, A.F. (2001). *Promoting a global community through multicultural children's literature.* Westport, CT: Libraries Unlimited.

Wawrychuk, C., & McSweeney, C. (1998). *The post office: Active learning about community workers.* Palo Alto, CA: Monday Morning.

Guided Comprehension Lesson Planning Forms

SAMPLE THEME–BASED PLAN FOR GUIDED COMPREHENSION

Goals and Connections to State Standards	Students will

Assessment
The following measures can be used for a variety of purposes, including diagnostic, formative, and summative assessment:

Comprehension Strategies	Teaching Ideas
1.	
2.	
3.	
4.	

Text	Title	Level

Comprehension Centers
Students will apply the comprehension strategies and related teaching ideas in the following comprehension centers:

Technology Resources

Comprehension Routines
Students will apply the comprehension strategies and related teaching ideas in the following comprehension routines:

GUIDED COMPREHENSION PLANNING FORM

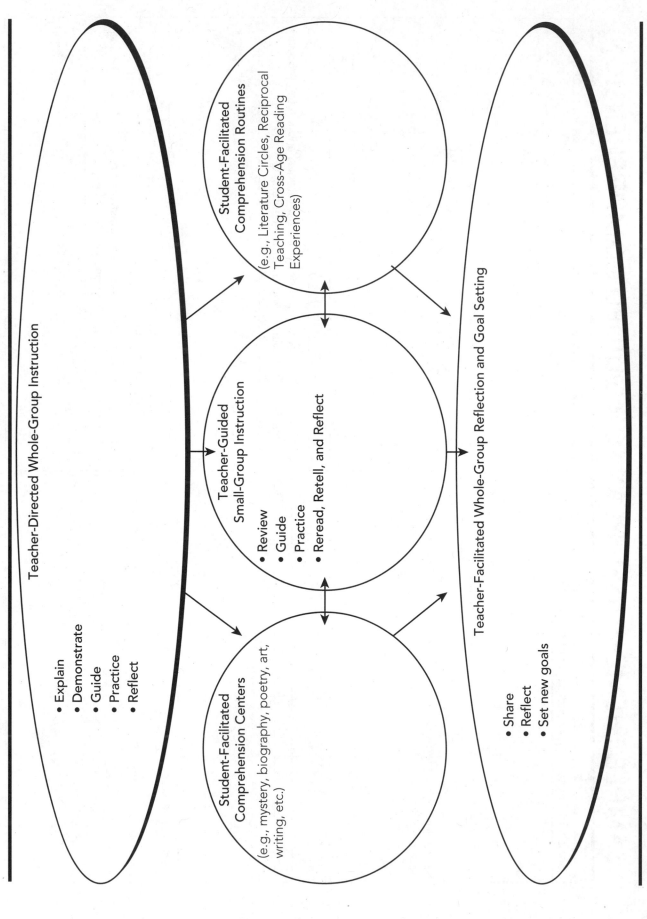

Teacher-Directed Whole-Group Instruction

- Explain
- Demonstrate
- Guide
- Practice
- Reflect

Student-Facilitated Comprehension Routines

(e.g., Literature Circles, Reciprocal Teaching, Cross-Age Reading Experiences)

Teacher-Guided Small-Group Instruction

- Review
- Guide
- Practice
- Reread, Retell, and Reflect

Student-Facilitated Comprehension Centers

(e.g., mystery, biography, poetry, art, writing, etc.)

Teacher-Facilitated Whole-Group Reflection and Goal Setting

- Share
- Reflect
- Set new goals

SAMPLE 60– AND 90–MINUTE GUIDED COMPREHENSION SCHEDULES

60-Minute Schedule		90-Minute Schedule
20–25 minutes	**Stage 1** — Teacher-Directed Whole-Group Instruction	**20–30 minutes**
20–25 minutes	**Stage 2** — Teacher-Guided Small-Group Instruction	**40–50 minutes**
20–25 minutes (one group)		**40–50 minutes (two groups)**
Students not meeting with the teacher are working on centers and routines.	**Comprehension Centers Comprehension Routines**	Students not meeting with the teacher are working on centers and routines.
10 minutes	**Stage 3** — Teacher-Facilitated Whole-Group Reflection and Goal Setting	**10 minutes**

REFERENCES

Allen, M.B. (2002, May). *Reciprocal teaching: A Guided Comprehension routine*. Paper presented at the 47th Annual Convention of the International Reading Association, San Francisco, CA.

Alvermann, D.E., Phelps, S.F., & Ridgeway, V.G. (2007). *Content area reading and literacy: Succeeding in today's diverse classrooms* (5th ed.). Boston: Allyn & Bacon.

Anderson, R.C. (1994). Role of the reader's schema in comprehension, learning, and memory. In R.B. Ruddell, M.R. Ruddell, & H. Singer (Eds.), *Theoretical models and processes of reading* (4th ed., pp. 469–482). Newark, DE: International Reading Association.

Anderson, R.C., & Pearson, P.D. (1984). A schema-theoretic view of basic processes in reading comprehension. In P.D. Pearson, R. Barr, M.L. Kamil, & P. Mosenthal (Eds.), *Handbook of reading research* (pp. 225–253). New York: Longman.

Askew, B.J., & Fountas, I.C. (1998). Building an early reading process: Active from the start! *The Reading Teacher, 52,* 126–134.

Au, K.H., & Raphael, T.E. (1998). Curriculum and teaching in literature-based programs. In T.E. Raphael & K.H. Au (Eds.), *Literature-based instruction: Reshaping the curriculum* (pp. 123–148). Norwood, MA: Christopher-Gordon.

Baker, L., Afflerbach, P., & Reinking, D. (1996). Developing engaged readers in school and home communities: An overview. In L. Baker, P. Afflerbach, & D. Reinking (Eds.), *Developing engaged readers in school and home communities* (pp. xiii–xxvii). Hillsdale, NJ: Erlbaum.

Baker, L., & Wigfield, A. (1999). Dimensions of children's motivation for reading and their relations to reading activity and reading achievement. *Reading Research Quarterly, 34,* 452–481.

Ball, E., & Blachman, B. (1991). Does phoneme awareness training in kindergarten make a difference in early word recognition and developmental spelling? *Reading Research Quarterly, 26,* 49–66.

Baumann, J.F., & Kame'enui, E.J. (1991). Research on vocabulary instruction: Ode to Voltaire. In J. Flood, J.M. Jensen, D. Lapp, & J.R. Squire (Eds.), *Handbook of research on teaching the English language arts* (pp. 604–632). New York: Macmillan.

Bean, T.W. (2000). Music in the content areas. In M. McLaughlin & M.E. Vogt (Eds.), *Creativity, innovation, and content area teaching* (pp. 91–103). Norwood, MA: Christopher-Gordon.

Bear, D.R., Invernizzi, M., Templeton, S., & Johnston, F. (2007). *Words their way: Word study for phonics, vocabulary, and spelling instruction* (4th ed.). Upper Saddle River, NJ: Prentice Hall.

Beaver, J., & Carter, M. (2009). *Developmental reading assessment (DRA): Grades K–3* (2nd ed.). Lebanon, IN: Pearson Education.

Beck, I., & McKeown, M. (1991). Conditions of vocabulary acquisition. In R. Barr, M.L. Kamil, P.B. Mosenthal, & P.D. Pearson (Eds.), *Handbook of reading research* (Vol. 2, pp. 789–814). White Plains, NY: Longman.

Blachowicz, C.L.Z. (1986). Making connections: Alternatives to the vocabulary notebook. *Journal of Reading, 29,* 643–649.

Blachowicz, C.L.Z., & Fisher, P. (2000). Vocabulary instruction. In M.L. Kamil, P.B. Mosenthal, P.D. Pearson, & R. Barr (Eds.), *Handbook of reading research* (Vol. 3, pp. 503–523). Mahwah, NJ: Erlbaum.

Blachowicz, C.L.Z., Fisher, P., Ogle, D.M., & Watts-Taffe, S. (2006). Vocabulary: Questions from the classroom. *Reading Research Quarterly, 41,* 524–539.

Blachowicz, C.L.Z., & Lee, J.J. (1991). Vocabulary development in the whole literacy classroom. *The Reading Teacher, 45,* 188–195.

Bogner, K., Raphael, L., & Pressley, M. (2002). How grade 1 teachers motivate literate activity by their students. *Scientific Studies of Reading, 6*(2), 135–165.

Brabham, E.G., & Villaume, S.K. (2000). Continuing conversations about literature circles. *The Reading Teacher, 54,* 278–280.

Brabham, E.G., & Villaume, S.K. (2002). Leveled text: The good news and the bad news. *The Reading Teacher, 55,* 438–441.

Brooks, J.G., & Brooks, M.G. (1993). *In search of understanding: The case for constructivist classrooms*. Alexandria, VA: Association for Supervision and Curriculum Development.

Brown, L.A. (1993). Story collages: Help for reluctant writers. *Learning, 22*(4), 22–25.

Busching, B.A., & Slesinger, B.A. (1995). Authentic questions: What do they look like? Where do they lead? *Language Arts, 72*(5), 341–351.

Cambourne, B. (2002). Holistic, integrated approaches to reading and language arts instruction: The constructivist framework of an instructional theory. In A.E. Farstrup & S.J. Samuels (Eds.), *What research has to say about reading instruction* (3rd ed., pp. 25–47). Newark, DE: International Reading Association.

Casey, H.K. (2008). Engaging the disengaged: Using learning clubs to motivate struggling adolescent readers and writers. *Journal of Adolescent & Adult Literacy, 52,* 284–294.

Ciardiello, A.V. (1998). Did you ask a good question today? Alternative cognitive and metacognitive strategies. *Journal of Adolescent & Adult Literacy, 42,* 210–219.

Ciardiello, A.V. (2007). *Puzzle them first: Motivating adolescent readers with question-finding.* Newark, DE: International Reading Association.

Clarke, L., & Holwadel, J. (2007). Help! What is wrong with these literature circles and how can we fix them? *The Reading Teacher, 61,* 20–29.

Clay, M.M. (1991). Introducing a new storybook to young readers. *The Reading Teacher, 45,* 264–273.

Clay, M.M. (1993a). *An observation survey of early literacy achievement.* Portsmouth, NH: Heinemann.

Clay, M.M. (1993b). *Reading Recovery: A guidebook for teachers in training.* Portsmouth, NH: Heinemann.

Clemmons, J., Laase, L., Cooper, D., Areglado, N., & Dill, M. (1993). *Portfolios in the classroom.* Jefferson City, MO: Scholastic.

Cooper, J.D., & Kiger, N.D. (2001). *Literacy assessment: Helping teachers plan instruction.* Boston: Houghton Mifflin.

Cunningham, P.M. (2008). *Phonics they use: Words for reading and writing* (5th ed.). New York: HarperCollins.

Cunningham, P.M., & Allington, R.L. (1999). *Classrooms that work: They can all read and write* (2nd ed.). New York: Addison-Wesley.

Cunningham, P.M., & Cunningham, J.W. (2002). What we know about how to teach phonics. In A.E. Farstrup & S.J. Samuels (Eds.), *What research has to say about reading instruction* (3rd ed., pp. 87–109). Newark, DE: International Reading Association.

Daniels, H. (2002). *Literature circles: Voice and choice in book clubs and reading groups* (2nd ed.). Portland, ME: Stenhouse.

Daniels, H., & Steineke, N. (2004). *Mini-lessons for literature circles.* Portsmouth, NH: Heinemann.

Darling-Hammond, L.D., Ancess, J., & Falk, B. (1995). *Authentic assessment in action: Studies of schools and students at work.* New York: Teachers College Press.

Davey, B. (1983). Think-aloud—Modeling the cognitive processes of reading comprehension. *Journal of Reading, 27,* 44–47.

Dewey, J. (1933). *How we think: A restatement of reflective thinking to the educative process.* Lexington, MA: D.C. Heath.

Dixon-Krauss, L. (1996). *Vygotsky in the classroom: Mediated literacy instruction and assessment.* White Plains, NY: Longman.

Dixon-Krauss, L. (2001). Using literature as a context for teaching vocabulary. *Journal of Adolescent & Adult Literacy, 45,* 310–318.

Duffy, G.G. (2001, December). *The case for direct explanation of strategies.* Paper presented at the 51st annual meeting of the National Reading Conference, San Antonio, TX.

Duke, N.K. (2001, December). *A new generation of researchers looks at comprehension.* Paper presented at the 51st annual meeting of the National Reading Conference, San Antonio, TX.

Duke, N.K. (2007, October). *Comprehension throughout the day.* Paper presented at the annual conference of the Alaska State Literacy Association, Anchorage.

Duke, N.K., & Pearson, P.D. (2002). Effective practices for developing reading comprehension. In A.E. Farstrup & S.J. Samuels (Eds.), *What research has to say about reading instruction* (3rd ed., pp. 205–242). Newark, DE: International Reading Association.

Durkin, D. (1978). What classroom observations reveal about reading comprehension instruction. *Reading Research Quarterly, 14,* 481–533.

Dzaldov, B.S., & Peterson, S. (2005). Book leveling and readers. *The Reading Teacher, 59,* 222–229.

Edmunds, K.M., & Bauserman, K.L. (2006). What teachers can learn about reading motivation through conversations with children. *The Reading Teacher, 59,* 414–424.

Ehri, L.C., & Nunes, S.R. (2002). The role of phonemic awareness in learning to read. In A.E. Farstrup & S.J. Samuels (Eds.), *What research has to say about reading instruction* (3rd ed., pp. 110–139). Newark, DE: International Reading Association.

Fielding, L.G., & Pearson, P.D. (1994). Reading comprehension: What works. *Educational Leadership, 51*(5), 62–68.

Ford, M.P., & Opitz, M.F. (2002). Using centers to engage children during guided reading time: Intensifying learning experiences away from the teacher. *The Reading Teacher, 55,* 710–717.

Forman, E.A., & Cazden, C.B. (1994). Exploring Vygotskian perspectives in education: The cognitive value of peer interaction. In R.B. Ruddell, M.R. Ruddell, & H. Singer (Eds.), *Theoretical models and processes of reading* (4th ed., pp. 155–178). Newark, DE: International Reading Association.

Fountas, I.C., & Pinnell, G.S. (1996). *Guided reading: Good first teaching for all children.* Portsmouth, NH: Heinemann.

Fountas, I.C., & Pinnell, G.S. (2008). *Fountas and Pinnell benchmark assessment system: Grades K–2.* Portsmouth, NH: Heinemann.

Fountas, I.C., & Pinnell, G.S. (2008). *Fountas and Pinnell benchmark assessment system: Grades 3–8.* Portsmouth, NH: Heinemann.

Fry, E. (1977). Fry's readability graph: Clarifications, validity, and extension to level 17. *Journal of Reading, 21,* 242–252.

Gambrell, L.B. (1996). Creating classroom cultures that foster reading motivation. *The Reading Teacher, 50,* 14–25.

Gambrell, L.B. (2001, May). *It's not either/or but more: Balancing narrative and informational text to improve reading comprehension.* Paper presented at the 46th annual convention of the International Reading Association, New Orleans, LA.

Gambrell, L.B., Malloy, J.A., & Mazzoni, S.A. (2007). Evidence-based best practices for comprehensive literacy instruction. In L.B. Gambrell & L.M. Morrow (Eds.), *Best practices in literacy instruction* (3rd ed., pp. 11–29). New York: Guilford.

Gambrell, L.B., Palmer, B.M., Codling, R.M., & Mazzoni, S.A. (1996). Assessing motivation to read. *The Reading Teacher, 49,* 518–533.

Gibson, V., & Hasbrouck, J. (2008). *Differentiated instruction: Grouping for success.* New York: McGraw-Hill.

Gilles, C. (1998). Collaborative literacy strategies: "We don't need a circle to have a group." In K.G. Short & K.M. Pierce (Eds.), *Talking about books: Literature discussion groups in K–8 classrooms* (pp. 55–68). Portsmouth, NH: Heinemann.

Goldman, S.R., & Rakestraw, J.A. (2000). Structural aspects of constructing meaning from text. In M.L. Kamil, P.B. Mosenthal, P.D. Pearson, & R. Barr (Eds.), *Handbook of reading research* (Vol. 3, pp. 311–335). Mahwah, NJ: Erlbaum.

Goodman, Y.M. (1997). Reading diagnosis—Qualitative or quantitative? *The Reading Teacher, 50,* 534–538.

Goodman, Y.M., Watson, D.J., & Burke, C. (1987). *Reading miscue inventory.* Katonah, NY: Richard C. Owen.

Graves, M.F., & Watts-Taffe, S.M. (2002). The place of word consciousness in a research-based vocabulary program. In A.E. Farstrup & S.J. Samuels (Eds.), *What research has to say about reading instruction* (pp. 140–165). Newark, DE: International Reading Association.

Greene, K., Guthrie, L., Kotinopoulos, C., Mellos, S., Sullivan, J., & Trim, J. (Eds.). (2009). *Teaching comprehension strategies that develop oral language, vocabulary, and fluency.* New York: Guilford.

Guthrie, J.T., & Alvermann, D. (Eds.). (1999). *Engagement in reading: Processes, practices, and policy implications.* New York: Teachers College Press.

Guthrie, J.T., & Wigfield, A. (1997). *Reading engagement: Motivating readers through integrated instruction.* Newark, DE: International Reading Association.

Guthrie, J.T., Wigfield, A., Humenick, N.M., Perencevich, K.C., Taboada, A., & Barbosa, P. (2006). Influences of stimulating tasks on reading motivation and comprehension. *The Journal of Educational Research, 99*(4), 232–245.

Hansen, J. (1998). *When learners evaluate.* Portsmouth, NH: Heinemann.

Harris, T.L., & Hodges, R.E. (Eds.). (1995). *The literacy dictionary: The vocabulary of reading and writing.* Newark, DE: International Reading Association.

Harvey, S., & Goudvis, A. (2000). *Strategies that work: Teaching comprehension to enhance understanding.* York, ME: Stenhouse.

Hiebert, E.H. (1994). Becoming literate through authentic tasks: Evidence and adaptations. In R.B. Ruddell, M.R. Ruddell, & H. Singer (Eds.), *Theoretical models and processes of reading* (4th ed., pp. 391–413). Newark, DE: International Reading Association.

Hiebert, E.H. (2006). Becoming fluent: Repeated reading with scaffolded texts. In S.J. Samuels & A.E. Farstrup (Eds.), *What research has to say about fluency instruction* (pp. 204–226). Newark, DE: International Reading Association.

Hiebert, E.H., Pearson, P.D., Taylor, B.M., Richardson, V., & Paris, S.G. (1998). *Every child a reader*. Ann Arbor, MI: Center for the Improvement of Early Reading Achievement.

Hilden, K., & Pressley, M. (2002, December). *Can teachers become comprehension strategies teachers given a small amount of training?* Paper presented at the 52nd annual meeting of the National Reading Conference, Miami, FL.

Hill, B.C., & Ruptic, C.A. (1994). *Practical aspects of authentic assessment: Putting the pieces together*. Norwood, MA: Christopher-Gordon.

Holmes, K., Powell, S., Holmes, S., & Witt, E. (2007). Readers and book characters: Does race matter? *The Journal of Educational Research, 100*(5), 276–282.

Hoyt, L., & Ames, C. (1997). Letting the learner lead the way. *Primary Voices, 5*, 16–29.

Hunt, L.C. (1996). The effect of self-selection, interest, and motivation upon independent, instructional, and frustration levels. *The Reading Teacher, 50*, 278–282.

International Reading Association. (1998). *Phonemic awareness and the teaching of reading: A position statement of the International Reading Association*. Newark, DE: Author.

International Reading Association. (1999). *Using multiple methods of beginning reading instruction: A position statement of the International Reading Association*. Newark, DE: Author.

International Reading Association. (2000). *Excellent reading teachers: A position statement of the International Reading Association*. Newark, DE: Author.

International Reading Association & National Association for the Education of Young Children. (1998). Learning to read and write: Developmentally appropriate practices for young children. *The Reading Teacher, 52*, 193–216.

Johnson, D.D., & Pearson, P.D. (1984). *Teaching reading vocabulary* (2nd ed.). New York: Holt, Rinehart and Winston.

Johnston, P.H. (2000). *Running records: A self-tutoring guide*. Portland, ME: Stenhouse.

Keene, E.O., & Zimmermann, S. (1997). *Mosaic of thought: Teaching comprehension in a reader's workshop*. Portsmouth, NH: Heinemann.

Ketch, A. (2005). Conversation: The comprehension connection. *The Reading Teacher, 59*, 8–13.

Lasear, D. (1991). *Seven ways of teaching: The artistry of teaching with multiple intelligences*. Palatine, IL: Skylight.

Leslie, L., & Caldwell, J.S. (2010). *Qualitative reading inventory—5* (5th ed.). Boston: Allyn & Bacon.

Lewin, L. (1998). *Great performances: Creating classroom-based assessment tasks*. Alexandria, VA: Association for Supervision and Curriculum Development.

Lipson, M.Y. (2001). *A fresh look at comprehension*. Paper presented at the Reading/Language Arts Symposium, Chicago, IL.

Lipson, M.Y., & Wixson, K. (2009). *Assessment and instruction of reading and writing difficulties: An interactive approach* (4th ed.). New York: Longman.

Macon, J.M. (1991). *Literature response*. A paper presented at the Annual Literacy Workshop, Anaheim, CA.

Maring, G., Furman, G., & Blum-Anderson, J. (1985). Five cooperative learning strategies for mainstreamed youngsters in content area classrooms. *The Reading Teacher, 39*, 310–313.

McGinley, W., & Denner, P. (1987). Story impressions: A prereading/prewriting activity. *Journal of Reading, 31*, 248–253.

McLaughlin, E.M. (1987). QuIP: A writing strategy to improve comprehension of expository structure. *The Reading Teacher, 40*, 650–654.

McLaughlin, M. (1995). *Performance assessment: A practical guide to implementation*. Boston: Houghton Mifflin.

McLaughlin, M. (2002). Dynamic assessment. In B. Guzzetti (Ed.), *Literacy in America: An encyclopedia of history, theory, and practice*. Santa Barbara, CA: ABC-CLIO.

McLaughlin, M. (2003a). *Guided Comprehension in the primary grades*. Newark, DE: International Reading Association.

McLaughlin, M. (2003b). *Guided Comprehension in the primary grades: A framework for curricularizing strategy instruction*. Paper presented at the 53rd annual meeting of the National Reading Conference, Scottsdale, AZ.

McLaughlin, M. (2010). *Content area reading: Teaching and learning in an age of multiple literacies*. Boston: Allyn & Bacon.

McLaughlin, M., & Allen, M.B. (2002a). *Guided Comprehension: A teaching model for grades 3–8*. Newark, DE: International Reading Association.

McLaughlin, M., & Allen, M.B. (2002b). *Guided Comprehension in action: Lessons for grades 3–8*. Newark, DE: International Reading Association.

McLaughlin, M., & Allen, M.B. (2009). *Guided Comprehension in grades 3–8* (Combined 2nd ed.). Newark, DE: International Reading Association.

McLaughlin, M., & Vogt, M.E. (1996). *Portfolios in teacher education*. Newark, DE: International Reading Association.

McTighe, J., & Lyman, F.T. (1988). Cueing thinking in the classroom: The promise of theory-embedded tools. *Educational Leadership, 45*(7), 18–24.

Minick, N. (1987). Implications of Vygotsky's theory for dynamic assessment. In C.S. Lidz (Ed.), *Dynamic assessment: An interactional approach for evaluating learning potential* (pp. 116–140). New York: Guilford.

Morrow, L.M. (1985). Retelling stories: A strategy for improving children's comprehension, concept of story, and oral language complexity. *The Elementary School Journal, 85*(5), 646–661.

Mowery, S. (1995). *Reading and writing comprehension strategies*. Harrisburg, PA: Instructional Support Teams Publications.

Nathan, R.G., & Stanovich, K.E. (1991). The causes and consequences of differences in reading fluency. *Theory into Practice, 30*, 176–184.

National Commission on Teaching and America's Future. (1997). *Doing what matters most: Investing in quality teaching*. Available: www.nctaf.org/documents/DoingWhatMattersMost.pdf

National Institute of Child Health and Human Development. (2000). *Report of the National Reading Panel. Teaching children to read: An evidence-based assessment of the scientific research literature on reading and its implications for reading instruction* (NIH Publication No. 00-4769). Washington, DC: U.S. Government Printing Office.

Newmann, F.M., & Wehlage, G.G. (1993). Five standards for authentic instruction. *Educational Leadership, 50*, 8–12.

Noe, K.L.S., & Johnson, N.J. (1999). *Getting started with literature circles*. Norwood, MA: Christopher-Gordon.

Norman, K.A., & Calfee, R.C. (2004). Tile test: A hands-on approach for assessing phonics in the early grades. *The Reading Teacher, 58*, 42–52.

Ogle, D. (1986). K-W-L: A teaching model that develops active reading of expository text. *The Reading Teacher, 39*, 564–570.

Page, S. (2001). *Tips and strategies for independent routines*. Muncie, IN: Page Consulting.

Palincsar, A.S., & Brown, A.L. (1984). Reciprocal teaching of comprehension-fostering and monitoring activities. *Cognition and Instruction, 1*, 117–175.

Palincsar, A.S., & Brown, A.L. (1986). Interactive teaching to promote independent learning from text. *The Reading Teacher, 39*, 771–777.

Partnership for Educational Excellence Network. (2001). *Early childhood learning continuum indicators*. Harrisburg: Pennsylvania Department of Education. Available: www.avongrove.org/ples/pdffiles/earlychildhood continuum.pdf

Pearson, P.D. (2001a). *Comprehension strategy instruction: An idea whose time has come again*. Paper presented at the annual meeting of the Colorado Council of the International Reading Association, Denver, CO.

Pearson, P.D. (2001b, December). *What we have learned in 30 years*. Paper presented at the 51st annual meeting of the National Reading Conference, San Antonio, TX.

Pearson, P.D., Hiebert, E.H., & Kamil, M.L. (2007). Vocabulary assessment: What we know and what we need to learn. *Reading Research Quarterly, 42*, 282–296.

Peterson, R., & Eeds, M. (1990). *Grand conversations: Literature groups in action*. New York: Scholastic.

Pinciotti, P. (2001). *Book arts: The creation of beautiful books*. East Stroudsburg: East Stroudsburg University of Pennsylvania.

Pitcher, B., & Fang, Z. (2007). Can we trust levelled texts? An examination of their reliability and quality from a linguistic perspective. *Literacy, 41*(1), 43–51.

Pressley, M. (2000). What should comprehension instruction be the instruction of? In M.L. Kamil, P.B. Mosenthal, P.D. Pearson, & R. Barr (Eds.), *Handbook of reading research* (Vol. 3, pp. 545–561). Mahwah, NJ: Erlbaum.

Pressley, M. (2001, December). *Comprehension strategies instruction: A turn of the century status report*. Paper presented at the 51st annual meeting of the National Reading Conference, San Antonio, TX.

Raphael, T.E. (1986). Teaching Question Answer Relationships, revisited. *The Reading Teacher, 39*, 516–522.

Rasinski, T.V. (1999a). Making and writing words. *Reading Online*. Available: www.readingonline.org/articles/words/rasinski_index.html

Rasinski, T.V. (1999b). Making and writing words using letter patterns. *Reading Online*. Available: www.readingonline.org/articles/words/rasinski_index.html

Rasinski, T.V. (2010). *The fluent reader: Oral & silent reading strategies for building fluency, word recognition & comprehension* (2nd ed.). New York: Scholastic.

Rasinski, T.V. (Ed.). (2011). *Developing reading instruction that works*. Bloomington, IN: Solution Tree.

Readence, J.E., Bean, T.W., & Baldwin, R. (2004). *Content area reading: An integrated approach* (8th ed.). Dubuque, IA: Kendall/Hunt.

Rhodes, L.K., Shanklin, N.L., & Valencia, S.W. (1990). Miscue analysis in the classroom. *The Reading Teacher, 44*, 252–254.

Richek, M.A. (2005). Words are wonderful: Interactive, time-efficient strategies to teach meaning vocabulary. *The Reading Teacher, 58*, 414–423.

Roehler, L.R., & Duffy, G.G. (1984). Direct explanation of comprehension processes. In G.G. Duffy, L.R. Roehler, & J. Mason (Eds.), *Comprehension instruction: Perspectives and suggestions* (pp. 265–280). New York: Longman.

Rog, L.J., & Burton, W. (2001). Matching texts and readers: Leveling early reading materials for assessment and instruction. *The Reading Teacher, 55*, 348–356.

Romano, S. (2002). *Reading = Success: Literacy activities that promote home-school connections* [Emergent Literacy Course Syllabus]. East Stroudsburg: East Stroudsburg University of Pennsylvania.

Rosenblatt, L.M. (1978). *The reader, the text, and the poem: The transactional theory of the literary work*. Carbondale: Southern Illinois University Press.

Rosenblatt, L.M. (2002, December). *A pragmatist theoretician looks at research: Implications and questions calling for answers*. Paper presented at the 52nd annual meeting of the National Reading Conference, Miami, FL.

Ruddell, R.B. (1995). Those influential reading teachers: Meaning negotiators and motivation builders. *The Reading Teacher, 48*, 454–463.

Rule, A.C. (2001). Alphabetizing with environmental print. *The Reading Teacher, 54*, 558–562.

Samuels, S.J. (1979). The method of repeated readings. *The Reading Teacher, 32*, 403–408.

Samuels, S.J. (2002). Reading fluency: Its development and assessment. In A.E. Farstrup & S.J. Samuels (Eds.), *What research has to say about reading instruction* (3rd ed., pp. 166–183). Newark, DE: International Reading Association.

Samuels, S.J., & Farstrup, A.E. (Eds.). (2006). *What research has to say about fluency instruction*. Newark, DE: International Reading Association.

Samway, K.D., & Wang, G. (1996). *Literature study circles in a multicultural classroom*. York, ME: Stenhouse.

Schön, D. (1987). *Educating the reflective practitioner*. San Francisco: Jossey-Bass.

Schwartz, R., & Raphael, T. (1985). Concept of definition: A key to improving students' vocabulary. *The Reading Teacher, 39*, 198–205.

Short, K.G., & Burke, C. (1996). Examining our beliefs and practices through inquiry. *Language Arts, 73*, 97–103.

Short, K.G., Harste, J.C., & Burke, C. (1996). *Creating classrooms for authors and inquirers*. Portsmouth, NH: Heinemann.

Sippola, A.E. (1995). K-W-L-S. *The Reading Teacher, 48*, 542–543.

Snow, C.E., Burns, M.S., & Griffin, P.G. (Eds.). (1998). *Preventing reading difficulties in young children*. Washington, DC: National Academy Press.

Spielman, J. (2001). The family photography project: "We will just read what the pictures tell us." *The Reading Teacher, 54*, 762–770.

Stahl, S.A., Duffy-Hester, A.M., & Stahl, K.A.D. (1998). Theory and research in practice: Everything you wanted to know about phonics (but were afraid to ask). *Reading Research Quarterly, 33*, 338–355.

Stahl, S.A., Heubach, K., & Cramond, B. (1997). *Fluency-oriented reading instruction* (Reading Research Report No. 97). Athens, GA: National Reading Research Center.

Stahl, S.A., & Kuhn, M.R. (2002, December). *Developing fluency in classrooms*. Paper presented at the 52nd annual meeting of the National Reading Conference, Miami, FL.

Stauffer, R. (1975). *Directing the reading-thinking process*. New York: Harper & Row.

Stien, D., & Beed, P.L. (2004). Bridging the gap between fiction and nonfiction in the literature circle setting. *The Reading Teacher, 57*, 512–518.

Szymusiak, K., & Sibberson, F. (2001). *Beyond leveled books: Supporting transitional readers in grades 2–5*. Portland, ME: Stenhouse.

Tierney, R.J. (1990). Redefining reading comprehension. *Educational Leadership, 47*(6), 37–42.

Tierney, R.J. (1998). Literacy assessment reform: Shifting beliefs, principled possibilities and emerging practices. *The Reading Teacher, 51*, 374–390.

Tierney, R.J., & Pearson, P.D. (1994). A revisionist perspective on "Learning to learn from text: A framework for improving classroom practice." In R.B. Ruddell, M.R. Ruddell, & H. Singer (Eds.), *Theoretical models and processes of reading* (4th ed., pp. 514–519). Newark, DE: International Reading Association.

Tomlinson, C.A. (1999). *The differentiated classroom: Responding to the needs of all learners*. Alexandria, VA: Association for Supervision and Curriculum Development.

Tompkins, G.E. (2001). *Literacy for the 21st century: A balanced approach* (2nd ed.). Upper Saddle River, NJ: Merrill.

Tompkins, G.E. (2006). *Literacy for the 21st century: A balanced approach* (4th ed.). Upper Saddle River, NJ: Prentice Hall.

Towell, J. (1997). Fun with vocabulary. *The Reading Teacher, 51*, 356–360.

Tyner, B., & Green, S.E. (2005). *Small-group reading instruction: A differentiated teaching model for intermediate readers, grades 3–8*. Newark, DE: International Reading Association.

Vacca, R.T., & Vacca, J.L. (2008). *Content area reading: Literacy and learning across the curriculum* (9th ed.). Boston: Allyn & Bacon.

Vaughn, J., & Estes, T. (1986). *Reading and reasoning beyond the primary grades*. Boston: Allyn & Bacon.

Vygotsky, L.S. (1978). *Mind in society: The development of higher psychological processes* (M. Cole, V. John-Steiner, S. Scribner, & E. Souberman, Eds. & Trans.). Cambridge, MA: Harvard University Press.

Waldo, B. (1991). Story pyramid. In J.M. Macon, D. Bewell, & M.E. Vogt (Eds.), *Responses to literature: Grades K–8* (pp. 23–24). Newark, DE: International Reading Association.

Weaver, B.M. (2000). *Leveling books K–6: Matching readers to text*. Newark, DE: International Reading Association.

Wigfield, A., & Guthrie, J.T. (1997). Relations of children's motivation for reading to the amount and breadth of their reading. *Journal of Educational Psychology, 89*(3), 420–432.

Wiggins, G., & McTighe, J. (2008). Put understanding first. *Educational Leadership, 65*(8), 36–41.

Wood, K. (1984). Probable passages: A writing strategy. *The Reading Teacher, 37*, 496–499.

Yopp, H.K. (1992). Developing phonemic awareness in young children. *The Reading Teacher, 45*, 696–703.

Yopp, H.K., & Yopp, R.H. (2000). Supporting phonemic awareness development in the classroom. *The Reading Teacher, 54*, 130–143.

Zutell, J., & Rasinski, T. (1991). Training teachers to attend to their students' oral reading fluency. *Theory into Practice, 30*, 211–217.

Children's Literature Cited

Adler, D.A. (2007). *Cam Jansen and the mystery writer mystery*. New York: Viking.

Appelt, K. (1993). *Elephants aloft*. New York: Harcourt Brace.

Baker, C. (2004). *Rosa Parks*. New York: Scholastic.

Base, G. (1996). *Animalia*. New York: Abrams.

Bauer, M.D. (2003). *Wind*. New York: Scholastic.

Berger, M., & Berger, G. (2001). *What do sharks eat for dinner? Questions and answers about sharks*. New York: Scholastic.

Berger, M., & Berger, G. (2001). *What makes an ocean wave? Questions and answers about oceans and ocean life*. New York: Scholastic.

Berger, M., & Berger, G. (2003). *Whales*. New York: Scholastic.

Berger, M., & Berger, G. (2004). *Earth*. New York: Scholastic.

Brown, M.W. (1990). *The important book*. New York: HarperCollins.

Carle, E. (1977). *The grouchy ladybug*. New York: HarperTrophy.

Carle, E. (1984). *The very busy spider*. New York: Philomel.

Carle, E. (2002). *"Slowly, slowly, slowly," said the sloth*. New York: Philomel.

Charlip, R. (1993). *Fortunately*. New York: Aladdin.

Cronin, D. (2000). *Click, clack, moo: Cows that type*. New York: Simon & Schuster.

Cronin, D. (2002). *Giggle, giggle, quack*. New York: Atheneum.

Cronin, D. (2003). *Diary of a worm*. New York: HarperCollins.

Cronin, D. (2005). *Diary of a spider*. New York: HarperCollins.

Cronin, D. (2007). *Diary of a fly*. New York: HarperCollins.

Cronin, D. (2008). *Click, clack, quackity-quack: A typing adventure*. New York: Little Simon.

Cronin, D. (2008). *Duck for president*. New York: Atheneum.

Cronin, D. (2008). *Thump, quack, moo: A whacky adventure*. New York: Atheneum.

Cronin, D. (2009). *Dooby dooby moo*. New York: Atheneum.

Davis, G. (1997). *Coral reef*. Danbury, CT: Children's Press.

Day, A. (1992). *Carl's masquerade*. New York: Farrar, Straus and Giroux.

Day, A. (1995). *Carl goes to day care*. New York: Simon & Schuster.

Denne, B. (2001). *First encyclopedia of seas and oceans*. Eveleth, MN: Usborne.

Frasier, D. (2002). *Out of the ocean*. New York: Voyager.

Freedman, C. (2001). *Where's your smile, crocodile?* Atlanta, GA: Peachtree.

Geist, K., & Gorton, J. (2007). *Three little fish and the big bad shark*. New York: Cartwheel.

Gibbons, G. (2000). *Pigs*. New York: Holiday House.

Gibbons, G. (2009). *Tornadoes*. New York: Holiday House.

Gill, S. (2007). *Alaska*. Watertown, MA: Charlesbridge.

Harris, J. (1999). *The three little dinosaurs*. Gretna, LA: Pelican.

Hollander, J., & Mulazzani, S. (2004). *Poetry for young people: Animal poems*. New York: Sterling.

Johnson, A. (2007). *Lily Brown's paintings*. New York: Orchard.

Johnson, D. (2002). *Substitute teacher plans*. New York: Henry Holt.

Kranking, K. (1996). *What is a coral reef?* New York: Scholastic.

Laverde, A. (2000). *Alaska's three little pigs*. Seattle, WA: Sasquatch.

Levitt, P. (1990). *The weighty word book*. Albuquerque: University of New Mexico Press.

Milton, J. (1989). *Whales: The gentle giants*. New York: Random House.

Minters, F. (1994). *Cinder-Elly*. New York: Viking.

Mitton, T. (2002). *Dinosaurumpus!* New York: Orchard.

Nash, S. (2004). *Tuff fluff*. Cambridge, MA: Candlewick.

Numeroff, L. (1998). *If you give a pig a pancake*. New York: HarperCollins.

Pilkey, D. (1999). *Dragon gets by*. New York: Orchard.

Pilkey, D. (1999). *The Hallo-wiener*. New York: Scholastic.

Pilkey, D. (2002). *Ricky Ricotta's mighty robot vs. the Jurassic jackrabbits from Jupiter*. New York: Scholastic.

Pilkey, D. (2002). *Ricky Ricotta's mighty robot vs. the mecha-monkeys from Mars*. New York: Scholastic.

Pilkey, D. (2003). *Dogzilla*. New York: Harcourt.

Pilkey, D. (2003). *Dragon's Halloween*. New York: Orchard.

Pilkey, D. (2003). *Kat Kong*. New York: Harcourt.

Pilkey, D. (2004). *Dog breath: The horrible trouble with Hally Tosis*. New York: Scholastic.

Pilkey, D. (2004). *'Twas the night before Thanksgiving*. New York: Scholastic.

Pilkey, D. (2006). *Ricky Ricotta's mighty robot*. New York: Blue Sky Press.

Polacco, P. (1996). *Aunt Chip and the great Triple Creek Dam affair*. New York: Philomel.

Polacco, P. (1997). *In Enzo's splendid gardens*. New York: Philomel.

Polacco, P. (1998). *Thank you, Mr. Falker*. New York: Scholastic.

Polacco, P. (2001). *Mr. Lincoln's way*. New York: Scholastic.

Polacco, P. (2004). *An orange for Frankie*. New York: Philomel.

Polacco, P. (2005). *The Graves family goes camping*. New York: Penguin.

Polacco, P. (2007). *The lemonade club*. New York: Philomel.

Prelutsky, J. (1986). *Read-aloud rhymes for the very young*. New York: Knopf.

Rhodes, M.J. (2006). *Sea turtles*. Danbury, CT: Children's Press.

Scholastic First Discovery. (1989). *Ladybugs and other insects*. New York: Scholastic.

Shaw, N. (1986). *Sheep in a jeep*. Boston: Houghton Mifflin.

Shaw, N. (1991). *Sheep in a shop*. Boston: Houghton Mifflin.

Shaw, N. (1995). *Sheep out to eat*. Mooloolaba, QLD, Australia: Sandpiper.

Shaw, N. (1997). *Sheep trick or treat*. Boston: Houghton Mifflin.

Silverstein, S. (1974). *Where the sidewalk ends*. New York: HarperCollins.

Simon, S. (1988). *Jupiter*. New York: HarperTrophy.

Simon, S. (1988). *Saturn*. New York: HarperCollins.

Simon, S. (1990). *Uranus*. New York: HarperCollins.

Simon, S. (1995). *Volcanoes*. New York: HarperTrophy.

Simon, S. (1996). *The heart: Our circulatory system*. New York: Morrow Junior.

Simon, S. (1997). *Deserts*. New York: HarperCollins.

Simon, S. (1997). *Mountains*. New York: HarperCollins.

Simon, S. (1997). *Neptune*. New York: HarperCollins.

Simon, S. (1998). *Icebergs and glaciers*. New York: HarperCollins.

Simon, S. (1998). *Mercury*. New York: HarperCollins.

Simon, S. (1998). *Venus*. New York: HarperCollins.

Simon, S. (2002). *Baby animals*. San Francisco: Chronicle.

Simon, S. (2002). *Killer whales*. San Francisco: Chronicle.

Simon, S. (2003). *Earth: Our planet in space*. New York: Simon & Schuster.

Simon, S. (2003). *Hurricanes*. New York: HarperCollins.

Simon, S. (2004). *Pyramids and mummies*. San Francisco: Chronicle.

Simon, S. (2005). *Amazing bats*. San Francisco: Chronicle.

Simon, S. (2006). *Earthquake*. New York: Collins.

Simon, S. (2006). *Oceans*. New York: Collins.

Simon, S. (2006). *Stars*. New York: Collins.

Simon, S. (2006). *The universe*. New York: Scholastic.

Simon, S. (2006). *Whales*. New York: Collins.

Simon, S. (2007). *Penguins*. New York: Collins.

Simon, S. (2008). *Gorillas*. New York: Collins.

Simon, S. (2009). *Cats*. New York: Collins.

Simon, S. (2009). *Dogs*. New York: Collins.

Simon, S. (2009). *Wolves*. New York: Collins.

Slonim, D. (2003). *Oh, Ducky!* San Francisco: Chronicle.

Stevens, J., & Crummel, S.S. (2005). *The great fuzz frenzy*. New York: Scholastic.

Van Allsburg, C. (1990). *Just a dream*. Boston: Houghton Mifflin.

Viorst, J. (1981). *If I were in charge of the world and other worries*. New York: Atheneum.

Vogt, G. (2001). *Solar system*. New York: Scholastic.

Waber, B. (1965). *Lyle, Lyle, crocodile*. Boston: Houghton Mifflin.

Whipple, L. (Compiler). (1999). *Eric Carle's animals, animals*. New York: Philomel.

Wiesner, D. (1997). *Tuesday*. New York: Clarion.

Wiesner, D. (1999). *Sector 7*. New York: Clarion.

Wiesner, D. (2001). *The three pigs*. New York: Clarion.

Wiesner, D. (2006). *Flotsam*. New York: Clarion.

Wild, M., & Argent, K. (2000). *Nighty night!* Atlanta, GA: Peachtree.

Worth, V. (2007). *Animal poems*. New York: Farrar, Straus and Giroux.

INDEX

Note. Page numbers followed by *f* indicate figures.

process, of instruction, 8
product, of instruction, 8
project center, 37–38
prompts: for literacy histories, 344; for literature circles, 44; for reflection, 29–30
Puppet Theater, 33

Q

Qualitative Reading Inventory–5, 62
Question-Answer Relationship (QAR), 222–223, 283
questioning: evaluative, 250–251; paired, 175–179, 176f, 222. *See also* self-questioning
questions: generating, 22f; on goal setting, 30; for miscue analysis, 61; for reflection, 29; for text selection, 72; types of, 21–23, 224, 293
Questions Into Paragraphs (QuIP), 37, 245–246; research grid, 123f–124f, 284; in Seymour Simon theme, 120–125, 121f
quick clouds, 329
quilt square, 45

R

Rakestraw, J.A., 9–10, 69
Raphael, L., 68
Raphael, T., 8, 223, 232
Rasinski, T.V., 33–34, 66, 201–203, 207, 316–317
read-alouds, 73
Readence, J.E., 214
readers: and accessibility, 68; good, characteristics of, 9–10
Readers Theatre, 33, 203
reading: contexts of, 10; developmental continuum for, primary-level, 191–195
reading teachers: excellent, influence of, 8–9; and leveling, 74; and small-group instruction, 23–26; and whole-group instruction, 17–23; and whole-group reflection and goal setting, 27–30
Reading Time Just for You and Me, 358
read-pause-ask questions, 239
read-pause-make connections, 39, 240

read-pause-retell, 39, 240
read-pause-visualize, 240
Read the Pictures, 358
read the room, 38
reciprocal teaching, 51–53, 256–257; bookmarks for, 53, 330–331; implementing, 52–53; observation of, 350; in primary grades, 53–55; purposes of, 51; self-evaluation on, 332
reflection: center, 301; on comprehension strategies, 26; group work sheet, 310; self-reflection, 351–353; variety of components in, 28–29; whole-group, 27–30
Reinking, D., 12
repeated reading, 203
repetition, 205
required centers, 40–41; forms for, 333
rereading, 26
response, in literature circles, 44–45
retelling, 26, 246–247
review, of comprehension strategies, 25
ReWrite, 37–38
Rhodes, L.K., 340
Rhodes, M.J., 182
rhyme, 205; and phonemic awareness, 197
Richards, M., 204
Richardson, V., 6
Richek, M.A., 204
riddles, 205
Ridgeway, V.G., 68
rimes, 205
rime word wall, 201–202
RIVET, 234–235
Roehler, L.R., 9, 206
Rog, L.J., 67, 69–70
roles, in literature circles, 46–47
Romano, S., 359
Rosenblatt, L.M., 9
rotating schedule, 41
Ruddell, R.B., 8
Rule, A.C., 358
running records, 62
Ruptic, C.A., 28